CHASING HISTORY

CHASING HISTORY

A KID IN THE NEWSROOM

CARL BERNSTEIN

THORNDIKE PRESS
A part of Gale, a Cengage Company

Copyright © 2022 by Essential Reporting Enterprises, Inc.
Thorndike Press, a part of Gale, a Cengage Company.

ALL RIGHTS RESERVED
Thorndike Press® Large Print Biography and Memoir.
The text of this Large Print edition is unabridged.
Other aspects of the book may vary from the original edition.
Set in 16 pt. Plantin.

**LIBRARY OF CONGRESS CIP DATA ON FILE.
CATALOGUING IN PUBLICATION FOR THIS BOOK
IS AVAILABLE FROM THE LIBRARY OF CONGRESS.**

ISBN-13: 978-1-4328-9865-6 (hardcover alk. paper)

Published in 2022 by arrangement with Henry Holt and Company

Printed in Mexico
Print Number: 01   Print Year: 2022

For those in this book who put me on a path

And for Lance Morrow especially

And for Jeff Zucker

CONTENTS

Prologue 9
1. The Door. 19
2. Adrenaline 28
3. Initiation 48
4. Knowledge 60
5. Dry Run 85
6. Legman 96
7. Warthog 124
8. Night Beat 140
9. Hot Type 158
10. Inaugural. 172
11. Misfit. 195
12. Lift-off 217
13. Dictation 249
14. Local News. 266
15. Crises. 284
16. Off Campus 311
17. Ambition 341
18. America 364
19. Monumental 394
20. Growing Up 422
21. Civil Rights 449

22. Summer 476
23. Fort Holabird. 498
24. General Assignment 509
25. The Wheel 528
26. Flack 546
27. Leavings 553
Epilogue 569

ACKNOWLEDGMENTS 597
INDEX 605

PROLOGUE

I needed a suit.

I had a proper suit, a winter one, but I had never owned a summer suit — a necessity in the immense heat of Washington, D.C., where most of the senators and congressmen from farther down south began dressing in whites and wearing straw hats in mid-April, not long after the cherry blossoms were done blooming. If I was now to enter the grown-up world of work in the nation's capital, I would require a summer suit.

I meant to buy it at Woodward & Lothrop, the big department store on F Street. I had forty-five dollars in my pocket, saved up from my Saturday job at S. N. McBride's layaway department store on the edge of Swampoodle, a ramshackle neighborhood the trains passed through as they slowed toward Union Station. After buying my suit, I hoped to ascend to a higher vocation: the newspaper business. I knew almost nothing about it, except that as a child I'd always read the sports section and

9

the front-page news in the *Washington Post*. And at ages twelve and thirteen, after my family moved from the city to Silver Spring in the Maryland suburbs, I had a paper route delivering the final edition of the *Evening Star* from a red wagon.

On this June morning in 1960, I hitchhiked up Colesville Road to Georgia Avenue, and then I walked the half mile to the B&O railroad station diagonally across from the pool hall where on any other summer day (and too many during the school year) I was likely to be found.

I boarded the Capitol Limited, which carried me in air-conditioned luxury through Takoma Park and Northeast Washington, past Catholic University and the Old Soldiers' Home, whose ancients, some still in uniform, looked up from their wooden chairs on the lawn and waved when the engineer blew his horn in tribute. I had read in history class that Abraham Lincoln summered each year of his presidency in a cottage at the Old Soldiers' Home, when the heat downtown made life unbearable in the White House, which had been built over a swamp.

From Silver Spring, Union Station lay seven miles down the tracks, its marble colonnade facing the Capitol of the United States — worlds away from suburban Maryland, it seemed to me, though our next-door neighbor was a U.S. senator, Alan Bible of Nevada.

The senator's sons Billy and Paul were my schoolmates. Their father was something like the emperor of Washington, D.C., by virtue of being chairman of the Senate Committee on the District of Columbia.

Union Station was magnificent, modeled on some famous Roman baths, as the tour guides liked to point out. Usually when I took the train downtown, I'd linger in the station's pinball room, adjacent to the USO lounge, and test my skill at the machines until I'd exhausted a shotgun roll of forty nickels. That might take a couple of hours on a good run.

But on this day I headed straight for the streetcar up Pennsylvania Avenue, getting off at Tenth Street and then walking past Ford's Theatre and the house across the street where Lincoln died. Downtown Washington was territory I'd known from the time I was a small child. My father's old office, the one he'd had at 930 F Street until it was closed down during the Joe McCarthy business, was around the corner from where Lincoln was shot. And a few blocks west, at Fourteenth Street, was Garfinckel's department store, where my grandfather — my mother's father — had gone to work as a cuffer in the men's tailoring department after he got off the boat from Russia. Next to Garfinckel's, F Street stopped abruptly at the Treasury Department — adjacent to the White House, which my class from grammar school visited almost

11

every year. My maternal great-grandmother, a tiny woman with shriveled skin, still lived downtown, on Seventh Street, just beyond the big department stores, atop a little photo studio where the youngest (and strangest) of her five children snapped portraits, sometimes of congressmen or a clutch of local businessmen.

I'd been disoriented by our move from the city to the suburbs. The jumble of downtown Washington, where the shrines and emblems of the nation gleamed next to squat mercantile buildings and faded antebellum rooming houses, had for me an enchantment of familiarity. I'd turned sixteen on Valentine's Day and felt much more adult now, with a work permit in my wallet and my underage employment at McBride's — technically illegal, like some of its layaway interest rates — behind me as well.

I walked past the sooty Hotel Harrington and the television studios of WTTG and the DuMont network, where every couple of weeks I danced on *The Milt Grant Show* with other teenagers — white ones, because the Black kids danced on a different day of the week. Woodward & Lothrop, my destination, was a turn-of-the-century pile that Washingtonians called Woodies. It was the biggest department store in the city and took up a full square block.

My mother and father, in the early 1950s, had taken me with them to join the sit-ins at

12

Woodward & Lothrop to desegregate its Tea Room. In those days, Union Station was the only place downtown, besides the government cafeterias and a few others owned by a man named Evan Sholl, that would serve Black customers at tables. They could stand and eat at the lunch counters inside the dime stores and department stores but were forbidden to sit.

On F Street, a block from Woodies, a legless vendor of pencils worked his turf on a dolly with roller-skate wheels, propelling himself with his hands and arms while a pet monkey held tight to his shoulder. I'd seen the man many times and had wondered about him. Flush with cash this day, I asked him for two pencils. I extended a quarter.

It was not often that I towered above the person I was talking to — or his monkey. The vendor seemed gabby, wanting to talk. He asked me where I was going, and I told him I was heading to Woodies to buy a suit. He was wearing tattered pants that had been cut off and sewn or folded somehow to cover the stumps of his legs. He suggested that perhaps I'd like to buy half a dozen pencils. He asked my name, and when I told him, he brightened and said his name was Bernstein too, Eddie Bernstein, which made me suspicious, and that his monkey was named Gypsy, which sounded about right.

To prove he was Eddie Bernstein he produced

his vendor's identification, then asked which Bernsteins I was from. I was sure we weren't related; there were no Bernsteins outside our immediate family who were kin that I'd heard of. Plus, this Eddie Bernstein said that his family was from Florida. He asked how much I wanted to spend on a suit. I told him maybe forty dollars.

"You should go see my friend Louie," he said. "No-Label Louie." He was insistent, but in a friendly way. He said that Louie sold suits at a steep discount, probably half of what I'd pay at Woodies, and that if I asked for Louie himself and told him Eddie Bernstein had sent me, I'd get an even better deal. I'd brought along a picture of a blue cord summer suit I liked, clipped from the pages of a magazine, though I didn't show it to him.

He pointed east and said Louie's store was on D Street near the intersection of Seventh, a patch I knew well because my great-grandmother and the photo studio were almost around the corner. I bought four more pencils from Eddie Bernstein and headed down the street, past my father's old union office.

Louie Goldstein's "haberdashery," as its owner referred to his store when I walked inside, was conspicuous from the sidewalk because of its big electric sign — unusual downtown, where almost everything shut down by six o'clock in the evening except for

14

a few restaurants and bars, and the peep show movies and burlesque house on Ninth Street. Louie was wearing a beret (something else not often seen in the neighborhood) and smoking a cigar. Eddie had been truthful about the quantity of suits. There were thousands of them, maybe five or six thousand, rack after rack, stacked halfway to the ceiling from the front of the store to the back. In one aisle, there was just enough space for a two-sided placard with pasted photos of well-dressed customers: NO-LABEL LOUIE'S — WE WON'T BE UNDERSOLD! One of the pictures showed the Senate majority leader, Lyndon Johnson, in a suit by Louie.

I told Louie I wanted a cord suit for the summer, which he agreed was just right for someone my age, and after he'd taken the tape measure that was draped from his neck and determined my size, he came back with three or four. One was almost cream-colored, not blue. Looking closely, I could see that the stripes were light brown. This suit would look best on me, Louie said, because I had so many freckles.

He had me stand on a box in front of a three-way mirror, the same way my grandfather did when he'd fit my clothes in his tailor shop (which was hardly bigger than Louie's dressing room). Louie was right that the cream-colored suit looked best.

I could have the suit for twenty-five dollars,

15

no questions asked, including alterations. I was thinking I should take the suit to my grandfather, who was a master tailor. But Louie said his man in the back could do it on the spot if I wanted, nothing needed to be taken in, just the pants cuffed and a button on the waistband moved a little bit, and he would sell me a tie that went with it for two dollars.

While he pinned the pants, I told him about my grandfather, and about my grandmother, who worked the sewing machine in the shop. Meanwhile, Louie expounded on the no-label concept and his eye for excellence, and about his own grandfather, who'd gotten off the boat in Baltimore in the 1850s, and how the business had prospered during the next decade by making uniforms for Union soldiers.

When the suit was ready and I tried the whole outfit on, I quite liked the look. I decided right then that I would wear it out of the store — and with the money I'd saved, I'd go to lunch at the Occidental Restaurant next door to the Willard Hotel near the White House.

On afternoons when our dancing was done and *The Milt Grant Show* had signed off, I'd always stop to buy a newspaper from the stout woman who fed the pigeons and gave treats to children at her newsstand at Eleventh Street, in front of the old Evening Star Building — the tallest structure on Pennsylvania Avenue except for the Old Post Office Tower. "Annie" was the only name I'd ever heard her called, and she never had much to say, except to the pigeons, but she often greeted her regular customers by name. She invariably addressed me as "young man," as she did on this day.

The Star Building was shuttered now; the paper had moved the previous year to new offices and a modern printing plant in Southeast Washington. Standing outside the old building made me think about what I might say at my job interview the following week at the paper. I hoped it would lead to getting my foot in the door there, and maybe put my life on a different track.

I was also thinking about lunch.

The Occidental Restaurant wasn't the kind of place women or families went to in the daytime; it felt more like an old-fashioned gentleman's club. I'd been there more than a few times with my father. We'd order oysters or clams fresh up from the Chesapeake, and crab cakes or, in the spring, shad roe from the Potomac. I'd never been to the Occidental by myself, but the host at the door seemed to think nothing of sitting me down at a choice table near the window, no different from the other men in their summer suits. He led me past the framed photographs on the wall that the restaurant was famous for, signed by presidents and congressmen and senators and generals and cabinet secretaries going back to when the Willard Hotel first opened.

Abraham Lincoln stayed at the Willard the night before his inauguration, and Ulysses S. Grant bunked there when he came to town to consult with the commander in chief.

After the maître d' had seated me and I'd tucked the white cloth napkin in my lap and looked around, I saw that J. Edgar Hoover, the FBI director, whose picture was prominent in the entry gallery — and who like me and my mother had been born not far from this part of town — was eating lunch by himself in one of the booths. I hadn't realized how much his face looked like a bulldog's. He had a barrel chest and small hands, which I noted on a piece of paper with one of the pencils I'd bought from Eddie Bernstein.

I didn't want to give myself away by staring, so I read the copy of the *Star* I'd bought from Annie, which at that moment was filled with news about the coming presidential election between John F. Kennedy and Richard M. Nixon.

1

THE DOOR

My becoming a copyboy was really my father's doing. He rightly feared for my future — a concern that was based on hard facts, most of them having to do with the pool hall, my school report cards, and the Montgomery County Juvenile Court. It was the opinion of experts at all three institutions that the odds were against my ever amounting to much. Selling shoddy merchandise on layaway to poor people from Swampoodle was another reason my father wanted to steer me toward more respectable work.

There had been no father-and-son discussion about my difficulties, unless you counted the time he told me how he had struggled and saved to get through college during the Depression. My father's eyes had filled with tears as he told the story. It was the only time I ever saw that happen at home, though it was not uncommon for his eyes to glisten when he marched on a picket line. My father was, until recently, the principal organizer of the United

19

Federal Workers / United Public Workers of America and was regarded as a saint by the people to whom he devoted his life. These were not the circles favored by the Washington *Evening Star,* the town's "conservative" newspaper.

But my father's preference for the *Star* — over the far more liberal *Washington Post* — went deep. In a company town in which the federal government was the company, being the government columnist was a position of importance, and the *Star*'s Joseph Young had covered a strike by my father's union with fairness and faithfulness to the facts. Whereas the *Post*'s Jerry Klutz (his actual name) had been more intent on uncovering if the union's leaders included members of the American Communist Party and, by inference, what role Moscow had played in determining whether U.S. government cafeteria workers should get their pay raised to a dollar an hour.

My father became a source for Joe Young. And it was Joe Young who said a word to Rudy Kauffmann and got me a job interview at the *Star.*

Rudolph Max Kauffmann II was the grandson of the first president of the *Evening Star* and cousin of the current one. Though his title was production editor, he was sometimes called the Clown Prince, which, later on, I came to think was unfair and more than a little cruel. As a youth, he had wanted to become a geologist, but after four years of Princeton his father had put an end to that dream and ordered him to join the family business. Rudy complied, but his career at the paper was not a glorious one. Basically, he hired the copyboys and, from a fair distance, was responsible for their supervision. His portfolio included the *Star*'s generous civic and charitable programs that served the city's children and the poor.

"That's quite a suit you got yourself, boy."

Rudy Kauffmann wore half spectacles, and he looked down his nose to see me. He had a friendly face.

I thought I was pretty well turned out, in my cream-colored suit and the pickle-colored tie Louie had selected for me. But Rudy Kauffmann seemed to have his doubts.

"Boy, I thought your dad told Joe Young you were almost finished high school?"

"Sir, I'll be in twelfth grade this coming year," I replied. I told him that I'd turned sixteen in February, but he still looked skeptical.

Before taking the elevator to his office on the third floor, I'd lingered in the lobby and studied a mural testifying to the *Star*'s long witness to history. There were front-page headlines — LINCOLN ASSASSINATED, SENATORS WIN PENNANT, UNITED NATIONS BORN, SURRENDER: JAPS STRIPPED OF CONQUESTS — and pictures of General MacArthur and Charles Lindbergh and presidents, kings, and queens posing with members of the three

21

families who had owned and run the *paper* almost since its founding in 1852: the Noyeses, the Adamses, and the Kauffmanns. In some of the photos, the owners were standing next to the presses and were wearing funny little hats made out of folded newspaper pages. On an office directory posted in the lobby, the names of the families were all mixed up with one another by the time of Rudy Kauffmann's generation; there were Noyeses and Kauffmanns listed in almost every department, including some executives with both names.

To catch up with the second half of the twentieth century and get the paper out to the suburbs faster, the *Star* had moved from downtown to its brand-new building at 225 Virginia Avenue on the edge of Capitol Hill, a state-of-the-art news production facility, all cinder block and concrete except for two floors of picture windows in the front.

"I thought Joe Young said you were in high school," Rudy Kauffmann said again.

The immediate problem, I gathered, was that I was too short to be a copyboy. Or too young, or too young-looking. Not only was I five foot three (and still growing), I was freckled from head to toe. One summer I'd smeared a whole bar of butter over my face because the man who pumped gas at the Tenleytown Amoco station told me — while I filled up my bicycle tires — that the butter would make my freckles go away.

The bookcase behind Rudy Kauffmann contained what looked like a century's worth of leather-bound volumes of the Proceedings of the Geological Society of America, and the top of his desk was covered with crystals and other geological specimens. Some were cut open down the middle like cantaloupes, and as he spoke, he ran his fingers along the veins where it looked like the fruit had been scooped out.

"When you're ready to graduate, come back and we'll see if there isn't a part-time job for you here," he said.

This was a disappointment. I had been assured by Louie that the suit would make me look older. I had also calculated the odds of my graduating from high school, which did not seem good. Even if I was on my best behavior, and assuming I took up studying, graduation was almost a year off. And that presumed I could pass chemistry.

Abruptly, Rudy Kauffmann put down the cantaloupe and started to get up; I became aware of a wizened man who had entered the room, advancing with the aid of a walking stick. His gnarled left hand gripped the knob — an ivory animal, a bobcat, it looked like. The man was bent like a parenthesis, with a bald head that shined like the rock that was split open on Rudy Kauffmann's desk, onto which the ancient fellow now tossed a sheaf of papers.

"Guest list and program — for the Press Club event," he said.

Rudy Kauffmann looked confused.

"What am I supposed to do with them?"

"Read them! Your cousin Sam told me you should look them over."

"Why?"

"He expects you to preside at the dinner, Rudolph."

The old man's exasperation was palpable. He looked at me for the first time — more at my suit than at me, I thought.

"Joe Young sent him here — knows his father. He wants to be a copyboy. Carl Bernstein."

Rudy Kauffmann had at least remembered my name.

"Meet Mr. Gould Lincoln, the senior editorial writer of the *Star*."

Gould Lincoln definitely belonged to the nineteenth-century side of the newspaper. He nodded at me and said, "I started here as a copyboy, but in those days we called them office boys. I was fifteen." He paused. "In 1895."

I took the opportunity to inform the senior editorial writer that I was a year older than he'd been at the start of his newspaper career — adding that I'd taken a journalism class in tenth grade and had brought some clippings from the school newspaper for Mr. Kauffmann to read. In fact, there were just three

24

stories, the total output of what I'd written; I did not mention that I'd been demoted on the paper's masthead to circulation and exchange manager because of my meager production.

Rudy Kauffmann explained that he and Mr. Lincoln had business to attend to, but he promised to read my clippings and led me to a door at the back of his office.

The door by which I had entered was at the end of a dim, quiet corridor of the sort you would find in any ordinary place of business. The door through which Rudy Kauffmann now led me opened into another universe. People were shouting. Typewriters clattered and chinged. Beneath my feet, I could feel the rumble of the presses.

In my whole life I had never heard such glorious chaos or seen such purposeful commotion as I now beheld in that newsroom. By the time I had walked from one end to the other, I knew that I wanted to be a newspaperman.

I walked as slowly as I could to take in the whole scene, while Rudy Kauffmann (like a man tugging on a leash against a very determined puppy) led me down the middle aisle of the reporters' desks running from the big windows at the Virginia Avenue end of the newsroom to a huge crescent-shaped desk in the middle of the room, which seemed about a football field away.

People ran here and there — copyboys, I guessed they were, though they were all fully grown and looked to be in their twenties — and men shouted *"Copy!"* and everybody seemed to be on the most urgent errands in the nation. Except (I noticed) that after one of them had yelled *"Copy!"* and somebody came to pick up a piece of paper, a few of the men around the crescent would go back to playing a gambling game with dollar bills folded lengthwise in half, staring at the serial numbers on the bill of the opposite player.

What the copyboys did, Rudy Kauffmann said, was anything the reporters or editors asked. They pretty much made it possible for the whole place to function. At that moment a copyboy came racing through with a cart loaded full of newspapers — that day's late-afternoon edition, with a red streak down the right side, the same edition I delivered in my neighborhood in Silver Spring. They'd just come off the presses. Rudy Kauffmann reached into the cart and handed me one. The pages were still warm.

After that, I telephoned every two or three days to remind Rudy Kauffmann that I was available. One day I took the trolley to the Capitol, walked over to the *Star* building, and sat outside his office with a typewritten autobiography of half a dozen pages that I'd written for an English class assignment. I was worried what he might make of my story, but he was amiable enough when I handed him the pages. He asked whether I could type, which I could, and he sent me to an office on the ground floor for a typing test and an examination by the *Star* nurse. And he told me he would be in touch soon.

When I phoned him two days later, he said I was hired — and to report to work the following Monday. My pay would be twenty-nine dollars a week.

2

ADRENALINE

"Boy, you didn't tell me you could type like that," Rudy Kauffmann said when I reported to his office on the sweltering morning of August 1, 1960. Typing was apparently what had gotten me hired.

That school year, I'd taken Typing I with the girls; it was the single subject in which I'd received an A since Miss Ottenberg's eighth grade English class, where we'd been forced to read *Paradise Lost*.

Aside from being the only boy in the course, the reason I'd decided to study typing — part of the Home Economics curriculum at Montgomery Blair High School — was that I'd come to hate shop classes by then. Starting in junior high, there'd been metal shop, and then wood shop, and thereafter a couple of variations of each, resulting in a junkpile of odd-shaped, useless objects that my mother refused to throw away. One piece was notable for its occasional appearance in the family kitchen: a wooden hors d'oeuvres tray fashioned in three shades of walnut, with rolled handles and a fanned mahogany fish I'd cut with a jigsaw and then pocked with holes to display dozens of colored toothpicks.

So the typing class had come as a big relief. From the start, my fingers seemed to fly across the keys. This unnatural facility enabled me to type close to ninety words per minute, which meant that I could probably become a civil service clerk if all else failed. I also recognized that typing went with newspaper work. I'd gathered that much from movies about reporters — and also from my tenth-grade journalism class, though I'd learned little else there, despite what I'd bragged to Rudy Kauffmann and Gould Lincoln. I'd memorized the stuff about the five *W*'s of newswriting and was confident that, with a little help, I could typewrite a passable newspaper story based on the Who, What, Where, When, and Why. But what impressed Rudy Kauffmann was my speed with the keys. Even the "dictationists" in the newsroom, he said, couldn't type as fast as I could. He didn't explain who the dictationists were or what they did.

Beyond that, he said, there wasn't much else for him to tell me about newspaper work.

He dialed zero on the black rotary telephone on his desk and announced he was turning me over to Phil Kelley, the head copyboy.

The last thing I expected in a head copyboy was that he could be as old as Rudy

Kauffmann was. Judging from his appearance, Phil Kelley was approaching the forty mark pretty hard, though there was something of the man-child aspect about him, perhaps because of the way he was dressed, or perhaps because his eyes didn't quite work together in conventional fashion. I wouldn't have called him cross-eyed; instead, one of his eyes was definitely looking to right angles of the other one, so they seemed to be working in opposition behind his thick glasses. Phil Kelley wore rumpled khaki pants and an unpressed short-sleeved white shirt open at the throat; his complexion was sallow and his arms had no muscular definition. The whole package suggested a powerful aversion to the out-of-doors.

"Well, good luck," Rudy Kauffmann said, and he pretty much shoved me out the door and under Phil Kelley's wing.

At ten o'clock in the morning, the newsroom was calmer than on my first visit. Phil Kelley seemed to appreciate that I needed time to take everything in. He set out to give me a kindly and thorough tutorial about newspapering, as practiced at the *Evening Star*. I was struck by the seriousness of his devotion to the paper.

The newsroom seemed huge — disheveled and colossal, even grander than the grandstand at Griffith Stadium, with rows and rows of ordered seats almost swamped by the accumulated debris of the journalism trade. I noted clumps of objects heaped on almost every desk: dictionaries and thesauruses; phone books and yellow pages from numerous jurisdictions; faded clippings from the paper's library — the "morgue," Kelley called it — brittle and scattered like dead leaves; blue-bound editions of the *Congressional Directory* and green-baize-covered copies of the *Social Register* (invaluable, I was to learn quickly, because they contained unlisted phone numbers); stacks of old newspapers; mountains of magazines and reference books, along with futile notices from the library chasing after exactly those same overdue materials; and (Kelley pointed out when they occasionally poked through the litter) pari-mutuel betting slips that had been purchased upstairs in the composing room from an assistant to Aloysius E. Baker, the foreman whose hideaway office provided enough privacy and a sufficient number of telephone lines to stay in touch with the tracks at Pimlico, Shenandoah, Charlestown, and Laurel.

Only the more fastidious staffers had an unobstructed view from their desks, so high had the landfill in their immediate neighborhood often grown. Each reporter's desk was of institutional gunmetal, painted a sickish shade of pinkly brown, with shoebox drawers stacked from top to bottom on the right and a shallow rectangular indentation hollowed in the desk's center to accommodate a type-writer. Some reporters used newer models — dark brown with green keys — but others had brought their light tan, very dirty Royal desk models from the old building on Pennsylvania Avenue.

Maybe fifteen or twenty reporters were on hand. Some had their feet up on their desks, some were typing with furious concentration (often using the hunt and peck method), some were finishing their breakfast and reading the paper, some were hard at work on the cross-word, some shouted into telephones. No one talked quietly.

The decoration of the place, like the layout, was altogether functional: a vast acreage of desks set upon a tract of brown linoleum that had been scarred and burned by an army of chain-smoking reporters who thought it pru-dent — less of a fire hazard — to stamp out their cigarette butts on the floor rather than use the ashtrays perched atop the towers of combustible papers on their desks.

Kelley led me to the back of the newsroom so that I might consider the entire spectacle. What I was looking at now, he told me, was the heart of the newspaper: the people who produced the words, at work on their floor of the newspaper factory.

The copyboy's job was to mediate between the thinking part of the operation and the mechanical part, between making the words and getting the paper out. The people who produced the words could think and type and do all kinds of magic with sentences, aided by their mighty powers of observation and inquiry. But they had almost no interest in the production side of the enterprise, centered in the composing room above us, where the stories were set in type, and directly beneath our feet, where the giant presses were housed.

Every day more words were printed in the newspaper than were in a good-sized novel; and during the course of the day these inked pages were corrected and rewritten and scrambled and updated five times. None of this could happen without copyboys. Kelley grabbed a couple of pencils and, with a flourish, handed me a notebook. This, he indicated, was to be the fundamental tool of my new trade. It even announced itself as such, with reporter brand printed on the cover above a carmine logo of a male figure on the run taking notes. The notebook was distinguished also by the way it opened, not right-to-left like a school notebook; instead it flipped over itself, bottom to top. I knew that stenographers used notepads of a similar shape and approximate size, but I sensed already that the object of what I now wanted to do with my life was the opposite of stenography.

Here was the geography of the newsroom. Starting from the big picture windows at the far end — the only opening to the outer world — Kelley and I advanced to the interior by passing down that center aisle through a region of jangling telephones and clattering typewriters under a wash of fluorescent lights. Then the newsroom grew wider to accommodate the crescent-shaped desk, its top covered in gray-black linoleum so that from the back of the room in the morning light it had first appeared to me like a shimmering river in the distance. And indeed the purpose was to move the flow of copy downstream, from reporter to city desk or national desk or rewrite bank, then to the news editor, who presided over this river of news and logged the stories and identified their place of landfall in the paper. He then sent them further downriver to the copy desk, where a "slotman" (who sat in the slot between the two wings of an adjacent U-shaped desk) would oversee the strict policing of the newspaper's wording — the final stop before the stories were sent to be set in type. At each port of call, editors in shirtsleeves bent over the copy, wielding pencils. One editor wore an old-fashioned green eyeshade and garters on his sleeves. He had bright red hair, and tufts of it sprouted above the eyeshade.

Beyond the news desk and the copy desk, in the deepest recess of the great long room, lay the Sports Department, which was a different world. The Women's Department was located in a separate part of the floor entirely, far from the main action.

Among the important people Phil Kelley wanted me to immediately know about — spelling their names and explaining what they did and instructing me to note exactly where they sat — the initial three were women: Miss McGrory, Miss Ottenberg, and Miss Werner, as he referred to them, almost as a unit. Mary McGrory wasn't in the newsroom that morning. Kelley announced that she was the best writing stylist on the paper and that her *prose* (he emphasized the word) and point of view were informed by her Boston Irish sensibility — which he said he understood even though he was from Kansas City. I had noticed that her desk seemed to be uniquely in order and tended to. It was adorned with a red rose in a vase and with framed pictures of children — not her own, Kelley explained, but kids from St. Ann's orphanage. He was certain she would pull me into her service, sooner rather than later, to help out at the orphanage and run her errands.

Mary McGrory's byline was well known, even to a kid like me. She had worked as a book reviewer at the *Star* until Newbold Noyes Jr., the paper's assistant editor at the time, had plucked her to cover the Army-McCarthy hearings in 1954; he'd had a sixth sense that a woman of her unusual perceptiveness, coming from the outside, might be able to see the senator from Wisconsin more clearly than the beat reporters on Capitol Hill did — and might better capture his manner and his particular menace.

The other two women were recent winners of the Pulitzer Prize, Kelley said, pausing for effect. Mary Lou Werner had won the previous year for reporting on so-called "massive resistance" to school desegregation in Virginia, led and conceived by Senator Harry Flood Byrd; and, this past May, Miriam Ottenberg had been awarded the Pulitzer for investigative reporting. Kelley told me Miss Ottenberg could be a terror, and that I should take care around her.

Of all the names of reporters on the *Star*'s staff, hers was the most familiar to me, because the Ottenberg family owned the town's major Jewish bakery. Since the Civil War the Ottenbergs had been the principal supplier of fresh seeded rye bread consumed in the nation's capital.

Miriam Ottenberg's desk, high on the disorderly scale, was about forty feet in front of Miss McGrory's. Piled on it were books about the Mafia and bound sets of transcripts of hearings of the Kefauver Committee on organized crime from a decade before. I'd read some of her stories: hard-boiled exposés on baby brokers, marriage counselors, fake charities, crooked investment companies, and home improvement rackets. She operated in a tough world and knew her way around. She'd won her Pulitzer for a series of articles about shady used car dealers. These days, she covered the Justice Department and the FBI.

As Kelley and I approached, she stood at her desk studying a piece of typewritten copy, a short, compact, intense-looking woman who seemed irritated at the moment and full of coiled energy. I noticed that she was wearing a gold necklace and that as she read, she rocked back and forth on her high-heeled shoes, not teetering, but in an athletic sort of way. She was maybe forty or a little older.

With a start, I thought of my eighth-grade English teacher, also a Miss Ottenberg. It had never occurred to me to find out if she was part of the Ottenberg rye bread family; mostly, I'd been baffled by her inexplicable enthusiasm for John Milton. She had been pretty and soft-spoken, with stylish black-framed eyeglasses. Now I saw the possibility of a family resemblance.

When Kelley introduced us, Miriam Ottenberg's fierceness vanished. She smiled, and sized me up for a second, and asked if I was related to Leo Bernstein, who owned several of the city's banks and swaths of valuable D.C. real estate. I wasn't, but my mother, like Miriam Ottenberg, had been in his graduating class — 1932 — at Central High School.

My mother had been very popular at Central, Miss Ottenberg said.

Built at the turn of the century atop one of the city's greatest hills, with a sweeping view of the city below, Central was the city's pre-eminent white high school for fifty years. It even had an indoor swimming pool.

As a way of compensating for past inequality — and to meet the era's constitutional standard of "separate but equal" schools for Blacks and whites — Central was transferred to the "Negro Division" of the D.C. school system and renamed Cardozo.

Soon after, in May 1954, the Supreme Court decided *Brown v. Board of Education,* ordering desegregation of the nation's public schools. Its companion case, *Bolling v. Sharpe,* specifically directed an end to Washington's segregated school system. I was in the sixth grade at Janney Elementary when our class was integrated under *Bolling* and *Brown.*

For the record, J. Edgar Hoover had also gone to Central High — valedictorian of the class of 1913. And yes, Miriam Ottenberg said, my eighth-grade teacher was her second cousin, Regina.

As Phil Kelley guided me around the crescent, he raised his voice over the racket coming from the adjacent, half-enclosed wire room. Inside this bullpen were the teletype machines — maybe twenty in all — that brought to the *Star,* by electronic circuit, news from around the world, provided by the Associated Press, United Press International, and the International News Service, along with columns and features distributed by the North American Newspaper Alliance and other syndicates. There were separate machines for national news, foreign news, state news from Maryland and Virginia, and the Dow Jones stock ticker. I was scribbling in my notebook, jotting down one detail after another, hoping to make sense of it later.

Suddenly one of the machines sounded an insistent series of bells: four loud rings, an interval of silence, then repeating again — over and over — for half a minute. It meant that a story marked URGENT was coming, Kelley said, though the phrase he used was "moving over the wire." Five consecutive bells, which occurred infrequently, meant that a BULLETIN — a much higher category of urgency, and so marked — was about to come in. The system was like the bells in a firehouse: four alarms, five alarms, and so on. The attendant in the wire room, another copyboy, bent expectantly over the ringing machine. When it chattered out the beginning of its URGENT story, he ripped the top of the paper out of the teleprinter and ran it to a dignified-looking middle-aged gent who sat at the far end of the crescent — the Star's foreign editor.

"Must be something from the Congo," Kelley guessed. The Belgian Congo was in a state of anticolonialist revolution. The foreign editor walked to the middle of the crescent to confer with a couple of the other editors.

Hardly anyone else in the newsroom took notice of the URGENT; they remained immersed in their own tasks.

Kelley further explained the wire room's codes. I wrote *FLASH!* in my notebook, complete with exclamation point. Ten bells ringing over and over signified that a story marked FLASH! was about to move over the wire. FLASH! was reserved for only the biggest news. The dropping of the atomic bomb was a FLASH!

From our left I became aware of the clattering of more typing, like the sound of a mild hailstorm. This came from the dictation bank, where six or seven of the younger men and women in the newsroom — all of them at least half a dozen years older than I — were seated at another elongated slab of gray linoleum. Wearing headsets as they typed, they would now and then interrupt the reporter dictating the story ("Is that *C* for Charlie?" "What's the slug?" "Is that *B* for Boy?").

Stories were coming in from Dwight Eisenhower's summer White House in Rhode Island; from the Virginia state capitol in Richmond; from the District Building across the street from the Occidental Restaurant — city hall, or what passed for it in the powerless D.C. government; from the United Nations; from reporters on the street covering local news and police stories; from members of the *Star*'s staff assigned to the presidential

40

campaigns of John F. Kennedy and Richard M. Nixon.

The cacophony was swelling with the approach of the next edition's deadline. Even the newsroom switchboard operator, whose outsized wooden console and tangle of wires abutted the dictation bank, was hollering: "Who can take Cecil with Ike in Rhode Island? He's got a five-minute window."

Between rounds of golf at the Newport Country Club, President Eisenhower was trying to counter Soviet interests in Cuba and the Congo. Moscow was about to stage a show trial of Francis Gary Powers, the pilot of an American U-2 spy plane shot down by a Russian missile that spring.

I now understood the reason for all the paste pots I had seen on supply shelves near the back of the newsroom. The editors, as they marked up stories and moved paragraphs around, tore off pieces of copy with metal rules in order to slap together separate blocks of words into coherent chunks. In a practiced motion, pulling the paste-laden brush from the pot, the deskman would swish it at the bottom of a strip of copy and, with the heel of his hand, pound the ripped pieces together. At least fifteen editors and rewrite men (there was one woman, too, I noticed) were seated around the crescent, reading copy or talking on the telephone or with reporters who came up to the desk to discuss their stories, while galley proofs — narrow, column-length versions of stories set in type — were passed from editor to editor.

Police and fire dispatchers droned in competing monotones from a battery of radio receivers on the city and state desks, and I tried to guess from their different local accents which were from the District and which were from Prince George's County or Alexandria or Rockville.

In the center of the crescent, across from the news editor, sat the city editor of the *Evening Star,* with deputies seated across and next to him. This was Sidney Epstein. Kelley instructed me to put several stars next to his name in my notebook; he would tell me more about him later.

To the city editor's immediate left sat Mary Lou Werner — Ludy, Phil Kelley called her, and introduced me. Between juggling telephone calls, she said she would be pleased to take me to lunch sometime soon — to "explain how the place really worked." She told me she had started as a copygirl at the *Star* when she was seventeen. I was dazzled. I was even more impressed when I went to the newspaper's library later that week to read the stories that had won her a Pulitzer Prize. I also learned that Ludy was thirty-four years old — very young to be so accomplished, as the story about her winning had noted.

About eleven thirty, the presses, two floors

down, began their low rumble to produce the *Star*'s first edition of the day. I felt the vibration coming through the floor.

Copyboys were allotted forty-five minutes for lunch. Before I headed upstairs to the company cafeteria, Phil Kelley suggested I think about joining the Newspaper Guild, of which he was the shop steward. He left no room for doubt that if I didn't sign up, I would not get along well with my fellow employees, especially because there had been a Guild strike at the *Evening Star* in 1958, the first newspaper strike in the city for decades. I was glad to inform him that my father had been a union organizer, and before I headed upstairs to the company cafeteria, he gave me a form to fill out to join the Guild.

At lunch I tried to sort out my thoughts and catch my breath. I paged through the first edition of the paper, amazed that I had watched it all come together.

I tried to connect the stories and the bylines to people I'd met, and to decipher the confusing odds and ends scribbled in my reporter's notebook. I would not have made a good stenographer. That day I began to invent my own abbreviations and shorthand symbols. Later I would draw a diagram of the newsroom on two facing pages of my notebook, and though art was another subject at school that had eluded me, my rudimentary sketch served as a kind of template that I would constantly update and fill in with more detail.

I noticed that the pencils Phil Kelley had handed me were not the usual ribbed and yellow variety, like the ones in school or that I had bought from Eddie Bernstein. These were thick, black, rounded, with no erasers — copy pencils, according to their manufacturer's stamp. They seemed to assume a bold certainty that in other circumstances might have been considered presumptuous.

That afternoon, around three thirty, the newsroom erupted. What I'd seen in the morning had been an ordered chaos, rhythmic and deliberate in its coordination. This was something different.

I didn't hear what caused the eruption, but I found out soon enough. A police call on the city desk squawk box reported the possible electrocution of at least two victims at one of the city's public swimming pools.

Suddenly Sidney Epstein — with a flick of his finger as if hailing a cab, or with a subdued barking of a last name — summoned reporters to the city desk. They came running. They listened to him for a few seconds and then tore out of the newsroom. Four or five were dispatched to the Banneker School playground in the Shaw neighborhood, where the pool was located. It was on Georgia Avenue, just a few blocks from the laundromat

44

my father now owned and ran. Other reporters headed to police headquarters; one rushed to Casualty Hospital and two to Freedmen's Hospital on the Howard University campus, not far from Banneker. The paper's photo editor appeared at the city desk; he had already sent three photographers to the playground. Sidney Epstein instructed two rewrite men and another reporter to get ready "to unload the legmen" — which meant to get new details from other reporters who would be phoning in from the scene. He told Phil Kelley to assign copyboys to fetch clips from the library for the rewrite men: he wanted all the stories of previous incidents involving electric shock at local swimming pools, the history of the Banneker playground, and background on the community it served. The deadline for the main afternoon edition had already passed, and the deadline for the last Red Streak Final — sold only on newsstands — was five thirty. The Red Streak could be "replated" — deadlines extended and an altered, later version printed — but it would reach only some of the newsstands.

I felt, for the first time, the adrenaline of a newspaper rising to a story. The details as they emerged were horrendous: an electrician had been repairing wiring near the pool when the underwater lights suddenly went on about three fifteen p.m. A ten-year-old boy was electrocuted, and so was a lifeguard who jumped into the pool to try to save him. Both were pronounced dead at the scene. A second lifeguard had also been shocked and taken to Freedmen's Hospital. Jim Moser, a veteran legman who ordinarily worked for the state desk in Virginia, was in the newsroom when Sid Epstein began dispatching reporters, and he was now on the scene interviewing witnesses. Moser learned that the nine-year-old son of the electrician had accompanied his father to work that day. While his father worked on the wiring, the boy had accidentally thrown the switch that powered the pool lights.

All of these details and more, phoned in by other reporters, were assembled in the story that appeared with an eight-column headline across page one — the entire width of the page: TWO ELECTROCUTED IN POOL HERE. Pushed down the page was the story it had displaced, about the Cuban leader Fidel Castro's first year in power.

Sidney Epstein himself edited the Banneker story, pasting pieces of it together from paragraphs turned out piecemeal by the rewrite men. I studied him from a distance. Beyond him, Jerry O'Leary, a burly rewrite man, pounded his typewriter. Now and then he growled *"Copy!"* and tore out the paper with his left hand while with his right he reached for a fresh sheet.

During the seventy-five or so minutes

between the police dispatcher's first call on the squawk box and the last paragraph of the story reaching the composing room upstairs, Sidney Epstein presided over the operation with crisp, unhurried calm — a master at work. Though the prestigious national staff and its news report dominated the front page on most days, there was little question about who was the leader of the newsroom and the person on whom most eyes fell when things were happening.

I understood the drama only in bits and pieces that afternoon: the horror of the event, Sidney Epstein's calm, the gathering of facts, the making sense of them, the speed of the paper's reflexes, the way the truth emerged from confusion and coalesced into a coherent story. Later that night and in the coming days, I studied what had occurred and put the pieces together. It was a lesson in the workings of the *Star* and the values of the newspaper trade.

3

INITIATION

Phil Kelley was off the next day, but he had assigned me to work in the wire room, learning how to pull copy off the teletype machines and deliver it to the appropriate desk — city, state, national, foreign, or telegraph. "Telegraph" was the old-fashioned term for the desk that handled all news from around the country, outside the metro area, because those dispatches arrived by electrical telegraph wire — primarily via the teletype machines of the wire services.

Tony Maggiacomo, the assistant head copyboy, was to be my instructor in these and related matters. He stood about six foot three and had been discharged from the navy earlier that summer after a two-year absence from the paper. He told me it wasn't necessary to call him Mister or Ensign Maggiacomo — Tony would be all right. I seemed to amuse him.

Tony hadn't grown up in Washington, as I had, but even though he came from Rhode Island and graduated from Brown University, he had become a sort of unofficial *Star* historian and seemed to know everything there was to know about the relationship between the paper and the city.

As I had long been aware (and he noted), Washington was a city divided, not just between north and south, Black and white, but also between the political transients and the permanent people who remained in the capital from one presidential administration to the next. Of those permanent people, the city's upper crust liked to call themselves "cave dwellers" (so entrenched were they), and many of the *Star*'s feature pages and its women's section still paid close attention to their comings and goings. I'd known something about the cave dwellers — and had met many of them as a child — because my grandfather took in their cleaning and altered their suits and dresses.

The *Star* understood this division between permanent and transient Washington better than its main twentieth-century rivals: the *Post,* the *Daily News* afternoon tabloid, and the *Times-Herald,* owned by out-of-towners. The Noyeses and the Kauffmanns — permanent people themselves — had had the good sense to put the writing and editing of the paper mostly in the hands of savvy and crafty locals who knew the city as only natives of the town or those who had done their apprenticeship in the streets and alleys of the capital could.

Jeremiah Aloysius O'Leary Sr., born in Swampoodle, had arrived at the paper in 1919, and he still covered the Senate (he also attended Mass every day before heading to Capitol Hill). His son, the rewrite man Jerry O'Leary Jr., had started as a *Star* copyboy at age eighteen. Sidney Epstein, Mary Lou Werner, Miriam Ottenberg, and something like a third of the staff of the paper were born in the city or nearby.

Taking advantage of this well of local knowledge, the *Star* presented, on the whole, a more balanced, thoughtful record of events in the capital, less complicated by ideology than the politically liberal *Washington Post*. At the same time, Deke DeLoach, the assistant director of the FBI, was the godfather of Jerry O'Leary Jr.'s kids, and for that reason (and others), J. Edgar Hoover, a hometown boy, was often able to play the *Star* like a pipe organ.

The *Evening Star* had been the city's dominant paper for more than a century, in advertising revenue and in the quality of its news reporting. But the newspaper business in Washington was changing, Maggiacomo noted. In 1954 the *Washington Post* bought the *Times-Herald,* which published ten editions a day between morning and evening, and eliminated any morning competition. It also picked up the *Times-Herald*'s syndicated features and comics — a significant circulation booster. Suddenly the *Post* had four pages of premier comics, which helped so-lidify its hold on the city's readership. Within a year, the circulation and profits of the newly named *Washington Post and Times-Herald* (though everyone still called it the *Post*) had exceeded that of the *Star.*

I continued to pull copy off the wire ma-chines while Maggiacomo turned from his-tory to the work at hand, explaining the jobs of the paper's subeditors to me and who did what.

The news desk — at the center of the cres-cent, fifteen or twenty feet away from the wire room — was presided over by the little red-headed man in the green eyeshade, Belmont Faries, who, in addition to his role as traffic manager for all the stories that went into the paper, was also the stamp and coin editor of the Sunday *Star.* It told you something about the slightly archaic character of the paper that it had philately and numismatics pages.

Belmont Faries sorted the news of the na-tion and the world with a gnome-like skill, at the same time that he kept track of the alter-nate universe of coins and stamps; he studied catalogs through the course of the day as presidencies and earthquakes and revolutions — and fires and murders and train wrecks — came and went.

Now, all of a sudden, Tony looked wor-ried and glanced at his watch. "Uh-oh, it's past noon," he said. I looked up at the line

51

of large double-sided Seth Thomas clocks that hung over the middle aisle of the newsroom. I noticed that their coordinated minute hands measured time not smoothly, but with a tense, jerky sprocketing from one minute to the next.

I was baffled that the arrival of noon would put the assistant head copyboy in a state of anxiety, especially an assistant head copyboy who'd done two years aboard ship. He sucked in his breath and said, "The carbon paper was supposed to have been washed fifteen minutes ago."

I thought about this. My father owned a laundromat. He'd opened it after Senator James Eastland of Mississippi had made a speech about my father's union, linking it to the Communists or some such, and in doing so had brought about wholesale career changes on the fringes of Washington's workforce — from white collar to blue collar — in a single afternoon. (And this was how the neighborhood laundry business in D.C. became a left-wing refuge in the 1950s.) Sometimes I worked in the laundromat, helping my father feed bleach and soap into the tops of the washing machines. But I had never heard of washing carbon paper.

Ensign Maggiacomo grew more agitated. Grabbing a wire basket, he ordered me to follow him. For the next fifteen minutes we scoured the newsroom, picking up every piece

52

of carbon paper from every desk — rather, I was the one who picked up every single piece of carbon paper, holding the wire basket at arm's length, trying to keep it away from my cream-colored suit from Louie's.

I should stop here to explain about carbon paper. Carbon paper was essential to the newspaper and a big part of a copyboy's job. Every reporter's story was typed onto what were called "books" that made four copies. A book was a sort of club sandwich, with copy paper on the top and bottom and middle, like the bread, and carbon paper was inserted where the turkey, lettuce, and tomatoes would be. The books were assembled every morning by the copyboys — messy work. The sheets of carbon paper were thick and double-sided. Touching the stuff turned your hands purple. A copyboy who wasn't careful would leave his fingerprints all over the newsprint — and anything else he touched. If you thought about how many stories went into a news-paper every day, plus how many more didn't get into print, it gave you an idea how much carbon paper littered the newsroom by eleven thirty in the morning, after the night shift and the first edition of the paper.

By the time I'd collected all the filthy sheets, I had a stack that was more than two feet high and extremely hard to manage in a basket only six or so inches deep. Holding the stack as far in front of me as possible, I maneuvered from the newsroom into the hallway, and then to the men's room.

I pushed the door open with my shoulder. I was relieved to be there; I had noticed that a lot of people in the newsroom were watching me. I began loading the carbon paper into one of the white porcelain sinks, using the tips of my fingers. The carbon paper filled the sink bowl to just under the faucet, and still the basket was half full. I would have to do two loads. As carefully as I could, I turned on the water so that it would hit the carbon paper in the center of the pile. But this was one of those faucets designed to act as a kind of nozzle. It sprayed like a fire hose, sending up an explosion of violent indigo that caused me to fly backward, but too late. Even as I leaped back, I could see in the mirror that my beautiful cream-colored suit now looked like a leopard's skin in a rainstorm.

I was thinking, also, how I might kill that sailor.

Then in the mirror I saw that I was not alone. I had been joined at the row of sinks by Newbold Noyes Jr., the august scion of the *Evening Star*'s founding families and the assistant editor of the paper.

He was watching me closely. Now and then he caught his own visage in the mirror and patted his hair. But instantly his eye would come back to my suit, which he studied with undisguised amazement.

"What are you doing?" he asked.

"Oh, it's noon, Mr. Noyes," I answered, pleased with myself for knowing who he was. "I was just washing the carbon paper."

This did not seem to be the answer he was looking for. I followed the editor's eyes as he took in the spectacle, not merely the jacket but the trousers as well, all blotched and empurpled.

"Is this some kind of fraternity joke?" His voice was rising. I thought it was a stupid thing to say, although I got his basic thrust, which was that he disapproved of copyboy hazing being conducted, so messily, in his place of business. It occurred to me that he was addressing his complaint to the wrong party.

"Go back in that newsroom, and you tell whoever told you to come in here that if I ever hear of something like this happening again, if I ever see any more of this initiation rite business — I presume that's what this is, an initiation rite, right?"

I shrugged.

"Heads are going to roll, beginning with the head copyboy's head, and furthermore you can be damn sure —"

And then he started to laugh.

Hazing aside, what I learned that first week became the foundation of my understanding of the newspaper business. Phil Kelley wanted me to work two full days on the copy desk, which was presided over by Earl Heap, the "slotman" and famous newsroom curmudgeon. Heap sat in the slot — hence the title — within reach of five or six copy editors on either side of the horseshoe-shaped desk. Upon his (usually grumpy) command, a copy editor would edit a story one last time, making sure it was grammatical and logical, using a thick blue pencil to vet each paragraph for the Linotype operators who set stories in type in the composing room.

In the front of my notebook, I kept a chart of these printers' marks and symbols, the language of my new trade. I studied it assiduously: subhead indicated by inverted brackets, every capital letter underlined three times, the start of each paragraph delineated by an elongated L-shaped bracket.

The copyboys were the stevedores in the process of moving copy downriver. Most of us would sit dockside, on a bench between the wire room and Mr. Faries's news desk, waiting for the cry of *"Copy!"* — it could come from anywhere — to signify that another story, or part of it, was about to move downstream and get swept by the current into the paper. On deadline, stories were written in short "takes," at times of only a sentence. At any particular moment, maybe thirty or forty stories were in various stages of transshipment to their ultimate destination in the newsroom — the copy desk.

"Copyyyyyy!" the reporter would yell, and whichever of us was next up would run and grab the book of typed copy from the reporter's outstretched arm like taking a baton in a relay race, then sprint back down the center aisle to stacks of wire baskets where we would strip the books of their carbon paper and in almost the same motion flip them, airborne, into the in-basket of the appropriate desk — city, state, or national. Then an editor would read the copy, reach for the paste pot, and stick the new section of the story — called an "add" — to the previous few paragraphs. Finally he'd yell *"Copy!,"* and wait for another copyboy to take it over to Earl Heap, who would grunt and complain about a split infinitive, fix it, and hand it to one of his copy editors.

Finally, after all their tinkering, the copy was ready to go upstairs to the composing room. This was accomplished by means of the hay baler, which is what Heap had named the conveyor-like contraption that rose above the end of the copy desk and rattled and shook and occasionally chewed up the copy if you didn't load it right — folded in thirds like a letter getting ready for an envelope. You jammed the copy between two interfacing rubber belts that, running in a loop, grabbed and cinched the copy — and your finger, too, if you weren't careful. Though I hadn't yet seen it with my own eyes, this same means of transmission was reputed to convey more than a few of the wagers involving horses to the other part of the composing room's floor, usually at night. After you jammed the paper between the belts, the hay baler would carry the copy along a track just under the ceiling until it disappeared upward through a hole. The arrangement reminded me of my friend Johnny Gianaris's HO gauge trains in my old neighborhood — the envy of every boy in Tenleytown — moving on tracks up from his basement and into the living room above.

Copyboys had other assignments that depended on what shift they were working. The six a.m. and seven a.m. copyboys made up the carbon-paper books in the morning, replenishing them through the day. If you worked the eight a.m. shift, you ran the galley proofs, meaning you raced back and forth between the newsroom and the composing room all day, up and down the iron-treaded steps that passed through a manhole in the ceiling near the wire room and the copy desk. Two other copyboys tended the wires at all times, ripping the AP and UPI copy from the machines, sending the flow of stock quotations from the Dow Jones wire to the business editor, firing off telexes to Crosby S. Noyes, the *Star*'s sole full-time foreign correspondent and the brother of Newbold Noyes Jr. Another copyboy was assigned to fetch page proofs from the composing room. Altogether, there would be twelve to fifteen copyboys working at any given moment of the day, and two or three at night and through the early hours of the morning.

I would learn that the day had a sort of elastic rhythm of deadlines and press times — the whole operation would tighten and relax, breathe in and breathe out, as the stages of the cycle unfolded. The first-edition deadline was nine o'clock in the morning, with the presses running at eleven. Eleven o'clock was also the deadline for the second edition, which would start coming off the presses at one in the afternoon, which in turn was the deadline for the three o'clock edition. And so on. The last edition of the day was the "stocks final," which included the closing quotations from Wall Street.

It was in the composing room that I could see how the whole process came together, and it was on the page proof itself, especially the page one proof I fetched, that I perceived the miracle of the daily newspaper, put out in these five different editions every day with more print than *Paradise Lost,* and twelve times more interesting to my mind. And it only cost a nickel.

4

KNOWLEDGE

During the school year, I had arrived for class each morning in a fog that wouldn't lift until midafternoon, when I made my way to Jim Myers Silver Spring Recreation Center, the fancy name of the local pool hall.

Now, arising in darkness to work the six o'clock early-morning shift during my second week on the job, I arrived in the *Star* newsroom fresh-faced and chipper — and capable of learning with miraculously little impairment, it appeared.

Stacks of out-of-town newspapers — their first editions, called the "bulldog," printed before midnight, bundled and wired — had arrived before me, to be doled out around the crescent. Despite deadlines and the incessant pressure of fast-breaking news, the editors usually managed to page through all the papers before lunchtime. I tried to do the same, working my way through the *New York Times, New York Herald Tribune, Wall Street Journal,* New York *Daily News, Philadelphia*

Inquirer, Baltimore *Sun, Boston Globe, Richmond Times-Dispatch,* and *Chicago Tribune.* And later in the day, the afternoon papers: the *Washington Daily News, New York Journal American, Baltimore News-American, New York Post, Richmond News-Leader,* and *Annapolis Capital Gazette.* Plus the *Washington Post,* which I digested in great gulps at breakfast in the company cafeteria and further deconstructed throughout the day with an increasingly jaundiced eye, comparing its stories to those by our own reporters covering the same events. And I read, from front page to back, the *Washington Afro-American,* published each Saturday.

There seemed hardly a day that magical August that wasn't thrilling, either in the nature of the news, or observing the people I was working with, or when I took account of the luck of my situation. I understood that I'd been given a front-row seat, though I was just an apprentice. I felt as if I was being let in on tremendous secrets.

During my first week, Phil Kelley had presented me with a yellow employee identification card with my name typed just below the ornate logo of the *Evening Star* against a filigreed background that looked like a banknote — so it couldn't be counterfeited, I guessed. I signed it on the back and took this tangible symbol of my exceptional new status to be laminated at one of the photobooth parlors on

Ninth Street. No matter that fifteen hundred other employees of the *Star* from ad salesmen to secretaries carried the same card.

I made sure the new ID was the most visible item in my wallet: atop my Maryland driver's license, my Social Security card, and the Montgomery County library card customized from a batch my friend Ron Oberman and I had prepared in tenth grade to facilitate our purchase of pitchers of beer at Phil's Tavern across the District line, where the legal drinking age was only eighteen.

One afternoon, Phil Kelley ordered me to take a cab to Burning Tree Country Club in Bethesda. There I was to meet up with a *Star* photographer, Paul Schmick, who'd been assigned to get some shots of President Eisenhower playing golf. My instructions were to rush his rolls of film back to the office. First, though, I had to find Schmick. My *Star* ID got me past a single Secret Service agent in the clubhouse and then into the caddy room, where upon presentation of the ID, the caddy chief volunteered to escort me to a practice green where the president of the United States was sinking putts. Ike was wearing a straw hat, and he was hardly ten feet from where I was standing. It was the first time I'd ever seen a president up close, though my mother had told me that she'd taken me as a one-year-old to watch FDR's hearse pass by the White House.

Schmick was crouched with his Leica on the edge of the green. I was so close I could see the brown spots on Ike's hands — I resolved to make a note of it later. I started to walk toward Schmick, but he signaled me with horrified urgency to halt until the president had finished his putt. Then, a few moments later, he held his finger to his lips to enforce silence while we completed our transaction. Schmick turned his body away from the president, opened the back of his camera, and handed me a roll of 35-millimeter film, then a second roll from his pocket, and shooed me on my way.

Another day, Phil Kelley sent me to the Capitol, to the United States Senate, which was only a fifteen-minute walk from the newsroom, to pick up a committee report from Jeremiah O'Leary Sr. Striding past a long line of tourists seeking entry to the building, I flashed my ID at a Capitol policeman, headed to the elevators designated for senators and press only, and announced "Carl Bernstein, *Washington Star*" to the Senate page operating the wood-paneled car that awaited. He glanced at my opened wallet, and I was whisked nonstop to the press gallery.

There I found Mr. O'Leary in a crowded anteroom where perhaps twenty correspondents from newspapers around the country had desks. He was typing away with two fingers but kindly rose and introduced himself when the gallery clerk took me to him. He stood hardly above five feet — about eye to eye with me. He had been covering Capitol Hill for the *Star* since Woodrow Wilson was president. Mr. O'Leary, as I would always call him, handed me an envelope with the report enclosed. Behind him, a set of ornate glass double doors led to the press gallery proper — rows of cushioned seats directly above the Senate floor, reserved for reporters accredited to cover the Congress of the United States. Without my asking, he told me I was welcome to sit inside and watch the debate below if I was interested, that there was no hurry to get the envelope back to the office.

I sat myself down in one of the press seats in the first row, almost directly above the vice president's chair, though the senator occupying it and presiding pro tem over the chamber was unfamiliar to me. I leaned over the brass rail to get a fuller perspective, until I noticed an usher moving toward me, and I pulled myself back before he could admonish me. Barely a dozen members of the Senate were on the floor, but I recognized Everett McKinley Dirksen of Illinois, the Republican minority leader, who was wearing a bow tie. Another senator, in fits and starts, was reading remarks about farm policy into the *Congressional Record* while a stenographer took it all down. Two or three reporters lounged in the gallery seats, bored by the proceedings. I pulled out my reporter's notebook and, just to get the feel of things, started taking notes. It didn't take me long to realize that it was almost impossible to keep up with a speaker's words for more than a couple of sentences — that the reporter's only hope of conveying a real sense of what was occurring was to wait and identify the essence as best as you could, to almost feel it in the cadence of speech and context of subject matter and then to get the most relevant or telling excerpts down between quotation marks as precisely as possible, while at the same time compressing the important concepts through some tight paraphrasing. This was not made easier by my unfamiliarity with farming, although my great-aunt Annie had grown up on a Yiddish-speaking tobacco farm commune in Charles County, Maryland, and there were still several small farms in Silver Spring when we moved from the city in 1955. You could hear roosters from Ron Oberman's house near Forest Glen Road; the western part of Montgomery County beyond Gaithersburg was still largely farmland.

That day on Capitol Hill, I invented for myself a system to register my personal observations and interpretations of what I was witnessing and to note particular details about a scene: I simply drew a box around them — Dirksen's blue-and-white-polka-dotted bow tie; the arrival on the floor of Senator Stuart Symington, whom I recognized from the televised Army-McCarthy hearings ("Sanctimonious Stu," McCarthy had called him); the fact that the senator holding forth seemed almost as uninterested in his own words as were Dirksen and Symington and the few other senators present, who were talking amiably among themselves.

Several were wearing white suits, I noted. I was again decked out in my cream-colored number from Louie, now restored to its original glory by the miracle workers at the National Institute of Dry Cleaning — the largest employer and biggest building in all of Silver Spring, both a trade association and research facility located across from the B&O Railroad station. It had been my grandfather's idea to send the suit there — it was where he went with hard cases of stains — and I was admonished by the institute's experts that I'd been lucky they could get rid of the leopard spots, warning me that carbon paper was often lethal to cotton. This again put me in high dudgeon about Tony Maggiacomo, who had done nothing by way of apologizing for his mischief.

At some point while I was scribbling in my notebook, my next-door neighbor Senator Bible entered the Senate chamber below me. Though he was a Democrat, I could see him chatting easily with Dirksen, with his arm around the minority leader's back. As fascinating and as useful to me as all this was,

66

after about twenty minutes of what even I could tell were desultory proceedings, I knew it was time to leave.

I thanked Mr. O'Leary for inviting me to sit inside, and when I mentioned that I'd seen my neighbor on the floor, he asked if I wanted to say hello to the senator. Leading me by the arm, he took me by a back stairway to the Democratic cloakroom, where he dispatched an assistant sergeant at arms with a note for Senator Bible, who soon came off the floor. I had never seen so many spittoons in one place as in that cloakroom, though only one seemed to be in actual use. It was hard to make out much of anything through the tobacco smoke generated by all the senators — easily three times as many legislators as I'd seen from the press gallery — and their various retainers.

Senator Bible was surprised, of course, to see me in the company of Mr. O'Leary, but when I explained that I now worked at the *Star* he invited me to join him in the Senate dining room for lunch sometime. This was an altogether different proposition from eating with him and Loucile, his wife, and Billy and Paul in their kitchen at home, which I'd done a number of times.

In my third week of employment, Phil Kelley assigned me to the wire room. The excitement of reading wire copy as it came into the building from around the world was built on a certain grand premise of privileged knowledge. Even Maggiacomo seemed a little stirred by the idea that he was involved in something important. At any given moment, the copyboys in the wire room probably knew more about what was going on around the country and the globe than almost everybody else on the planet who wasn't lucky enough to work in a newsroom, or wasn't employed up the George Washington Parkway at the CIA where Mr. O'Leary's other son, Jerry O'Leary Jr.'s brother, was believed to work.

What I was reading and pulling off the machines — the news in pieces, in its rawest form — had not yet been in the headlines. Only a smidgen would be read by an announcer on the hourly radio broadcasts of the news and the fifteen-minute TV newscasts (including cigarette commercials) on the three networks at the dinner hour.

August was usually the doldrums in the news business, when reporters took their vacations, but not this year: Soviet premier Nikita Khrushchev was planning to come to America for the United Nations General Assembly meeting in September, and Ike was under pressure from the Democrats and his own party to keep the Soviet leader from traveling outside Manhattan; Senator Kennedy and Vice President Nixon were gearing up for the final stretch of their campaigns for the presidency; Congress was still in session because Eisenhower insisted that it pass a modicum of civil rights legislation; and for a change, the Washington Senators weren't in last place — they'd been edging in and out of the first division of the American League for days, with Harmon Killebrew hitting tape-measure home runs over the Griffith Stadium fence. Given the weight of all this, not to mention railroad strikes in the West, war in the Congo, and Castro in Cuba, I could hardly keep up with the BULLETINs and URGENTs that, with jarring frequency, were sounding the AP and UP and INS bells.

In quieter moments, after delivering copy to Mr. Faries on the news desk, I was able to engage him in a discussion of U.S. postage first-day covers — the only part of my stamp collection that hadn't been stolen at an eighth-grade science fair — to which he was not only amenable, but he'd even promised to bring me a catalog devoted to collecting them.

Some nights, before I fell asleep, I conjured the notion of ten bells sounding in the wire room and tried to imagine what the story might be. And then one Saturday afternoon, it happened. I counted four and then five bells on the A-wire of the Associated Press — but the ringing didn't stop. Five more pealed in rapid succession as I rushed toward the machine. There was a brief pause, then the insistent ringing resumed: ten bells in rapid succession. I waited for the machine to type its news. MOSCOW — AUGUST 19: THE SO-VIET UNION HAS LAUNCHED . . . Here, as the machine often did after a few words, it stopped typing, as if to catch its breath before delivering more, like a hiccup, in the remainder of its lead paragraph: A SPACECRAFT CARRYING TWO DOGS INTO ORBIT. The Soviets had brought the spaceship back to earth twenty-four hours later, with the dogs still alive.

I tore the paragraph off the wire and ran it to the foreign desk, then raced back to the machine, which in the next sentence — after ten bells again, and typing out the story's identifying "slug," SPACEDOGS ADD 1 — reported that the dogs had orbited the earth eighteen times, almost half a million miles. Within a minute, most of the editors around the crescent had rushed from their desks to crowd into the wire room to read the coming paragraphs over my shoulder.

Phil Kelley, Tony Maggiacomo, and a third copyboy, Mark Baldwin, joined the crush and worked the machines with me. Baldwin had recently been rehabilitated as a copyboy after trying to slip a fake obituary into the paper about the (fictional) architect of an underwater city designed for the Washington Channel of the Potomac and Anacostia Rivers. So skillfully and plausibly had he crafted the idea — describing the underwater city as an integral part of a controversial urban renewal and slum-clearing plan for Southwest and Northeast Washington — that the obit had sailed past an assistant city editor and the copy desk without a hitch. But Sid Epstein got a look at a galley proof and his face turned red, and he killed the story.

To me, the space dogs seemed even more unbelievable than Baldwin's phony obit. Half a dozen wire machines were now providing additional parts of the story. Instead of copyboys running take after take from the machines to the editors at the crescent, the editors now ripped the wire copy from our hands as soon as we'd torn off a paragraph.

The subsequent bulletins laid out the details of the story, which were astounding.

BULLETIN: Radio Moscow said the spacecraft weighed four and one-half tons. Its passengers had also included rats, mice, flies, plants, microscopic water organisms, fungus, and some seeds.

BULLETIN, ADD 1: The rats, mice, and flies were chosen because they breed quickly. This could enable the Soviet Union's scientists to assess whether cosmic radiation in space would cause physical changes several generations in the future.

"Get Hines in here! Somebody find Hines!" the national editor shouted. Bill Hines was the *Star*'s reporter covering the U.S. space program — probably the best science reporter in the country.

71

But this news was wholly unexpected; it was only three years after Sputnik. This was more like science fiction. And the Russians were crowing, triumphantly announcing the historical first of sending animals into space and returning them alive.

The commotion in the newsroom was even greater than what had been set off by the swimming pool electrocution story. Almost every reporter appeared to be on the phone; within minutes, dictationists were taking down Garnett Horner's account of the initial White House reaction and the statements of congressional leaders — stunned chagrin. The United States had not yet tried to send any large creature beyond the earth's atmosphere. And almost as amazing as getting the dogs up there, to my mind, Soviet scientists had watched them on television screens during the flight. They had been able to see the animals move and eat their food while orbiting the earth.

REDS LAND ANIMALS FROM SPACE SAFELY, announced the Star's headline soon after. REPORT FIRST RETURN FROM SHIP IN ORBIT.

The last paragraph of the story on the front page (just before the "jump" to the story's continuation on an inside page) noted that the launch and return had been announced during the sentencing phase of the trial in Moscow of the American U-2 spy plane pilot Francis Gary Powers. His plane had been downed by a Soviet missile at an altitude of 70,000 feet. It did not seem an accident of timing that these humiliating events were occurring on the eve of Nikita Khrushchev's trip to New York.

Powers was from Virginia — and Mary Lou Werner and George Porter, the state editors, had for months flooded the story with reporters who had earned the trust of the pilot's lawyers and members of his family. He could face the death penalty. "All news is local" was more than a cliché, I was learning. POWERS' FAMILY PLANS PLEA TO RED PRESIDENT was the off-lead of that day's paper (the second most important story on the front page), next to the space dogs.

Less prominently, the front page carried a photograph of former president Harry S. Truman and Senator Kennedy above the headline TRUMAN, KENNEDY BURY ALL THEIR DIFFERENCES / EX-PRESIDENT PLEDGES FULL SUPPORT. Truman had thought Kennedy green and callow, and prior to the Democratic convention he had backed the candidacy of Senator Symington, his fellow Missourian.

And in an adjacent column, above the byline of David Broder, the *Star*'s new chief political reporter: NIXON WARNS OF RED APPEAL TO NEW NATIONS.

I had been studying Sid Epstein ever since the electrocution story. The figure he cut was about as far from your ink-stained wretch as a newspaperman could be. He would even whistle sometimes while he read copy, which I gathered was a sign that the piece was on the money.

Sid Epstein's physical presence was commanding: an inch or two above six feet, but loose-limbed, like an athlete. His eyes were a piercing brown and his smile was unforced, and all of this was set off by custom-made suits and monogrammed shirts from the Lewis & Thos. Saltz haberdashery on F Street, button-down oxford pastels and striped neckties, not too bold but in perfect contrast to the larger scheme. The whole effect was mesmerizing for a newsroom, and much too elegant. You did not expect the city editor to look like something out of *Esquire,* though Sid Epstein did not strut like a major peacock. Tony Maggiacomo said you knew Sid Epstein was really mad when his face turned red and he addressed you in a whisper.

It was also clear that he inspired a measure of fear almost equal to the awe in which his troops held him. I had seen both aspects in the days immediately following the swimming pool electrocutions, when half a dozen reporters had been assigned to find out why the D.C. Recreation Board had once again proved incompetent, tragically so this time. There was a parade marching to and from Sid Epstein's desk, and at the completion of each conversation the enhanced motivation of the reporter was evident. Phil Kelley and Tony Maggiacomo had assured me that Sid Epstein's talents as an editor and leader were unearthly — and it was now impossible to miss his single-minded fierceness to be the first to get the story, to get it right, and to write it tight, through five editions a day. It was also conspicuous that he encouraged in his troops a camaraderie that he, however, did not join in.

Rather, he hovered above the proceedings, aloof but always definite and exacting. When he gave orders, he was ruthlessly clear. I came to realize that his personal remove from his reporters was part of what made him such an effective leader; it contributed to his mystery because (as he wished it) we knew almost nothing about his life outside the newsroom. It was rumored that he went riding in Rock Creek Park every Wednesday afternoon, his day off, with a beautiful riding instructor. After I'd heard the tale from enough people to give it credence, I would sometimes walk through the park hoping to get a glimpse of Sid Epstein and his Guinevere in their equestrian finery, but I never sighted them.

He would arrive each morning precisely at eight forty-five, remove his suit jacket, and fit it onto a hanger on the coatrack in his small office on the east side of the newsroom. But he did not linger there. Instead he would proceed to his preeminent position at the center of the news desk, seat himself in a green-padded aluminum swivel armchair, roll his sleeves with just one measured turn, and then motion to a copyboy in the wire room less than twenty feet away, which was how I first came to be addressed by him. "Hey, kid," he said, and he beckoned me with his finger.

The breakfast that he then ordered — and that I fetched from the cafeteria upstairs many times thereafter — rarely varied: a toasted, buttered bagel and coffee, light with one sugar, with a side of grits in a Dixie Cup. And for his wife, Eleni, the paper's fashion editor, who arrived with him each morning and would appear some ten minutes later from across the hall in the women's section, a bacon and egg sandwich on a kaiser roll, coffee regular.

Eleni used only her first name in her byline: *By Eleni, Star Fashion Editor.* Eleni Sakes Epstein was a first-generation Greek American, of which the capital had an unusually large population. This indicated another peculiarity about Washington: Greeks probably outnumbered Italians five to one. This was because Baltimore, forty miles to the north, was one of the country's biggest port cities, and large Italian families arriving as immigrants had tended to stay there. Most Greek immigrants arriving at Baltimore in the first half of the twentieth century were men looking

76

for work, and most of them found jobs in Washington, often in occupations dominated by Italians in other places. These included the rackets, many of which were controlled by the uncle of my playmate Johnny Gianaris. In any other city, the rackets would have been run by Italians, but we had no Italian mob in Washington. J. Edgar Hoover, perhaps in part because of this, for decades was famous for not believing there really was a consequential Mafia in America, maintaining instead that it was something made up by journalists in New York. Likewise, we had more Greek restaurants than Italian ones. In a city with a population of more than 750,000, I knew of only three Italian restaurants, the most popular being A.V. Ristorante Italiano on New York Avenue, which from the outside looked like a low-rent funeral parlor; Gusti's near Dupont Circle, where my friends and I went for pizza after school dances; and the Roma in Cleveland Park. In Silver Spring there was the Villa Rosa, where a talented guitarist, Charlie Byrd, played with a trio and customers were drawn more to the music than the food. He had been my guitar teacher after we moved to Silver Spring from Tenleytown.

When the news broke about the space dogs, it was characteristic that Sid Epstein had not rushed to the wire room but had remained at his desk, dispatching reporters into the street to gather reactions from ordinary citizens.

One thing I had noticed about Sid Epstein was that the greater the pressure and the bigger the story, the more important it became for him to stay calm in the storm, to take measure of all the howling and then pay it no mind. He seemed a completely self-possessed man. Even pushing deadline on a huge story, with eight or nine reporters calling in details as he conferred with his deputy, Coit Hendley, and marked up the copy, he had an air of equanimity.

His desk, except for a metal spike with carbon copies of old stories impaled on it, a paste pot, a ruler, and the telephone, was always kept clear. While he read copy, his knee would gently bounce up and down, and if he was deep in thought, he'd lightly roll his pencil back and forth across his desk with his fingertips; when he took it up again to write it might as well have been a baton between the fingers of an orchestra conductor. Almost everything he did in the newsroom seemed methodical, but he brought an artistry to his work, or so it looked to me in those early, impressionable weeks as I settled into my new newspaper life. I sensed that he would figure in it wherever it took me.

In the last week of August, Phil Kelley assigned me to work the four-to-midnight shift. The shift had a rhythm altogether its own, dictated by the squawk box and whatever mayhem and murder was occurring on the streets, which might be considerable, especially in the summer months.

After sundown, there'd be fewer than a dozen or so people in the newsroom: a night city editor, an overnight dictationist, another copyboy in the wire room, a couple of copy editors, plus the night police reporter, who'd be out on the street with the cops and fire trucks more than he'd be in the office. I was the lone monitor of the squawk box each night when Emerson Beauchamp, the night city editor that summer, went out to dinner and left me with instructions to call the restaurant and summon him back if anything consequential were to happen. By this he meant some kind of extreme bodily harm occurring in the fancier parts of the city or in the bars downtown where members of Congress and visiting foreign dignitaries had been known to get into altercations with women not their wives or con men nearby, and the cops would be called. I had high hopes of being dispatched to such an event, but mostly that week, I beat a path back and forth to the cavernous library behind the newsroom with its rows and rows of file cabinets as tall as I was, stuffed with newspaper clippings (in alphabetical order by name or subject) in thousands of letter-sized manila envelopes organized front to back.

Out of curiosity, I looked up my parents in the files, knowing of my father's run-in with

Senator Eastland's committee. To my surprise, there was an earlier clipping, from June 1944, with a picture of my mother and me as an infant, from the *Washington Post*.

Victory Baby of the Week

Carl Milton Bernstein was born three months before his father, Pvt. Alfred Bernstein, went overseas, but Uncle Sam never gave the leave necessary to allow the two to meet. Today, Father's Day, is Carl's parents' fifth wedding anniversary. He and his mother are living at 1601 Argonne Pl. N. W., with her parents, Mr. and Mrs. Thomas Walker. Just before embarking, Pvt. Bernstein wrote his family not to feel badly about his leaving. He said there was a job to be done if they were to lead the kind of life they wanted. Formerly attached to the Senate Committee investigating railroads here, Bernstein was supervising investigator for the West Coast of the Office of Price Administration at the time of his induction.

Next I decided to systematically look up subjects relevant to my new profession, beginning with Sidney Epstein, and I spread out the clippings at a long table at the back of the room.

A story written when he'd been named city editor of the *Star* said that his parents, Abe and Ida, had owned a small restaurant on

Seventh Street. He had begun his career as a copyboy at the *Washington Herald* in 1937 — when he was sixteen — and dropped out of George Washington University in his freshman year to become a full-time reporter. He, too, had graduated from Central High School, five years after my mother's class.

By the time he was twenty-one, he was known as a crack rewrite man. He joined the U.S. Marines in 1942, served two years in the South Pacific, and came home a captain. By then the *Herald* had merged with the *Washington Times,* and he became the city editor of the combined paper. The *Post*'s purchase of the *Times-Herald* in 1954 created a sudden realignment of the town's journalistic resources, and the *Star* snagged some talented writers and editors (along with a share of oddballs and boozehounds). Sid Epstein was one of the prizes of the *Times-Herald* that the *Post* lost to the *Star.*

I found a pile of stories he'd written for the *Times-Herald,* including one accompanied by a photo of him as a twenty-two-year-old marine wearing standard-issue khaki and a foxhole helmet clamped tight with a chin strap. The effect was not quite as impressive as when he'd stride into the newsroom in full Lewis & Thos. Saltz regalia, but the crease in his uniform trousers was as crisp as that in the civilian slacks he wore in the oppressive Washington humidity.

81

The story carried the byline of Staff Sergeant Sidney Epstein, with a dateline of Guantánamo Bay, Cuba. It was about the sacrifices the troops were making as they shipped out to war, and their fears. Just under a column's length, about seven hundred words, the piece was perfectly fashioned — even elegant — in its taut storytelling: about young men and boys from city and countryside getting ready to transfer to a troopship that would take them to the European theater, where GIs were fighting and dying by the thousands. A private first class talked about the letter he'd written to his girlfriend back home and how if he got back in one piece they'd get married. A master gunnery sergeant talked about the odds of his company's getting overrun. A military policeman from North Dakota, who had never met a foreigner, tried to imagine guarding a stockade filled with German prisoners. And from that clip I began to understand not just Sidney Epstein's sensibilities as a writer and young reporter, but also something about great rewrite men and deadline stylists and the elements of what made the best of them.

Sid Epstein's way with words — and his rigorous insistence on stories being verified from every available angle — was also reflected in his pencil editing. That week on the night shift, I'd take the carbon copies from the metal spike on his desk and examine the stories he'd edited during the day. There was sureness to his touch, and when he was finished with a piece of copy, it had often achieved a kind of flow and patina that wasn't there in the original typed version. The words were now as they were meant to be: an easy progression of simple paragraphs that allowed the complexity and context of the story to come through. Reading his clips and his edits, I began to sense the way he worked and what he valued: at heart, it seemed to me, he was a storyteller who built his tale cleanly, with an accumulation of detail that came from careful observation and multiple sources of information, so that it resonated yet had its corners solidly nailed down. You trusted the story.

This was what had marked the clip I'd read from Guantánamo in 1942, and this was what he was able to do with someone else's copy. He'd find whole paragraphs that were best excised, no matter how attached the writer might be to the flower of the prose; he would make a perfect box around the offending typewritten lines and draw an X from corner to corner. In my few weeks at the paper I had overheard complaints and grumbling from some reporters that he was butchering their best work. But from what I could see, his excisions were unerring.

By the end of that first month, it was clear to me that the best job to aspire to in the

world was city editor of the *Star* — and that
if and when I ever grew up, I wanted to be
Sid Epstein. Substantively, temperamentally,
sartorially.

5

DRY RUN

In the first few weeks of my apprenticeship, I filled a dozen notebooks with what I was learning about the newspaper, how to be a copyboy, the news of each day, and which reporter was covering what story. At night or on the train back to Silver Spring I studied what I'd written, and in capital letters appended a note of interpretation. One late afternoon, I walked from the *Star* building to Reeves Bakery on F Street for strawberry pie, and then, to quench my journalistic curiosity (or so I imagined it), I searched out Eddie Bernstein. He seemed thrilled that I'd landed a job at the newspaper, and he was not in the least put off that I was asking him a lot of questions about himself and scribbling some of his answers in my notebook — just for practice.

Though I continued to go to school, I never really cracked a book after that summer, which wasn't much of a stretch from my regular practice. But now, entering my senior year, I had an excuse not to study: I was a working newspaperman. I announced the fact around Montgomery Blair High School by carrying a reporter's notebook stuck smartly into my back pocket, its REPORTER BRAND legend visible to anyone walking behind me.

In class I imagined myself taking notes, say, standing over a body, or discussing a heist with a cop, or from a sitting position with my notebook braced on my knee during an interview or press conference, scribbling away, flipping the pages up over the spiral, struggling to keep pace with the president's outpouring of words.

My mother and Phil Kelley had assumed that I'd work Saturdays and most holidays until the end of the school year — the same as I'd managed at McBride's in the tenth and eleventh grades. But I concocted a better plan, and I sketched out its details in my reporter's notebook before presenting it to the appropriate parties: I would work at the *Star* every Saturday, plus either Friday or Sunday each week, and occasionally both; midweek, I'd put in another late-afternoon shift from three to eleven p.m. To further accommodate my vocational education, I arranged my school schedule so that my final class each afternoon was an unsupervised study hall in the school library; and preceding the study hall on Mondays, Wednesdays, and Fridays, a gym class that would have no bearing on my academic record if, as a result of inattention or nonattendance, I got a D or an F. My enlightenment appeared ensured all around. Three times a week I could escape the school grounds by one thirty, take the train to Union Station and be at the *Star* by three, and get back home and into bed not long after midnight. I overcame the objections of my mother, who attempted enforcement of such matters in our family, by assuring her I'd have adequate time to do homework during my evening shift. I implied that there was little else to do while I was sitting at the city desk with the night editor after seven o'clock or so. In sum, I figured out a way to put in a four-day workweek until I graduated in June. Or didn't.

My self-accelerated plan to become a real newspaperman was unexpectedly advanced when a list of upcoming citizens association and civic association meetings for the fall was posted on the copyboys' bulletin board in the second week of September. Mark Baldwin explained to me the significance of these events: they were meetings of neighborhood organizations that, in a city with no self-government, came as close to being sanctioned bodies of advisory authority as existed in the capital of the United States. It had been during one of these meetings, Mark told me, that he had dreamed up his idea for an underwater city in the Washington Channel and spun it into an obituary of its designer — which nearly got him fired. (His inspiration had been a presentation by the District of Columbia army engineer commissioner, the official responsible for overseeing public works in the capital.)

Sid Epstein had decided that instead of full-fledged reporters covering these neighborhood meetings, copyboys and dictationists could boost their pay at the rate of $7.50 per meeting and, more valuable, could attain some reporting experience.

I asked to cover the September 18 meeting of the Petworth Citizens Association as my first bona fide reporting effort. This was a calculated choice. First, the gathering of this group of citizens was only a few days away. Second, I knew my way around the Petworth neighborhood. My great-aunt Rose and great-uncle Itzel lived in a bungalow on Allison Street in the heart of Petworth. Many weekends I'd been shipped off to their house, and I had happy memories of the place; there had been a cherry tree in the backyard with actual fruit, and Aunt Rose had made terrific pies out of the cherries I picked. Third, Petworth was a residential neighborhood with important history and institutions in its midst: the Old Soldiers' Home (and Lincoln's summer cottage); Fort Stevens, from which federal troops had fled when the British came to sack the city in 1814; and old Mr. Marriott's first big restaurant, which he opened when my mother was a teenager; now there were Marriott Hot

Shoppes all across the region, and if the one in Silver Spring was too crowded after a football game or sock hop at the armory, teenagers from Montgomery County would drive down Georgia Avenue to the one in Petworth, three miles away.

I arranged to use the family's '58 DeSoto for the night of September 18, and instead of skipping study hall that afternoon, I read up on Petworth from local history books in the school library. I also stopped at the Petworth Hot Shoppe for a Mighty Mo double burger at dinnertime.

The parents of many of my classmates had moved their families from Petworth to Silver Spring in the mid-1950s, soon after the Supreme Court had ruled in *Brown v. Board of Education* and *Bolling v. Sharpe*. Barnard Elementary, where the Petworth citizens were to meet, had been the white grammar school attended by many students now at Blair. Like the city itself, and the effect of white flight to the suburbs, Barnard now had a majority of Black students, as did nearby Roosevelt High School, which had once been the white high school attended by most Jewish pupils in Northwest Washington. Petworth, a working-class and middle-class neighborhood of single-family homes, was now 60 percent Black.

I was unprepared for what I encountered when, a quarter hour before the meeting's eight o'clock start time, I took my seat in the school auditorium, several rows from the front but close enough to get a view of the whole show and hear from both the front and back of the hall. What I saw was a sea of white faces — *only* white faces.

I introduced myself to the president of the association, who was effusive in her appreciation that the *Star* was covering the meeting. By then, perhaps 150 people had seated themselves, and still every face in the place was white. The president's name was Annabelle Gustavson Weaver, and she would be happy to help with anything I needed to report my story. So I took a deep breath and asked: *Could you tell me, ma'am, why none of the Black residents of this neighborhood are here?*

She was not the least put off by my ignorance and educated me on the spot about community meetings in the District of Columbia. *Citizens* associations, she explained, were neighborhood organizations whose membership was all white. *Civic* associations — including the Petworth Civic Association — were all Black. I was covering the monthly meeting of the Petworth Citizens Association. The separate citywide umbrella organizations for the two communities were the Federation of (white) Citizens Associations and the Federation of (Black) Civic Associations.

While I tried to absorb that, and wrote down what she had told me, I again took my

90

seat — and had already filled several pages in my notebook when Mrs. Weaver gaveled the meeting to order. A secretary read the minutes of the previous meeting, in which there had been a unanimous vote to write a letter of protest to the District commissioners about the D.C. Transit Company's decision to close down the Georgia Avenue streetcar line that ran from downtown, through Petworth, and all the way to the D.C.–Silver Spring border. The secretary noted that the save-the-streetcar movement, favored by both the Federation of Citizens Associations and the Federation of Civic Associations, was failing. Streetcars — trolleys — had been the city's main mode of public transportation up until the fifties, when they started giving way to buses, and by now the whole metropolitan area was choked with automobile traffic. Which was another reason the *Star* was losing circulation: it couldn't get the paper out to the newer postwar suburbs until late in the afternoon.

Next, an amiable public servant from the city Highway Department attempted to brief the group on current road construction projects. He might as well have read a declaration of war upon those present. For fully forty-five minutes, he and his department were vilified for disturbing the peace and tranquility of decent people all over the capital, not just in Petworth. The primary concern of the Highway

Department — it was alleged — was to make it easier for members of Congress and their staffs to get to work and to get out of town quicker.

The highway man also bore the brunt of the citizens' outrage that nearby Sherman Circle was inaccessible by foot because of construction underground to shore up the little park in the middle of the circle and to make sure the statue of the general and his horse didn't come tumbling down on their way to Atlanta.

Mrs. Weaver then introduced a K-9 patrol officer from the Seventh Precinct — and a very large German shepherd. Both got the undivided attention and admiration of the audience, as the officer explained how dogs were fearsome crime-fighting tools for Petworth. He put the shepherd, named Mazie, through some paces (most involved sniffing) that he claimed would discourage loitering. The final business of the association this night, accompanied by applause, was a unanimous resolution to commend the Police Department for its effective use of dogs to reduce crime.

How to turn all this into a coherent newspaper account was vexing. I had not expected I would need to master the intricacies of highway development and urban planning to be a reporter. Nor did I have a hint of how anything that had transpired at the meeting could be made interesting to the reader.

When I got to the newsroom that night and gave Emerson Beauchamp a rundown on what had occurred, it didn't seem any clearer to him than it did to me. "Keep it to one take, and let's see what you've got," he said. One take meant a single page.

To me, the most important aspect of the whole business was that there were separate associations for white and Black citizens, but Beauchamp said this was a well-known fact of life in the city and had been reported more than once.

I went to one of the reporter's desks deep in the newsroom. I tried a dozen different ways to tell the story, and I did more staring at a blank page than I did typing. I focused several attempts on Mazie the K-9. Finally, I arrived at my story.

The Petworth Citizens Association last night resolved to urge the National Capital Parks to restore Sherman Circle to its original condition prior to underground construction work undertaken in recent months.

Leonard A. DeGast, Project Development Engineer for the District Department of Highways, spoke to the group about highway developments in the Washington area.

Some members of the association were displeased with plans for newly proposed highway routes. One woman said, "It seems as though you want to tear Washington up so other people can drive through and tear it up."

In other action, the group voted to commend the Police Department for their effective job of curbing crime and loitering through the use of dogs.

The meeting, held at the Barnard Elementary School, was presided over by Mrs. A. G. Weaver, Sr.

Emerson Beauchamp was a thin, professorial man in his early thirties with round black spectacles, whose ambition was to become the *Star*'s drama critic; he had arrived at the paper from Frankfort, Kentucky, where his father was a former lieutenant governor of the state. During my week on the night shift, he had been generous in taking time to show me how he edited a story, pointing out the weakness or strength of a noteworthy sentence or paragraph in the overnight copy entrusted to his judgment. I had seen how meticulous his approach was.

Now he invited me to sit beside him on his side of the crescent, across from where Sidney Epstein would be during the day. He read through what I had written, following the words with his pencil. I was relieved he was changing so few of them and excising relatively little. "Resolved" became "voted." Sentences became a bit tighter. The highway man's job title shifted to lowercase.

"You're really getting the hang of it," he said and explained each change. I wondered what page my story was destined for.

Then he wrote the words DRY RUN above the story's slug, drew a big X through the whole thing, and said, "Next time, you'll be ready to write for the paper." And he told me to save a copy of what I'd written — that someday I'd want to look back at it.

I folded the top copy in half and stuck it between the pages of my notebook.

6

LEGMAN

A week after the Petworth experience, my first published story appeared on page B-18 of the local news section, five paragraphs in length totaling six column inches. Its brevity didn't matter. I had now reported and written a story for a great American newspaper. From the meeting hall to my typewriter to news-stands and two hundred thousand homes.

It reported the opposition of the LeDroit Park Civic (Black) Association to locating a public housing project in the adjacent neighborhood of Swampoodle. The quality of the prose was half a notch better than my dry run in Petworth. (Still it took me more than two hours to compose.) I will admit that the thrill of seeing it in print was difficult to contain, but I managed nonchalance in the newsroom. Not, however, with my parents — who seemed encouraged.

It was a tradition at the paper that upon publication of their first story, copyboys and dictationists (and copygirls in the women's section) were presented with a leather-covered scrapbook embossed in gold with the *Star*'s logo — the same as given to newly hired reporters upon joining the staff. Phil Kelley handed mine over when I arrived for work the next day. At lunchtime, I retreated to the mailbox area at the back of the newsroom. Using a Linotype rule made of lead, I carefully tore my story from the newspaper and, brandishing the brush from one of the paste pots shelved nearby, cemented this diminutive account of heroic civic effort to the approximate center of the first page of the scrapbook. Then, upstairs in the cafeteria over a sandwich, with my oversized scrapbook opened wide, I read and reread what I'd written as if it were set down for the ages in iambic pentameter.

Because I was considerably younger than the other copyboys and dictationists, it would have been my almost certain destiny to cover civic meetings and little else in the coming months were it not for the happy coincidence that George Porter, the state editor for Maryland and Virginia news, lived a half mile from our family's house.

I had hardly noticed Mr. Porter. My attention was focused on his deputy, Mary Lou Werner. She seemed the glamorous epitome of a great modern newspaperwoman. The stories that had won her the Pulitzer, on massive resistance to school desegregation in Virginia, conveyed drama and history. The term "massive resistance" — so artful and evil all at once — had been invented by the state's senior politicians for their strategy to obstruct school integration ordered in *Brown v. Board of Education*. "Integration anywhere means destruction everywhere," Virginia's governor proclaimed in his 1958 inaugural address.

Ludy Werner's extraordinary reporting had revealed the machinations and private deliberations and even the bigoted language of the state's elected leaders as they shut down hundreds of public schools rather than integrate. In their place, the state government established an elaborate system of tax-funded "private academies" — and tuition grants — for whites across Virginia, while schools for Black children were left underfunded, dilapidated, and miles apart.

What made Mary Lou Werner's stories so remarkable were her unconventional choices about what constituted "news" — which facts and scenes to highlight and the context they conveyed. She'd developed sources deep inside the "Byrd Organization," which since the 1920s had ruled the state's politics under the firm grip of Senator Harry Flood Byrd, an apple farmer who owned not only most of the orchards in the state but the politicians as well. And she described the plight of Black children denied decent education, and their parents' sadness and hardship.

In story after story, she evoked the elements

of a great human drama, not least the inculcation of hatred among white children caught up in the struggle through no fault of their own. Most of her stories had been written on deadline, and more often than not dictated from a telephone booth outside a schoolhouse or a courthouse or the statehouse in Richmond.

A generation earlier, Ludy Werner had graduated from one of those affected schools, George Washington High in Alexandria. She'd gone to work as a copygirl at the *Star* the year I was born, after she dropped out of the University of Maryland. Like several women on the staff, she became a reporter when so many of the men in the newsroom had gone off to war.

While I was eating my sandwich and admiring my story that afternoon, she emerged from the cafeteria line and invited herself to sit across from me. She was very pretty in a big-boned way, tall with dark, upswept hair. I guessed she was at least five foot ten, and she always wore flats. In the newsroom she talked as an equal to the guys and smoked Marlboros, and she seemed to be in perpetual good humor. Tony Maggiacomo said she had a boyfriend who was a few years older and worked as a lobbyist for the Maryland and Virginia Milk Producers Association.

In a hurry, but too late, I shut my scrapbook. Undeterred, she asked what I'd covered so far. I admitted to the dry-run experience and told her, in as few words as possible, about my subsequent assignment. She asked to see the story. She must have spent a full minute reading the three hundred or so words I'd suffered over at the typewriter, and her verdict was generous: she said I'd put together a fine account of what happened. I was full of questions that I wanted to ask about being a reporter, but she was loaded up with questions of her own, and by the time lunch was finished, she had elicited something like an edited summary of my life up to that point. The Silver Spring portion led her to interject that Mr. Porter, too, lived there, not far from Montgomery Blair High School.

Except for some of the copy editors put out to pasture and working part time, George Porter was probably the oldest editor on the crescent, older than my parents, older even than Earl Heap, which is to say he was about sixty. Later that afternoon, having been tipped off by Ludy Werner, he asked me where my house was in Silver Spring — almost around the corner from his, as it turned out — and he offered me a ride home.

Mr. Porter drove a green 1948 Oldsmobile — so slowly that he managed to make the trip from the *Star* building to Silver Spring take longer than either the bus or the train and hitchhiking the rest of the way, as I usually did. The extended commute provided plenty of time for Mr. Porter to tell me more about the history of the *Star,* one third of which he'd been there for. After my lunchtime interrogation I was grateful to be on the question end of this discussion, which also was about the expansion of the Maryland suburbs, and the transformation of Montgomery County from a semirural backwater to the county with the highest per capita income in America, a fact I'd heard recited by our teachers too often.

I had been anything but enamored with the place, at least our particular suburban enclave on Harvey Road, and the experience of having moved there in the middle of the sixth grade, on my eleventh birthday. I made, at best, a grudging adjustment to these new circumstances. My last good grades had been at Janney Elementary in Washington; since then, at Montgomery Hills Junior High and at Montgomery Blair, my grade point average had slipped below C; twice I'd had to attend summer school, after eighth and tenth grade, for algebra and then for Spanish.

I did not mention any of this to Mr. Porter, who clearly believed suburbia was one of mankind's great accomplishments. After five years I still missed my old neighborhood in Tenleytown, and my friends there. There were sidewalks in Tenleytown. Our little semidetached stucco house on Chesapeake Street N.W. was in a working-class quarter, far removed from the fancy homes of lawyers and doctors and diplomats and senators and congressmen that encircled us at a distance of less than half a mile.

For some reason, my utterly irreligious parents had decided to move me and my two sisters — Mary, born in 1947, and Laura, 1949 — to a largely Jewish neighborhood in Silver Spring, backing onto Sligo Creek Park. Sligo Creek was a murky culvert compared to the rushing waters of Rock Creek and its steep-sided valley that gave Washington so much of its character.

The Montgomery County Board of Education had officially designated my new public school, Parkside Elementary, as a progressive educational experiment in which students seemed to do everything but read and write, of which I was reasonably capable; much of our time was spent outdoors tending a rock garden, for which I had no facility. To my mind, the school's redeeming feature was that Sherry Robertson's kids went there: he was the nephew of Clark Griffith, owner of the Washington Senators, and had played in the outfield for the team, then gone into the club's front-office management. I spent as much time as possible with the Robertsons — and at the ballpark with them.

My next-door neighbor and first close friend on Harvey Road (on the opposite side of our house from Senator Bible and his family) was Ben Stein, whose father, Herb, was a celebrated economist. In Tenleytown, my closest friends' parents had been a barber (who was also an ex-con), a department store salesman, a divorced secretary at the Navy Annex, a Korean War widow, and a fireman. And Johnny Gianaris, whose uncle Pete, the gambling and numbers king, took us to Uline Arena to watch heavyweight prizefights.

Now I lived in a neighborhood in which teenage social life seemed to revolve around bar mitzvahs and country clubs. Ben Stein and I devised an entrepreneurial venture in junior high that continued when I'd worked at McBride's: a lox-and-bagel / Sunday *New York Times* delivery service for the eighty or so homes on Harvey Road. We took advance orders during the week and phoned them in to Hofberg's delicatessen, three miles away on the D.C. side of the line at Eastern Avenue. Early Sunday morning, Ben's older sister Rachel would drive us to pick up the big brown paper bags that Hofberg's had filled for each customer. At Mousie's newsstand on the Maryland side of the line we'd buy about fifty copies of the *Times* and stuff them inside the bags.

Mr. Porter became my primary source of transportation to and from the *Star* building on Saturdays — and in no time my friend and benevolent tutor. I'd start the day walking to his house from Harvey Road and sometimes have coffee with him and Mrs. Porter, who would fill a thermos with what was left from the pot, even though a coffee-and-pastry cart came through the newsroom every couple of hours.

I had assumed, from his manner and his accent, that Mr. Porter was from farther south than D.C., but he'd graduated from Central High too, in 1920, and had been born near the old Eastern Market. His first newspaper job was as a freelancer for the *Sporting Bulletin,* founded in the closing years of the nineteenth century to cover baseball. He seemed altogether the southern gentleman of another era — a gracious, soft-spoken man in rimless eyeglasses. It was hard for me to imagine him even interested in the likes of Walter Johnson, the Big Train, probably the greatest pitcher in history. And yet Mr. Porter had not only covered the Washington Senators' championship season (its last) in 1924, but he'd become good friends with Johnson in the clubhouse. He and Mrs. Porter even socialized with the Big Train and his wife. It had been baseball writing, Mr. Porter told me, that had landed him freelance assignments from the *Star* while he was working for the *Sporting Bulletin;* in 1927, Rudy Kauffmann's father hired him as a local reporter for the Maryland and Virginia desk. Then he told me something amazing that I had never read on the back of any baseball card: Walter Johnson had lived in Germantown and been elected to the Montgomery County Council in the late 1930s; he'd even run (and lost) as a Republican candidate for Congress. Walter Johnson had become a politician.

On our ride to work on the second Saturday of that October, Mr. Porter asked me if I'd noticed any special preparations being made at Montgomery Blair High School for the following night, when Senator John F. Kennedy was scheduled to hold a campaign rally in the boys' gymnasium.

I had. All week, Secret Service men and Kennedy's advance people had been inching their way around the school grounds. On Thursday and Friday, gym classes were canceled; electricians were hooking up outdoor speakers in the stadium bleachers and behind the gym so that Kennedy's speech could be heard by folks unable to get seats inside. Maryland was a critical state for the Kennedy campaign — a toss-up, Mr. Porter said — and this would be JFK's last appearance in the state before Election Day. National polls showed the race with Nixon very close. I told Mr. Porter my intention was to get inside the gym for the speech, and I volunteered to arrive there early and take notes on the scene inside and out. What I would do with such notes I had scant idea, but Mr. Porter seemed to think I could be useful because of my familiarity with the school grounds.

Later that morning in the newsroom he took me over to Paul Hope, the chief Maryland political reporter, who was assigned to cover the rally. Mr. Porter told him that I was a student at Blair who could supply details and color on the crowd and its reactions to Kennedy.

The next afternoon was a hot Indian summer day, perfect weather for my cream-colored suit. With special care, I took my *Star* employee card and punched a hole in the laminate, removed a shoelace from my gym sneakers, and threaded it through the hole so I could hang my political reporter's credentials around my neck. I wanted to be sure that I would not be mistaken for a student when it came time to cover the arrival of the candidate's motorcade.

Kennedy's rally was scheduled to begin at six that evening. When I left home at three, Dale Drive was already cordoned off by the police halfway to Colesville Road. By the time I reached the Grove — the maple-shaded front lawn of Montgomery Blair High, designated for student smoking — several thousand people were penned between barricades adjacent to C-Building, where my locker was, and maybe another thousand people were lined up to pass through a sort of funnel the police had fashioned to move them into the gym. From Sligo Creek Parkway, on the far side of the football field, thousands more were making their way to the stadium. At least half the crowd, probably more, were students, and not just from Blair. At the stadium, there were chants of *We Want Kennedy!* I moved through the crowd taking notes, holding my notebook up in front of me at chest level so that people could see, from the notebook and the credentials around my neck, that I was a reporter. I made a note about the way that the noise from the chants reverberated against the concrete stands. Red, white, and blue posters with the candidate's picture (KENNEDY: LEADERSHIP FOR THE 60S) dominated the landscape, held up by hundreds of people in the crowd or staked into the football field and planted around the school grounds, which, except for the Grove and the stadium area, were barricaded to block access to other buildings.

Paul Hope had said he would be arriving with Senator Kennedy's caravan in a press bus, and that I could be the most helpful if I met up with him after the event to tell him what the crowds had been like as the motorcade approached. Hope would be in the gym for the senator's speech, and I would stay outside with the overflow crowd, probably at the stadium. He said there would be a pressroom set up somewhere inside the school, and that's where he'd go to write after Kennedy and his entourage had left Blair. I told him I'd try to meet him there, but he seemed dubious; instead we agreed to meet at Ertter's Market next to the Grove and I'd unload my notes to him outside.

The sun was just setting when it became apparent that the crowds were going to over-flow the whole school area and spill onto the lawns of the houses on Dale Drive and Wayne Avenue. Many of their residents had put Kennedy signs in their windows, and the mood was festive, almost like a beach party. Younger people had transistor radios and lis-tened to live broadcasts on WDON that were being announced by Don Dillard, the disc jockey revered by teenagers from Rockville to Takoma Park and even around Coolidge High on the D.C. side of the line.

I asked a police captain how many people he thought were there, and he said at least twelve thousand — maybe twice the size of the crowd that Adlai Stevenson had drawn during the 1956 campaign when he had spo-ken at Blair. All that history was news to me. Both my parents had hoped that Stevenson would win the presidential nomination again in 1960; they did not like what they called Kennedy's "saber rattling" at the USSR, among other things.

When the crowds first heard the sirens com-ing from the direction of the Georgia Avenue Hot Shoppe a mile and a half away, they started cheering. I made my way toward the A-Building steps, where the principal's office (which I knew all too well) was just inside; I could see that Mr. Shaw, Blair's principal, was part of a greeting committee waiting for the motorcade. At the bottom of the steps an area had been roped off for the press, guarded by motorcycle police and men in suits. With the most natural and matter-of-fact motion of which I was capable, I presented the laminated ID hanging from my neck, holding it between my thumb and forefinger, pronounced the magical words *"Washington Star,"* and was admitted to this sanctum by somebody who seemed to be in charge. Inside, there were almost as many newsreel and TV cameramen as reporters.

I thought of Sidney Epstein's example, staying calm in the midst of a storm. I can say with truthfulness that I inclined that way myself, whether it was simply my nature or was something I had learned, from necessity, in extricating myself from the jams I was always getting into. But I had never been to a political rally and had never seen anything like the frenzy and hysteria of a Kennedy rally. It was impossible to think that Vice President Nixon, though favored in the polls, could inspire anything like what was occurring this day in Silver Spring.

The motorcade came into view. Kennedy stood on the backseat of a Buick convertible, tanned, trim, and tall in a dark suit and white shirt with a gray-blue tie. I tried to get all the details down, but there were too many; too much was happening. Flashbulbs were popping like fireworks, set off by photographers in two side-by-side convertibles behind the candidate's. The photographers looked like clowns in a clown car, standing and leaning every which way to get an angle for their shots. The screams from the crowd were overpowering. Then, without any warning, JFK put his left foot onto the right fin of the Buick while it was still moving through the cavern, braced his right hand on the shoulder of an aide running next to the car, and jumped to the pavement. He went straight for the crowd. The shrieks, mostly from girls and even from many of the grown women, sounded like something between agony and ecstasy; I'd never heard anything like it except maybe at the 1957 Alan Freed rock-and-roll show at the Paramount Theater in Times Square in New York, when Jerry Lee Lewis had thrown his jacket into the crowd and it got ripped to shreds by girls fighting over it.

Something similar happened when John F. Kennedy got out of his car at Blair. It was almost frightening. From what I could see, he seemed to revel in the spectacle, just like Jerry Lee, a big smile creasing his face as he walked against the ropes and thrust his arms into the crowd, pulling himself back only when the tugging at his jacket and hands seemed a little dangerous. One woman tried to get her arm around his neck in a hammerlock and kiss him, she was so excited, and he pulled away.

There were other dignitaries with him.

I recognized Senator Estes Kefauver and Pierre Salinger, Kennedy's press secretary, and then I saw Blair Lee III, who was the chairman of the county Democratic Party. Lee's sister, Elizabeth Lee Scull, lived in the oldest house in Silver Spring, on a wooded plot of land adjacent to the Harvey Road subdivision, with the only private swimming pool I'd ever seen and a bomb shelter stuffed with canned goods and shovels and sleeping bags and short-wave radio equipment. It was no wonder that the Scull children, David and Betsy, were extremely popular in our neighborhood.

I'd met Blair Lee a few times, when he'd come over to swim at his sister's house, along with those of us on Harvey Road who didn't belong to country clubs, which included Ben Stein and me.

A rostrum had been set up on the walkway leading to the boys' gym so Kennedy could address the crowd outside. Following the other reporters who were in the pen, I ran out and continued down the street behind the candidate. It took him fully ten minutes to get there, not because his way was obstructed but because he chose to move back and forth from one side of the street to the other as the noise and excitement crescendoed. Salinger and some of the others urged him to proceed to the microphone, but he paid no attention; instead, he seemed to bask in the experience.

When he finally got to the podium and Blair Lee III managed to get the crowd to settle down to expectant murmurs and punctuated shouts — which was as quiet as it got — the place erupted again when he introduced Kennedy as "The next president of the United States, John Fitzgerald Kennedy." *We want Kennedy!* the crowd shouted for another two minutes, and they wouldn't quiet down until JFK, who was laughing, gave up and started speaking over their chanting.

After this buildup, and from everything I'd read of Kennedy and seen on TV and the fact that Mr. Porter had said that the candidate was going to make a major speech in the gym, the last thing I expected — even if it was just introductory remarks to the crowd outside — was the hodgepodge I now heard. Right off, he talked about how happy he was to be in Southern Maryland, which was about forty miles down the road, and then he went on about how he represented Massachusetts in the Senate and how Senator Engle represented California, but only the president of the United States could speak for both Massachusetts and California and on behalf of the United States. My guess was that some page from a speech in California had gotten into the mix, but certainly Clair Engle was nowhere in the vicinity. (The only other senator in sight was Kefauver, who was from Tennessee.) Though I'm not sure JFK's remarks would have sounded any better in California, so convoluted did they seem.

What I didn't bother to write in my notebook, because I couldn't imagine how to put it in a newspaper story, was that it didn't seem to make any difference to the enthralled crowd — and maybe not to me either. Kennedy was hypnotizing. He stabbed his finger in the air. He quoted Dante about divine justice. And misquoted, I was pretty sure, Charles Dickens about the best of times (if Kennedy won). And then he was off and running with a poem by T. S. Eliot, "And the wind shall say: 'Here were decent godless people / Their only monument the asphalt road / And a thousand lost golf balls.'" Which the crowd went wild over, I suppose because Ike played so much golf, but it seemed to me to also describe aspects of Silver Spring and some neighbors who spent inordinate hours at the Indian Springs Country Club on Colesville Road.

This muddle from the candidate was, if I got it right, intended to say that he had inherited the mantle and clear vision of Franklin Delano Roosevelt, whereas his opponent was actually two opponents, "the old Nixon and the new Nixon," one of them wanting America to go to war in Indochina and the other being unconcerned about what the Chinese Communists were doing in Tibet. Probably most students in the crowd knew from the front pages of newspapers that Kennedy and

Nixon were trying to outdo each other on being tough with the Communists.

Altogether, the senator's speech outside didn't last more than two minutes. When he was finished the mob went even wilder than when he'd arrived, chanting *We want Kennedy!* again and again. The girls and women screamed even louder, and pushed at the ropes, and the candidate kept waving. Then he went right up to the ropes to shake hands and reached inside the mob, or that part of it that was pushed back against the walkway leading to the gym. It took another full five minutes to cover the three hundred feet. I timed it and made a note for Paul Hope. But the best part, I have to admit, was walking right behind them with my press card dangling from my neck and not a few of my fellow students from Blair looking at me bug-eyed as if they'd seen a ghost, though I was marching quite purposefully and (every bit the professional) peering down at my notebook as I scribbled, and then up at the candidate and then into the crowd, and then I'd scribble something more, by this time probably just for the fun of it.

I could have gotten inside the gym with the rest of the press corps, it was becoming apparent, but Mr. Porter and Paul Hope had made it clear that I was to concentrate on the crowd outside. So when Kennedy and his entourage went inside, I headed back down

Wayne Avenue to the football stadium. To my surprise, a section of folding chairs had been set up in the end zone and roped off with a sign that said RESERVED, PRESS, so I went there. Somebody had really cleaned up the place, because the previous day the Blair Blazers had lost at home, a rare event, 10–7 to Wheaton High.

This evening, the Kennedy noise was even louder than when the Blazers scored a touchdown, though the people sitting in the stadium and standing on the field and behind the bleachers couldn't actually see Kennedy. His remarks outside the gym were piped through the loudspeakers set up around the school grounds. The chants — *KEN-ne-dy! KEN-ne-dy!* — bounced from the gym to the stadium like an echo. Only after Blair Lee III introduced him inside the gym and after several more minutes of cheering did the place calm down, inside and out. Somebody from the campaign had put mimeo'd texts of the speech Kennedy was about to give onto the press seats in the end zone, but the first thing out of his mouth wasn't in his prepared remarks, and it got the place going crazy again. "If we can get the voting age to sixteen, we can skip this election," he said. "Otherwise it might be close." I wrote it down.

Sitting in the end zone, as I followed the rest of his remarks from the text, it was apparent to me that covering a candidate's speech was

115

a lot easier than I'd imagined, because you were freed up from the task of taking notes on what he was saying, except when he went off script. Which in this instance was hardly at all, so there was plenty of time to make boxes on the pages of my notebook, mostly about how frantic the crowd was, and to put stars next to the things I thought I should tell Paul Hope.

In his remarks to thousands standing outside the gym, Kennedy had talked about the "vitality" of the nation, the renewed "vigor" and confidence he would bring to the White House, and the need for a more "vigorous" society. Reading the text of his speech and listening to it resound through the speakers in the stadium, and the cadence of his voice, it was impossible not to notice how often he was using these V-words. He was referring to himself, really, when it came to what he called "the vigor, the vitality, the good judgment, the sense of history, the sense of the future, the foresight of the next president of the United States."

I didn't think the substance of Kennedy's formal speech was much more interesting than his convoluted warm-up remarks outside. But what he was doing seemed to me beyond the capability of Paul Hope or almost any reporter to articulate in a simple news story. I'd seen it that morning when JFK appeared on *Meet the Press,* and it was the same force that had whipped the crowd into delirium. It was about him and his manner and a new kind of presence in our politics. Even if he was talking rote about the need for a higher minimum wage, increased federal aid to education, and guaranteed medical care for the aged tied to Social Security, Kennedy drove home his central message as much in his body language and the use of his hands and fingers as his words. The Republicans, Eisenhower and Nixon especially, had made America weaker, and now the Communists were winning. He would make us stronger.

I was surprised that Kennedy said nothing in his speech, directly, about civil rights, especially since Eisenhower was pummeling the Democrats in his final months as president, accusing them of ducking a great moral issue. Nor did Kennedy say anything about the opposition to his candidacy on grounds that he was Catholic. That day the *Star* had featured a front-page story about a call by some evangelical Protestant leaders for a nationwide anti-Kennedy rally.

I didn't know what to make of the end of Kennedy's speech, which seemed almost tacked on. In his closing words, it wasn't clear if he was attempting to address the religious question, or civil rights, or the Communists, or just talking about himself. He noted that when Lincoln had to face the question of slavery, he wrote to a friend, "I know there is a

God, and that He hates injustice and slavery. I see the storm coming, and I know that His hand is in it. If He has a place and work for me — and I think He has — I believe I am ready."

Kennedy told the crowd that he was ready. Whatever he meant, the place erupted, first inside the gym — people were stomping their feet and banging on the wooden stands — and when the people in the street heard the ruckus, they got even wilder. By the time Kennedy retraced his steps back to the Buick on Wayne Avenue, it was bedlam, and the cops were having a tough time keeping people from mobbing the motorcade as it tried to get under way. And even after the motorcade had been out of sight for five minutes, the people still didn't leave. They seemed stunned.

I decided to take the chance that I could get inside A-Building. I flashed my ID at security, walked past the principal's office, and headed for the school library. I spotted Hope among perhaps twenty reporters who were either milling around or banging away on big Royals that had been rolled over from the typing classroom.

Mr. Shaw was there too, trying to tell the reporters about the wonders of Montgomery Blair High, but they showed no interest whatsoever. It was plain to see that Mr. Shaw was surprised by my presence. I introduced him

118

to Paul Hope and explained that I was now working at the *Evening Star.* The last time Mr. Shaw and I had spoken was when Detective Sergeant Pay of the Montgomery County police had come into the school to arrest me and two of my classmates for defacing public property. We had climbed onto the roof of C-Building and painted ELECT JIMMY PROCTOR in big white letters that were visible from a large swath of Silver Spring. Jimmy Proctor, who was celebrated for his work on customizing cars, but not for his academic ability or school citizenship, was the renegade candidate that a similarly inclined group of us had put up for president of the student body against Ron Bogley, who had been class president every year since Parkside Elementary. Our slogan was "Enough Is Enough — Proctor for President." And we almost won. Mr. Shaw had launched a major investigation of the offensive signage, and we were summoned to his office a few days later. After a very few words from the principal about his disappointment, Detective Sergeant Pay took us forthwith in his unmarked cruiser to the Silver Spring police station and booked us as juvenile offenders.

I didn't know much about Paul Hope except that he had come to the *Star* from the *Alexandria Gazette,* which bragged, with apparent truth, that George Washington had been a subscriber at Mount Vernon. Perhaps it was a better newspaper back in the 1780s. I paid the *Gazette* no mind, even though there was a lot about Alexandria that was interesting because of its history. Ever since I'd been given my first three-speed bike when I was ten, I'd ridden on many summer days across Memorial Bridge, by the Lincoln Memorial, into Virginia and up to Robert E. Lee's mansion, where I'd sit on the grass and enjoy the view of the city far below. Sometimes my friends from Tenleytown and I would bike over to the southern side of the river and fish under the willows for porgies and catfish. I always threw mine back — partly because the idea of my mother cooking a catfish was something not worth considering.

The Civil War had taken place a century earlier but continued to define the landscape of Washington, D.C. Much of the carnage had occurred within an hour or two's drive from the *Star*'s newsroom. The capital of the Confederacy lay just ninety miles due south, at the other end of Jefferson Davis Highway from Alexandria. One hundred years after Appomattox, the war's shadow still cast a pall over our days. And General Lee's mansion on Arlington Hill, with its majestic view of Washington and of the river separating North and South, represented for us far more than Lee's ghostly inhabitance.

In my notebook, I had put big stars next to

120

what I thought Paul Hope might be most interested in; this proved providential, because I must have had more than a hundred pages of notes, and by the time I'd left the stadium I was scribbling back to front on the reverse sides of the pages.

But Hope was patient, perhaps because the stars started right around the time when the police lieutenant told me there were probably twelve thousand people in attendance — so we got off to a good start. Hope hadn't known about Adlai Stevenson's rally, either, and said he'd check to make sure it was true. I told him about the woman who had grabbed Kennedy and tried to kiss him. And that many of the earliest arrivals were teenagers, thousands of them, carrying Kennedy signs.

It probably took us about twenty minutes to unload all the notes he wanted. Hope was seated at one of the typing tables from the Home Economics Department, typing away. I was standing next to him. "Good job, Bernstein," he said, and I hoped Mr. Shaw heard him.

Walking back to Harvey Road I tried to guess what Paul Hope would choose to lead the story with — and debated what my choice of a lede would be. Probably how tough Kennedy said he'd be on the Communists, I decided.

Monday was not a workday. It was the only day of the week that I'd programmed myself to remain at school all day. But at lunch, instead of heading to the cafeteria, I hitchhiked to Mousie's at the District line to buy a copy of the first edition of the *Star*. Forgoing the pinball machines, I hurried into Hofberg's to order a pastrami sandwich on Ottenberg's rye and to see what Paul Hope had done with our story. It was a few pages inside the front section of the paper. He'd led with Kennedy telling the wildly cheering audience that "the tide of the campaign" had begun to move in his direction, and noted that a crowd estimated at more than twelve thousand had jammed the gymnasium and football stadium and that local Democratic Party officials had said the crowd was bigger than when Adlai Stevenson had spoken at Montgomery Blair in '56.

Almost all the details that weren't about the content of the speech itself — perhaps half a dozen or so paragraphs out of about twenty in total — had come from my notes. At home that morning, I had studied the *Washington Post*'s account of the rally. The *Star*'s story was better, I thought, because it had more crowd detail; it was apparent that the *Post*'s reporter had arrived at the rally with the motorcade and didn't have a legman to help him.

Usually when I played the pinball machines I was able to rack up some free games on the first few nickels I'd play. I tucked the paper under my arm and headed back to Mousie's, and on my first nickel I won the super jackpot: fifty free games. I didn't go back to school that day, and went fewer and fewer days thereafter.

7

WARTHOG

Now about Ted Crown.

Ted Crown couldn't type, and he was no more capable of writing a coherent newspaper story than he was of composing a sonnet. But it was apparent to all who knew and worked with him that he was one of the great police reporters in journalistic history, though his vocational brilliance was vastly complicated by his racism and the way he played at police department politics. So when the D.C. chief of police decided there should be a woman precinct sergeant, it was Crown who put the kibosh on the idea and told the chief that, if he persisted, the *Star* would run a front-page story on Inspector Blick's vast pornography collection, which (among other things) was sort of a lending library that went out to the squad commanders. Ted Crown prevailed.

The man looked like a warthog, and he sounded like a warthog, too. Accordingly, his manner of speech was much imitated around the newsroom. To talk like Crown you had to purse your lips and grunt, out from the throat and through your nose — *ueowehh, ueowehh.* That snuffling, rooting noise preceded almost every clause he uttered.

Each morning he'd call Herman Schaden, the rewrite man whose job it was to figure out what it was that Ted Crown was trying to tell him about the previous night's carnage and carnal excess.

"*Ueowehh, ueowehh,* good morning, Hummin," Crown would begin, and then he'd move smartly to the point: "*Ueowehh, ueowehh,* at 2:14 in the a.m. three men and a maiden lady of their acquaintance became apprehended — *ueowehh, ueowehh* — on the steps of the Bethel Tourist Home behind Thomas Circle while beating about the head a man she had enticed from his 1955 Cadillac El Dorado convertible with promises to, *ueowehh, ueowehh,* perform oral sodomy upon his circumcised pecker." This was Crown's way of saying that the john was Jewish. Crown didn't assign Jews any higher rhetorical regard than he did dark-skinned people, a measurement of which was that he occasionally pointed out that his grandfather had owned four slaves in Prince George's County, Maryland, right up until the emancipation.

Crown's distinctive manner of speech owed a lot to the El Producto cigar people. He always had a stogie in his mouth except when he ate, and even then the cheroot was close at hand. He would chomp down on the cigar, so the spittle would run down the side of his mouth, all brown and crudded. What Herman Schaden heard every morning was all manner of gurgling and slurping of tobacco juices — the only way Crown knew how to talk and breathe at the same time.

It was because Herman Schaden managed to translate Crown into a known tongue, using words fit to read in a family newspaper, that Herman was called the Magician. Herman could make words jump like trout.

In the afternoons, after he'd finished turning Ted Crown into "By J. Theodore Crown, *Star* Staff Writer," Herman would often go to the National Zoo, which was his regular beat, and he'd sometimes invite me to tag along with him. It was there that he pointed out to me the similarity between a warthog and Ted Crown. Herman was a master of simile.

The *Star* being an afternoon paper, Crown arrived early, around six thirty in the morning, at the press room on the third floor of police headquarters, which was located in the old municipal building on Indiana Avenue. Johnny Burch of the *Daily News,* the Scripps-Howard afternoon tabloid, showed up around the same time. Al Lewis of the *Washington Post,* the odd man out, shuffled in around ten. His first deadline for the following morning's edition would be hours away.

"Good morning, Jewboy," Crown would

call. Lewis was given to wearing regulation blue Metropolitan Police sweaters, and he held his pants up with a belt buckle made out of a Metropolitan Police badge — or with a brass buckle fashioned into a Star of David, which he wore less for reasons of piety than for the subversive pleasure he took in getting a rise out of Crown and Burch and goading them to still more redneck abuse.

Crown, Burch, and Lewis reminded me at times of the Three Stooges, or a dysfunctional family at the grotesque end of the scale: love, hate, and recreational sadism. They had outlasted chiefs and inspectors, and they knew their way around headquarters better than most of the cops did.

Lewis, a nervous, bantam-sized man, talked smooth, like a racetrack announcer. He didn't smoke, or to my knowledge drink, except for Pepto-Bismol, a big pink quart jar of which was the only permanent object on his desk at police headquarters aside from the telephone. I once saw Lewis drink a full jar of the stuff in a single day, and it was said to be on account of Crown and Burch's torment. They were so merciless with Lewis that he developed a bleeding ulcer. By the time I came to witness it, the torment had been going on for more than a quarter century, and all three of them insisted it was good-natured. Which was possible.

I first arrived at police headquarters, on the

order of Sid Epstein, to deliver to Ted Crown his biweekly paycheck. "Hey, kid. Go down to headquarters and give Crown his check — maybe you'll learn something," he said.

The pressroom, facing south from a central corridor, was just to the right of the third-floor elevators. The furnishings were minimal: three bulky wooden desks, their bare tops stained by decades of spilled coffee and pocked by the carved initials of flatfoots and commanders who counted themselves friends of the house and had whittled away their spare hours in the company of its three long-term occupants. From a speaker mounted high on the wall, the voice of a police dispatcher droned on in the background.

On one wall, directly behind Johnny Burch's desk, was an enormous street map of the District of Columbia. The slatted back of Burch's wooden chair was parked up against the map, about two square feet of which, say from Florida Avenue to Mount Pleasant Street, was covered with plastic. This was on account of Johnny Burch leaning back in his chair so his head rubbed up against a sizable swath of Northwest Washington, leaving a dark, greasy smear and eventually a hole in the plastic, which had to be replaced every six months or so.

The room was uninhabited when I arrived that Tuesday morning. Half-eaten sandwiches and wrappers were slopped on Crown's and

Burch's desks. Both men were voracious eaters, especially in comparison to Lewis, whose midday meals were arranged in a lunchbox with meticulous care by his wife, Gladys — the "Jewess," as the other two called her, or sometimes "Queen Esther," but not to her face when she would occasionally show up at headquarters, which was contrary to all protocol of the place.

Down the hall I could hear Crown's grunt, so loud and exercised that a couple of secretaries had peeked out of their offices to see what the commotion was about. It took me a moment to register Crown's unusual music and start to understand it. "Mister Depooty Roy Blick, Doooo Nut You Dare Uhh-Tempp Tew Shovel Yet Anudduh Weeel-Barrow of Your Blick-Shit Lies in the Vicinity of This Fort Estate — Because You Have Finally Become Hoisted Upon Your Own Leotard." Or so I caught its gist.

And at that moment, Ted Crown, John Burch, Al Lewis, and a fourth man marched with indignant purpose into the hallway, the last man stomping off in the opposite direction, stabbing the air with his middle finger and growling something crude and dismissive. The man wore a black, ten-gallon Stetson, his white hair curling out from beneath the brim. He appeared to be missing an eye, and as he gestured with one hand he pushed back the brim of the Stetson with his opposite hand, which sported a pinky ring the size of a thumb. This peculiar figure — peculiar in almost every regard, I would soon come to learn — was Deputy Police Chief Roy Early Blick, commander of the Metropolitan Police Morals Division, whose exploits combating vice in Washington were legendary.

Blick had been promoted from inspector to deputy chief a couple of years earlier, after he testified before a congressional subcommittee that it was his "informed" estimate that there were about 5,000 homosexuals in Washington, D.C., 3,750 of whom were employed by the government, including at least 350 at the State Department.

Most of Blick's famous (and highly specialized) campaign against iniquity was conducted through his division's Prostitution and Perversion Squad. This outfit operated under his direct personal and vigilant supervision, which meant that the division's Gambling, Bootlegging, and Narcotics Squads were severely neglected. Blick's imbalanced priorities accounted for a glut of dope, illegal booze, and after-hours clubs, all of which flourished in the city. Meanwhile, anything having to do with sexual organs, their display or attempted use, Blick claimed as his own bailiwick and fiefdom.

Part of Blick's renown was the result of his appearances in court, where he spent almost as much time as he did in the public men's rooms of the nation's capital. Not only did he personally collar many of the (mostly) men arrested in nighttime raids conducted by the Prostitution and Perversion Squad, but he insisted on making grand appearances himself before the few judges brave enough to protest that his policing subjected homosexuals to regular and systematic harassment and entrapment. He denied it. Rather, he proclaimed, he and his officers were committed to the health of the community and the enforcement of laws passed by the Congress of the United States that governed illegal sexual conduct in the capital. As a *Star* rewrite man had put it, "He is a bird dog on the trail of alleged degeneracy."

If there was a single figure in law enforcement whom Blick regarded as his superior and treated with deference, it was J. Edgar Hoover. The two collaborated closely.

Blick's role as enforcer of public morality was enhanced by his swoops on the peep show emporiums and dirty book stores on Ninth Street, the fruits of which formed the nucleus of his astounding pornography collection. Portions of this unlikely municipal library were arranged loosely by sexual preference on the floor-to-ceiling bookshelves that lined two walls of his office near the pressroom.

After the man in the Stetson stalked off, I followed the three reporters into the pressroom. I still had Crown's paycheck envelope in my hand. The three ignored me and grabbed their telephones. Crown, instead of asking the newsroom operator to get him rewrite, asked to be connected to Sid Epstein himself, to alert the city editor that the chiefs' report on the Lafayette Square police brawl had at last arrived.

In a flash, I understood: all this commotion had to do with the moonlit hand-to-hand combat that had occurred the previous May outside the Lafayette Square men's room, directly across Pennsylvania Avenue from the White House. The battle had been between (on one side) Blick and his deputies from the Prostitution and Perversion Squad and (on the other side) officers of the United States Park Police. Representatives of both law enforcement agencies had been loitering in the park for the same purpose that night: in preparation to "arrest deviants," as the new report put it. They had ended up fighting and flashing their badges, howling "Police!" and trying to arrest one another.

It was a defining moment in the history of local law enforcement. From a certain perspective, it was perhaps a fascinating mess, but after order was restored the authorities decided that this embarrassing spectacle must never be repeated. And so began demands for the reform of the Morals Division of the Metropolitan Police Department. This reform idea even figured, indirectly, into the agenda of the President's Commission on Pennsylvania Avenue — supervised by Jackie Kennedy herself — and the wholesale restoration and beautification of Lafayette Square, including the conversion of its men's room to a storehouse for gardening implements.

I'd first learned about the battle from Walter Gold, the *Star*'s night police reporter, who had rushed to the scene when he heard a policeman-in-trouble call on the Park Police frequency of his battery of car radios, followed by a plea for reinforcements from a fellow park officer. Then, on the Metropolitan Police frequency, he heard what sounded like Roy Blick's voice shouting for help. Gold hit the gas, and when he arrived in General Lafayette's square there were about a dozen men rolling around and fighting on the ground. Many of them were in uniform, and, as it turned out, all of them had guns and badges. Finally (Gold had said in a memo to the city desk), Blick and his principal deputy ordered the whole lot of them, at gunpoint, to stand down while the situation got sorted out. Blick also chased Gold out of the park under threat of arrest.

Since then, to little avail, reporters had been trying to find out exactly what had happened that night. Jokes abounded, of course. But, otherwise, a curtain of silence descended in both police departments, so effective that not even Crown, Burch, and Lewis could penetrate it.

133

Now the report had come out, signed by the chiefs of both the United States Park Police and the Metropolitan Police. It placed unequivocal blame on a single park policeman, a ten-year veteran of the force, who stood accused of "failure to work harmoniously" with the D.C. policemen who had been lurking around the "comfort station" in plainclothes under the moonlight.

For Sid Epstein's benefit, Crown briefly removed the cigar from his mouth as he elaborated upon the tale in the chiefs' report — "a dispicuable whitewash," Crown called it, and harrumphed, "Pluuupostperous." Meanwhile, on the other side of the room, Burch was telling his editors at the *Daily News* that Blick had prevailed in covering up whatever it was that had actually occurred.

Breaking off in midsentence from Sid Epstein, Crown snatched the paycheck from my hand and commanded that I run to Blick's office and get a copy of an appendix to the report.

The two-room sanctuary to which Crown dispatched me — behind an entryway counter that opened with a buzzer — was dominated by a cast-iron safe with its enormous doors swung open on its hinges. I was surprised to find Blick himself seated at a desk across from the safe, his Stetson now perched atop a coatrack, his demeanor calm and impassive. He showed no hostility when I told him that Ted

134

Crown had sent me to pick up the appendix to the report. I studied his sightless right eye, which had been lost in a Prohibition-era raid when a tear-gas canister misfired from the launcher gun that Blick was wielding in a rum house. Blick led me to the second room of his suite and introduced me there to his principal deputy and factotum, Detective Sergeant Louis Fochett. Fochett had a remarkable mustache. It looked like a brush for a vacuum cleaner. A bookshelf on one side of the room was lined with different editions of *Lady Chatterley's Lover* by D. H. Lawrence, which the courts had ruled, though obscene, could be sold in the United States because of its inherent artistic merit.

The decision had put a dent in Blick's book-seizing operation. But movies were another matter. The lower shelves of the bookcases on the opposite wall were filled with eight-millimeter film canisters, and a movie projector was set up on a desk in the middle of the room facing the back wall from which a full pull-down movie screen was suspended. Several wooden chairs were balanced on either side of the doorway, which I presumed were for visitors to the movie show.

Even though I was just a copyboy and he did not know me, Blick treated me as if I were an official emissary from the *Star*. He assured me that Sergeant Fochett was the real hero of what had occurred in Lafayette Square on the night in question, and that the report and its appendix would finally put to rest all the innuendo that hung over the incident — regardless of what the likes of J. Theodore Crown and company wished to believe.

Fochett nodded and handed me two copies of the supplement.

"You're welcome here anytime," Blick said.

I scanned the report as best I could during the fifteen-minute cab ride back to the office. It stated that the versions told by the park policeman and the three undercover D.C. cops he initially encountered in the park were in direct conflict. The park policeman had lied, the report concluded, with Blick asserting that the park officer had set off the confrontation by pulling his gun and threatening to kill the whole undercover posse of the Prostitution and Perversion Squad if they did not leave the square. Blick said his men had acted properly throughout.

According to the park policeman's account, the trouble started when he saw three scruffy-looking men near the "comfort station" and asked one of them what he was doing there. Told that it was none of his business, he placed the man under arrest and led him, struggling, cursing, and screaming for help, to a police call box in the park.

At that point, the park policeman saw the two other men coming toward him. He used his skill in judo to toss one into the shrubbery and flick the other into a flower bed. Significantly, the tossed individual was Sergeant Louis Fochett, who, though supine, was recognizable to the park policeman by his mustache.

Fochett's fellow officer raised himself from the flower bed, grabbed the park policeman's nightstick, while the other two started to rush him. It was at that moment, the park policeman said, that he put his hand on his pistol and warned the city cops not to come any closer.

Blick's plainclothesmen told a different story. The arrested man said he attempted to show his badge but was ignored and instead dragged toward the call box and hit with a nightstick when he shouted for help. So he grabbed the nightstick and threw it into the bushes as Fochett and his partner rushed to help.

Sid Epstein decreed that there should be three stories: one for the last editions of that afternoon's paper and, for the next day, a full account with a sidebar about Blick and his unusual work.

Gerry Herndon, the afternoon rewrite man, composed the sidebar — a masterful summary of Blick's career "in the twilight zone of law enforcement." It also discussed the giant safe in his office. Inside that iron hulk and its card indexes, apparently, were Blick's handwritten notations for every alleged or suspected sex

137

offender he had dealt with or received information about in his quarter century of work in the Morals Division: tens of thousands of individuals. The dossiers were not limited to residents of the Washington area; there were entries on citizens from all the states and from numerous countries abroad. As Herndon noted, inquiries from federal agencies — and J. Edgar Hoover's office — arrived by the dozens on Blick's desk each week to be checked against the names on the index cards in the safe and their information passed on for security and federal personnel matters. "The safe belongs to the District of Columbia, but the lock belongs to me," Blick said.

Ted Crown had told Herndon that he was all but certain that Hoover himself had intervened with the chief of the Metropolitan Police to ensure that the Lafayette Square investigation and report would cause no harm to Blick or his operation. But that suspicion was based on secondhand information from a single source, and it wasn't strong enough to justify being published in the newspaper, Sid Epstein said.

The overnight story, under Crown's byline, identified the park policeman as Private James E. Thomas. The last paragraph stated, "Thomas, who is a Negro, said yesterday he was given no formal hearing and planned to appeal his suspension to higher federal authorities."

Crown was sure that Blick had had an easy time setting Thomas up to take the fall because Thomas was Black and the three D.C. cops were white.

That was another confounding aspect of J. Theodore Crown. He was certainly bigoted, but he had allegiance to the facts and to getting the story right.

8

NIGHT BEAT

To understand Walter Gold, the *Star*'s night police reporter, the analogy was often drawn in the newsroom of the attraction of a moth to a flame. But that would be unfair, especially because moths don't sense danger. Walter was as respectful of fire as he was drawn to it, and he studied it. Often, when I arrived to work the night shift in the office, there would be a stack of past issues of *FIRE: The Magazine of Firefighting and Fire Prevention* sitting on the city desk, which meant that Walter was out on the street cruising in his 1958 Pontiac Bonneville V-8.

This was no ordinary automobile. The Pontiac had come off the assembly line with giant fins that had dual red taillights protruding from them, so from the rear it looked like a cross between a shark and a booster rocket. Inside, a row of police and fire radios stretched clear across the front-seat console, and the car had a specially compartmentalized trunk with a bracket that secured a firefighter's ax. A set of fireman's boots resided behind the spare tire, and a running coat stamped with the insignia of the Bethesda–Chevy Chase Rescue Squad (of which Walter was a member) was folded front side up to facilitate quick entry into burning buildings.

For weeks that fall I'd agitated with Emerson Beauchamp to let me go out riding with Walter, on the grounds that the experience would make me more useful to the desk. He finally relented one night in early December.

My first ride in the Pontiac, I was rewarded by a three-alarm fire that took down the better part of a vacant warehouse on the edge of the city's railroad yards.

To watch Walter Gold at the scene of a good fire was to witness a ritual, a sort of fire dance. When he arrived on location, Walter would spring open the trunk of the Bonneville by hitting a button under the dashboard. He would then jump from the car and put on his running coat and boots in something under twenty seconds. I was to cover many fires in the coming months of my apprenticeship, but never did I find it necessary to dress for the occasion. Then again, I was never overcome by a desire to run into a burning building with the firemen.

When I rode with Walter, his fireman's hard hat would be moved from its natural riding position on the passenger seat and stowed behind us, next to a pile of ropes and pulleys

141

and other lifesaving paraphernalia on the backseat. If we were responding to a fire call, he'd reach back and clamp the helmet onto his head even before we neared the scene, siren blaring and red light flashing.

There was constant static coming out of the squawk box as it picked up competing voices of dispatchers talking in fragments about potential emergencies. Most involved car crashes or minor property damage, but Walter would twiddle the dials until he heard something more interesting, even if it was twenty miles away. Then he'd floor the gas pedal, as if the Pontiac had been built for stock car racing. The voices that filled the car were confusing, a dozen jurisdictions talking at once. In addition to the Metropolitan Police, a babble poured in from the U.S. Park Police, the National Zoo Police, the U.S. Capitol Police, the Federal Aviation Police, and the foreign embassy police, which went under the name Executive Protection Service. Washington, D.C., it occurred to me, probably had more police forces than any other municipality in the world, and Walter had radio reception for each of them, plus those in the outer jurisdictions that sprawled halfway to Fredericksburg in Virginia and Hagerstown in Maryland.

Like the other reporters, Walter had a proper desk in the newsroom, but I never saw him working at it except to open his mail or make a private phone call. He preferred to take a seat at the city desk, across from the night city editor, and do his office work there, in between reading through the stacks of magazines devoted to what Emerson Beauchamp called "fire journalism."

But there was much more to Walter's prodigious talent and his beat than that. He had an easy rapport with the cops at crime scenes, and he was as adept as Ted Crown at pulling information out of men who spoke in the law enforcement patois, a tongue that now and then was as mysterious as Basque.

Murder, of course, would be the high point — professionally speaking — of any first-rate police reporter's evening on the job. But there were always more fires than homicides. They broke out in every part of the city and here and there in the counties almost every night. Less obsessive reporters were content to cover 95 percent of them by means of a telephone call. Not Walter Gold — he had to be there. That was terrific for me. His desire to witness the flames firsthand meant that my knowledge of the geography and culture of my native city and its environs was expanded over the next few months to include streets and shortcuts and back alleyways and whole neighborhoods and their people that I would never have come to know otherwise.

Walter may or may not have been born to his assignment. His father was Bill Gold of the

143

Washington Post, whose six-times-a-week column of homespun local news, "The District Line," was perhaps the most popular feature in all the city's newspapers. In a town whose grandees regarded the place as a great world capital and saw themselves as participants and observers in Monumental Events, Bill Gold concerned himself with the communal life of the city. He was a master of puns, a relentless fundraiser for local charities, a promoter of neighborhood Bingo games, a recorder of the birthdays of waiters and bus drivers and nurses and checkout clerks and of the birthing of their dogs and cats. The formula was unbeatable.

Walter was twenty-six, ten years older than me, but we had a lot in common. He'd graduated from Bethesda–Chevy Chase High School, our fierce rival at Montgomery Blair, and from the University of Maryland. He and I had plenty to talk about in the car, and not just related to the job. We listened to the same disc jockeys, got our flattop haircuts from Milton Pitts, the barber in the Glover Park shopping center on Wisconsin Avenue, and had skipped school to ride the roller coaster at Glen Echo Amusement Park.

Part of Walter's responsibility as the night police reporter was to leave a memo for the dayside desk and for Ted Crown about anything that had happened overnight. So toward the end of his shift, he called each of the District's twelve police precincts and the headquarters of each of the suburban counties and fire departments to check in. It was a tedious routine. Walter was happy to pawn off the phoning part of the business to me whenever I was around, and I was more than happy to accept. I tried to write the results in story form, and with some regularity I'd find what I had written — about a double car wreck fatality or some such — in the newspaper almost word for word the next day.

This division of labor freed Walter for an extra hour or so to read more deeply into the intricacies of fire and police work, or to extend his cruising time, or to meet up with his friend and co-owner of the night Larry Krebs — Krebsie, as Walter called him — of WMAL radio and TV. The stations were owned by the *Star,* and providentially so: of late, they had been a steadying source of income for the company as advertising started to falter at the paper.

Others called Krebs the Penguin because of his funny waddle-walk and the fact that he almost always dressed in a black trench coat, except in summer. He and Gold called their occupation "playing the street." Krebs jangled when he walked, owing to a giant chain on his belt that held two dozen keys or more; most of them fitted the various call boxes around the city, the fire boxes painted red and the police boxes blue. Krebs, too, drove a big Pontiac, the trunk of which was even more overstuffed with gear than Walter's because Krebs was expected to film and deliver live reports from crime and fire locations.

Gold and Krebs worked in effortless tandem. One would head off to a fire in Northeast while the other would show up for a knifing in LeDroit Park and summon the other by walkie-talkie if the event turned out to be worth reporting. It was not uncommon for Krebs to interview Walter on the air for details of a murder. And the two shared certain journalistic techniques. They both carried a supply of glazed doughnuts and thermoses full of coffee, which were helpful in encouraging cops to talk. The on-camera portions of their interviews with policemen and rescue workers were professional enough, if a little stiff and perfunctory, but afterward Krebs and Gold would take the cop or fireman aside and, fresh from stardom, the guy would spill his guts "on background" — meaning that the reporters could use his information but could not reveal where it came from, since, strictly speaking, only the commanding officers were supposed to talk to the press. Krebs and Gold were masters at becoming confidential with cops and firemen at the scene, speaking their language. I saw now how important that was for a reporter.

There was a human dimension to the way Gold and Krebs conducted their business, a decent and perhaps more civilized way of interviewing than practiced by some reporters I was to study over the next months, including a few luminaries on the national staff. Gold and Krebs didn't run from the scene or close their notebooks the minute they'd learned something — as if the person they were talking to was a mere conduit to be used for a story. They offered the people they interviewed sufficient time to explain conversationally what had occurred. It was only after some basis of mutual respect and purpose had been established that they would begin asking probing or direct questions.

I grasped that, while they could be cynical and hard-boiled in private conversation, Gold and Krebs were capable of great tenderness. They sought an understanding of the people and situations they covered. Perhaps it was because of their rescue squad training.

One other thing I picked up on: both of them carried rolls of nickels and dimes in their pockets so they'd never get cut off in the middle of calling in a story from a telephone booth.

After I'd ridden with Walter Gold on special occasions in my early months at the paper, I was able to persuade Emerson Beauchamp and John Kopeck (the night city editor when Emerson was off reviewing plays) to let me accompany Walter routinely, for a couple of hours, once I'd finished my other night copy-boy duties.

On one especially cold December night, I set out with Walter about eleven o'clock and we headed straight to St. Elizabeths Hospital in Anacostia, where one of the psychiatric patients had set fire to a mattress in his dormitory. When we got there, about a hundred patients in their pajamas were jumping up and down in the freezing cold. Some were crying and screaming.

A consequence of Washington's being the U.S. capital was that the first psychiatric hospital run by the national government had been established in Anacostia in 1852. Originally called the Government Hospital for the Insane, it took in the mentally ill among the civilian population of the District of Columbia along with those in the U.S. Army and the U.S. Navy. The best view of the capital city, strangely enough, was enjoyed by the people committed to the national insane asylum, though not on this night. In daylight, the eight thousand inmates of St. Elizabeths Hospital (there was no apostrophe in the changed name) could look out from a series of bluffs at the monumental city across the Anacostia River — a bird's-eye view from a height that appeared almost equal to the top of the Washington Monument. A few hundred feet directly below the hospital was Bolling Air Force Base, with its southernmost runway

148

edging the riverside. From an inmate's dormitory window, jet fighters would streak by at eye level. The Sacred Cow — the presidential plane used by Roosevelt, Truman, and Eisenhower — was parked in full view.

My cousin Stanley Walker owned a liquor store a few blocks from St. Elizabeths, and my grandfather, Stanley's uncle, had taken me for Saturday drives in Anacostia to enjoy the view and to get away from my grandmother. Popsy, as I called him, would tell me stories of how his family had settled nearby after they'd gotten off the boat and taken a bus over from Baltimore. Southeast and Southwest Washington was where the greenhorns — poor Yiddish-speaking immigrants from Russia and Eastern Europe — settled in the late nineteenth century. My grandfather's other daughter, my mother's only sibling, was buried nearby in the old Jewish cemetery; she died in the influenza epidemic of 1918. My mother had once told me that her uncle Dave — who still lived above the photo studio with my great-grandmother on Seventh Street — had briefly been hospitalized at "Saint E's," as D.C. parlance had it; this was a great shaming family secret that she was somewhat vague about.

Not far to the east of the asylum, many of my parents' closest friends still lived in little garden apartments around Trenton Terrace — which in the 1950s had become a haven for young left-wing families, most of whom worked for the government. I'd spent many Sundays at union picnics there, eating hot dogs and singing songs like "Union Maid" and "Which Side Are You On, Boys?"

In the cold night air, while the St. Elizabeths patients were being herded to a heated auditorium on the other side of the grounds, Walter Gold's pager began sounding. The gizmo was an experimental prototype that the Motorola radio company had distributed to several thousand doctors. Somehow Walter had gotten hold of one. He sprinted for a phone booth while I stayed with the patients. It was a disturbing scene: mental patients, many of them paranoid schizophrenics in their pajamas, traumatized and barefoot in the freezing cold; bursts of revolving lights from fire trucks and ambulances; the noise of the water being pumped to the trucks from hydrants; nurses, orderlies, and D.C. firemen handing out blankets and trying to calm the patients.

The inmates' dormitories were firetraps, constructed recently from flimsy materials to contain the flood of new patients charged with petty crimes and remanded by the courts to St. Elizabeths. The two solid brick Gothic wings of the original hospital — one built for white patients and the other for Black patients — had long since been converted to administration buildings. I had my notebook out when a nurse came up to me to complain that the only inmate the press had ever cared about was the poet Ezra Pound. He'd been released from St. Elizabeths two years earlier, after a campaign on his behalf waged by Ernest Hemingway.

Walter came running back for me after about ten minutes. The page had been from John Kopeck on the city desk, informing him of a possible fatal shooting in the 1200 block of Nichols Avenue, not far away.

With the Pontiac's red light flashing, we raced down Nichols Avenue to the Anacostia Flats. Metropolitan Police cars were stretched bumper to bumper across the intersection at Talbert Street, a roadblock. Walter Gold's reportorial approach to a murder, I learned, was the opposite of his demeanor when arriving at a fire: instead of running toward the scene, he now affected an almost languid pose — not much different, I was to observe in coming months, from the way homicide detectives would sidle casually to the vicinity of the deceased, gravitating toward the uniformed cops who had arrived first and had already radioed for a morgue wagon. The homicide detective would get there, a little late, to take charge of the scene, a sort of celebrity.

When we arrived, a lieutenant and a sergeant, both in plain clothes, were standing next to several uniformed patrolmen whose flashlights were trained on a prostrate male figure lying close to the gutter. The cops had ripped open the man's jacket, where blood seeped from his chest — alarming and repellent quantities of it. I followed Walter and pushed myself between a couple of detectives for a closer look. I had never seen a dead body before.

The man appeared young, maybe in his early twenties, with light skin and wide-open, striking blue eyes. I couldn't tell if he was white or Black. I thought about him and his life. Did he have a mother and a father who would now get the terrible news? What had he been doing — if anything — that might have gotten him killed?

"Any ID yet? Anything about who shot him?" Gold asked one of the detectives. I had taken out my yellow *Star* employee card, but Walter told the uniformed lieutenant presiding, "He's with me."

I could see now what looked like the entry wound in the middle of the chest, but the most conspicuous aspect of the dead man — at least I presumed him to be dead, though now I wondered about it — was the immense erection straining beneath his pants.

In my notebook I'd written down the names of the uniformed officers from their shields, and, phonetically, the name Malachi, which was how Walter Gold had addressed the detective sergeant, as if they were old friends.

And a series of question marks — ?????? — about the erection.

"Just another Proctor shot another Swann," Malachi said. "They're cousins — always after each other." Proctor, the shooter, was already on his way to police headquarters in handcuffs, to be booked and interrogated. Swann (he spelled it for Walter, with two *n*'s) was DOA: "Nothing here of interest to the newspapers."

"Angel lust," Walter said, with a nod to the deceased's unusual state of arousal. "Can't put that in the paper."

"Yeah — never fails to amaze," the cop responded, with a laugh.

Malachi explained to Walter and me some of the anthropology of the Proctors and Swanns, describing them as large interracial clans, part white, part Black, and part Native American, who for generations had intermarried. They kept pretty much to themselves, but now and then they feuded violently. Hundreds of people named Proctor and Swann lived in Southeast D.C., Malachi said, but most of the clan was in Maryland, in the tobacco counties — around Upper Marlboro, the Prince George's County seat, and Charles County.

By now Larry Krebs had arrived, and Walter briefed him. Krebs offered coffee all around, then began filming the scene from a distance. The coroner also showed up, and homicide-squad photographers shot pictures and took measurements around Swann's body. Proctor had used a .44 Magnum on his cousin.

Later, in the car heading back to the office, I mentioned the erection. Walter said he had seen it often enough in victims of fatal shootings and knifings — something to do with the body's postmortem reaction to trauma. I wrote down in my notebook, "Angel Lust." And in large letters surrounded by a box: "Proctors / Swanns."

Walter wrote a three-paragraph note for Ted Crown about the shooting, giving him the location (a slum neighborhood) and the apparent circumstances (a family dispute) that would dictate the coverage (minimal, two paragraphs inside) that the shooting would get in the next day's paper.

I went to the library, to the file cabinets that contained clips of stories going back decades. First, I looked up those filed under the name Swann. They filled a whole drawer.

Many were about individuals with the last name Swann who had been arrested over the years, often for misdemeanor crimes in Southeast Washington and in Charles and Prince George's Counties. Still other accounts focused on resourceful men who were hunting and fishing guides, a big business downriver past Accokeek. In addition to guides named

Swann, many of the hunting and fishing and trapping outfitters mentioned in the stories were owned by men named Proctor.

I took the clips about the guides and laid them out on the big new copying machine at the back of the room. It took less than a minute a page to make copies, and I put the duplicates in a big envelope to take home with me.

I also pulled the files about St. Elizabeths, curious about the Ezra Pound / Ernest Hemingway connection. I was stunned to discover that Mussolini's brain had ended up at St. Elizabeths Hospital for study. This bizarre news was included in one of the articles about Pound. He had been a prominent supporter of Mussolini before and during World War II, and the reason he'd landed in St. Elizabeths was to keep him from being hanged for treason (nineteen counts) for aiding the Axis through his wartime radio broadcasts.

It would be four in the morning before I got back to Silver Spring.

The next day I called my cousin Stanley at the liquor store. If anybody would know about people named Proctor and Swann in his part of town, I figured, it would be Stanley. He told me he cashed the checks of quite a few people named Proctor and Swann, but he didn't know much about them except that

155

they were good customers and showed up usually on paydays.

I asked for his mother's phone number — my great-aunt Annie, who had grown up on the tobacco farm close to the hamlet of Waldorf in Charles County. Nearly everybody in my mother's family of that generation spoke English with a Yiddish accent, but not Aunt Annie, who talked with a Southern Maryland twang that, if you didn't understand the far lowland counties, would be considered hillbilly speech. Even her Yiddish twanged. She was surprised to hear from me — it was the first time I'd ever telephoned her in my life.

I told her I'd gone to work for the *Evening Star,* which she already knew about from Cousin Stanley and Uncle Charlie, she said. She agreed to answer a few questions to help me understand the story I was helping to cover.

When she was growing up, I asked, did she know people nearby named Proctor and Swann?

"Oh, you mean the Wesorts," she said without hesitation.

Wesorts?

"It's from, 'We sorts of people are different than you sorts of people.' They're a big, separate community down there. Everybody knows them. All intermarried. They come from indentured servants. Proctors, Swanns,

156

Johnstons, Bealls, and a couple of other names. Some of the local people call them blue-eyed Nigras."

She promised to make borscht and tell me more about the Wesorts if I came over to her apartment on Tilden Street. I said I would.

9

HOT TYPE

It had taken me almost no time to recognize that Sidney Epstein was a mighty presence at the *Evening Star*. It took me a while longer to comprehend that Aloysius E. Baker, the foreman of the composing room, was Sid Epstein's equal in the exercise of authority and in the eyes of the people who worked with him.

Every piece of type that was cast and set in place in our newspaper factory was under Baker's jurisdiction. The empire over which he ruled — with an iron hand and a union contract that brooked no nonsense from management — was directly above the news-room and occupied the exact same amount of space. But it seemed bigger. Maybe it was the absence of windows or the fact that there were no desks and almost everybody worked standing up. Rather than a forest of desks, there was a sea of "turtles," heavy brushed-steel tables with oily gray surfaces, higher than a man's waist and set on casters, each used to build a single page in the daily or Sunday newspaper.

Every page was composed, literally, within a rectangular metal form, called a "chase," that replicated the size of a newspaper page and served as a fence to contain the tens of thousands of pieces of type inside. Amazingly, the type was cast from molten lead right there in the composing room. Three rows of Linotype machines extended almost the full length of the floor, each the size of a giant loom in a textile mill and each emitting a racket of clicking and stitching sounds.

Sometimes when I went to fetch proofs in the composing room I would scoot up the metal stairs through the hole in the newsroom ceiling a few minutes early and stand by one of the Linotype operators and, fascinated, watch him work.

The operator, seated at a keyboard and working from single-take segments of newsroom copy, transformed the words letter by letter into pieces of metal type fashioned from hot lead. When he struck the key, the lead was in a molten state, and then the machine would magically spit out single lines of solidified hard-set type in word form. Each line stacked itself upon the previous one, the whole stack of type exactly a newspaper column wide. It was this miracle machine, invented in the late nineteenth century, that had upended the basic system of movable type going back to Gutenberg. Phil Kelley had explained all this to me the first time he took me upstairs to watch. On occasion, the words in the *lines of type* produced by the machine were exactly the same as in the piece of copy I'd snatched only a few minutes before from a reporter's hands.

During the workday and through the night, there were probably three times as many printers on the composing room floor as reporters in the newsroom. I'd gotten to know a few of them by name, and they were generous in explaining the intricacies of their work. Watching a printer at his craft with finished type was like watching a fine Sunday artist at work on his sketchpad, so swift and perfect were the movements of his hands and the coordination with his eye.

The eye part was probably harder, because a good printer was expected to read backward and upside down. He had to be able to spot a line of type or a single word or letter that needed correction, working from a full page proof or column-long galley proof on which an editor or proofreader had identified an error or specified a change in the copy. So, working from the right-side-up image in his head from the proof, the printer would look down at the maze of upside-down-and-backward type in the chase, locate the corresponding pieces of miscast type, and — using a shortened link of column rule as a tool — pry a line or bank of type from the story, lift it between his fingers and set it down outside the form, then pick up the new type and wedge it into the cavity he'd just made, meanwhile swinging the mallet with his other hand — *bang!* — until the whole thing clapped together and the typefaces were all secure and level.

Al Baker was a giant who looked a little too rough even for the roughhouse into which the composing room sometimes deteriorated. But it was his job to maintain order, as well as to make sure the pages of the newspaper got put together. A scuffle upstairs might cause an edition of the paper to go to press three or four minutes late, in which case Aloysius E. Baker would convene a chapel meeting after the press run was finished. A chapel meeting was what the printers called their union gatherings, though there was nothing remotely holy about the International Typographical Union except the size of the paychecks it earned for members of the printing trade. A printer's pay was as high as a reporter's salary, which after the 1958 Newspaper Guild strike by newsroom employees at the *Star* had reached $155 a week for a journeyman reporter with eight years' experience. It had been the first newspaper strike in the city since the 1920s, leaving a powerful undercurrent of militancy and resentment in the newsroom — and respect among reporters for the printers, who had refused to cross the picket lines.

Because perhaps a third of the *Star*'s printers were deaf, chapel meetings were conducted in both English and sign language. The first day I'd climbed up the stairs to the composing room I'd been stunned to see almost as many people signing as making vocal conversation. Phil Kelley explained to me the history of deaf people in the newspaper vocations, which had to do not only with the god-awful noise from the machinery but also with the nature of the printing trades themselves, which didn't require a lot of talk — just hard work.

In Washington, the tradition of hiring deaf people in the newspaper business ran deeper, and the number of deaf employees was higher than anywhere else in America because of Gallaudet College, the country's principal center of higher education for deaf people. It was a liberal arts school, but it also offered excellent training in the printing trades.

When I'd worked selling layaway merchandise at McBride's, I would occasionally walk over to the tree-shaded Gallaudet campus a few blocks away with my lunch bag. On some buildings the original name of the school — before it was abbreviated by Congress in 1956 — was faded but still visible: GALLAUDET COLLEGE FOR THE DEAF AND DUMB. Usually, when a fight erupted in the composing room, it was because a hearing printer had referred to a deaf printer as dumb.

As a native of the city, I did not need Phil Kelley to tell me that, next to talking, printing was the biggest industry in Washington.

Washington never had big factories that turned out conventional goods, the nearest assembly lines being in Baltimore, forty miles up the road. No, our factories were word factories, the largest of which was the Government Printing Office, an enormous pile of red brick that occupied most of a city block up North Capitol Street from Union Station. More people worked at the GPO — some seven thousand printers — than at any other building in Washington, including the Capitol.

The actual words printed and, in effect, embalmed by the government printers amounted to the collected works of the federal government — a stultifying and ever-growing accumulation of books and periodicals and pamphlets. Every word uttered on the floor of the Senate and the House of Representatives and in all the congressional hearing rooms was transcribed and preserved and, in many cases, I'd say, read only by the printers, proofreaders, and court reporters who were responsible for taking it all down and getting it into type. Truckloads of these publications arrived in the newsroom and went straight into trash bins, though occasionally the Department of Agriculture would issue a helpful primer on how to grow tomatoes on the vine. And there were people on the *Star*'s business and national desks who knew how to find stories, and even secrets, in this avalanche of verbiage.

The single government document that had a sizable readership was the *Congressional Record,* a daily compendium, half as thick as the D.C. telephone book, of the proceedings of the House and Senate. When I'd arrive for the six a.m. shift, copies had already been delivered to the newsroom. I doled them out to editors on the national, city, and state desks along with the first editions of the out-of-town newspapers. Everyone familiar with the *Congressional Record* knew, however, that it had a certain cheerful dishonesty about it, that it was at least in part a work of fiction, because of the tradition of "congressional courtesy" that allowed a congressman or senator to change his words after he had spoken them, whether to make them grammatical or to readjust their emphasis after a tide of negative telegrams from offended citizens. As Gerry Herndon had once written, the statesman could give himself a mulligan.

One advantage the deaf printers may have had was that they couldn't hear Aloysius E. Baker's voice. In opera (which, along with zoology, I learned a smidgen about from Herman Schaden, because he reviewed classical music and sometimes had an extra ticket), Baker's vocal range would have been called basso profundo. He was accustomed to speaking over the din of the machinery, and if he was calling a chapel meeting, you could hear him from one end of the composing room to the other. I imagine the deaf printers could feel the vibration too.

It was in that same voice on an afternoon in January that he summoned Sid Epstein, at the very moment that the city editor was attending to the back of the row of chases making sure that all of his pages in the second section of the paper — the local news section — closed on time and were in perfect shape.

I was in the front of the composing room with Baker, both of us standing over the split page (which is what the first page of the city section was called), when he hollered out to Sid Epstein. Though I had been at work at the *Star* for less than six months, I knew a lot for a copyboy, including how to read upside down and backward. I had trained myself to do it on days when I ran the page proofs. On this occasion, I handed the printer making up the split page a corrected proof that called for throwing out a few lines of type in the lead story and inserting new copy related to yet another arrest of Dallas O. Williams, the Badman of Swampoodle. I tried to be extra helpful by putting my finger on the lines of type to be replaced; I even used the nail of my forefinger to separate the first line to be discarded from the rest of the story.

The printer seemed amazed at my abilities, and he remarked upon it to Baker, who had taken to calling me Alfalfa because my cowlick reminded him of the character in the *Our*

Gang comedies. And now, as Sidney Epstein approached the chase, the foreman remarked to the city editor how clever and helpful I was proving to be for the printers.

I will leave it to the imagination how Sidney Epstein in his sherbet- colored shirt from Lewis & Thos. Saltz looked standing next to Aloysius E. Baker in his ink-stained smock, his belly keeping the rest of him a full column rule's distance from the edge of the chase that held the split page.

I stood with pride between them, as Al Baker remarked upon my facility for reading upside down and backward.

Then I noticed Sid Epstein's face begin to turn red. The next thing I saw was Al Baker's huge forearm; it moved in what seemed to be slow motion past my face and down to the column 8 side of the page on the right, the lead column that contained a couple thousand pieces of type describing Dallas O. Williams's latest remarkable altercation with the Metropolitan Police. I saw Al Baker's ham hock of a fist push all that type toward column 1 and the direction of oblivion as it dropped off the edge and fell toward the floor, suspended in sight, silver shards, thousands of pieces of lead dropping off the edge and then hitting the smooth concrete, sounding like some atonal orchestral mistake against the flat register of the composing room machinery.

Then column 2 headed toward the abyss,

followed by columns 3 and 4, as Aloysius's forearm now pushed across the surface of the chase with incredible momentum and the rest of the page accelerated downward, the noise a crescendo of metal notes as they hit the floor and Sid Epstein's wingtip shoes.

Sid Epstein, his eyes furious and his face now crimson, fixed on Al Baker's round head. I had no idea at that moment what had caused Baker to throw his fit, nor was I to learn much about what transpired between him and Sid Epstein afterward. I knew only that there was now no split page for the next edition of the newspaper, and that it would take an hour, at least, for every Linotype machine operating at unaccustomed speed to set the type for a new split page, and that more than a hundred thousand subscribers were going to get their newspapers late. And I knew that this was not good.

"Go downstairs, kid," Sid Epstein said to me.

In the newsroom, I decided to keep my own counsel about what I'd witnessed, at least until after Sid Epstein came down. I had no doubt that he would explain it to me. Until now our dialogue had mostly been confined to matters of coffee and perhaps grits — but once he had remarked that Emerson Beauchamp thought I'd done a good job covering a meeting of the D.C. Association of Oldest Inhabitants and its campaign to save the city's doomed street-cars. So already the city editor, I was sure, had taken more than routine notice of me.

I waited. When Sid Epstein came downstairs from the composing room, I saw that his color had improved, and I was not at all surprised that he sought me out by the wire room.

"Kid, in my office."

Sidney Epstein's bare office was mainly used for tasks he didn't like: scheduling the staff, interviewing job applicants who were friends of the Noyes and Kauffmann families, and disciplining reporters, usually for some incident related to drinking, or for mistakes that got into the paper, which might also have been related to alcohol. There were times Sid Epstein would come out of the office and shake his head, his jaw clenched like he couldn't believe some of the things he had to deal with.

He told me to take a seat at Coit Hendley's desk directly across from his. He rolled a pencil back and forth with his fingertips across the leatherette surface of the desk while tapping the heel of his right foot. He cleared his throat. He seemed a little miffed.

I was scared and putting two and two together. I'd heard tales about copyboys being fired for gumming up the production process.

"Kid, what do you want to be when you are older?"

"A reporter," I answered with not a second's hesitation.

"Not a printer?"

"No, definitely not a printer." The question surprised me.

"Then I want you to make me a promise," Sid Epstein said. He had a gentle way of speaking. I'd never heard him raise his voice, even the time he fired a reporter after a drunken, racist tirade at a cleaning woman in the newsroom.

"Would you make me this one promise?" he repeated.

"Okay," I said.

"But first tell me why you think you can be a reporter."

I explained about carrying my reporter's notebook everywhere, studying how the reporters went about their business, and all the citizens meetings I'd covered, and riding around with Walter Gold at night. But mostly, I said, I was good at getting information. "I've always been interested in secrets," I said, though I doubt I knew exactly what I meant. But it was also true. Even though I was only sixteen, it seemed as if my whole life there'd always been secrets going on around me. Like when the FBI kept watch on our house when I was little, for instance, although I didn't tell Sid Epstein about that.

"And I can type ninety words a minute," I said.

"You sure you don't want to be a Linotype operator or something?" Sid Epstein asked. "Then you could type all day."

169

"Definitely not, sir."

"Or a printer? You seem to like being in the composing room so much; you're sure you don't want to be a printer?"

"I'm sure."

What had happened upstairs, he now explained to me, was that I had violated the cardinal rule of the composing room: I had touched a piece of type, which was a sphere of activity reserved for members of the International Typographical Union.

"Al Baker's been on my ass for two years — since I became city editor — and I've been on his for the same time," Sid Epstein said to me. "You gave him his big chance." He wasn't mad at me, but he was furious at Al Baker. I had allowed Baker the opportunity to humiliate the city editor. All because I had "tainted" the split page when I put my finger on the line of type.

"Understand me?"

Baker had seized on the technicality and destroyed the whole page.

"Here's the promise you have to give me," Sid Epstein said. The way he said it was very quiet, almost a whisper, which had the same effect as if he were shouting at you. But the way he said it also conveyed that he was sharing something very important, like he was letting me in on the conspiracy.

"Yes, sir."

"Until the day you die, you will never again touch a piece of hot type."

"I promise, sir."

Sid Epstein turned to his right and began leafing through a pile of papers on a cabinet next to his desk. From the pile he removed a sheaf of several pages, stapled and folded together, and began running his finger down the first page. It amazed me, not for the first or last time, how his nails stayed buffed.

He flipped to the next page and very slowly moved his finger from one paragraph to the next, finally stopping at a paragraph toward the bottom. This he proceeded to circle with a pencil; then he shoved the sheaf of papers across the desk to me. There was also a map pasted to the page.

"Here's your assignment for Inauguration Day. You go to Fourth and Pennsylvania and cover the crowd there, plus the parade when it goes by. Anything interesting. Phone in to rewrite at least every half hour. Be there at six a.m. Schaden will be the rewrite man. Don't try to write — just tell him what you saw."

At that moment, another copyboy stepped into the cubicle and laid down a split page proof on the city editor's desk. The lead story was about Dallas O. Williams's latest run-in with the law.

10

INAUGURAL

My plan was to walk over to Pennsylvania
Avenue on Thursday afternoon after work,
the day before the inauguration, to survey
the territory I'd be covering. I'd already been
to the bank and gotten myself twenty-five
dollars in rolls of nickels and dimes for pay
phones. Staking out the right phone booth
was essential. It would need to be accessible,
but not so accessible that I'd have to wait
to use it. Or maybe it was more sensible to
come in from the cold and use a pay phone
indoors. The weather bureau was predicting
that Friday's temperatures would be near
freezing.

I'd studied the tonnage of literature the
Inaugural Committee had prepared for the
press, especially about elements of the parade that were to step off immediately after
the swearing-in ceremony. A whole loose-
leaf binder was devoted to the marchers and
floats, with stupefying detail about the history of each organization and the dignitaries

172

who'd be passing by. Herman Schaden had been happy to lend me his copy.

Herman — the Magician — had already written parts of the "B-matter" for his story based on these handouts, describing, for instance, all the midshipmen and plebes and cadets from the service academies marching in perfect formation, thousands of them, and he'd composed masterful prose about the girls from the University of Texas twirling their batons, and the drum major beating his big bass drum. The drum was a big deal. According to the Inaugural Committee's literature, it was the biggest drum in the world — eight feet in diameter. Arturo Toscanini had once borrowed it for a performance of Tchaikovsky's *1812 Overture*.

I'd also gone back to the library and scrolled through the spools of microfilm from January 1957 to study the *Star*'s coverage of Ike's second inauguration, which sounded like a pretty dull affair. ("Our population grows. Commerce crowds our rivers and rails, our skies, harbors, and highways. Our soil is fertile, our agriculture productive," he'd said.)

I went to work Thursday hoping I could sneak into that evening's inaugural gala that Frank Sinatra was putting together with a cast of Hollywood stars such as Washington had never seen, and most of whom I had never heard of. To say that the nation's capital was not a glamorous town understated the case: as

Washingtonians, our ideas of celebrity tended toward Gypsy Rose Lee appearing at the Casino Royale supper club, or the cast of whatever Broadway musical had finally reached the capital's single legitimate commercial theater, or Rocky Marciano in town for a prizefight.

The great inaugural eve blizzard banished any thought of onsite preparation or rehearsal for my assignment. By six o'clock, eight inches of snow had fallen, and a traffic nightmare of historic proportions had seized the city. There was even consideration — reported in the *Star*'s final editions, but rejected in the end — of canceling the parade or parts of it.

I accepted Mr. Porter's offer to drive me home to Silver Spring. Truckers from the *Star* garage had put tire chains onto his vintage Oldsmobile. Behind the wheel, he handled the Olds with surprising dexterity, dodging abandoned cars and those slip-sliding backward down Sixteenth Street. It occurred to me that I might not be able to get to my assigned post from home the next morning under these conditions. So at Columbia Road, not more than a mile from Pennsylvania Avenue, I asked Mr. Porter to drop me off. The wind was fearsome, whipping swirls of snow and ice crystals that stung my face. I trudged through knee-deep drifts to my grandparents' apartment around the corner on Lanier Place. I'd lived the first two years of my life with them and my mother in that little apartment while my father was in the South Pacific. My grandmother and grandfather were more than a little surprised to see me at their door, soaked and shivering this snowy evening. And when I asked if I could stay overnight so I could be on time to cover the inauguration of the president of United States, my grandmother marked the occasion by making potato latkes.

She worried that I would need warmer clothes, and she instructed my grandfather to take me into their tailor shop directly across the street. For weeks, the two of them had been altering formal attire for local swells who would be going to the inaugural, including a number of senators and congressmen who were their regular customers. Inside the shop, he pulled apart rows of cleaned and pressed garments hanging from the steam pipes until he found something he thought would work to keep me warm — a full-length military officer's woolen coat.

While we were in the shop, he informed me that my grandmother, at age seventy, was studying to become a U.S. citizen. But he could not. Unlike her, he'd never learned to read and write English, a requirement for passing the citizenship test, even though his knowledge of the classics — in Yiddish, both poetry and prose — was formidable, and he read two Yiddish newspapers every day.

On inauguration morning, my grandmother, Ooma (as my two younger sisters and I called her), awakened me at five and laid out a big breakfast of bacon and eggs and lox and bagels. She fetched my grandfather's galoshes from the front closet and fastened the buckles after I tucked my pants into them.

In addition to my *Star* employee's card, now dangling from a brass chain around my neck (I'd bought the chain after the success of my shoelace experiment at Montgomery Blair), I was wearing an official inaugural parade press credential: a red, white, and blue badge with engraved lettering announcing the inauguration of President John Fitzgerald Kennedy and signed by the D.C. chief of police and Senator John Sparkman of Alabama, the inaugural chairman. "Here, kid, you'll need this," Sid Epstein had said to me, handing me the credential a few days before.

My thought was to hitchhike to Lafayette Square at the bottom of Sixteenth Street. Walking through the drifts of unplowed snow on the sidewalk would be impossible, and too many snow removal trucks were careening in the dark on Meridian Hill, one of the steepest in Washington, to consider descending on foot. I thought for a moment about my old Flexible Flyer sled; Ooma and Popsy had pulled me through the neighborhood on it when I was little.

On the hill, I flagged down a pickup truck with the insignia of the D.C. Highway Department — yellow lights flashing — and explained to the driver, who was supervising some of the clearing party, that I was a reporter covering the inaugural for the *Star*. He offered to take me as far as the Statler Hotel at K Street. The streets and sidewalks there, within sight of the White House, had been completely cleared. (To me, like many natives of D.C., the Statler was less a real hotel than a movie set. It was where *Mr. Smith Goes to Washington* had been filmed, with Jimmy Stewart roaming its corridors.)

Through the darkness, from Lafayette Square across from the White House, I could see the illuminated reviewing stand with the presidential seal, where after the swearing-in — and their ride down Pennsylvania Avenue — the new president, vice president, their families, cabinet members, and various VIPs would watch the parade. A television crew was setting up a pair of oversized cameras; this would be the first inauguration to be broadcast in color.

The lights were on in the White House. I drew a box in my reporter's notebook and tried to write a poetic riff about the snow-covered North Lawn — for whose benefit or use I had no idea, since far more experienced reporters would be composing their own odes.

I wondered about Ike and his last night in the White House. He'd had a pretty good final week as president, warning his countrymen in his farewell address that they should beware of the military-industrial complex. And Congress had granted him a last favor: he was restored to the rank of five-star general of the army. Eisenhower had been a grandfatherly sort of president. He'd been in the White House for half my life, and I was looking forward to watching him go by in the parade. He'd kept a kind of military distance from the press, but the reporters liked him well enough. When asked at his final press conference if he'd been treated fairly by the newspapers, he'd said, "Well, when you get down to it, I don't see what a reporter could do much to a president, do you?"

Before leaving my grandparents' apartment, I'd dialed the telephone number for the latest weather bureau report. Though the blizzard was over, the forecast called for twenty-mile-an-hour winds throughout the day and a high temperature of twenty degrees. With the wind howling, and still something like six hours remaining until the start of the parade, I figured this would be too much even for the Eskimos who, according to information in the briefing books, would be riding on the state of Alaska's float. I wrote that down in a clever sentence I thought I might offer to Herman.

In fact, I was freezing. Under my suit and military coat, I'd put on two sweaters from my grandfather, who'd also given me a couple of scarves that my grandmother wrapped me in, and an extra pair of earmuffs. I declined to wear a hat, despite their urging: I could not imagine a working reporter under the age of sixty dressed in a hat; but by the time the parade started I'd found a vendor selling knitted caps with "JFK" stitched on the front, bought one, and stuck it on my head.

I'd stuffed my pockets with fresh notebooks, a dozen sharpened copy pencils, two packs of Kool cigarettes, a Zippo lighter, a transistor radio, and an extra pair of gloves.

At Fourteenth Street, in front of the Willard Hotel, a contingent of troops was clearing the reviewing stands and bleachers — I'd never seen federal troops on the streets of the capital. I could not get a one of them to utter a word of news, because (they said) only their commanding officer was authorized to talk to the press.

Up and down Pennsylvania Avenue, what looked like a small army of Boy Scouts — almost two thousand of them, I was to learn — shoveled snow off the bleachers that lined the route. I took a notebook from my pocket and approached a scoutmaster. He explained that his small troop, from one of the Maryland beach towns on the Chesapeake, was assigned to be ushers in the stands. They had walked all the way from Anacostia, on the other side of the city, after the scoutmaster had to abandon his car in the snow. There were five of them, and as they ducked into the Raleigh Hotel to get warm, they were eager to tell me how they'd almost frozen to death. By now, sunrise was approaching and I tried to imagine how I could wring enough detail out of them to weave their tale into a coherent insert for Herman.

At Eleventh Street, in front of the old Evening Star Building, I stopped to buy copies of the *Post* and the *New York Times* from Annie. In her familiar hut, she had set herself up in the business of selling inaugural souvenirs as well as newspapers. But she was not in a celebratory mood. "Young man," she said, "what the Kennedy people have done is not right." During the night, trees along the avenue had been sprayed by inauguration work crews, and the cops had fired pistols during the height of the snowstorm to scare off the pigeons and starlings that were permanent residents of the neighborhood — sustained, in part, by Annie's peanuts. In all the times I'd bought newspapers from her, she'd hardly addressed me, but now I couldn't get her to stop talking about the iniquity of the new administration's policy toward pigeons.

Around Fifth Street I started searching for the right phone booth. Up and down the avenue, the wind was picking up in gusts, and blown snow once again covered the side streets to the north. It was obvious that I would need shelter from the cold during the proceedings. Between D and E Streets there was a Sholl's Cafeteria. Sholl's cafeterias were a Washington institution, famous for serving literally millions of people a year — tourists, diplomats, lobbyists, lawyers, bureaucrats, and bankers who appreciated the low prices and simple, good food. When he was vice president, Harry Truman would stop at Sholl's for breakfast on his way to the White House from his apartment on Connecticut Avenue. The half a dozen Sholl's restaurants in D.C. were unique in that from the 1940s and throughout the period of fighting for integration of restaurants downtown, they stood against segregation and served Black customers. Along with catsup and mustard and salt and pepper, each Sholl's table offered framed blessings for the meal — separate prayers for Christians, Jews, and Muslims.

There was no public phone booth inside Sholl's, but when I asked the manager where the nearest one was so I could report on the inauguration for the *Evening Star,* he said I could use the telephone in his small office behind the kitchen. Sipping coffee and spooning grits, I worked my way through the front sections of the *Post* and *Times,* making notes in my reporter's notebook of ideas that their coverage suggested to me. I then availed myself of the manager's telephone and reached Herman. He told me he was trying to juggle calls from a dozen reporters, and with the same gentle voice that he would use when we sat together at the zoo watching the animals he urged me to be brief. I rattled off descriptions of the color TV apparatus, informed him of the Boy Scouts' overnight predicament (with quotes), and reported Annie's indignation about the treatment of the avenue's pigeons that she regarded as pets.

From Fourth and Pennsylvania, where I found a police call box to lean against and take in the scene, I could see part of the crowd of fifty thousand on the Capitol grounds — the people with special invitations for preferred seating and standing rights to the inauguration ceremony itself. That was if I turned my head to the left. To the right stretched Pennsylvania Avenue to the Treasury Department and the White House almost a mile away. Sid Epstein had assigned me a plum vantage point. Behind me were the first parade units and floats and marchers who by nine o'clock had begun to assemble.

I was just near enough to where the actual ceremony would take place to hear the Marine Band, and to make some notes on the crowd's reaction to the announcements of the principal dignitaries' arrivals as each was escorted into the small area — invisible to me — where Kennedy would be sworn in and deliver his inaugural address. After playing "The Stars and Stripes Forever," the band struck up "The Washington Post March" — and I was left to consider, not for the first or the last time, why John Philip Sousa (a native Washingtonian like myself) had never written a march for the *Evening Star*.

More than a million people had been expected to line the parade route, but I doubted that that estimate would hold in this weather. The stands along the avenue were at most three-quarters filled, predominantly on the sunny, northern side of the street. When a deputy police chief who came to use the call box confirmed my suspicion, I ran back to Sholl's to tell Herman. I could also see that there were plainclothesmen working the crowd. Since riding around with Walter Gold at night, I'd learned to spot them by looking for a bulge below the knee in their pant legs. I flashed my credentials at one and asked if he had seen any action, but he said it was too cold — and people were too bundled up — even for pickpockets to operate. Everything within my sight or hearing, any detail, could be part of this story, I realized, if presented interestingly enough. Covering the inauguration of a president, even his parade, was different from turning out stories about citizens associations.

Most of the notes that I scrawled in my notebook had to do with the weather and the strategies that people in the crowd had invented to deal with the wind and Siberian cold. Up and down the avenue there were conspicuous green patches: families huddled together under green blankets or stuffed inside green sleeping bags. Some wore souvenir buttons naming the county in Ireland their families were from. I thought of the folk song sung by Pete Seeger — "No Irish Need Apply" — and wondered whether this was a theme I could somehow push into Herman Schaden's narrative. But it seemed a stretch. More promising was a contingent of perhaps forty Mormons dressed up like their ancestors making the trek to Salt Lake City. Along the avenue, dry goods stores were selling out of long johns. I found a first aid station at Fifth Street and learned from the medics that several people had already been treated for signs of frostbite, including some marines who had fainted at parade rest.

Mostly I kept my concentration on the street scene until, from loudspeakers off to the east, in the direction of the Capitol, I heard Marian Anderson sing "The Star-Spangled Banner." My parents had attended the great concert at the Lincoln Memorial in 1939 that Eleanor Roosevelt had organized when Miss Anderson had been forbidden by the Daughters of the American Revolution to sing at their headquarters at Constitution Hall because she was Black. Mrs. Roosevelt would be riding in Kennedy's parade, although it was said she did not like him much — because he had abstained in the vote to censure Joe McCarthy — and she had preferred Adlai Stevenson for president.

And now, for the first time, I felt something far more complicated than whatever details I would be reporting to Herman Schaden this day: yes, I was privileged to have my front-row reporter's seat for a great moment in history, but there was also a palpable stirring about its meaning for the country and perhaps the world that was impossible for me to detach from. It hadn't occurred to me that being a reporter could get so mixed up with feelings.

Still, I did not pay much attention to Kennedy's voice reciting the oath of office over the loudspeakers — "I do solemnly swear that I will faithfully execute the office of president of the United States . . ." I was looking around and trying to gauge the crowd's reaction — which was surprisingly restrained, I thought — as the chief justice proclaimed, "Congratulations, Mr. President."

Early on in his inaugural address, I caught the cadence of the new president. "Let the word go forth from this time and place, to friend and foe alike, that the torch has been passed to a new generation — born in this century, tempered by war, disciplined by a hard and bitter peace, proud of our ancient heritage — and unwilling to witness or permit the slow undoing of those human rights to which this nation has always been committed."

Kennedy orated for the ear and for the mind. There was elegance in the words and thoughts and delivery ("Let us never negotiate

185

out of fear. But let us never fear to negotiate.") and a sense of the sweep of history.

I remembered the gibberish I had heard Kennedy mouthing that day in Silver Spring three months earlier. Now we were in a different universe — though my comprehension of the most memorable aspect of his address was not immediate. Just as Kennedy proclaimed, "Ask not what your country can do for you — ask what you can do for your country," I was putting on a second set of earmuffs over my cap, ignorant of the fact that they would muffle the president's voice. In a few moments I was warmer, and I removed the earmuffs and put the transistor radio to my ear. I heard Howard K. Smith of ABC News recapitulating the new president's words, and I finally understood what the crowd had been cheering about.

Kennedy's speech lasted less than fifteen minutes. Just that quickly, the Eisenhower era was over. There was real excitement in the air — a sense that America was on the verge of something very new. Kennedy felt like an adventure.

But for now, I reminded myself, Sid Epstein had sent me to cover a parade.

I hadn't realized that Ike wouldn't be in the parade. He was heading off to his farm in Gettysburg, Howard K. Smith said on the radio. I'd been counting on the former president's passing by me as the idea for a scene I'd give to Herman, though I hadn't quite worked it out.

The parade started forty-five minutes late. By then I had taught myself to take notes in fur-lined leather gloves, removing the right one for a few seconds to jot down details or leaving it on to record a single bulky word or two.

Ike's familiar four-door bubble-top Lincoln convertible — with the bubble now tucked away — came into view at Third Street. But in place of the seventy-year-old president and Mamie Eisenhower were the new First Lady and her husband in the backseat. And though people standing curbside were shouting "Mr. President! Jack, Jack!" there were oohs and ahhs and shouts of "Jackie! Jackie!" that right away signaled another aspect of the newness of this American experience.

Eight weeks earlier, Mrs. Kennedy had given birth to their son John Jr. The First Lady was thirty-one years old, and, at forty-three, JFK was the youngest elected president in American history — succeeding the oldest.

When the president's car neared, I turned my notebook back to front, deciding I would get down everything I saw or heard at important moments and sort it all out later. Keeping that kind of record in a separate place from my other notes seemed sensible, and variations of this method would thereafter become part of my regular reportorial routine. I noted that Kennedy seemed to study the crowd as the car passed in front of me, and he pointed out, for his wife's benefit, the enthusiasm from the stands directed toward the new First Lady. I wasn't sure if this was the kind of thing Herman Schaden was interested in hearing about from me, especially because I knew he'd be tracking the procession on a television set in the newsroom. But from the outset it struck me that this day was very much about the both of them. It was disarming to witness Kennedy's ease, gliding down the avenue, president of the United States, and savoring the moment with his wife.

Mary McGrory had made much of the fact that the president's wife had attended the Sorbonne and that her hand in the inaugural program was significant. The presence at the ceremony of some certified intellectual heavyweights on her guest list — like the writer John Steinbeck and the musician Leonard Bernstein — had captivated more than a few reporters in their advance stories.

Then there was the whole Kennedy family entourage, more than a hundred of them listed in the briefing books, including the president's father and mother. It was hard to imagine a president having living parents, but JFK was only two years older than my own mother. Several cars behind the bubble-top, the new attorney-general-to-be of the United

States, the president's younger brother Robert F. Kennedy and his wife, Ethel, were seated high on the back of another open car. I had already made a call to Herman about a bus marked kennedy family that was parked at the edge of the Capitol grounds. Its driver told me it was designated for the dozens of children of the president's siblings and his in-laws, who were to be delivered to their own reviewing area of the parade inside the Treasury Department, next to the White House.

The biggest surprise of the day, or so I phrased it to Herman, was the extraordinary welcome for Harry Truman, now aged seventy-six. "Give 'em hell, Harry! Give 'em hell!" echoed down the avenue from a lot of people who were delighted to see the former president back in town. All I could remember of his presidency was the day a group of Puerto Rican nationalists tried to assassinate him at Blair House, and that his daughter Margaret sang opera.

Whoever designed the parade seemed to have almost deliberately contrasted the old order with the new. This was a ceremony in which the past handed off to the future. My father had worked in 1948 for the election of Franklin Roosevelt's former vice president Henry Wallace, who'd run on the Progressive Party ticket for president. Now Wallace turned up in one of the cars not far behind Truman, along with President Woodrow

189

Wilson's widow, Edith. And then another car with Eleanor Roosevelt and Teddy Roosevelt's daughter Alice, who had lived in the White House as a teenager. I did not see it, but when Kennedy's car reached the reviewing stand in front of the White House, he half-stood and doffed his black top hat to his aged father in the reviewing stand.

Then the parade proper began.

The first float, ahead of those from the fifty states, was from the District of Columbia. NO TAXATION WITHOUT REPRESENTATION was spelled out on a carved Styrofoam model of the capital's marble monuments that, when I lifted my eyes, were visible in their actuality. I was sure that Sid Epstein would want to know how the crowd reacted to the float, but from my perch it was clear that there was almost no interest in the subject. I asked a couple of people near me if they knew that the citizens of Washington couldn't even vote for president, and they looked at me as if I didn't know my American history and asked if I was sure of that. I was.

A few weeks earlier, I'd asked Senator Bible if he thought congressional representation for the District's citizens was on the horizon. I'd taken him up on his offer to have lunch at the Capitol. Over bowls of Senate Bean Soup in the members' dining room, he told me there was no chance that the southerners from his

190

party — or the Republicans — would ever allow it to happen, even though he believed it should. He didn't need to tell me this was because the city had a Black majority.

Since I'd gone to work at the newspaper, it had become clearer to me — and even more so after listening to President Kennedy's inaugural address — that almost everything important in Washington that wasn't about the Communists seemed to come down to race in one way or another. Ike had failed to get his party to embrace civil rights. Before him, Truman had appointed a commission and signed a historic report on the effects of segregation in the nation's capital; it hadn't made much of a difference. Kennedy had been sworn in by Chief Justice Earl Warren, who had written the unanimous opinion in *Brown v. Board of Education* and *Bolling v. Sharpe*. When Warren's open limousine went by there were loud boos (just like for the Soviet ambassador) and even some people yelling, "Lynch him!"

To me, it was conspicuous that so many southerners played major roles in the inauguration. Vice President Lyndon Johnson, who was in the car behind the new president and First Lady, had been sworn in by the Speaker of the House, Sam Rayburn of Texas, his mentor. Senator John Sparkman of Alabama, the inaugural chairman, rode in the bubble-top with President and Mrs. Kennedy. Senator George Smathers of Florida was Kennedy's best friend in Congress and had helped plan the inaugural balls. Except for Johnson and Rayburn, all those southerners — and pretty much the whole Congress from below the Mason-Dixon Line (except for Maryland) — were still adamant in their opposition to desegregation in America. Kennedy was going to have his hands full, given the civil rights demonstrations that were already under way.

I'd seen Lyndon Johnson order a sandwich a couple of times in Wagshal's delicatessen on Massachusetts Avenue; and when I was nine and ten years old my schoolmates and I from Janney Elementary earned quarters carrying grocery bags from the A&P behind Wagshal's for the wives of quite a few of the men who'd just passed by.

Getting raised in D.C., I thought sometimes, was akin to living in a small town that also happened to be the capital of the United States. Washingtonians had a kind of double vision of these people — as ordinary neighbors, but also as historic figures.

Growing up around such recognizable individuals — whether from north, south, east, or west — was different from encountering them in movie newsreels narrated by big, booming voices or watching them on the TV news. Mrs. Johnson and Mrs. Nixon shopped at the A&P regularly, though both of them had their own help for the bags. Riding my bike, I was used to passing by Justice William O. Douglas as he walked on the C&O Canal towpath. At Griffith Stadium, it was common to see real senators watching the baseball Senators. Some of them lived in apartments in the Argonne, above my grandparents' tailor shop, and when I was little, I'd go with my grandfather to deliver their cleaning.

A sizable contingent of Texans from the university alumni association had been given preferred seating in the stands near me with tickets they'd gotten from Lyndon Johnson's office. Some of them were swigging from pocket flasks. When the Longhorns' marching band passed by, they commenced hooting and hollering. A cowboy dressed as Buffalo Bill rode a real bucking bull who wasn't pleased to have a cowboy on his back. Each time the cowboy tried to tip his hat to the crowd, the bull sensed another opportunity to throw him onto the Pennsylvania Avenue streetcar tracks. Though the cowboy managed to hang on, he finally came down — *wham!* — on the beast's withers and thereafter ceased trying to tip his hat.

I spotted the Big Bertha bass drum of the marching band as it came around the corner, pulled by a couple of college strongmen behind a solid line of tubas. The thing was so big the drummer had to jump up to reach its center and whack at it. So he looked like a jack-in-the-box, which is how I described him to Herman Schaden. The majorettes in their formation looked just as Herman had depicted them, except they were shivering, and when they strained to catch their batons, I could see that a few of them were wearing pajama tops under their uniforms.

By the time the parade ended, the sun had set, and the crowd — especially at the Capitol end of Pennsylvania Avenue, where I was — had dwindled hours before. I walked across the Capitol grounds, now deserted, and down Independence Avenue to the office. There were more people in the newsroom than I'd ever seen except for election night, most of them writing and editing pieces for the next day's paper and getting ready to cover the inaugural balls.

Herman — still at his desk — told me to write a memo with anything I might have for the main parade story that Jerry O'Leary would be writing overnight for tomorrow's first edition. I went to the rear of the newsroom, found a vacant typewriter, and flipped through the pages of my notebook, first front to back and then back to front. I was surprised how much detail was in there and typed a full five pages of something meant to approximate what I thought an actual insert to a story would look like. When I turned it in, I saw that Sid Epstein took a copy for himself.

"Good job, kid," he said the next day, when he dispatched me to the cafeteria for his and Eleni's breakfast.

11

MISFIT

Now that I had covered the inauguration of the president of the United States, Mr. Adelman's chemistry class interested me even less. My underlying problem was how to graduate from high school. While Mr. Adelman prattled on about the periodic table of the elements, I concentrated on the notes I'd taken from my latest conversation with Eddie Bernstein. Or practiced writing ledes about Roy Blick. Or made lists of follow-up stories I intended to do based on nuggets of information gleaned from the events and people I was covering.

High on my list of individuals to interview were Gover M. Kookogey and General Ulysses S. Grant III, both of whom I'd met at a meeting of the Association of the Oldest Inhabitants of the District of Columbia, an assemblage of do-gooders of grand civic intention drawn from the ranks of the capital's most ancient pooh-bahs. Which is how Phil Kelley had described them when he warned me to be extra careful in my reporting because some

Kauffmanns and Noyeses might be present at their meeting. As for General Grant, he was the grandson and namesake of the U.S. president and in his own right had gotten himself appointed chairman of the United States Civil War Centennial Commission. This outfit was gearing up to reenact the great battles in full regalia, followed by ceremonies at which "Taps" would be sounded and solemn speeches intoned. General Grant had promised a press pass for any battles I wanted to attend. According to information I found in the *Star* clips, both the general and Mr. Kookogey had been born in 1881.

On Valentine's Day 1961, my seventeenth birthday, I was summoned to the office of the twelfth-grade guidance counselor, Joe Good, who was also the head football coach. Coach Good presented me with an official note to be returned with a parental signature; the note repeated in writing the stern warning he was delivering to me in person. Both Mr. Adelman and Colonel Johnson, my Spanish teacher, intended to fail me if I continued the path I was on. Unless I passed both courses, I would not graduate in June.

Colonel Johnson had failed me once already, in tenth grade, and I'd had to go to summer school to repeat first-year Spanish. Still I liked him more than almost any of my other teachers at Blair, because he was interesting. He stood straight as a stick at the blackboard and squinted through thick glasses the color of nicotine as he told stories about the action he'd seen in World War II, and about the Spanish-American War, in which his father had fought; they'd both gone to West Point. The peak of his own career, he told us, had been as the United States military attaché in Chile in the early 1950s — which he was sly about discussing in class and hinted was cover for being a spy. Sometimes I took notes on what he said about the Chile part, though almost never the Spanish language.

Mr. Adelman seemed to have arrived in Silver Spring straight from the Bronx with his shirttail hanging out of his jacket, and he acted oblivious to the mockery attending his lectures and the exaggerated nasal New York accents in which Pete Ohlheiser and Dickie Edelman and Bootsie Tenley mimicked him with hilarious perfection. Mr. Adelman definitely was not a spy, and except for his speech patterns I hadn't heard much of anything he'd said since September.

One of the things Coach wanted to know in the five minutes I was in his office was why I couldn't concentrate on my studies, as if this defect of mine was a sudden surprise to him. He must have been the fifth guidance counselor to have asked me the same question, and I never had much of an answer, except to say that if something interested me I could focus on it just fine. About the only subjects that

I'd never struggled with were U.S. History and English, and my senior year was turning out consistent in that regard. I was on track to get a B in American Literature because half the final semester grade would be based on a book report. We were studying the modern novel.

Whatever my disdain or lack of interest in school learning, it wasn't because I disliked the experience of Montgomery Blair. There were aspects of my life as a teenager in Silver Spring that I regarded as downright fulfilling. One was playing poker with Ron Oberman and Buddy Rubin and Peter Berman, in a game that had started in eighth grade and continued through the summers and the Saturdays we worked at McBride's. Whoever won big the previous week had to buy six-packs of beer for the whole table. Now that I was earning upwards of forty or fifty dollars a week at the *Star* (when overtime and citizens meetings pay were figured in), I didn't hesitate to push out a big bet and bluff. I had a winning streak for a while, until the others, Berman in particular, figured out what I was doing.

And though I wasn't a jock, if I really thought about it, the best things about Blair tended to be sports-related: the rituals and bragging rights and letter-sweater stuff passed down from decades of our school dominating the county in football, baseball, and basketball. I avoided covering citizens meetings on evenings when basketball games were scheduled. That season, Bob Windsor scored thirty-eight points in the final (a record) to clinch the Maryland state title for the Blair Blazers. The championship parade on Georgia Avenue, past the firehouse and through the Silver Spring business district, seemed almost as important to the grown-ups who lived near Blair as to its students.

Windsor was in the lead car, with the top down, next to Sonny Jackson. Even though everyone admired Bob for his accomplishments in basketball, baseball, and football, Sonny was the real hero of Montgomery Blair. He stood barely five foot six, but he could dunk the basketball, and he'd outscored almost every other running back in the county. In eleventh grade he was already being scouted by major league baseball teams. You couldn't get a seat near Sonny Jackson in the school cafeteria at lunchtime unless you got there early.

Sonny lived in Takoma Park and not in Lyttonsville, where most of the other Black kids at school lived, across from the county dump in a hamlet of shotgun houses. Its first residents had been descendants of slaves once owned by the Blair family.

Riding maybe forty cars back from Sonny and Bob, the whole celebratory scene gave me goose bumps, especially because I was sitting next to Nancy Immler, who I'd had a crush on since seventh grade and was always looking for ways to impress. I told her how different this was from President Kennedy's inaugural parade, which I had covered for the *Evening Star*.

The next Monday I signed my mother's name to the guidance counselor's report and returned it to Coach Good.

The way I looked at it, Silver Spring was more a relic of small-town life than it was some perfect leafy middle-class suburb, and it was about a thousand miles mentally distant from Washington, D.C., by my calculation. We had our own little train station, an armory where the National Guard drilled, a shopping center on the main street with a dozen storefronts for most necessities from groceries to jewelry to 45 rpm records, a movie theater that showed first-run films in Technicolor, an ice cream parlor, a public library, eight filling stations, and about fifty thousand people, three thousand of whom were teenagers enrolled at Blair.

A model railroad Christmas display was put up in a window of the Hecht Company department store every holiday season that I liked to spend time looking at, with a little train going in circles around the miniature landmarks of the town. About the only thing missing was the curved blacktop band of the new circumferential highway that had been under construction since I was in ninth grade.

I don't know who at Blair was the first to figure out that an unopened, unpoliced six-lane highway was perfect for nighttime drag racing, but Richie and Ronnie Cohen, who owned otherwise identical red and white 1960 Chevy Impala convertibles (bought by their father, a major home builder), and the Proctor brothers' crowd, which was working class and ran heavy toward hot rods, would be laying down rubber beginning at what was to be the Franklin Avenue interchange and accelerate all the way to University Boulevard and later, when the pavement was extended, to Langley Park, a distance of four miles.

These heats turned out to be practice sessions for the sanctioned drag racing that went on at Aquasco Speedway in southern Prince George's County on weekends. Just for the fun of it, and knowing that my windshield would get cindered in an actual race, I sometimes took the family four-door '58 DeSoto, big fins and all, onto the Franklin Avenue ramp; even though it had push-button automatic transmission and couldn't keep up with the Proctor brothers, it could do zero to sixty in less than eight seconds. I once raced the thing at Aquasco and turned in a respectable quarter mile in under seventeen seconds.

Weekday mornings, the same cars — and a hundred others — would be in the student parking lot, windows down and all radios tuned in unison to WDON from up the road in Wheaton. Most white teenagers in Silver Spring and upper Northwest in the District listened to Don Dillard before and after school. (The call letters of WDON were named for him by his father, who owned the station.) Don played not just rock and roll but a lot of Black rhythm and blues and doo-wop music, and rockabilly. Ron Oberman and I had been taking the trolley to shows at the Howard Theater downtown since junior high. We heard James Brown, Dinah Washington, Duke Ellington (who was born in D.C.), and Bo Diddley, who lived on Rhode Island Avenue. As soon as we turned sixteen and got our driver's licenses, we drove three hundred miles to the WWVA Radio Jamboree in Wheeling, West Virginia, which broadcast on a fifty-thousand-watt clear channel and was akin to the Grand Ole Opry but not as corny. We had an inkling that we'd been deposited at a magical musical crossroads. Sometimes we'd go hear Patsy Cline, when she'd sing on Jimmy Dean's TV show on WMAL. She was from nearby Winchester, Virginia, in the Shenandoah Valley. Every couple of months, in Arlington, there were fiddle festivals sponsored by WGAY, the station owned by the country music promoter Connie B. Gay. There were hillbilly music clubs in the far Maryland and Virginia counties on both sides of the river, plus the Shamrock, an Irish bar where the Country Gentlemen played blue-grass on M Street in the heart of Georgetown.

Until Rudy Kauffmann hired me as a copyboy, the best thing that had happened in my life, hands down, was when I went to the 1957 Alan Freed Christmas rock-and-roll show in Manhattan. I'd gone to New York City to visit my cousins on my father's side and to see my friend Paul Keegan from summer camp. When Paul and I arrived at Times Square, the police had blocked off most of the area for tens of thousands of fans trying to get tickets to the Paramount Theater, but the two of us managed to sneak inside through one of the exits as people were streaming out between shows. I'd pinned the souvenir program from the show onto the bulletin board in my bedroom in Silver Spring: Fats Domino, Chuck Berry, Buddy Holly and the Crickets, Danny and the Juniors, Frankie Lyman and the Teenagers, Dion and the Belmonts, the Everly Brothers, Jerry Lee Lewis, the Coasters, Bill Haley and the Comets, Jo Anne Campbell, and Little Richard. At Blair, we'd worn black armbands for a week in tenth grade when the plane went down with Buddy Holly and Ritchie Valens and the Big Bopper.

That year I'd started going to Friday night "socials" at the armory; sometimes they were sock hops, at which Don Dillard was the announcer. These were huge events that attracted teenagers from the District and Maryland as far away as Rockville and Hyattsville — from the Catholic schools, too, even cadets from St. John's College High School on Military Road. There could be two thousand people jammed on the armory floor, and sometimes fights broke out, over girls more often than not. The big draw was not just Don Dillard but also the house band, Link Wray and His Ray Men. They were from Accokeek in Charles County, or at least that's where they had settled, on a chicken farm not far from where my aunt Annie grew up in tobacco country. I first heard Link Wray when I danced on *The Milt Grant Show*. His big hit "Rumble," which was an instrumental with a lot of electric feedback, had been recorded by Grant when I was in the eighth grade. Its sound was over-powering because Wray had punched holes in his amplifiers.

I tried to play "Rumble" on my nylon-string acoustic guitar (in front of the mirror of my bedroom), which of course could not be done, and I was forced to admit my playing was a yard short of hopeless, even though, before taking lessons from Charlie Byrd, I had studied downtown with Sophocles Papas, who'd been a student of Segovia himself.

So growing up in Silver Spring wasn't altogether unpleasant. I just itched to get out as fast as I could type.

A few weeks after my seventeenth birthday, driving the family DeSoto from the armory with Ron Oberman and Peter Berman in the car on a Friday night, I pulled up at the stoplight at Colesville Road and Fenton Street in front of the Hecht Company. Larry Marine, our classmate since junior high, was stopped in the next lane in his '56 Bel Air hardtop V-8, gunning his engine.

We lit out in a screech heading for the circumferential. I was doing close to ninety behind the county library when I saw the flashing lights of a police cruiser in the rearview mirror, and at that moment Oberman, who was in the backseat, shouted, "Bernstein, I think he's got a gun out." The thought of being shot at was even worse than the prospect of my parents coming to bail me out again. I slowed down and ended up with the car rolling onto the lawn of the Maryland National Capital Park and Planning Commission. Two policemen jumped out of the cruiser, snatched me out of the DeSoto, and then threw me against it so hard I thought my back was broken.

They took the three of us to the Silver Spring substation, where Officer Pay — who, as usual, had been keeping peace at the sock hop — booked me, and again I was scheduled for an appointment at the County Juvenile Court in Rockville.

That night, lying in bed, it occurred to me that I did not want Sid Epstein to find out I was a juvenile delinquent.

■■■■

Among my privileges as a copyboy was being assigned to the Sunday Department and its leader, Ed Tribble, whom Sid Epstein had replaced as city editor in 1958.

Mr. Tribble and Sid Epstein could not have been more different characters, despite the fact that they were about the same age and both were thoroughbred clotheshorses. Even in winter, Mr. Tribble wore shiny brown penny loafers and argyle socks — probably because he was from the South, I decided. Instead of a suit jacket, he'd arrive at the office in a bright-colored cardigan sweater that he'd wear throughout the day. He not only dressed the part but looked and acted like a professor, in a tweedy sort of way, with his soft Georgia accent and horn-rimmed spectacles and — as I was to learn — the care he took constructing a paragraph as he edited. The sentences would come out smooth and cultivated and clarifying, but still unpretentious. Sid Epstein's edits were far more brisk and energetic.

Tony Maggiacomo said that the minute Sid Epstein became city editor, Ed Tribble had seemed relieved of a mighty burden. I could see that the thoughtfulness of Mr. Tribble's personality was well suited to the Sunday Department, which was as hushed a place as the newsroom was rowdy. His domain included the weekly arts and music and books pages, which were all shuffled together with "The Week in Perspective."

The pieces that ran in the "Week in Perspective" section were called "thumbsuckers." John Cassady, the national editor, was the first person I'd heard use the term, when he told Miss McGrory to take some of the more nuanced and interpretive points in one of her stories — about the Kennedy family's love for touch football — and save those details for a thumbsucker to run in Ed Tribble's section. She'd been happy to oblige, the clear implication being that thumbsuckers were a way to expand on the simpler aspects of news and report with a more analytical bent and colorful palette than in a straighter "just the facts, ma'am" news story narrative. It also helped that Ed Tribble had more space available in his section than Cassady could ever offer on deadline. Sometimes Sid Epstein would roll his eyes when one of his reporters suggested that a topic was ripe for a thumbsucker, but later he would have to admit that Ed Tribble's pages were the perfect place to get beyond the breaking news and provide more depth than deadline-reported pieces or ordinary feature stories.

I presumed that Sid Epstein's life beyond the office, beginning at the cocktail hour, was one altogether glamorous whirl as he swept, together with his wife the fashion editor, into fancy society events to which the rest of the local staff would never be invited. Whereas Ed Tribble, after the final edition was off the presses, ran a regular salon at which he held court until late into the evening from his genteel precincts across the hall from the newsroom. Maggiacomo explained to me that the origins of these soirees went back to the old Star Building on Pennsylvania Avenue and a restaurant to which much of the same crowd would still head out for drinks sometimes — the Chicken Hut on Eleventh Street, kitty-corner from the Old Post Office Tower.

Among the reasons the copyboys appreciated working in the Sunday Department was that Ed Tribble seemed as accepting of us sitting with our feet up on the file cabinets and listening to the chatter as anyone else. Almost anything was likely to come up for discussion, from the troubles with Castro that had confounded Ike and now vexed Kennedy, to the trial of Adolf Eichmann in Jerusalem that spring, to the latest office gossip (which was incessant). Sometimes red wine would be poured into plastic cups from the cafeteria, which seemed to me a really grown-up way to drink.

A lot of information laid out between glasses of wine didn't make it into the paper or hadn't yet been confirmed for accuracy. David Broder, the political correspondent who'd come to the paper to cover the 1960 election, seemed to know ahead of time almost every appointment President Kennedy was planning to make. He had a story to tell about each of Kennedy's retainers, though Miss McGrory, who was worshipful of the new president, had much better tales about the people who went way back to JFK's Boston Irish days.

Many of the habitual participants who gravitated to these discussions were reporters on the national staff — Miss McGrory in particular, who attributed some of the finer points of her writing style to Ed Tribble's counsel and pencil work. Plus the critics — architecture, art, music, drama, movies — and John Rosson, the assistant photo editor, who reviewed restaurants and got to put the tab on his expense account. And a gaggle of cityside reporters, most of whom had worked under Mr. Tribble in the newsroom, plus a few dictationists too. I was amazed at the easy camaraderie; there didn't seem to be many distinctions of rank.

Dawdling in the right-hand lane of rush hour traffic on Sixteenth Street on one of the last evenings of March, Mr. Porter missed the turn at Colesville Road as we headed back to Silver Spring. He eased the Oldsmobile toward the left lane at East-West Highway, and I asked him where we were going.

Mr. Porter was a man of not many words, except when we'd sit in the parlor of his house with Mrs. Porter and the two of them were regular chatterboxes.

"Bethesda," he said.

During the ride from the *Star* building, we'd talked a bit about the demonstrations in Maryland: on Route 40, north and east of Washington to the Delaware line, to integrate the restaurants where African diplomats were being denied service on their way to the United Nations and New York; and in Montgomery County.

The United States capital of my childhood was a Jim Crow town, and my parents had been among those trying to change that during the late 1940s and 1950s. When I was in grammar school, all the public swimming pools in the District of Columbia had been drained by order of the City Recreation Board rather than allow Black families to swim in them.

Now, for the first time, Glen Echo Amusement Park, near the Potomac Palisades at the far end of Bethesda, would be opened to Black people; its owner had announced his capitulation a few days earlier. From the time I'd been nine or ten, I'd taken the trolley — it was the last stop on the Cabin John line — to spend sweltering summer days at Glen Echo, swimming in its Crystal Pool and riding the roller coaster. I'd placed smartly in a Howdy Doody look-alike contest there, too, and received as my prize the opportunity to squirt Clarabell, the *Howdy Doody Show* clown, with his signature seltzer bottle.

The same group of pickets that had forced Glen Echo to desegregate — Black students from Howard University and white home-owners from the Bannockburn neighborhood nearby — were provoking ugly resistance on Bethesda's main shopping strip on Wisconsin Avenue. The so-called American Nazi Party, started by a local man named George Lincoln Rockwell, had organized some of the coun-terdemonstrators. A few were wearing Nazi uniforms.

Mr. Porter said he wanted to see the con-frontation for himself. We drove slowly by several men and women holding signs reading NIGGERS GO HOME. Mr. Porter said it was sickening. You could grow up with segrega-tion, he said, and it could be all around you and just the way life was, but — at least when he was a boy — nobody had ever tried to change it in a concerted way, at least not that he had been aware of. Now he was the chief editor of news about two states, Maryland and Virginia, where on some days probably half the big stories had to do with segregation and integration. Haynes Johnson, who was probably the local staff's best writer-reporter, had been working on a multipart series for months, to be called "The Negro in Washing-ton." Mr. Porter said it was going to be almost as long as a book.

The center of the Bethesda demonstrations was the Hiser movie theater on Wisconsin

Avenue. I'd never gone to the movies there, but in junior high, if Silver Spring Lanes was overcrowded on a Saturday, we'd go bowling at the duckpin alley downstairs at the Hiser, even though the pinball machines weren't as good as the ones in Silver Spring.

As Mr. Porter slowed the car even more, we inched past pickets and counterdemonstrators at Gifford's ice cream parlor, a block from the Hiser. Going to Gifford's main branch, in Silver Spring, was a ritual that I'd presumed every Blair student had enjoyed at least once or twice; its banana splits and sundaes and shakes were far superior to the Hot Shoppe's. If there was ice cream cake served in the gym for some special school event, it came from Gifford's. And in the warm months, Gifford's on Georgia Avenue was packed with kids from Blair. It had never occurred to me that Sonny Jackson would not have been allowed inside the door or served at the counter or at one of the tables.

I asked Mr. Porter if I could take a closer look at what was happening outside the Hiser. He said okay, but to be sure to be back at the corner for him to pick me up in ten minutes.

Most of my experience with the Montgomery County police had been with Detective Sergeant Pay, but on this evening the uniformed policeman who stopped me at the sidewalk was firm but polite. I showed him my *Star* identification card. He said I could go only as far as where about twenty-five Black and white picketers were marching together in front of the theater. Many held signs demanding that the theater's owner, John Henry Hiser, Bethesda's most prominent real estate owner and businessman, integrate his movie house. Hiser had vowed that he'd sell the place before he'd ever allow a ticket to be sold to a Black moviegoer. Behind the picketers, a phalanx of policemen, their billy clubs at the ready, kept the pro-segregation demonstrators at a safe distance.

I wasn't sure what I was looking for, and it appeared both sides were getting ready to go home for the night. More as a way of introduction than anything else, I approached a young Black woman who seemed to be in charge of the pickets — she couldn't have been more than twenty or twenty-one — and she handed me some literature. She told me that if I needed any information, there was a contact list inside, and she circled her name. I asked how long they were willing to keep demonstrating.

Until she could watch the movie show, she said.

Later that week, I was assigned to cover the monthly meeting of the all-Black D.C. Federation of Civic Associations. Its first order of business, to my surprise, was a discussion of the case of Private James E. Thomas of the Park Police. A resolution had been drafted stating the federation's concern that — as Officer Thomas maintained (and Ted Crown had speculated) — he was being made a scapegoat in the Lafayette Square police battle because he was Black. Not only had he been suspended from the police force and his previously stellar career denigrated, said the resolution, but he was now being slapped with a multimillion-dollar lawsuit filed against him and the Park Police and the federal government by Sergeant Louis Fochett, aide-de-camp to Deputy Chief Roy Blick, the perverse commander of the Metropolitan Police Morals Division and its Prostitution and Perversion Squad. Fochett claimed to have been manhandled in the brawl.

There was no real debate on the resolution — it was obvious it would pass, perhaps unanimously. But as the motion to take up the resolution was introduced, one of the men present asked to address the room. He spoke in the deep-voiced cadences of the southern church, and he was spellbinding. He paced in front of the fifty or so people in attendance, his voice rising and falling in rhythms of outrage as he condemned the silence of the municipal authorities who had done nothing to come to Private Thomas's defense. The man said flat-out that it was because Thomas was Black and Blick and Fochett were white.

In my notebook, I tried to write a description

of the speaker, not for the newspaper or any story I would write, but because of the drama he was introducing in the room, and I wanted to see if I could capture it. He was a firebrand, wound up and ready to strike as his sentences unreeled with a pulsing indignation. Why, he asked, in a town where crime was rampant and on the increase, should three Metropolitan Police detectives be stationed in Lafayette Park in the first place, lurking in the bushes to entice and arrest homosexuals, instead of solving real crimes? Some in the room appeared uncomfortable when he introduced that subject, and they seemed put off by the speaker's militancy. But he won them over, mostly, and when he finished, many applauded.

At the close of the meeting, a crowd gathered around the speaker. I introduced myself as a reporter for the *Star,* and he said his name was Julius Hobson, spelling it for me. When I asked which civic association he was from, he said he was there simply as a citizen of the District of Columbia. He introduced me to two younger men he was with: the Reverend Walter Fauntroy and Stokely Carmichael. He told me that Mr. Fauntroy was the pastor of the New Bethel Baptist Church and had lived in Washington all his life, and that Mr. Carmichael was a student leader at Howard University and one of the organizers of the Route 40 sit-ins.

Carmichael seemed impatient, apparently

over the fact that I was there representing the *Evening Star*. Why hadn't the *Star* sent a Black reporter to cover the meeting? he demanded. I was defensive: the *Post*'s reporter, who had already left because he was on deadline, was also white. Still, I knew the *Post* had at least two Black reporters on its staff. The *Star* had none.

When I went back to the newsroom, the most I was able to extract from my notebook were the basic facts about the resolution the federation had passed, and I worked in a vivid paragraph-long quote from Julius Hobson. But Emerson Beauchamp killed the quote, and my story the next day ran to barely five paragraphs buried near the dime-store ads in the back of the local section. I was dismayed that the quote had been excised. It seemed to me that the real news of the meeting was in Hobson's words, and their fury and context about the police and race. I could not understand why the *Star* would shy away from this.

A few days later, at home, I read through the literature I'd been given by the woman at the Hiser Theater demonstration. One of the names on the contact list, with the same number he'd given me, was Stokely Carmichael.

12

LIFT-OFF

A lot of my difficulties at school were a result of the Russians trying to beat us in the space race — or so I told myself. Almost from the moment the first Sputnik satellite was launched when I was in the eighth grade in 1957, our curriculum in the Montgomery County school system began to change. More math. More science. Mr. Adelman's chemistry class wasn't the half of it.

Until Sputnik, I might have stood a chance of getting through science-based courses with a C — not great, but not entirely a disgrace either. Now science classes became more intense and rigorous. If the classwork required solving equations or spending time in the laboratory with a Bunsen burner or a bullfrog pickled in a tank of formaldehyde, I was resigned to getting a D — if I was lucky. Or if I sat next to Robin Zehring, who sometimes offered help with the answers and was handy with an X-Acto knife.

I decided I had better concentrate. So after

Easter recess, during which I worked at the newspaper every day including Easter Sunday, plus overtime hours because the Communists were on the verge of taking over Laos, I decided to go to school more and cut back my copyboy schedule to Saturdays and Sundays, plus one night a week for citizens meetings. And I got one of the brainier girls in my Spanish class to tutor me in the school cafeteria at lunch.

My reacquaintance with the classroom felt like a major sacrifice. The news, including the local news and what was going on in the neighborhood associations I was covering, had become a blizzard of big stories. Consequential ones. Not just the ones about Castro or Indochina or Khrushchev or President and Mrs. Kennedy getting ready to visit General de Gaulle in Paris. The Twenty-Third Amendment to the Constitution, giving the citizens of the District of Columbia the right to vote in presidential elections, had finally been ratified by three-quarters of the states. My mother had never voted until we moved to Maryland. Now Washington, D.C., would have three electoral votes — equal to the least populous state, Alaska.

D.C. residents would be able to go to the polls in 1964. Everyone had an opinion on what the minimum voting age should be. Republican and Democratic Party operatives were showing up at neighborhood meetings, and I was determined to cultivate them. One was Phil Guarino, a member of the Republican National Committee, who spoke at a meeting of the Brightwood Civic Association that I was assigned to cover. I already knew him well enough from his real job as the owner of Phil's Tavern on Georgia Avenue. His establishment was where Oberman, Berman, Buddy Rubin, and I went to drink pitchers of beer on Friday and Saturday nights, because Phil's was known to specialize in serving underage teenagers with dodgy IDs. It also had great pizza, which Phil would bring to the table himself and engage in friendly banter with us. Guarino's argument to the civic association was that he represented the party of Lincoln, traditionally the party that Washington's Black middle class had identified with through Reconstruction and most of the twentieth century. In my notebook, I put three stars next to that. Meanwhile, he insisted that the minimum voting age should be twenty-one, as it was in most of the states.

Now that D.C. had the vote, President Kennedy said that he would welcome real home rule for the capital and would like to see the District commissioners, who were appointed by the president, replaced by an elected mayor and city council. I again sought out my neighbor Senator Bible. One Sunday morning I knocked on his kitchen door — less than ten yards from our front door — and Loucile

Bible let me inside. Her husband told me, with his feet up on the ottoman in their living room, that even though he was in favor of home rule and might be able to bring along a majority of his committee, Congressman John McMillan of South Carolina, the chairman of the District Committee in the House, would never allow a bill to get to the floor for a vote. McMillan was among the congressmen who had signed the so-called Southern Manifesto vowing implacable resistance to integration. I wrote a memo to the city desk reporting what the senator had told me — "off the record," I specified — and gave it to Coit Hendley, the deputy city editor. Grace Bassett, who covered the House District Committee, got some more information, turned it into a page one story, and sent me an appreciative note with a copy to Sid Epstein, which I pasted into my scrapbook. After that I tried to eat dinner in Silver Spring with the Bible family in their kitchen every chance I got.

On the morning of Wednesday, April 12, when I turned on the radio, instead of playing rock and roll Don Dillard was talking about a man the Russians had sent up into space and brought back down to earth.

Newspaper people hardly ever watched TV news, which they considered crude and amateurish and somehow phony, a kind of playacting. Now, while I was still putting on my clothes, I ran downstairs and switched on Dave Garroway on the *Today* show, who was reading bulletins about the cosmonaut Yuri Gagarin and the five-ton spaceship that had carried him to outer space and back. I tried to imagine what would be going on in the *Star* newsroom and decided that I could be helpful. I hitchhiked to the B&O station instead of heading to school and got to the paper by ten.

Phil Kelley right away told me to sit down in a chair directly behind Earl Heap and do whatever Mr. Heap told me to do, which mostly turned out to be him shouting at me to run this piece of copy or that one straight up to the composing room through the hole in the ceiling. A specially designated bank of Linotype operators was tapping out the type for a slew of front-page stories, and Al Baker himself snatched the copy from my hands.

"So, Alfalfa, you're back at it," he said, though he'd seen me probably half a dozen times since he'd thrown his fit over my touching the type.

I kept my hands behind my back and murmured something, though I was tempted to tell him that my skill at reading upside down and backward had improved.

"Sid Epstein must be a brave man to let you upstairs again. On this, of all days," he said. He tousled my hair and said he was glad I had learned my lesson without too much pain, except for the few thousand dollars it had cost the *Star*.

When I came back down through the hole, I could tell from my elevated view that the commotion of the previous summer about the space dog story was nothing compared to what was going on in the newsroom now. Newbold Noyes had come out of his office to run things. Noyes and Herb Corn, the managing editor — who seemed to me to be about a hundred years old and as a rule had all the animation of one of the city's marble statues — were personally overseeing the story from inside the rim, which by then was so crowded there was barely room to move. Bill Hines, the chief science and space reporter, was wedged in next to the national editor with the telephone cradled to his ear as he took notes on the typewriter from his sources in the U.S. space program and turned the notes into copy.

While he was still on the phone, Hines was advising John Cassady on who to call at the National Aeronautics and Space Administration about the rocket that had shot the cosmonaut out of the earth's atmosphere. "Get hold of the engineers at Cape Canaveral," he barked, and the national editor obeyed him as if Hines were his boss. Cassady started writing down names and phone numbers Hines was reading out of a pocket-sized leather telephone book. I made a mental note to begin carrying one, though I wasn't sure whose phone numbers I'd list.

Even Earl Heap, who I regarded as perhaps the most cynical man I had ever met, seemed astonished at the copy he was moving. "Jesus, will you look at that," he said as the first wire-photo of Gagarin crossed his desk and he read the caption. It showed the spaceman wearing what looked like a football helmet left over from the Knute Rockne era. He handed it to me and told me to get it upstairs.

It was an amazing story, a wonder, but it became more complicated and dangerous because it was the Russians who'd pulled it off.

During the flight, Gagarin had traveled at something like 17,000 miles per hour while radioing back to earth how great the view was.

SOVIET ASTRONAUT ORBITS EARTH IN 5-TON SHIP AND LANDS SAFELY read the banner headline in the *Star*'s third edition. The off-lead story was KHRUSHCHEV DARES WEST TO CATCH UP.

A preeminent British astronomer was quoted — in one of the takes of copy I ran upstairs — as saying that it was the greatest scientific achievement in the history of mankind.

I could tell that some people in the newsroom were trying to decide whether it was a good thing or a disaster.

Around two o'clock, Phil Kelley said he was trusting Mark Baldwin and me with a special assignment. He would need the information on our driver's licenses to send over to the Secret Service so we could get into President Kennedy's press conference at four o'clock at the State Department auditorium. From there, Kelley wanted us to dictate a running official text back to the newsroom. The Night Final was going to be held open an extra hour and a half to get in anything the president said about the Russian spaceman.

Phil Kelley explained that the text would be handed out several pages at a time, about ten minutes behind the reporters' questions and the president's actual words. Baldwin and I would dictate the text over the phone to a dictationist, and that way the national desk would have the president's exact language while editing Jack Horner — Garnett D. Horner, the Star's White House reporter — who would begin dictating his story the minute the press conference ended. The paper would run a boxed, abbreviated text on the jump page.

Baldwin had already been to one of Kennedy's press conferences and Tony Maggiacomo had taught him how to do this particular job.

So when the Secret Service man waved us inside, Baldwin told me to grab a seat in the back row of the auditorium, where the newsreel photographers were set up on tripods; he took a seat farther down front. This disappointed me because he would be much closer to the president than I would.

The auditorium wasn't all that big — there were more seats in the Silver movie theater on Colesville Road in Silver Spring — but this was the fanciest theater I'd ever been in. The seats were high-backed and covered in red leather. After I'd sunk down in the cushion, I stood up to take in the complete scene as reporters started to fill up the room. They were keyed up, talking, gesturing. This was the whole White House press corps, not just from the United States but from all over the world. It took me another couple of minutes to realize that the reporters weren't going to sit down until after the president arrived.

To either side of the auditorium stage, two TV cameras trailing big cables on the floor were trained on the podium from which the president would speak. The presidential seal on the rostrum was lit for the cameras, and a pair of American flags were placed — I noticed — just close enough so they would stay framed on television behind the president.

In Ed Tribble's salon I'd picked up that Jack Horner and a lot of other White House reporters believed the whole notion of televising a presidential press conference had, since January, turned covering the presidency upside down. No president before Kennedy had ever held an on-the-record press conference with cameras and microphones transmitting live, though only the ABC network actually put it on the air while it was happening. But

JFK couldn't have been happy he'd scheduled a press conference for this day, I imagined.

It was his ninth in the twelve weeks since the inauguration.

In short order, a set of double doors opened to the right of the hall near the stage and Kennedy entered, followed by his press secretary and a few staff people. Even before he motioned everyone to sit, I found myself making notes. I put quotation marks around the first words out of his mouth: that it was sixteen years to the day since Franklin Roosevelt had died. But he didn't say any more about this, and then he observed that it was also the sixth anniversary of the announcement that a vaccine had been discovered to prevent paralytic polio. Ninety million Americans had since gotten the Salk vaccine, he said. Which got me to thinking about my classmates in grammar school who had been in iron lungs and how terrified we all were of getting polio. And also about Powell Hill, my closest friend in our old neighborhood on Chesapeake Street, whose stepfather wore iron braces on his legs and hitched them into place whenever he sat down. For a while at Janney Elementary, parents hadn't let their children play on the playground after school. Later that afternoon, when I went back through my notebook, I saw that I'd written myself a reminder to call Powell and ask about his great-great-uncle and namesake, the Confederate general Ambrose

Powell Hill, who was killed at Petersburg; I thought it might give me something to talk about with General Grant.

I'd figured that the president would make a statement about the spaceman, but he went straight to questions, which to my surprise were as much about what was going on in Cuba as about the Russians putting a man into space.

How far would he go in helping an anti-Castro uprising or invasion of Cuba? Kennedy was asked.

There had been rumblings for days that some kind of military action by anti-Castro forces was imminent or under way in Cuba. But President Kennedy, from where I was sitting in the back of the hall, seemed unequivocal in saying that there would not be, under any conditions, an intervention in Cuba by American armed forces. And that he would make sure that Americans would not be involved in any actions inside Cuba.

Soon enough the president was asked about the Soviet man in space, for whom he professed admiration. He said he'd sent Khrushchev his personal congratulations, and a note to Mr. Gagarin too. To me it sounded as if he wanted to put the blame on Ike for falling behind in the space race, and he went on about how he'd put together his own task force on booster rockets and the like just before the inauguration. He did not mention that in two weeks' time the United States would be sending up the first American astronaut, on a fifteen-minute suborbital flight into space. Suddenly the U.S. effort seemed puny after the Soviets' achievement.

Baldwin had grabbed a seat on the aisle, in the same row as Jack Horner. After ten minutes, young women from the White House press office began handing out mimeographed copies of the text of the first part of the press conference to those seated on the aisle, who passed the pages along. Baldwin jumped up and ran his copy to me in the last row, where he'd parked me so I'd be closest to the phone booths in the lobby.

Phil Kelley had told me to call the newsroom operator as soon as I got the first pages, and she would connect me with a dictationist and tell the national desk that the text was coming. There must have been twenty or thirty telephone booths stretched across the lobby. Several were occupied by messengers holding them for reporters.

Even though I had never taken dictation myself, much less dictated anything to the newsroom, I knew enough from working there eight months how to do it, pretty much. Jane Daugherty, the dictationist I was connected to, helped explain the process to me — like reminding me to say "upper case."

So, if the president's words in the text were, *Well, Mr. Castro has a choice to make. We hope he'll choose the sensible course. Next question,* I'd say to the dictationist, "Well, comma, Mister Castro has a choice to make, period. We hope he'll — apostrophe after 'he' — choose the sensible course, period. Next question, period paragraph."

I spent the rest of the press conference in the phone booth, and about every five minutes Baldwin would reappear with another couple of pages. The purple ink from the mimeograph drum hadn't even had time to dry. It occurred to me that I'd never get to see anything but the first ten minutes of a presidential press conference, which turned out to be the case on this day. Still, it really was exciting.

Kennedy cast almost all the events he was being asked about in a single context: a worldwide struggle in every sphere between the United States and the Communists. In Cuba, in space, at the UN (where Red China had been excluded but was determined to become a member), in Laos.

Unfamiliar as I was with covering presidents, I thought he was getting his point across effectively, at least from what I was reading.

The fact that the Soviets had put the first man in space did not represent a weakening of "the free world," he said, but there was no question that the total mobilization of the Communist bloc over the past year was a continuing source of danger. We were going to have to live with the danger, he went on, probably through the rest of the twentieth century.

I could see how the press conference format worked to convey his charm and humor, both of which were infectious, even for reporters who were supposed to be strictly objective. There was some laughter. When he was asked about the Republicans — whom he called "the grand old p-a-h-d-y" — he talked about how old their ideas were and how they were opposed to any kind of government health care because it was "socialized medicine." He was totally at ease. He even appeared to be having a good time, which seemed strange under the circumstances, what with the implicit humiliation of the Americans by the Russians. Later, back in the newsroom, I heard that Cecil Holland found out that Kennedy had had a rehearsal with his press secretary, Pierre Salinger, to cover some of the points they thought the reporters would pursue.

The way I knew that the press conference was over was that I could feel the floor shaking inside the phone booth, from so many reporters running up the aisles to the other booths around me.

Kennedy's shortest answer of the day preoccupied Mark Baldwin and me in the taxicab on the way back to the office. Someone had asked Kennedy about the fact that the White House News Photographers Association didn't allow

Black members. *Did the president feel that an organization attached to the White House should have such a policy?* he was asked. He was unequivocal in his reply: "No." He hoped the association would change its policy, because "everyone comes into the White House," and that was the way he wanted to see it.

The *Star* had no Black reporters, so it was obvious to Baldwin that the color barrier in our own Photo Department wouldn't be breached in the foreseeable future.

Like so many things in Washington, even getting to the State Department by taxicab had involved a racial choice. Whenever Blanche, the newsroom's switchboard operator, summoned a cab for one of the reporters, she dialed LIncoln 4–1212, which was the number for the Diamond Cab Association; it had been under contract to the *Star* almost as long as Gould Lincoln had been an editorial writer. All its drivers were white. Phil Kelley, who considered himself something of a renegade, and as shop steward of the Guild had unusual autonomy in the newsroom, made a point of calling the Capitol Cab Company, which had only Black drivers, whenever he would send the copyboys out.

Two days after Gagarin's return to earth, there was another eruption in the wire room. Bulletin after ominous bulletin crossed the teletype machines as I worked my shift. First there were reports of warplanes hitting Cuban airports. After that, there came a tumble of news (BULLETIN, URGENT) about a full-scale invasion of Cuba by sea and air. Pretty soon, the secretary of state, Dean Rusk, and the U.S. ambassador to the United Nations — Adlai Stevenson — were denying American involvement.

The Bay of Pigs had started out as a rumor and ended as a disaster and an almost paralyzing embarrassment for the new president. It was supposed to be a secret CIA operation, but plenty of people knew about it, including the Russians and the Cubans and some American newspapers. Even I, a seventeen-year-old copyboy, knew about it.

I'd heard all about the hush-hush project weeks earlier, while I was having dinner with Rupe Welch. Rupe was bitter and scathing on that night, because someone at the paper had just killed his story reporting the badly kept secret of what the CIA and a force of Cuban exiles were about to attempt. Kennedy and everyone else would have been better off if the full story had come out and the thing had been canceled.

Rupert Welch was from Buffalo and sounded that way, as if a clothespin was holding his nose closed. He was shrewd and alert and cynical and kind, all at once. Short and sturdy, his neck thick and his chest and belly pushing out in front of him when he walked, Rupe dressed and talked like a cop. He covered the night police beat at headquarters. He liked to prowl the city's after-hours clubs, where he was well known, between midnight and dawn.

A twenty-five-year-old former paratrooper, Rupe had just been finishing up his three months on the *Star*'s reporter training program, which was Sid Epstein's invention. The city editor had been concerned that the copyboys and dictationists who wanted to rise through the ranks didn't have enough reporting experience outside the newsroom to make the jump. The program was intense: trainees spent time with beat reporters at police headquarters, on the Hill, and at the District Building covering welfare, housing, city planning, and transportation.

Rupe had chosen to do his in-depth reporting project on the large Cuban exile community in D.C. Most Cubans in Washington had settled around Columbia Road in the Adams-Morgan area, where my mother grew up and where my grandfather had his tailor shop. In the course of interviewing a former radio broadcaster from Havana who was one of the community's leaders, Rupe learned that there had been an extensive recruiting effort for an invasion that was intended to happen sometime in the spring. Rupe followed the tip by going to a big social event at the Dupont Plaza Hotel, where several men told him in detail about being recruited by U.S. government agents for training and dispatch to Cuba as part of an invasion force. When Rupe asked if the CIA was behind the recruiting, other Cuban community leaders said yes.

Harry Bacas, the editor who ran the training program, agreed with Rupe that the invasion-in-waiting story was too important to be delayed as part of a larger series on the Cuban exile community. Bacas told Rupe to write it, and it went up through the tiers of editors and the news desk and the slot and onto the front page. But after running in the first edition, the story was killed — by whom was not clear, though Sid Epstein was aware what had happened; neither Rupe nor Bacas ever got a satisfactory explanation, though later it became clear that Ben McKelway, the paper's editor in chief, had signed off on the decision to kill it.

I told Kelley that I had almost no more schoolwork to do; I was just waiting for my final exams in a few weeks. Which he said was no business of his anyhow, and given what was going on with the news, he could use me at the paper as much as I could work. That was the thing about the news, you never knew what was going to break.

So it was that Kelley again sent me over to the president's press conference in the State Department auditorium, the day after the Bay of Pigs fiasco. I sat in an aisle seat next to a row of reporters with White House credentials hanging around their necks. I was much closer to the president than the last time, maybe midway back in the auditorium. Now that I knew the drill, I was sure there would be plenty of empty telephone booths to head back to, once the first sheaf of mimeographed transcripts arrived. I made detailed notes about my perception of the president's appearance and state of mind, as if I were Walter Lippmann, the famous columnist, whom Kennedy happened to mention in one of his answers.

The mood was grim.

Kennedy opened by reading prepared remarks, saying he was not going to comment specifically about what was going on in Cuba. His head was sunk down to his chest almost, and when he looked up after that, and for the whole time I was able to watch him, he never smiled. There was none of the easy banter of the previous press conference.

Right away, he took responsibility, and said that victory had a hundred fathers and defeat was an orphan. When, in no time, the operation in Cuba came to be called the Bay of Pigs disaster, with a capital D almost, it was Kennedy's disaster. And yet, amazingly, his poll numbers went up.

I was curious what Rupe Welch would be feeling now that the invasion had become the biggest story in the world. He'd probably be angrier at the *Star* than at Kennedy. Rupe had a military swagger about him. He was the kind of guy who would have joined up with the Cubans and hit the beaches himself if he weren't a reporter.

Kennedy had lied outright for days. That was what surprised me so much. I knew I shouldn't feel disappointed — and I was still excited to be there at his press conference, especially with the chance to see the president from closer up. I knew how important it was to keep reportorial distance from the story. But I felt let down, in a muted kind of way. Even Ike smudged the truth sometimes, and presidents were rightly expected to keep secrets. The previous night, Kennedy had invited Nixon to the White House to brief him on what was going on in regard to Cuba, and Ike was going to meet with the president this very night. Kennedy was scrambling, I thought.

As I stuffed dimes into the pay phone, my immediate concern was to dictate an accurate text of his remarks. It didn't go very well because the Ivy League dictationist I'd been given was new to the *Star* and anyway she was a slow typist. And we were on deadline. The whole press conference had run about half an hour, but at the rate we were moving, the other copyboy would be back in the newsroom with the full mimeographed text before I'd finished dictating the first ten minutes of the event itself. And the telephone booth was stifling. I hoped the desk would realize I wasn't the one setting this snail's pace.

Almost every name that Kennedy had mentioned, except perhaps General de Gaulle (I was careful to spell out "small d-e"), was unfamiliar to her, or at least the spelling. "L-I-P-P-M-A-N-N," I spelled out for her. "Radziwill" was as foreign to her as the name itself, though the front pages were full of news about Jackie Kennedy's jet-set sister. Sandy Vanocur of NBC News, a TV correspondent known to almost every print reporter in town, and whom the president had called on by name, sounded to her like *vinegar* and precious minutes evaporated trying to get it right. Dictating a story — and taking dictation, I was learning — required not only quick fingers but a nimble mind and some knowledge of the news.

The president, in his chagrin, tried to enlarge the perspective. He set out to give a kind of tutorial to the press on how he saw the struggle between the Communist world and the West, between the Soviet Union and the United States. Each question about the Bay of Pigs and the Russian cosmonaut — and the comeuppance of America these weeks, though the reporters used more diplomatic language — led Kennedy to another elaboration of what must have been his deepest thinking.

Outright he'd stated that the Communists were at an advantage around the world because of how effectively they suppressed dissent, liquidated the opposition, and forced people out of their native countries to be refugees. They were especially effective in seizing power in democracies and aspiring democracies. These were the problems Americans were going to have to confront in this decade.

He cited another country, Vietnam, as "one of the great problems facing the United States" that could persist through the decade. Seventy or 80 percent of the people there had endorsed the elected government, he said, but Vietnam was in danger of falling to the Communists because of operations carried out by a small, well-disciplined guerrilla force.

Washington and Moscow were muscling each other, exchanging threats over Cuba. Meanwhile, he said, Castro was turning Cuba into a Communist camp.

Kennedy noted that secret information about what had occurred in the past few days and about the role of the CIA and the U.S. military had been printed in the newspapers. One of the problems of a free society, not faced by dictatorships, he pointed out, was how to handle information under such circumstances.

I tried to think this through, to see things as he saw them. It seemed to me that Kennedy had a point that national security had to be considered, especially if lives were potentially in danger. At the same time, though, I didn't think I'd trust the government every time it raised the flag of national security.

Worse, Kennedy seemed ready to make the conduct of the press the issue in the Bay of Pigs disaster, rather than the conduct of the president himself and the advisers around him who secretly had given the go-ahead to the clandestine operation.

A few days after my encounter at Blair with Coach Good, I'd brought Mr. Tribble some galley proofs for the upcoming Sunday front thumbsucker page. As usual, piles of books crowded the working space on either side of his desk, and the table behind him was stacked even higher with extra copies of editions sent by publishers for review. He reached into the pile back there and handed me a volume that was thicker than the telephone book. He said he thought I'd enjoy it, because it was a novel about Maryland and offered an amusing way of looking at the state's history.

I did not mention to him that it had taken me almost a whole semester to reach the end of *Paradise Lost* — and that I couldn't imagine staggering through a piece of literature of this poundage and subject matter.

The way he knew that I was from Maryland, or at least that I lived there, was from a discussion during his salon a few evenings before, when I'd gotten up enough nerve to open my yap, because I knew something about the topic at hand.

Mr. Tribble had just announced that Newbold Noyes had put him in charge of a special section the *Star* was planning for the coming summer, to mark the opening of the first section of the new Capital Beltway. That was the official name to be conferred on the circumferential highway that had been under construction for half a dozen years. Mr. Tribble took off his horn-rimmed glasses and shook his head at how dumb an idea he thought the whole subject was. So I said maybe it would be interesting if someone were to write a piece about the fact that teenagers had been the original test drivers for the Beltway, and that even now, if he wanted, he could get someone from the photo department to head out to Silver Spring on almost any night and get some good flash pictures of students from Montgomery Blair hauling ass around the highway — though of course that's not quite how I put it. He thought my notion was a fine idea, considering how boring any coverage of highways and municipal planning tended to be. I offered to give him Jimmy Proctor's phone number.

The book Mr. Tribble had presented me, all nine hundred–plus pages of it, was called *The Sot-Weed Factor*. After I'd gotten only a few pages in, I realized that "sot-weed" was

240

what the English in colonial days had called tobacco. I'd never been a fast reader and, as much as I thought I enjoyed reading books, it was sometimes hard for me to read straight through them, even the detective novels or historical biographies I liked best; I'd often have to go back to the previous chapter and read it again, a difficulty that had gotten worse by tenth grade. This wasn't true of newspapers, however. I could read a full column of news, straight down from top to bottom, in no time. And remember almost everything.

But with this *Sot-Weed Factor* doorstop, by an author I'd never heard of called John Barth, I seemed to fly through the pages. From the start it struck me as an amazing piece of storytelling, not least because of its main character, Ebenezer Cooke, whom the author described as "Poet and Virgin" and who referred to himself as "P/V" when he signed his full name. In the novel, Ebenezer was appointed by Lord Baltimore to be the first poet laureate of Maryland.

I doubted that Mr. Tribble or even Mr. Porter, the state editor himself, was aware that in the second half of the twentieth century there was a real poet laureate of Maryland. I had in fact met him, Vincent Godfrey Burns, when he came to our sixth-grade class at Parkside Elementary School wearing a cape and reciting doggerel about the Russians threatening our American democracy and Christian way of life.

Not only was *The Sot-Weed Factor* maybe the funniest novel I'd ever read, it put ideas into my head about the world around me, in particular the Maryland world, that had never occurred to me. All the territory that Ebenezer was exploring around the Chesapeake and along the Potomac and on the Eastern Shore across the bay — where Blair kids would skip school and drive to Ocean City — was familiar ground to me. On weekends, since before I could walk, I'd gone with my grandparents to the bay beaches on the Western Shore of the Chesapeake near Annapolis.

Now that we had driver's licenses, my friends and I spent a lot of time going up and down Route 301 near the West River until we got to Waldorf, where there were dance parlors with slot machines and live music. Two hundred fifty years after Ebenezer had traipsed the area, the road was still lined with tobacco fields, including those on the farm where my aunt Annie's family still tended them. Upper Marlboro, the county seat of Prince George's, still had tobacco auctions on Saturdays.

The Southern Maryland counties — Charles, St. Mary's, Westmoreland, and Calvert — were the only places in America outside Nevada that allowed slot machine gambling, and they held a particular fascination after a rumor swept through the Blair

student parking lot one morning that someone had won a five-hundred-dollar jackpot.
The other rapture some of us shared with
Ebenezer was Baltimore itself — named for
his patron and forty miles straight up U.S. 1
from Silver Spring — where we'd go in illicit
wonder to the Gayety Burlesque Theater on
the city's notorious Block and watch our favorite stripper, Chili Pepper. Once, I'd caught
her G-string when she took it off and threw it
into the audience. It lived in a cigar box in the
closet of my room in Silver Spring.

While Ebenezer spent page after page struggling to protect and preserve his virginity,
we sought to undo all vestiges of ours, with
little success, though technically mine had
been lost a year earlier in Hagerstown to a
hooker named Peg. Phil Sklover and I drove
eighty miles to her doorstep. She had been
well known to my counselors at Camp Airy
— adjacent, as it happened, to Camp David,
the presidential retreat in Western Maryland.
I'd preserved the information of her where-
abouts: thirty miles to the northwest of the
camp. The journey that night in Sklover's father's four-door Buick with just the two of us
was filled with expectations more memorable
than the event itself.

Ebenezer had been commissioned by Lord
Baltimore to write a Marylandiad to sing the
praises of colonial Maryland. By the time
I had finished the first chapter of his story,

I went to the *Star* library and found a 1950 U.S. Census directory for the Eastern Shore counties of Maryland. Sure enough, there was a listing for Vincent Godfrey Burns, in St. Michael's.

The bad news that I would not graduate arrived in May, on the day it came time for the class of 1961 to be measured for caps and gowns. I would not be needing those items, Coach Good informed me. Mr. Adelman was determined to give me an F in chemistry.

Awful as I was at math, I was able to figure out my exact grade-point average, down to the decimal point, and realized that — if Mr. Adelman showed mercy and gave me a D, which was also the grade I was going to receive from Colonel Johnson in Spanish — I might just have enough credits to graduate.

That was because of an unexpected A-minus in my American Literature class.

The A-minus came with a note from Mrs. Wubnig, who was not known for being lavish with praise, and certainly not praise for my work; she'd handed me mostly C's, D's, and F's on tests.

Part of the course had been to write a book report. Under ordinary circumstances the book report would have accounted for less than half my final grade, but mine turned out to be something different. It had combined my view and excitement about the book with original research that went beyond what was in it. The caliber of the writing and the narrative I'd created in the report exceeded anything she'd thought I was capable of, though Mrs. Wubnig's note was tactful enough not to say it that way.

My book report was on *The Sot-Weed Factor,* and the character of Ebenezer Cooke, poet laureate of Maryland (and virgin), whom I compared with the real-life contemporary poet laureate of Maryland, Vincent Godfrey Burns. I'd driven to the Eastern Shore and found Mr. Burns, dressed in his cape, on an old tobacco farm near St. Michael's. When I told him I wanted to write an account of his laureateship for the *Evening Star* he was thrilled, and — when I could get him to stop spouting vitriol about the current president of the United States — he had quite a tale to tell. I hadn't told Mr. Porter yet about my visit, which I intended to submit as a piece for the paper. But with nothing else to write a book report about, I sketched out the story for Mrs. Wubnig.

As to how I was finally allowed to graduate, I never did get a straight story — not from Coach Good, not from my parents, and not from Mrs. Wubnig, though I know she had something to do with it. And I had no desire to do any further reporting on the matter. What it came down to was this:

A meeting had been convened in Coach's

office, originally for the purpose of informing my parents why I wasn't going to graduate. But before that meeting took place, there had been another powwow, called by Daryl W. Shaw, the principal with whom my dealings during three years at Blair were well documented. From what Coach told me, the principal preferred not to have me around for another year, even if Mr. Adelman preferred to give me an F. And Miss Wubnig, speaking on my behalf, declared that no earthly purpose would be served for anyone involved if I was forced to repeat the twelfth grade, although there was also the option of repeating chemistry with Mr. Adelman in summer school. He had no interest in that solution.

In the end I got a D in chemistry, and Godspeed.

That summer, for a month after graduation, I studied harder than during all my years at Blair. As a Maryland resident, I was entitled to attend the University of Maryland with a reduced in-state tuition of three hundred dollars a semester. But my grades were too low for admission. Still, Maryland residents could take an equivalency test to determine if their knowledge was equal to what a capable high school graduate should know. Somehow, I passed, was admitted to the university in College Park without probation, and waived past the basic English and government-and-politics courses required of freshmen. For my essay on the test, I wrote about Ebenezer again.

Meantime, Tom Dimond, who was the fastest typist on the dictation bank, and whose trajectory at the paper I paid attention to, was called up for active military duty at Andrews Air Force Base in the fall. He told me that I should apply for his slot on the dictation bank. It seemed unlikely to me that Sid Epstein would want to put me, a seventeen-year-old, in that job. But Dimond said he'd been only nineteen when he went from copyboy to dictationist — and, he said, I'd made an impression in the newsroom.

The only advice I sought about whether to apply was from Mr. Porter. He said he'd speak to Harry Bacas, who, along with running the training program, supervised the dictationists. Mr. Porter must have also said something to Sid Epstein, because in the next few days the city editor seemed (or so I imagined) to take a little more notice of me when I delivered his coffee. Harry Bacas told me he'd consider me as he would anyone else: there would be at least half a dozen other applicants, each a college graduate, but all of my work would figure in any decision — the citizens association and civic association meetings and the other assignments I'd had, and my familiarity (from the president's press conferences) with the dictation process. Plus Phil Kelley's evaluation. And there would, of course, be a typing test.

My biggest concern was that, knowing how much was at stake, my fingers would shake. Otherwise, I figured I could out-type anyone who took the test.

13

DICTATION

It was Dimond who told me to be sure I knew how to spell *Khrushchev*. There were three unlikely *h*'s embedded in there — a typist's equivalent of a trick question.

So when it came time to take the typing test and the Soviet leader's name came up in the front-page story that Harry Bacas dictated to me, I breezed right through — first reference Premier Nikita S. Khrushchev and thereafter just Khrushchev about two dozen times — so fast he might as well have been Farmer Jones from Kentucky with no nuclear missiles in the cornfield.

Two days later, Sid Epstein looked at me like I was some kind of wizard, and said, "Kid, where'd you learn to type like that?"

I started to tell him about being in typing class with the girls at Montgomery Blair but thought better of it. He told me I would start the following Monday on the dictation bank.

During my first week there, I could see that being able to spell Khrushchev without a halt put me at an advantage; some of the other dictationists were stumped by the time they got to the second *h*. The carriages of their typewriters would suddenly stop for a few seconds and go haltingly forward . . . *clack* . . . *clack* . . . *clack* . . . and there might be Xxes over the first or second try.

Earl Heap wouldn't berate an experienced reporter for a spelling offense or a mistake in grammar, but he didn't hesitate to march over to the dictation bank and admonish us for some infraction or other — especially if, for instance, we misspelled it *supercede* instead of *supersede,* or *advisor* instead of *adviser.* And although I could manage Khrushchev just fine, there were occasions in my early months on the dictation bank when Heap found a reason to come and wag his finger and educate me.

Being a dictationist meant thinking like a reporter, not a copyboy. Before, I'd spent hours filling paste pots from five-gallon jugs of the stuff. Now I commanded a typewriter, not just typing the reporters' stories as they phoned them in. I was becoming an apprentice reporter myself.

During my first week as a dictationist, Soviet and NATO tanks faced off in Berlin. So Khrushchev's name came in handy. Not everything the full-fledged reporters were covering was earth-shattering. You could doze off listening to Gil Gimble trying to goose up

250

the proceedings of the Metropolitan Washington Park and Planning Commission.

The volume of words processed via dictation at the *Star* was enormous compared to that at a morning newspaper like the *Post*. Most of their beat reporters came back to the office late in the day to compose their stories, with the luxury of time to gather their thoughts and choose their words and rise to writerly heights — whereas at the *Star,* reporters had to compose their breaking stories directly over the phone from notes in their notebooks and off the top of their heads, to meet a noon or two o'clock or three o'clock press deadline. They would fumble and mutter and curse under their breath, and they would cough into your ear sometimes, since most of them smoked, and you could tell when the phone booth would get filled up with smoke because you could hear them opening the door to get some fresh air.

Some were skilled at the art of dictating and could rattle off a coherent story into the telephone just as easily as if they were seated at a typewriter. Miss McGrory, whose prose danced across the newspaper page, was able to pirouette almost as deftly inside a telephone booth on deadline as when she returned to the office late in the afternoon to write an overnight account for the next day's paper, with a pack of Marlboros next to her and time taken for a glass of wine back in Ed Tribble's salon. Still, she hated dictating and preferred to agonize over every word — she'd spend an hour on one sentence at her desk.

In my first weeks, as I got to know individual reporters over the phone, I learned how I could be helpful to them and judge their moods and, when they started to curse and get balled up, keep them calm and organized. Even the best of them could get lost in midsentence or have trouble coming up with the right word or phrase. Sometimes they would dictate a paragraph that contradicted the one preceding it. Or get a middle initial wrong.

I was expected to know the spelling of names including middle initials, whether they were D.C. Engineer Commissioner Edwin W. Clarke (with an e) or U.S. District Court Judge Alexander (no middle initial) Holtzoff or Nikita S. Khrushchev. After only a couple of weeks, I could tell you the middle initial of every important member of the U.S. Senate.

The *Star* staff was a compelling cast of characters. Working with them over the phone under the pressure of deadline, I learned the peculiarities of each — their skills, habits, weaknesses. Every dictationist knew that the *Star*'s senior White House man, Jack Horner, who dictated in a deep and doomy voice that sounded as if he spoke from beyond the grave, began each story with the words "President Kennedy today . . ." Older dictationists recalled that every story from Horner during

Ike's administration had begun "President Eisenhower today . . . ," so by the time Blanche the switchboard operator had shunted Horner to one of us, we were a step ahead and had already typed out the beginning of his lede.

The terror of the dictation bank was Bill Hines, the high-energy, ferocious science reporter who dictated his space stories from Cape Canaveral or Houston so fast that most of the dictationists would seize up and fall hopelessly behind, and when they finally begged him to stop so they could catch up — or, worse, asked him to repeat whole paragraphs — Hines (who did not suffer fools gladly and barely managed to suffer intelligent people) would sputter and fume. On the first suborbital flight, Martha Angle had done such a good job taking his impossible dictation that she was rewarded with a twenty-five-dollar savings bond. After that, Hines insisted that he dictate to Martha, which was a huge relief to everybody else and a source of pride to Martha, as the only one who could ride the beast.

On my second day on the dictation bank, Harry Bacas gave me a *Star* style book — a pamphlet-sized document of less than fifty pages that set forth the rules and eccentricities of English usage and grammar that (I presumed) someone named Noyes or Kauffmann had slapped together in some distant time. It took getting used to: government bodies "indorsed" certain policies rather than "endorsed" them. People who worked for an employer were "employes," not "employees," as if the newsroom were on the wrong side of the Atlantic. If the presidential motorcade had driven from the Capitol at one end of Pennsylvania Avenue to the White House at the other, we would say that it arrived at 1600 Pennsylvania Ave. N.W. at 6:13 pm, not 6:13 p.m. with periods. Sen. (not Senator) Bourke B. Hickenlooper (R-Iowa) had introduced a bill to indorse an enlarged U. S. — not "United States" and with a space between *U.* and *S.* — Navy nuclear fleet to challenge the Soviet Union at sea. (David Broder, who had come to the *Star* after working for the *Congressional Quarterly* and writing part time for the *New York Times* for five years, persisted in reverting — to Earl Heap's frustration — to *Times* style. Hence he would lead the same story with "Senator Bourke Hickenlooper, Republican of Iowa," etc.)

Oddly enough, dictationists were apt to write more words that got into print each day than anyone else on the staff. As part of our duties, dictationists wrote almost all the obituaries, probably three or four a day by each of us, plus short items about meetings of community organizations and church groups. Mr. Porter or Ludy Werner would tell a dictationist to pick up a call from one of the local "stringers" who covered a hundred or so counties in Maryland and Virginia. They would have news of a town or county board meeting, or a fatal car wreck, or a fiddlers' convention, and we would rewrite them from our notes.

Obituaries were the essential proving ground — basic training — in competence, accuracy, and speed. They also offered the chance to tell an unconventional tale of an unconventional life. I was fascinated and amazed at the details of some of the lives I discovered just after they ended. Writing obits was a lesson in what you might find if you were curious. There might be a war hero, a moment of glory a long time ago. Or someone's bizarre accomplishment.

Many of the obits — a surprising number — were about people who died as a result of car accidents, fires, murders, suicides, falls from horses and balconies, even being shot by deer hunters' arrows. The hardest obits to write were about children, especially if I had to get the information from a parent or sibling.

Early on, Earl Heap caught a misspelling I'd made in the first name of a surviving relative. Sid Epstein beckoned me to roll my chair over next to his. In almost a whisper, he said, "This is the only time the family you're writing about will deal with a newspaper in their lives. It's very important to them that you get all of it right. Writing an obit is a big responsibility — and you'd better live up to it." He had never struck me as a sentimental sort, but

255

there appeared to be genuine feeling in what he said. He also meant to teach me a lesson that extended beyond writing obituaries.

I started to think more about the lives of the people I was writing about.

Not long after that, the public relations director of the D.C. Salvation Army phoned in obit information about one of its volunteers: the tiny woman who beat the big bass drum outside Salvation Army headquarters downtown. In the lede I wrote, "The little 89-year-old lady who braved rain and wind and snow and cold for the last 12 years at her post outside the Salvation Army Harbor Light Mission is dead. Known only as 'Aunt Laura' to those who passed by her big drum at Ninth and I streets N.W., Mrs. Laura Eastwood died Monday at District General Hospital after suffering a series of strokes."

The quote in the next graf had come from the Salvation Army flack. "'I love my God,' the sea captain's daughter from New Bern, N.C. declared at her 89th birthday celebration in March. 'Not 14 years old, I gave my heart to God in the Masonic Opera House in New Bern, and oh, I'm glad that he has spared me this long.'"

All this appeared next to a great headshot of her with a bonnet tied beneath her chin and buttoned up in her Salvation Army uniform. Then, "Her companion with whom she lived, Mrs. Annie Crawford, said Aunt Laura's

256

playing of the violin was always accompanied by the chirping of Aunt Laura's numerous birds — a holdover from the days when she was a professional bird breeder."

Sid Epstein told Harry Bacas it would be good to see more stories like that on the obit page.

In fourteen months of being a copyboy, I'd seen that the dictationists already had one foot on the next rung up the journalistic ladder, but I hadn't understood their unique place in the social order of the newsroom, and their pivotal role. Being a copyboy — wondrous as it was — had been like attending grammar school by comparison. You could succeed just by paying attention to Phil Kelley's orders and being wise to Maggiacomo's practical jokes and showing some initiative.

By November I had grown to almost full height — a hair under five foot seven. Of the dozen or so dictationists in November 1961, I was the youngest, though not the only one who hadn't graduated from college yet. Mark Baldwin, who was two years older than me and the second-youngest, had been awarded the *Evening Star* scholarship to George Washington University. Upon graduation he was supposed to go on to the training program and then — assuming success — the reporting staff. Like in the army, getting the *Star* scholarship meant that you had to sign up for staying at the paper for at least two more years after graduation day.

Next to Tom Dimond, the dictationist I felt particular kinship with was Clare Crawford, who had grown up in Silver Spring, attended St. Bernadette's Academy on Colesville Road, and graduated from the University of Maryland three years before I showed up there. She had been a copygirl in the Women's Department and hoped for a slot on the training program but was languishing there, waiting.

Like Clare, most of the dictationists were in their early and midtwenties and had graduated from big state universities. A few had worked for smaller newspapers.

Generally speaking, we did not seem an overeducated bunch. But that was already starting to change. Mort Kondracke, who was stationed at Fort Meade in the Army Intelligence Corps and worked part time until his discharge, had graduated from Dartmouth. The *Star* was on the verge of recruiting so many Yale Whiffenpoofs and *Harvard Crimson* editors and Columbia Journalism School graduates that soon the ivy might as well have been growing out of their typewriters. They were not all from eastern schools, however. Ben (Benjamin Franklin) Forgey — a handsome, brainy addition to our ranks — had gone to Berkeley.

All through my first month as a dictationist, the Cold War and the hair trigger of

Berlin dominated the newsroom's attention. Ominous reports with an implication of imminent peril, even of war, maybe nukes, came through our headsets from reporters at the Pentagon, the White House, the State Department. Some were about aboveground nuclear tests that the Soviets were conducting and about Kennedy's response. Another was dictated from the Carter Barron Amphitheater on Sixteenth Street — where Broadway musicals and the circus performed when they came to town — about a demonstration by an organization called Women Strike for Peace that was protesting both U.S. and Soviet nuclear tests. Its founder, Dagmar Wilson, whose daughter I once had a date with, was a good friend of my parents'. I guessed my mother was probably among the demonstrators.

The Berlin Wall had gone up in August. Tom Dimond would arrive in the office to type up his stories in his air force uniform.

Most of the *Star*'s middle-aged reporters were veterans of World War II or Korea. Two of the paper's best rewrite men — Jerry O'Leary Jr. and Charles McAleer — were lieutenant colonels in reserve units and had been in a good-natured race to see who would be first to make full colonel. Now, in the Berlin crisis, their weekend training schedule was doubled. They showed up some mornings at their desks in uniform, with campaign ribbons on their chests and their officers' caps next to their typewriters.

Given what was happening in Berlin and Moscow and the Pentagon and White House and State Department, I now found it harder to focus on the stories dictated from the District Building or the courthouse in Rockville. Hearing Dick Fryklund at the Pentagon putting together a paragraph in my ear about tanks on the move in Germany was a different order of reality.

Six weeks after the wall went up, Khrushchev ordered Stalin's body removed from its place next to Lenin in the great mausoleum in Red Square. Stalin's statue in Berlin, within sight of the American and Soviet tanks, was pulled down as well.

The Berlin crisis and Stalin's posthumous fall carried enormous implications in the Cold War. The city of Stalingrad returned to its original name of Volgograd and the Stalinallee where his statue had towered over Berlin near the wall was now Karl-Marx-Allee. Stalin was being demystified by his own people.

Unlike the *New York Times* or the *Washington Post,* the *Star* had no bureau or resident correspondent in Moscow, and the paper relied on stories filed by the wire services.

It was an article of faith at the *Star* that we were a newspaper far superior to the *Post* in almost every regard except the comics pages:

local coverage, national coverage, the quality of writing.

But the absence of a foreign staff — except for the globe-trotting Crosby Noyes and a part-time Asian correspondent — rankled and became a topic of unhappy conversation after the crisis began with the Soviet ultimatum that all Allied occupation forces be withdrawn from Berlin.

Now about Harrigan's.

Just as I had been accepted into Ed Tribble's salon while a copyboy, the same was true at Harrigan's saloon now that I was a dictationist. The reporters and editors there didn't seem to pay much attention to my age. I'd already discovered that a dictationist who was good at his job — good in the trenches — tended to forge a bond with the reporters.

Harrigan's was the *Star* staff's refuge and reward. Reporters and assistant desk editors and dictationists flocked there for lunch, after the main city edition deadline at one o'clock. They arrived in carloads from the newsroom and singly from their stations in the District Building and the Capitol. Late in the afternoon, after the final edition had gone to press, a lot of the same people returned "to wait out the rush hour," as they said, which lasted long after the last traffic jam of the evening, and sometimes past midnight.

When the paper moved in 1959 to its new

building in Southeast D.C., Harrigan's was discovered in the slightly desolate landscape a stone's throw from the Maine Avenue Waterfront and its antebellum restaurant row and seafood market, which were in the process of being torn down for urban renewal and "redevelopment." My whole family, with my grandparents, would often have dinner upstairs on the New England Restaurant's screened porch and watch the boats in the channel. Now the entire waterfront and the neighborhood beyond were the subject of a titanic struggle between advocates of public housing for the displaced citizens of the "Old Southwest" — most of them impoverished Black people — and opponents who wanted luxury high-rise apartments to dominate the redeveloped landscape.

Parts of the neighborhood looked like pictures I'd seen of Berlin in 1945, after the bombing, but Harrigan's was a survivor in the rubble. It occupied a cozy white-painted brick building, with two fireplaces inside and a terrace outside where, in the warm months, a jazz trio struggled to play loud enough to be heard above the noise from the nearby Southwest Freeway. Its drummer was Phil Trupp, whose father had worked part time on the copy desk at the *Star* and the *Post*. I presumed Phil's moment of truth arrived when the freeway noise became unbearable, and he got hired at the *Star* as a dictationist a few months after I'd first put on my headset. He'd recently graduated from the University of Maryland.

It was Jim Lee, another dictationist, who introduced me to Harrigan's. Jim was close to thirty years old and looked like something between a middle linebacker and a roly-poly cherub, with a disposition that ran the same gamut. About ten of us left the newsroom together and pooled up in three cars for the ride on the freeway past old St. Patrick's Church — about the only sizable structure still standing in that part of town. Entering Harrigan's, I saw that seven or eight men and women from the newsroom were already finishing up, seated at the long line of tables that ran from one end of the front room to the other, facing the bar. Father Hartke, head of the Drama Department at Catholic University, whom I already knew from rewriting his handouts a couple of times, was also there, as was Lucianne Von Steinberger Cummings. Lucianne was a PR woman with major accounts and an office in the National Press Building. She was big and brash and blond, and kind of a pied piper with a wicked tongue who came to figure in the social lives of many of us at the Star, in part because she was able to get free tickets to almost anything happening in town.

That first afternoon I noticed that most of those present drank martinis — big birdbath martinis served in a frosted glass. Occasionally my father would drink a martini, but until that afternoon I had never had one. I ordered the same as everybody else, and the bartender — Morris Engel, though I didn't know his name yet or that he was the owner of Harrigan's and had appeared as an actor in many of Father Hartke's productions and at the New Arena Stage Theater in Southeast — didn't bat an eye.

I watched how the others sipped their martinis, and after the first medicinal sting, it was not difficult to enjoy the taste. The first time I had tried any kind of alcohol was at a party in a friend's basement in seventh grade, when I was twelve. His parents weren't there at the time, and I must have consumed about half a bottle of some amber-colored whiskey. The next thing I remember was being driven home by the kid's parents in the front seat of a Lincoln sedan with a shoebox tied around my neck so I wouldn't mess up the Naugahyde upholstery. And my mother's horrified look as I stumbled through the door.

But I liked the taste of Morris Engel's martini, though I didn't order a second one that afternoon, as many of the people at the table did. Two or three reporters drank ginger ale and said they were on the wagon. When I got back to work, I was able to take dictation and type without impairment. The next few times I went to lunch at Harrigan's — still limiting myself to a single birdbath — I found that martinis made it easier to be sociable and at ease and engage in conversation with these people, most of whom seemed dazzling in one way or another to me.

14

LOCAL NEWS

I will admit that I did not know what the word *matriculate* meant until freshman orientation week, most of which I skipped because of what was happening in the news.

An unfortunate consequence of my late admission to the university was that no regular dormitory space was left on campus. Underachievers like me — whom the university had taken a chance on — were designated academic "overflow" and assigned living quarters in a sprawling mobile home development built on the far side of U.S. Route 1. "Trailer park" would be too genteel a term for the place. Seven or eight hundred mobile homes had been set up on an island of gray gravel. In a thunderstorm, the water table would rise and flood the whole complex. Beneath the gravel was mud.

Each mobile home was divided in half, for two students per half, with enough room for each to walk to the door if the other was either not present or gave way by climbing into his bunk bed. The mattress on each bed was so thin that we might as well have been sleeping in a jail cell.

In addition to being on academic probation, my roommate, for all I knew, could have been on probation with the Maryland State Police too. Within weeks of the start of the semester, I was missing sweaters, pens, and ten-dollar bills, and I didn't dare take off my Montgomery Blair high school ring because I figured it would end up in a pawnshop in another county.

I did not accuse him directly, because I had no proof. He grew sullen and defensive when I asked, "You didn't by any chance see my . . ." I knew almost nothing about his life. All questions of mine were greeted with a shrug or "I dunno."

He was also an early riser: if I slept in late, he'd turn the thermostat up to about 90 degrees and leave me there to cook. It was not a good situation. I stayed away from our tin-sided "dormitory" altogether, except to sleep. I studied at the student union or, until closing time around eight, at the Dairy Bar. Often I thought the best thing about the University of Maryland was the cows, who lived not far from the trailer dorms. Because it was a state land-grant university, Maryland received agricultural stipends from the federal government, including funds for an experimental dairy farm that dated back to the mid-1800s.

And the farm made great ice cream, sold in the Dairy Bar retail store and ice cream parlor on Route 1.

My struggle to get a high school diploma had been so taxing on my parents that I owed it to them to give formal education another chance. On the last day of orientation, I submitted my list of courses for the semester: Advanced Freshman Comparative Literature; Principles of Government and Politics; State Government and Administration; Public Speaking; Orientation to Physical Education (required); and Basic Air Science — ROTC, also required, for the same reason the cows were there, to maintain the university's status as a land-grant college.

I rarely showed up for Phys Ed, and once every week or two, I'd march up and down the drill field for Air Science. As for the classroom part of ROTC, I simply absented myself altogether by the middle of the semester. A noncom would call the roll at the start of each class and students marched to their desks in alphabetical order, starting at the back and moving to the front, and then sat down. Because my name started with B, and there were upwards of a hundred of us, I was in the backmost row, and I simply walked out the rear door once the noncom hollered "Bernstein." I'd been issued the same air force uniform — regulation blue-gray trousers and shirt and jacket, with a garrison cap — as

268

Tom Dimond's active-duty apparel. It itched from head to toe and was worn both to class and on the drill field. Usually I stripped out of regimental dress the minute I could, but sometimes my schedule was too tight and I'd change into civvies after I got to the *Star,* in that men's room adjacent to the newsroom. Colonel Newcomb, our commanding officer that semester, spent a lot of time boasting that America's superior airpower would clean the Soviets' clock if they kept making trouble in Berlin.

On days when the colonel scheduled a test, I'd hang out at the Dairy Bar and read the text for a couple of hours, and then I'd take my seat for class instead of heading out. I managed to get a C or a D on most ROTC exams.

My favorite course was State Government and Administration, not because of the subject but because of the professor, Dr. Elbert Byrd Jr. He was a member of the Byrd family of Virginia, West Virginia, and Maryland, which, like the Lees, had controlled or dominated much of the politics of all three states in various generations. This Byrd was from the southwestern Virginia branch and spoke not in the drawl of his Maryland or upriver Virginia cousins, but in the hard-edged twang of the hollows. Something I wrote on an early exam caught his attention, and we established a dialogue about what was going on in

Maryland politics and the state generally in regard to race and civil rights and — strange as it sounded — land use policy being debated in the legislature and county boards.

On Tuesdays, Saturdays, and one evening shift a week, I worked on the dictation bank. At least one other night a week, I'd take an assignment from Mr. Porter or Ludy Werner. She seemed confident that I could cover the intricacies of planning and zoning, and I shuttled during the winter between meetings of the Maryland National Capital Park and Planning Commission (on whose lawn I had been arrested, across from Bobby Pustilnik's house), to the Prince George's County Greenbelt Preservation Board and other agencies better known by their initials than their actual names. Their proceedings were deadly dull 90 percent of the time. My normal pattern was reversed: I fought to stay awake while on assignment for the *Star* but was wide-eyed and alert in the classroom. Or at least in one or two of them.

The *Star*'s chief writer on matters of urban planning was Robert J. Lewis, who also was the paper's real estate editor. He was the object of frequent pranks by the copyboys, owing to his absentmindedness and his inability to throw anything into a trash can; rather, a book or pamphlet or old story draft or three-hundred-page report became a fixed object on his desk, piled so high that he became almost invisible behind the mountain. It became a running gag to hide his telephone in the bottom drawer of his desk and then call Blanche and ask to be connected to Robert J. Lewis, at which point his phone would ring and he would start ferreting through the mess on his desk, setting off little avalanches of paper. He almost never seemed to remember the joke.

Lewis's stories, like so many of the planning meetings I was covering, could be hideously dull, but at the same time he had a feel for the human element of his subject, and I took note, especially of his coverage of what was happening in the Southwest redevelopment wars. He wrote a weekly column on urban affairs that ran on the split page of the Saturday paper. That winter he devoted a whole column to a new book written by an uncredentialed citizen activist in New York City named Jane Jacobs. It was called *The Death and Life of Great American Cities*. I bought a copy and immersed myself.

Bob Lewis's manner when dictating was halting, his sentences convoluted, and his voice almost a whisper. I alone volunteered to take his dictation, after I started reading Jane Jacobs's book. When he'd finished dictating, I'd engage him in a discussion of Jacobs's contrarian principles about planning and zoning. When I saw Lewis in the office that winter, sometimes I'd go sit next to him behind the mountaintop and continue the conversation.

I learned that he was a shy man, something unusual in a reporter, or so I thought, but the fact that he had his perch at the *Star*, and knew he could use it to get hold of almost anyone he wanted to respond to his inquiries and phone calls, seemed to compensate for his reticence. I noticed that he did more book-and-reading research than most local reporters. And I could see the dividends.

At College Park, I was disengaged from the usual collegiate experience. I joined no university organizations, nor did I make new friends there. My only concession to school spirit was to buy University of Maryland–embossed loose-leaf notebooks. In class, as often as not, I'd take notes in my reporter's notebooks. I did maintain close friendships with old pals from Blair and Harvey Road who also were at Maryland, including Ron Oberman, who I helped get hired at the *Star* as a copyboy. And Rita Sitnick, who was a junior and lived on campus. She was the older sister of my closest friend on Harvey Road; I'd had a crush on her since she was in the eleventh grade. Now I would meet her at the Dairy Bar sometimes and — with my stature as a real newspaperman (as I saw it) — I got up the nerve to ask her out, though it wasn't altogether clear whether we were going on real dates or were just two close friends who'd grown up on the same block. One thing was sure: it was possible to be a much more interesting person to almost anyone if you could converse on the basis of what you'd learned being a copyboy and a dictationist and hung out at Harrigan's and went to the president's press conferences.

Still, I was a teenager — a seventeen-year-old — though I didn't like to admit it.

My first-semester grades were, for me at least, something to behold — the first time since moving to Montgomery County that I was pleased to show them to my parents.

Professor Byrd gave me an A.

Largely on the strength of my recycled *Sot-Weed* expertise, I received a B in Advanced Freshman Comparative Literature. There were three C's — and a D in Phys Ed.

I hadn't bothered to apply for a place in the regular men's dorms for the second semester, figuring I would find a room to rent off campus. In December, Tom Dimond moved into a house in Arlington with four other reporters, on a leafy street above the Arlington palisades. At Harrigan's one night I asked if they had room for one more, and it turned out there was a small bedroom available. I grabbed the opportunity, without thinking too much about the one-hour-plus commute to College Park. I paid my $300 in-state tuition, registered for the spring semester, and chose, among my courses, two that I thought might actually be enjoyable: Philosophy for the Modern Man, which, according to the

273

course catalog, meant I would read Plato and Descartes and, for the continuing Phys Ed requirement, Recreational Sports. This was, in truth, a course in sailing, undertaken twice a week on the West River near Annapolis, located happily about two miles down the road from the slot machine parlors on Route 301. Between the cows and the breeze on the river, the University of Maryland didn't seem to be an altogether awful place, but to hedge my academic bet, I decided to add a fourth day each week to my work schedule at the *Star.*

Not only did moving into the Arlington house mean I was living with a group of reporters with substantial newspaper experience among them, but the addition of a fourth workday put me into a whole new rhythm and level of engagement with newspapering. Two of the workdays began in late afternoon, with a break for dinner at which I'd join my housemates and other reporters and dictationists who had headed to Harrigan's for the rush hour. The only time I really studied was on Sundays, at the office, where I was the lone dictationist on a day when there was usually no major news and almost no dictation to take except if President Kennedy and his family were out of town in Palm Beach. Then, the presidential "news" was likely to be about the president and First Lady going to church or sailing. Working Sundays also meant that if there was a homicide or a big fire, I'd get dispatched to the scene, or sometimes to D.C. General Hospital, where there were sure to be some cops with firsthand details. In a heated hospital holding room, cops tended be more talkative than when they were bouncing on their toes outside on a freezing street corner or rushing back to headquarters or the precinct. I also made friends with, and got the phone numbers of, some homicide detectives. A couple of them knew a second cousin on my mother's side who had been on the squad in the 1950s, before he became an FBI agent. I had never met this cousin, except once at a funeral for my great-aunt Tante Haya Sura, but I did not tell them that.

On the morning of February 14, 1962, my eighteenth birthday, I reported at nine o'clock to the old Blair Mansion in Jessup Blair Park, at Georgia Avenue and Blair Road in Silver Spring, to register for the draft. This was a mere formality, I was certain. I could not be dragooned into the army as long as I had a legitimate student deferment by virtue of being enrolled and in good standing at the University of Maryland. President Kennedy and his secretary of defense, Robert McNamara, had sent one thousand "military advisers" to South Vietnam in October, and the number had grown to more than three thousand by the first of the year.

I had been present that month — in a phone

booth in the back of the State Department auditorium — when Kennedy had declared that "the United States is determined to help Vietnam preserve its independence," but he'd hedged on the question of whether the United States would ever commit regular ground forces to the civil war there. Through my headset in the newsroom, and at Harrigan's, I'd begun to hear an undercurrent that the United States was heading for a major on-the-ground commitment of troops to prop up the anticommunist regime in Saigon.

Blair Mansion — Silver Spring's local head-quarters for the Selective Service — had been built by the founder of the town, Preston Blair (Montgomery Blair's father), who was the publisher of the Washington *Globe* newspaper and resided most of the time at his grand house on Pennsylvania Avenue across from the White House. There was a portrait of President Kennedy inside the Blair Mansion's entry room — as in most every U.S. government building — and a photograph of General Lewis B. Hershey, who had served as head of the U.S. Selective Service since World War II and whose buzz cut and spectacles reminded me of Colonel Johnson in Spanish class. The draft board clerk examined my university registration certificate for the spring semester and a copy of my grades from the fall, which I was proud to present. I filled out some paperwork, was given a draft card that I stuck in my wallet, and left. Later, when I started having nightmares about getting drafted, the man who always whispered in my ear until I awoke in a sweat was General Hershey, with his bristling buzz cut and bottle-bottom glasses.

The addition of Phil Trupp to the dictation bank was a turning point for our little corner of the newsroom. Having Trupp at the adjacent typewriter was like being in the presence of a kind of glorious exotic, because of the unusual way his mind worked: lightning fast, often ingenious, almost never traveling in a strictly linear fashion or burdened by conventional wisdom. He brought with him a warehouse of knowledge of things I knew almost nothing about, including jazz, obscure science bordering on the occult, movie arcana, and a photographic memory of the complete works of Mickey Spillane and Gertrude Stein. He was enthralled by the newsroom and what we were doing at this stage of our lives; more than once he sighed that the whole experience, to his mind, was like being in Paris in the twenties, though when I looked out the window I still saw the Southeast Freeway. The farthest I had ever been from home was Asheville, North Carolina.

He also said he was the nephew of Bobby Troup, the Hollywood jazz band leader, actor, and songwriter who had written the song "(Get Your Kicks on) Route 66" and was

277

married to Julie London, the sexiest woman alive, no question, either to listen to (especially when she was singing "Cry Me a River" in that deep, inimitable voice of hers) or to look at. Sometimes Trupp would bring me a promotional copy of one of her albums as a gift, including *Whatever Julie Wants, Julie Gets,* with a picture of her on the cover naked except for a fur coat draped over her body and champagne and jewels set out on its train. He promised that if she ever came through town, he'd make sure I met her.

When our shifts were the same, Trupp, Jim Lee, and I would head to Harrigan's together at the end of the day. One September evening, on the back terrace where Trupp had played the drums before setting his sights on newspapering, Lee was running through a litany of famous copyboy and dictationist moments. He concluded with the tale of Herb H., a dictationist who decided that he'd been passed over too many times for promotion, and quit. On his way out the door, Herb stopped in the office of Sam Kauffmann, the president of the *Star,* and defecated on his desk. The next morning — as it was related over the years — Jack Kauffmann, his son and then head of the advertising department, entered the newsroom, summoned the whole staff, and demanded in a shout to know, "Who shat on Daddy's desk?"

Jim Lee, Trupp, and I also talked about

Mark Baldwin's good fortune to still be working at the paper after his fake obit attempt, and the Kauffmanns' generosity in continuing to pay for his education.

I will admit here that it was my idea, not Phil's or Jim's, to build on and perfect Baldwin's concept of a fake obit. We decided not to do it for the *Star*. That would be too dangerous and might result in all three of us being fired. Our project would be to slip a fanciful obituary into the pages of the *Washington Post*.

I invented a character, upon whom Trupp and Lee improved, a fellow in his eighties who had made a name for himself on the Washington burlesque circuit as a one-man band and had once performed for the president of the United States.

It was drilled into every dictationist to confirm the funeral arrangements with a funeral home, or, if the obit was of someone important enough to rush into print before funeral arrangements had been made, to find a surviving relative who could supply details on the life and death of the subject. (Conversely, if a funeral home called with an obit, we had to make sure the essential biographical details were consistent with the knowledge of a member of the family.) All this was to ensure accuracy and to avoid the possibility of being tricked into running a phantom obituary.

That night, back at the house in Arlington,

I worked up more biographical details, and the next morning Trupp and Lee arrived in the newsroom with additional garnishment. At lunch, the three of us put the final touches on his life. It was agreed that I would phone in the obit to the *Post,* posing as the son and only survivor of our subject. We figured the odds were long at succeeding, because there would be no funeral home that a *Post* reporter or obit writer could reach to confirm the extravagant specifics of the information we were going to supply.

I went downstairs to a public telephone booth in the lobby at about three o'clock, calculating that the *Post* newsroom would be at its most hectic to meet its own first-edition deadline. I dialed DEcatur 4-6000, asked the operator to connect me with whoever wrote obituaries, and was passed on to an editor on the city desk. I told him I had an obit about a musician who had once been commended by President Woodrow Wilson, and he passed me on to a reporter whose name I was not familiar with. The reporter knew a good story when he heard one — I could sense his enthusiasm for the possibilities of an extraordinary obituary — and he outdid himself asking for further illuminating details about our man's career, a few of which I made up on the fly. Then he wanted to know which funeral home would be handling the arrangements. I explained that I was calling from Sarasota,

Florida, and was in the process of choosing a funeral home in Washington to handle the burial. I added that I would be on a train for D.C. for the next twenty-four hours, accompanying my father's casket (it would be in the mail car), and thus could not be reached until I'd arrived in Washington. And there were no other survivors.

The next morning, Saturday, September 15, 1962, the lead item on the *Post*'s obituary page announced CHARLES MOORE, ENTERTAINER, 84. Its double-deck headline was the most prominent on the obit page.

The *Post* reporter had done a spectacular job of writing about Mr. Moore's life.

Charles J. Moore, a Washington vaudevillian, who once received personal congratulations from President Woodrow Wilson for his ventriloquy, died yesterday following a stroke in Sarasota, Fla. He was 84.

Mr. Moore was born in Washington and attended public schools here until he was 16.

Then he collected a set of drums, a harmonica, tambourine and banjo, and set out to make a name for himself as a one-man band in the District's old burlesque circuit.

During World War I Mr. Moore offered his talents to the American Red Cross and toured Army installations here and in Europe.

A master of ventriloquy, he would dress

his dummy, Van Rudy, in the garb of Kaiser Wilhelm and carry on satiric dialogues, lampooning the Kaiser.

The dummy's name was, to us, an obvious reference to Rudy Kauffmann, though we hoped it wouldn't be obvious to Sid Epstein.

Mr. Moore said his proudest moment came after his performance at a benefit in Washington when he met President Woodrow Wilson and received his congratulations.

After World War I, Mr. Moore gave up ventriloquy to study magic. For nearly 15 years he apprenticed under Blackstone, the magician, before setting out on his own.

After he was invited to join the International Brotherhood of Magicians, he played theaters around the country, including the old Capitol and Palace vaudeville houses here.

He used the name "Henri the Mystical."

During World War II, Mr. Moore made two trips to Europe for the U.S.O. before his health began to fail around 1943. He spent the remaining war years performing for the armed forces in the U.S.

In 1948, Mr. Moore retired and entered a rest home in Sarasota, where he died. He is survived by his son, Charles Jr., of New York. His wife, Flora, died in 1936.

When I got to the newsroom, I saw that Sid Epstein had a copy of the obit — neatly trimmed to size — on his desk. Jim Lee arrived. Phil Trupp arrived. We tried not to look toward Sid Epstein's desk or, too often, at each other. Our greatest fear was that he would ask one of us to confirm the obit and write it up for the *Star*'s obituary page, and that we would crack up in the process. Or betray our unnerved condition.

For what seemed like the better part of the morning, Sid Epstein rolled his pencil back and forth across his desk, otherwise cleared except for the *Post*'s obit. The constant up-and-down movement of his right knee had, to my eyes, reached an unusual state of agitation, and his face got redder and redder. Then he seemed to calm, and he would talk across the desk with Coit Hendley in hushed tones, and the process would start over again. Finally he picked up the clipping, scrunched it into a ball, threw it into the trash can by his foot, turned his chair toward us, and gave a look that needed no words. There would be no scholarships for us. And a repeat of such an incident would bring a premature end to our newspaper careers, at least at the *Evening Star*.

15

CRISES

Strange things started happening on October 20, a Saturday. President Kennedy was in Chicago, on the first leg of a three-day campaign swing from the Midwest to the West Coast to help Democrats in the upcoming midterm elections. But suddenly he turned around and flew back to Washington.

The rest of the trip was canceled. The president had a cold, his press secretary, Pierre Salinger, said, "a slight upper respiratory infection." By the time Kennedy was back in the White House, his temperature had returned to almost normal. Instead of joining the First Lady at their estate in the Virginia hunt country, he would spend the rest of the weekend in the White House. This was all very odd, said David Broder, whose dictation I was taking from California, where he was covering Richard Nixon's attempt to become governor of the state.

Early Monday morning, I took dictation from Dick Fryklund, the *Star*'s Pentagon reporter, who was in Puerto Rico covering the annual Navy-Marine military exercises in the Caribbean, involving twenty thousand men and forty vessels. The exercises had been called off Sunday night because of "the dispersal of ships caused by Hurricane Ella," the Pentagon announced. So now as many as forty American vessels, including six large amphibious landing craft carrying thousands of sailors and marines, were scattered here and there in the Caribbean.

They were moving toward Cuba, almost certainly, Fryklund said. Among them was an aircraft carrier, and a destroyer, the *Joseph P. Kennedy Jr.,* named for the president's brother, who had been killed in World War II.

"Officers here say they were ordered by the Navy in Washington not to discuss Cuba 'either militarily or politically' with reporters," he dictated. I ripped the page out of my typewriter and hollered *"Copy!"*

By noon on Monday, the newsroom was in a state of heightened alert. I'd seen excitement in the newsroom before, but this was something entirely different, the adrenaline of a big story mixed now with foreboding and a measure of real fear. Jerry O'Leary's sources at the CIA — meaning, foremost, his brother, we all assumed — wouldn't say what this was about. Was Kennedy planning a second invasion of Cuba, this one for real? After the Bay of Pigs, President Eisenhower told Kennedy that that fiasco would embolden the Soviets to try something they would not have attempted before.

Tom Dimond phoned in from Andrews that the base — including his unit — was on standby alert. Jet fighters were being scrambled. Salinger announced to reporters in the pressroom that the president would address the nation by television and radio at seven that evening.

Whatever the president was going to say, it was apparent that some kind of mighty military operation was in the works. It might involve Berlin as well. Perhaps the "crisis" — the word used in the lead story to describe whatever was happening — involved a new Communist threat against that city. Salinger said that Kennedy had called a special meeting of the National Security Council for three fifteen, and a meeting of the cabinet at four thirty.

Eighteen congressional leaders were summoned to return to Washington. The air force sent planes to fetch them. The vice president made the long flight back to Washington from Hawaii.

It felt as if the United States was about to go to war — and not a limited kind of war, as in Korea, but nuclear war. And perhaps on American soil. Sam Eastman called Sid Epstein from the District Building to report that Civil Defense officials were ready to activate air raid sirens and prepare for the opening of bomb shelters around the city.

By three o'clock that afternoon, all of these murky and menacing lines of fact and rumor had been summed up in a front-page story that ran under the biggest headline I could remember the *Star* using: a double-deck eight-column banner, KENNEDY WILL SPEAK TONIGHT: 'MATTER OF HIGHEST URGENCY.'

Work came to a halt. The whole staff — reporters, copyboys, dictationists, editors — crowded around both sides of the city and national desks, where four television sets had been set up. Kennedy was behind his desk in the Oval Office. A hush descended over the newsroom. The president began to speak.

His voice was solemn and hard: rational, almost monotonous. He stared straight into the camera and it seemed possible from his words that he might be talking about the end of the world.

As Kennedy spoke, there seemed to be a shared recognition that we were passing into a new dimension. I was reminded of those scenes in a movie, in slow motion, when the car goes out of control and you know that in an instant there will be a terrible crash. This was life-and-death stuff.

It was difficult to absorb: American reconnaissance planes had discovered and photographed Soviet missile bases being constructed inside Cuba, and nearing completion. "The purpose of these bases can be none other than to provide a nuclear strike capability against the Western Hemisphere," Kennedy said. Already they housed medium-range ballistic missiles capable of carrying a nuclear warhead to Washington, D.C., and other American cities. These missile sites, he said, must be dismantled and removed.

Kennedy announced that he had ordered a naval "quarantine" of Cuba and warned the Soviets that ships under any flag would be intercepted and "turned back" if they tried to bring any more offensive weapons to the island.

He had ordered U.S. armed forces "to prepare for any eventualities." A hostile response by the Soviets "anywhere in the world . . . in particular, Berlin" would be met by "whatever action is needed." Any missile launched from or by Cuba against any nation in the Western Hemisphere "would be regarded as an attack by the USSR on the United States," resulting in "a full retaliatory response upon the Soviet Union." There it was.

The president had left himself — and the United States — no room to back down. Everyone understood that "a full retaliatory response upon the Soviet Union" meant that the same thing would be coming back in our direction. Washington, D.C., was ground zero.

■■■■

The next seventy-two hours were a sleep-deprived blur — work on the dictation bank until two or three in the morning, then a few hours of sleep at the Arlington house and back to the newsroom to take more stories over our headsets: from Horner and backup reporters at the White House, from several more at the State Department, from Fryklund and a team at the Pentagon, from the United Nations, from meetings at the Organization of American States, and from local reporters dispatched by Sid Epstein to cover the now expanding civil defense story.

I thought about all those air raid drills at Janney Elementary School in the midfifties, which had seemed exercises in unreality in an era when all the air raid sirens in the District of Columbia were tested several days a month at noon. Our classroom windows shook from the sound. Now, only a few years later, the focus on air raid shelters and warning sirens seemed chillingly real and justified — especially the more I learned from the stories our reporters were dictating and from what we in the newsroom knew about Soviet ship movements and other military details. The *Star,* and every other major news organization, had signed on to the stringent self-censorship rules promulgated by the Pentagon on the day of Kennedy's speech. The rules were tighter than those in place during World War II.

Sid Epstein had assigned Janet Koltun, ordinarily the paper's chief obituary writer, to report on the torrent of instructions coming from civil defense officials, from where to take shelter in public spaces to what canned goods and other lifesaving supplies ought to be stocked in home basements. Charlie Puffenbarger, one of the assistant city editors, asked me and a couple of other dictationists to help Janet compile listings of more than one thousand designated underground shelters in schools, federal buildings, hotels, and private office buildings, where 1.6 million people might shelter from the blast.

The list we finally put together dated to the time of my fifth-grade air raid drills. Almost eleven hundred spaces in D.C. buildings had been identified back then to serve as air raid shelters. Now our task was to make sure, through phone calls and city maps and directories, that the spaces still existed. We finished the list on Thursday the twenty-fifth — at what seemed like the most dangerous juncture in the crisis, when a dozen Soviet vessels were bearing down on the quarantine zone.

The next day's paper carried an eight-column italic overline above the *Star*'s masthead: *1083 Potential Fallout Shelters Listed by District, Page A-10.*

■■■■

On Wednesday, for the second time that week, I'd called my parents in Silver Spring. The first time had been on Tuesday, the day after Kennedy had announced the blockade. My sisters, now thirteen and fifteen, had gone off to school; they were frightened, my mother said, and she was going to pick them up afterward. Did I have any hopeful inside information about what was going on?

Everybody was frightened, I told her; even the reporters and editors at the *Star* were anxious, especially those who seemed to know the most.

My father, who had recently found work in a new profession — fundraising, for the Eleanor Roosevelt Institute for Cancer Research — had decided to stay home rather than getting on a plane for one of his weekly trips. My mother put him on the line. His attitude was frustration at both Kennedy and Khrushchev, though more so at Kennedy for "provoking" — the word he used — the Cubans in the first place with the Bay of Pigs invasion. The United States was committed to the destruction of Castro's rule and the Cuban revolution, and that was the underlying dynamic that had brought about the crisis.

When my mother answered the phone on Wednesday night, her voice was quaking. Twice in the past twenty-four hours the phone had rung and a male voice had asked if Mr. Bernstein was there, and then if this was Mrs. Bernstein. The first time she said yes, and that she'd get my father. Then the caller hung up. She wasn't sure if the voice on the phone was the same on the second call; again the man had asked for my father, and if this was Mrs. Bernstein. This time, my mother asked who was calling — and, as before, the man hung up.

"Talk to your father," she said to me and she put him on the phone.

My father said he knew what was happening. After the second call, they'd phoned old friends. Several had received similar calls. And then their friends had checked with other friends — all left-wing people — and the pattern was the same.

"It's the FBI," he said. "They want to know where people are in case there's a roundup to send people to detention camps."

I knew what he was referring to. There was a provision in the McCarran Internal Security Act of 1950 that gave the government authority — in a "national emergency" declared by the president — to apprehend and detain Americans deemed security risks. Ostensibly this law was aimed at people who might engage in acts of espionage or sabotage, but in reality it targeted people who had been suspected of being members of the Communist Party or who associated with such people, or simply had left-wing leanings. The authority had been sought by J. Edgar Hoover.

The senator who introduced this provision of the act was Hubert Humphrey of Minnesota, widely considered a great liberal. My father had long regarded the detention authorization as one of the dirtiest pieces of business in the McCarthy era, and he had a particular disdain for Humphrey because of it. President Truman vetoed the McCarran Act and Humphrey's proviso, but Congress passed it again over his veto.

President Kennedy had not yet declared a "national emergency," but my father thought that J. Edgar Hoover would be working to see he did.

The lead story in Wednesday's paper — about the interception of a Soviet tanker by U.S. vessels, and twelve other Russian ships that turned back before reaching the blockade — was written by Jerry O'Leary Jr. Though he was still a cityside rewrite man, O'Leary had reported for the national desk throughout Latin America and had covered Castro's rise in Cuba.

He was a regular at lunch at Harrigan's, a heavy drinker who was on and off the wagon, and a wonderful friend to newcomers and younger people as they settled in to the newsroom. I'd gotten to know him in my earliest copyboy days, working the early shift that coincided with his six o'clock arrival on the rewrite bank. When it came time to choose a successor to Ed Tribble as city editor, the two leading candidates had been Sid Epstein and Jerry O'Leary. O'Leary had never quite reconciled himself to the fact that Sid Epstein was chosen, and he regarded the city editor with considerable coolness. But Sid Epstein knew that there was no more skilled rewrite man at the paper, and none faster on deadline, and that O'Leary was as good a street reporter as had ever come through the newsroom. And of course O'Leary had literally been raised in the *Star* newsroom, starting as a copyboy when he turned eighteen and his father thought it was time for him to go into the family business.

Most news involving the FBI went through O'Leary, though he was happy to let Miriam Ottenberg handle the organized crime side of the street, a subject in which Hoover had little interest. O'Leary's sources at the FBI went up through the ranks, from the Washington field office to the top echelons of the bureau. First and foremost among them was Cartha "Deke" DeLoach, the bureau's number three man, who was considered a likely successor to J. Edgar Hoover in the event that Hoover ever retired. O'Leary's relationship with DeLoach was brotherly — too close, some people in the newsroom thought, given that DeLoach was the godfather to O'Leary's children.

■ ■ ■ ■

After Thursday's paper had been put to bed, I went to O'Leary's desk and asked him about the McCarran Act: Given the gravity of the crisis, did he think Kennedy might invoke its "national emergency" detention provisions? I'd gone back to the library to see how Kennedy had voted on the act as a congressman. He'd favored it.

O'Leary said my question was a good one. It hadn't occurred to him, but he doubted Kennedy would want to start fighting a civil liberties battle at the same time he was engaged in the greatest crisis of the Cold War.

He said he would ask someone at the bureau.

About half an hour later, he had an answer. Hoover, he said, had hoped the detention provision of the law could be used in the crisis, and the bureau had started making "pretext" phone calls to keep track of people. Hoover had tried during the Korean War to get Truman to use the law, and he had put together a list of more than ten thousand people to be swept up in dragnets and detained. Truman had refused outright. Though the list still existed and probably had been expanded, Kennedy had shown no interest in the idea either.

O'Leary said his information was off the record. He said nothing about the source. De-Loach, I was certain.

I went back to my desk and called my

mother and father and told them that I'd done some discreet checking and that it was extremely unlikely that Kennedy would declare a national emergency or that Hoover would be authorized to order any detention under the McCarran Act.

But the moment of anxiety — not merely the risk of nuclear war but also, on top of that, about Hoover and the McCarran Act, about mysterious phone calls, and the possibility of an FBI dragnet that might sweep up my parents as "security risks" and lock them up who knows where — had brought back the old drama and danger. It had shadowed my childhood, especially in the Joe McCarthy days. I'd felt a scalding shame, sometimes, and then was ashamed of my shame. The emotions were hard to sort out. My idealistic parents, having devoted their lives to causes they believed in, paid a price for their ideals — not least, I understood, the price of an emotional distance from their son.

I sometimes thought that, in the *Star,* I'd found a family that was less complicated, less fraught, than the one at home in Silver Spring. I was more comfortable in the newsroom with Sid Epstein and Jerry O'Leary and Mary McGrory and Haynes Johnson and Ludy Werner than I'd ever been at home.

Ironically, there was safety in journalism, a haven in reporting, especially the way the *Star* went about it: proceeding without judgment or predisposition to wherever the facts and context and rigorous questioning led, to some notion of the truth in all its complexity. I liked that place. And the comfort and purpose it gave me.

Now the crisis was showing signs of easing; Soviet ships had turned back when they encountered the American naval blockade. On October 28, Khrushchev, in effect, conceded, writing an open letter to Kennedy that Soviet missiles would be removed from Cuba and never again introduced there.

Becoming a dictationist had given me a major boost in pay, especially when overtime was figured in. My starting salary as a copyboy had been twenty-nine dollars a week; now I was earning sixty dollars base pay, plus double time on holidays. Already I'd bought some nice stuff from the Marimekko store in Georgetown for my room in Arlington: a printed rug, some knickknacks, and a molded oak Eames chair. For the first and only time since I'd stopped taking shop courses in junior high, I attempted woodwork. There was a beat-up chest of drawers in the bedroom, and I'd taken it onto the screened porch that summer, sanded it down by hand, painted it black, and bought new hardware for it. It looked passable, not professional.

By now I had a charge account at Lewis & Thos. Saltz and I filled a couple of drawers in the black chest with button-down oxfords and alligator polo shirts. I owned a blue blazer and some charcoal-gray slacks, a trench coat like Dick Fryklund's (and Cary Grant's in *His Girl Friday*), and two-tone brown-and-tan saddle shoes. The way I dressed for work wasn't near as flashy as that sounds. I'd just throw on my blue suit or, in spring or summer, a pair of khakis with the blazer, plus a white shirt. And when it was stifling hot, there was always my cream-colored outfit from Louie's, which my grandfather had let out now that I'd grown some.

More than most holidays, I was looking forward to Thanksgiving this year. The annual D.C. high school championship game between the first-place teams from public and Catholic schools was played on Thanksgiving Day in front of fifty thousand spectators on the Redskins home field at D.C. Stadium. Steve Guback in the Sports Department had asked me to do some work with him on the sidelines. He moonlighted for the weekly *Catholic Standard,* and sometimes I earned extra money writing captions for him and the *Standard* during football season. Harry Bacas said it was okay for the Thanksgiving game and that I could finish my dictation shift when I got back to the newsroom. I could also keep an eye out for any news in the neighborhood around D.C. Stadium, especially for the holiday travel and traffic story that Gerry

Herndon would be putting together. Afterward I would go to Silver Spring for turkey dinner, then I'd work the rest of the weekend: Friday, Saturday, Sunday.

The stadium was jammed to overflowing for the game between St. John's and Eastern. The cadets from St. John's College High School were an elite corps of the parochial school hierarchy in the Washington archdiocese. The cadets swaggered around town in probably the fanciest military dress between West Point and the Citadel, gray waistcoats and bloused double-breasted jackets with rows of red buttons. The school, started by the Christian Brothers in the nineteenth century, was not quite as highly regarded for its academic excellence as it was for its football teams.

Eastern High, near Capitol Hill, in my mother's time had been one of the four big white high schools in the D.C. public school system, but since the Supreme Court decisions in *Brown* and *Bolling,* its student body — like the surrounding neighborhood that straddled East Capitol Street between the Capitol and D.C. Stadium on the Anacostia — had turned overwhelmingly Black.

And that was the backdrop of what occurred at the stadium that afternoon. In the fourth quarter, with the Cadets ahead of the Ramblers by a touchdown, one of the Eastern players was thrown out of the game for unnecessary roughness. I was with Guback and Paul Schmick from the Photo Department on the Eastern side of the field, and Schmick kept snapping pictures as the ejected player charged from the bench back onto the turf and started swinging wildly at anyone in sight on the St. John's team. Players on both sides threw punches. The ejected player was injured by his own teammates trying to restrain him, and he had to be carried off the field on a stretcher. Looking up from the field into the stands, I could see that some of the fans were fighting, too. But knots of cops broke it up quickly enough and the game resumed. A semblance of order appeared to contain matters until the final seconds of the game, with the Cadets leading 20–7. The players on the field started swinging again, and this time the fighting spread through the whole stadium, almost like a wave. Cops tried to get the players off the field and establish a cordon between the east and west sides of the stadium. Guback and I sprinted toward one of the baseball dugouts to get a safe view; by the time we got there, thousands of people were rushing onto the field from the Ramblers' side of the grandstand; many were wielding splintered chair legs from the stadium seats as they headed toward the St. John's fans on the other side. The cops were overwhelmed, though they managed to push people toward the exit tunnels and set up some lines that kept the attackers from getting farther across the field.

The St. John's band was nearly surrounded by Eastern fans, and I saw a girl running away whose face was badly cut. I also watched a man get smashed in the face with a bottle.

I had taken special note before, when I'd been on the street with Walter Gold at the scene of some violent events, that real cutting and stabbing and shooting and fighting weren't anything like what you saw on television or in the movies. It not only looked different, it sounded different: awful, people shrieking in pain. Once, when Phil Sklover, Ron Oberman, Buddy Rubin, and I had visited the Block in Baltimore, we went to a bar where a fight broke out and people were slashed by broken bottles and kicked and punched. It was the real thing, not *Gunsmoke*.

The scale of the violence I was watching now in D.C. Stadium, and the fury of those attacking — mostly Blacks going after whites, though not entirely, and there was some aggressive retaliation and defensive violence from the Cadet side — was terrifying. Anyone caught in the crossfire was in grievous danger. Meanwhile, the cops had chased Schmick, Guback, and me from the dugout. This time the press cards hanging from our necks provided little protection. We were on our own.

From as safe a distance as I could manage on the field, I took more notes, and Guback did the same, but we tried to stay in sight of each other. The St. John's side of the stands was completely cordoned off by now, though there was still some fighting there behind the lines established by the police. Guback said we should try to move through that part of the stadium to the press parking lot directly behind the main entrance, which we were able to do. I wanted to find a pay phone to call in to the desk with a description of what we had witnessed, but the confusion and risk of a stampede made it impossible to maneuver on foot to locate one.

The *Star* cars had two-way radios, and once we elbowed our way to the parking lot, Guback took the wheel while I tried to reach the desk. Charlie Puffenbarger, who was doing double holiday duty on both the city and state desks, answered the call; before I could unload any information, he gave us a better sense of the scale of violence and response. Mobs had chased people onto the parking lots and into the streets; every available police unit from the northeast and southeast quadrants of the city, including Canine Corps dogs, had rushed to the stadium; fighting was reported as far as a mile and a half away. Dozens of people were on their way to hospitals.

Puffenbarger put Herndon on the line. He was able to give Guback some ideas about an escape route to circumvent the fighting and the scores of emergency vehicles converging on the stadium and surrounding area. Then

I began to describe what I'd seen from the field, with Guback supplying other chunks of information. It took us more than an hour to get back to the office, by which time Herndon had written a ten-paragraph story for the front page. Though it was skeletal in its account because of the early holiday-edition deadline, the story conveyed a sense of grim foreboding.

When we got back to the office, Puffenbarger was on the phone with Sid Epstein, who had taken command of the story from wherever he was having his Thanksgiving dinner. Guback and I wrote long, separate memos about what we had witnessed. Puffenbarger said to be sure to include all our observations about questions of race that might have played out in what we'd seen. Herndon would write a first draft of the next day's story — B-matter really, because the top of the story and more details would be put together in the morning by Jerry O'Leary (himself a former St. John's Cadet), along with information from reporters at police headquarters and the District Building who were being called in from their holiday weekend.

Because of the stadium riot, Sid Epstein arrived in the office early on Friday morning to supervise our follow-up coverage and the delicate questions of race raised by what had occurred. The chairman of the D.C. Board of Commissioners, Walter Tobriner, was urging that the annual championship game be postponed indefinitely, on the grounds that to hold it would be bad for the city, bad for sports, and bad for the schools. This formulation — I was sure — was also his way of warning that the specter of racial violence was a threat to the home rule movement and that it would be seized upon by the southern congressmen who controlled the District's purse strings and governance. I pondered what Senator Bible would think, and what role he might choose for himself in what was likely to be a defining event for the city's future. Tobriner had received a confidential report from D.C. Police Chief Murray overnight — Charlie Pierce had learned this at the District Building — but he refused to say what was in it.

I'd gotten to the newsroom for the eight-to-four shift. Sid Epstein was in deep conversation on the phone for what seemed like an hour with his back turned to me, and I wondered if he was talking with either Newbold Noyes or Ben McKelway about what the first-edition story would say. Bill Peeler, the sports editor, had come over to sit next to him, which was something I'd never seen before. Forty people had been treated by hospitals, several of whom were very seriously injured, and scores more had been hurt but declined hospital treatment. When the page one proofs for the first edition came down from the composing room, Sid Epstein and Peeler asked Steve Guback and me to read over the main story, to see if anything was inconsistent with what we had seen. The story was understated, but factually accurate, except for a single reference that minimized what had transpired as a "donnybrook." What the story lacked was proper context. Race was not mentioned until about the tenth paragraph, which noted antiseptically that most of St. John's students were white and that Eastern's enrollment was "predominantly Negro." A few grafs farther down, a deputy police chief was quoted saying that the "disorder and brawling" was "not necessarily a racial fight," that "Negroes had been fighting other Negroes as well." And that eight of the forty injured and taken to hospitals were Black.

Peeler ran three whole sports pages on the game, one of which was almost all pictures taken by Schmick and another *Star* photographer. Whether or not I had been in the midst of a real race riot, I wasn't sure. There had been racial epithets, no question, and racial antipathy; the front-page story described a "mob" that had crossed the field from the Eastern side in pursuit of St. John's students and fans on the other. Whatever had occurred, it was terrifying, both in its immediacy and, I thought, in the context of other things happening in the city and the country.

That morning additional reporters had been called to work at the District Building and in the Sports Department, and several more were dispatched to hospitals to interview students admitted from Eastern and St. John's. Because of the holiday, the newsroom was still almost empty: a single editor on the state desk, plus Sidney Epstein's unanticipated appearance and an extra rewrite man. I was the only dayside dictationist scheduled. Around a quarter to one, I heard Sid Epstein say "Jesus Christ," very loud, and he looked around the newsroom, a little bewildered, with the phone cradled under his chin. The few other local editors and rewrite men at work that hour were also on the phone, urgently it looked, and Sid Epstein gestured to me to get over there quick.

He told me there was a report of a passenger plane down near Ellicott City, between Washington and Baltimore. I was to get into a *Star* car and head there right away. George Porter would be calling some of his reporters from home to go there too. I'd get more information on the car radio as it became available.

By the time I'd gotten to the farm fields near Columbia, Arnold Taylor, the deputy photo editor working that day, radioed the coordinates of where the plane had gone down. He told me and a photographer in another car that the flight had left Newark, New Jersey, for National Airport around noontime.

There were fire engines coming from every direction when I got within a couple of miles of the location he'd sent, and I could see smoke rising from a field as I got closer. The police hadn't set up a security perimeter yet, so I pulled onto the edge of the field and got out of the car, maybe a hundred yards or so from where the firemen were clustered and spraying water and foam from long hoses attached to pumper trucks. Right away, the overwhelming stench registered, unlike anything I'd experienced. I did not know if part of the smell came from the pumper trucks, or from the twisted pieces of burning wreckage, or from what I could now see were body parts. I could not imagine the impact that would have caused such devastation, but an indication was that the front section of the plane had burrowed several feet into the ground. I could make out parts of the symbol of United Airlines on some of the metal pieces.

I tried not to think about the people who had been on the plane, or their families, or what it must have been like on board when the plane went into its fatal dive. I was certain that no one could have survived the crash and found a Hartford County police captain who judged the same when I showed him my *Star* ID. I told myself I needed to stay calm and consider what needed to go into a newspaper story. I took out my notebook. He was talking to a man who'd witnessed the plane coming down — James Clark, a Maryland state senator from the county. Senator Clark told us that he'd heard what sounded like an engine choking and looked out his window and saw a huge black cloud of smoke, and then heard three big explosions. He'd raced to the scene, but there was only burning debris when he got there. From where we were standing, I could see that some of the trees in the woods across the field were still on fire, where the plane had sheared off the tops. The senator asked the police captain if he knew how many people had been aboard. About twenty, the captain said. That's what he'd been told by his dispatcher, who was in touch with authorities at National Airport.

I asked Senator Clark if I could use the telephone at his house to call the newsroom. Trying to unload my notes and thoughts over car radio from D.C. Stadium the previous day had been a trial — and I didn't want to do that again. He said his wife was at the house and gave me directions. Mrs. Clark told me she had heard the plane coming down and rushed to a window; she could see the fireball from the explosion that followed. I called the city desk and Sid Epstein picked up.

Briefly, I told him what the crash scene looked like and said that I had quotes from two witnesses and the county police. He turned me over right away to Jerry O'Leary Jr. — and said to head straight back to the field afterward to find out anything else I could.

O'Leary already knew a lot more than I did. He'd used the criss-cross phone book (which listed phone numbers by street address rather than by name) to reach neighbors who, from several different vantage points, had watched the plane come down. He said the plane was a United Airlines Viscount l with a crew of four, including stewardesses, and thirteen passengers. It had been flying at about ten thousand feet. The angle at which it came down was so steep that the plane had cut a swath barely a hundred yards long — as I could see when I returned to the burned field.

Within an hour, investigators from the National Transportation Safety Board and the FBI had arrived and began securing the whole vicinity: taking pictures, putting stakes in the ground, unspooling tape measures. Ambulance crews searched for body parts, which were photographed. I was glad to leave near dusk without having to watch whatever further processing was to be done. Floodlights had been set up to help the investigators and fire crews through the night. The site was what I imagined a movie set would look like, though not a movie I wanted to see. Meanwhile, I had interviewed half a dozen witnesses who had heard or seen something — I'd found a few in the crowd who had gathered around the scarred ground, others whose doors I knocked on behind the scorched woodlands. It had been a bright, sunny fall day, with little wind, and the airplane seemed to have literally fallen from the sky. Some described something fluttering down just before the crash, as if the plane had begun to disintegrate in the air.

Sid Epstein had said I should come back to the office and write a memo of everything I'd seen. Inside the car, I noticed that the smell from the field had permeated my clothes or was in my nostrils. I felt sick, and I thought again about the people who had been on the plane.

When I arrived in the newsroom, I immediately headed to the men's room and, as best I could, washed my face and hands and arms, and even tried to scrub my hair with soap.

Puffenbarger was still on the desk. I sat down across from him and picked up the front section of the Red Streak Final edition. I realized that the two main stories on page one were the ones I'd worked on: the follow-up to the D.C. Stadium riot, which was the off-lead of the paper, and above it an eight-column headline:

17 DIE AS D.C.-BOUND AIRLINER CRASHES, BURNS NEAR BALTIMORE

16

OFF CAMPUS

The way I came to be reporting on the Supreme Court of the United States was that Mr. Porter handed me a pile of documents one afternoon and told me to check the details out with the attorneys involved and write a story of less than a dozen paragraphs for the first edition of the next day's paper. My lede announced:

A brief challenging the constitutionality of Bible reading and recitation of the Lord's Prayer in public schools was filed in the Supreme Court today by attorneys for a Baltimore housewife. . . . Madalyn Murray asked the high court to reverse a Maryland Court of Appeals decision permitting such exercises in Baltimore City public schools.

I never did meet Madalyn Murray, though I talked to her on the phone that week, and several times thereafter when follow-ups seemed in order. The experience taught me that even idealists are sometimes lousy people. When I first talked to her over the telephone, she cursed about Catholics, called them mackerel snappers, and made jokes about Justice Frankfurter's frankfurter and the like. She also proclaimed that "all Christians are animals" — and that they had been throughout history.

Not that my general feelings about praying in the public school classroom were much different from hers, but it seemed to me that there were more immediate issues confronting the country, like civil rights.

Madalyn Murray's uncharming manner didn't keep me from calling her during lulls on the dictation bank, and I passed along what she told me to Dana Bullen, our Supreme Court reporter. Later, Mr. Porter suggested to Bullen that he take me with him to hear the oral arguments in the case and help him out with background, since I knew Murray and he did not. Though I'd seen Justice Douglas walking the C&O Canal towpath above Georgetown a few times (he was a famous outdoorsman, and known by Supreme Court reporters to be a ladies' man, too), and had watched the chief justice go by in the inauguration motorcade, it was a lot different seeing the justices in their robes and listening to the court's marshal holler "Oyez! Oyez! Oyez!" Now they were asking Madalyn Murray's lawyer about what sort of praying had been imposed upon her son in his classroom in Baltimore, and why it should be deemed onerous in the eyes of the law.

In Montgomery County, we'd had no regular Bible reading or Lord's Prayer recitation, and no other religious observance except singing carols at the annual Christmas assembly at Blair; the school choir was renowned for singing "The Little Drummer Boy," and they'd been sent to a statewide caroling convocation in Western Maryland one season and had come back with a medal. Whereas at Janney Elementary, in D.C., my fourth-grade teacher, Mrs. Slye, had us read either the Lord's Prayer or the Twenty-Third Psalm every morning at the start of class, and about once a month she would lead us in formation across Albemarle Street to St. Columba's Episcopal Church for what she called "prayerful contemplation" and for psalm reading by the parish priest. Then, when I was in sixth grade, an act of Congress added the words "under God" to the pledge of allegiance to the flag.

I surmised from the justices' questions during oral arguments that they feared it was a slippery slope from reciting a simple prayer to forcing religion wholesale down the throats of impressionable children who might not wish it. The principle of separation between church and state was sacrosanct, one justice after another seemed to be saying — which

313

was what Murray's lawyer had argued, and he was a lot more pleasant about how he expressed himself than she was. I was thinking it was a good thing the justices never had to listen to her on the telephone.

Meanwhile, I pondered the fact that the marshal, after he'd done his final "oyez," proclaimed, "God save the United States and this honorable court!" And the fact that "in God we trust" was printed on the dollar bills in my wallet.

Madalyn Murray herself was in the Supreme Court chamber that day and held a little press conference outside on the steps, which I attended. Then I went into the court's pressroom and gave my notes to Dana Bullen, who was dictating back to the paper. His preparation for the case was prodigious. He'd even found out that Chief Justice Earl Warren regularly read aloud from the family Bible to his children and that, almost nightly before he got into bed, he read still more biblical passages to himself. I'd focused on the chief during the hearing. He was a head taller than most of his colleagues, and he spoke with quiet authority. Some of the other justices, I thought, were a little theatrical in their questioning from the bench.

After that day I started reading up on Earl Warren from the clips in the morgue. I learned that he lived at the Wardman Park Hotel, around the corner from where Sid

Epstein lived in Woodley Park, in a much less fancy brownish brick apartment house. Once, I drove into that neighborhood in the evening and made a loop past Sid Epstein's apartment and then around the driveway of the Wardman Park, thinking I might get a glimpse of either of these esteemed men away from their jobs and out of their work clothes.

Around the same time that I was raised to writing about the Supreme Court of the United States, I was suspended from the University of Maryland for getting too many parking tickets on campus. The fact that I'd made it through two whole semesters with respectable grades before the parking sheriff caught up with me seemed a pretty good run, given my approach to the academic life.

Since taking up residence in the Arlington house, more than an hour away from College Park, I'd made it my habit to park my car on Student-Faculty Lot A, within reasonable walking distance to my classes. The alternative was a vast parking area reserved for off-campus commuters near the milk-cow barns and about a mile from the nearest classroom. Hiking was not part of the curriculum I'd signed up for.

From Parking Lot A, I could make it to the newsroom in forty-five minutes flat after finishing class and jumping into my new car — a 1962 red Renault Dauphine my parents had given me for my eighteenth birthday that Valentine's Day. The gift celebrated my promising grades in the first semester. It marked my coming-of-age and also the demise of my '53 Chevrolet. The Chevy was notorious among my friends for the tendency of its steering mechanism to lock during a tight parking turn: when that happened, I'd have to jack up the car, kick the suspended right or left wheel to undo its seizure, lower the jack, and then return to the driver's seat to finish turning.

I had been dutifully paying off the parking tickets in batches every month or so, but I'd overlooked the fine print in the student manual that said you could be suspended for parking too many times in the wrong place. I'd accumulated close to a hundred parking violations by the time the university authorities lowered the boom.

There was no question in my mind that I would return to school eventually: it was the only safe haven from being drafted into the U.S. Army. The suspension was for the remainder of the fall semester, after which I could apply, pro forma, for readmission upon promise of good behavior. I figured I'd tuck myself back into the protective custody of the university system come spring: I did not want to push things with General Hershey.

On the other hand, I'd say the period of my suspension from the university was the happiest fall and winter of my life. It was the first time since kindergarten that I had experienced those months without having to go to school.

Living in the Arlington house now that I didn't have to study, or even feel guilty about not studying, meant that for pretty much twenty-four hours a day my life was focused upon newspapering and the newspaper people I worked with. I could concentrate unencumbered on the assignments the state and city desks gave me and on dreaming up feature stories of my own.

Compared to my family's three-bedroom, single-bath home in Silver Spring, the Arlington house was a mansion. There were six bedrooms on three floors, with a separate dining room, and even a butler's pantry. My little bedroom was behind the kitchen, with space enough for a single bed, a long desk I'd made out of a door from the lumberyard and a pair of sawhorses, plus the black chest of drawers I'd refinished. There was nothing imposing about the house from the outside, a white-painted brick mock Colonial in an ordinary suburban neighborhood. Our neighbors were civil servants, salesmen, teachers, merchants, and — we surmised, considering that the CIA's new headquarters was just a few miles down Spout Run and up the George Washington Parkway — a spy or two. Because of our erratic schedules, plus waiting out the rush hour at Harrigan's, we didn't get to know many people on our street.

Along with Tom Dimond, my housemates were Walter Wurfel, who had arrived at the *Star* earlier that year from Stanford and the Columbia School of Journalism and was covering Fairfax County in northern Virginia; John Fialka, a Yale graduate and Wurfel's classmate from the J-school, who was now studying law at Georgetown while making up his mind whether he wanted to be a reporter or a lawyer; Ken Campbell, another Yale graduate, who was on the *Star* training program and had a couple of years' experience at a string of local papers in upstate New York; and Kim Willenson, a cub reporter at the *Washington Post* fresh from J-school at Columbia after two years in the army. Wurfel and Fialka were twenty-six, Campbell twenty-four, and Willenson and Dimond twenty-five. I had yet to turn nineteen.

Wurfel assumed the role of housemaster. He'd signed the lease for the place, kept the books, and collected the rent, and he did things like post signs next to the kitchen sink saying DISHES MUST BE DRIED BEFORE THEY GO IN CABINETS.

We were a convivial group. We gathered in the living room late evenings as one or another arrived home from the newsroom or from an assignment around town, while Fialka read law books in the corner. A pitcher of chilled martinis was at hand, along with a well-stocked bar, and cases of beer were stacked in the pantry. Wurfel had played trumpet in his high school band, and I'd brought my guitar with me from the trailer dorm, along with my clothes, textbooks, and an engraved silver wristband given to me by my high school girlfriend Gerry Rebach. Wurfel and I arranged folk songs like "Goodnight Irene" and "This Land Is Your Land" in harmony for trumpet and guitar. The others either fled or sang along.

The talk was about the *Star* and its people and the newspaper business in general, and the events of the day. Ben McKelway had retired as editor in chief, a position the *Star*'s owners had bestowed on him in 1946. He had been the first editor from outside the three families that owned the paper. Newbold Noyes Jr. had succeeded him, restoring family tradition and faith in a gene pool that — if you listened to some grousing in the newsroom — was endangering the whole newspaper.

But Newby, as everyone called him, understood as well as any of the *Star*'s reporters that the owning families had made a series of business blunders in recent years, not least allowing Eugene Meyer to buy the *Washington Times-Herald* at a fire sale price and merge its useful parts with his *Washington Post*. Until that moment the *Star* had carried twice as many ads as the *Post* and had twice the circulation.

Now, less than a decade later, the circulation and revenue of the *Star* were half that of the *Post*. Since the Lincoln administration, the *Star* had supported the Republican Party in its editorial policies. But with Ike gone, Kennedy's New Frontiersmen had taken over the town, and the *Post*'s publisher, Phil Graham (Eugene Meyer's son-in-law and successor), was fast friends with both Kennedy and Vice President Lyndon Johnson, which made the *Star* even more the underdog newspaper — the outsiders — despite the daily excellence of our news coverage.

In our living room in Arlington, the talk about Kennedy and his presidency went on endlessly, though it consisted too often of gossip and rumors. What we did know that wasn't common knowledge we'd picked up from the national reporters when we took their dictation, or overheard in the newsroom, or imbibed at Ed Tribble's salons. The president of the United States was the big story, and the town revolved around him. Especially this new president with his novelty and glamour and family mystique.

Tom Dimond was himself a sort of star of the Arlington house. Of all the up-and-coming talents in the newsroom, Dimond's status was unique: admired by every editor, full of experience on the street, held in even higher regard than the Ivy Leaguers recruited for the training program, and considered likely, someday, to be one of the great reporters of his generation.

Now he reported daily to active duty at Andrews Air Force Base. There he had befriended a congressman from Oklahoma who was in his unit and who was furious that their air wing did almost nothing but sit around all day, with the commanding colonel often AWOL. The congressman had calculated it would be a good career move to remain in the reserves after his service in the Korean War, but he hadn't anticipated getting called up because of a crisis in Berlin, which kept him off the floor of the House for most of a year and a half. In secrecy, he encouraged Tom to begin investigating their do-nothing unit for the *Star*. The story became a minor scandal; it was picked up by the wire services and the New York papers and prompted editorials around the country.

Like me, Tom Dimond had been a neighborhood paperboy for the *Star*. He had also gone to Montgomery Blair High School — and he'd quit. When Rudy Kauffmann hired him as a copyboy in 1955 he was a seventeen-year-old high school dropout. Ed Tribble, then the city editor, thought Tom didn't know how to dress appropriately for the newsroom, so he'd personally taken him to a men's store on Fourteenth Street in his first week at the paper and bought him a suitable shirt and tie.

Our friendship was cemented by a shared

enthusiasm for the city and a native's intuition about the daily, sometimes grittier life of the place — not as the capital of the country but as our hometown, with its inbred peculiarities and its local cast of characters. Our Ivy League housemates, coming from elsewhere and transfixed by national politics and power, had little sense of this other dimension of the city. They did not love it as Tom and I did.

With no school to concern me, I worked forty hours plus overtime on the dictation bank five days a week and took on assignments at night from Mr. Porter, Ludy Werner, Harry Bacas, Coit Hendley, Emerson Beauchamp, Charles Puffenbarger, and on special occasions Sid Epstein himself.

Mr. Porter sent me to D.C. Stadium for Opening Day because Tom Brown, probably the greatest athlete in the history of Montgomery Blair High School, was starting at first base for the Senators in his first major league game. Because there had been so many stories in the papers about Brown's extraordinary talent in two professional sports (he had also been drafted by the Green Bay Packers to play professional football), Kennedy had mentioned to someone that he was looking forward to seeing him play at the opener. The Senators' manager had no choice but to start him.

The editors were giving me opportunities,

322

and watching me pretty closely. If I made a mistake — say, burying the lede of a story — I heard about it. A lot of the work was dull stuff, but they were bringing me along: zoning hearings, school board meetings, County Council deliberations, civil rights demonstrations in the Maryland and Virginia suburbs, meetings of business associations and labor unions: the clippings in my scrapbook reflected an expanding range.

I would also roam the city with my yellow "press card" for the sheer fun and fascination of it. I could go places that until now had been off-limits to me and meet people I would never otherwise have encountered. Sometimes I would approach these adventures with an idea for a story, but there were just as many times when I merely wanted to experience and observe. Harry Bacas had indicated he was willing to accept a piece — "If you have a really good idea" — for the weekly rotogravure *Star Magazine*.

I liked to work the late dictation shift that winter. If Rupe Welch was covering night police, something interesting was bound to turn up.

About one thirty one night, riding in a blue *Star* radio car after we'd left the scene of a supermarket burglary near Dupont Circle, Rupe said he had a special place he wanted to show me. But first he made me swear that I wouldn't tell anyone at the paper where we'd been. On Swann Street, he said, which puzzled me.

I thought I knew Swann Street well enough to be certain it was of no special interest — a five-block swath of row houses between Fourteenth and Nineteenth Streets N.W. It was the borderland between the Dupont Circle and Logan Circle neighborhoods: the area around Dupont Circle, where my mother was born on P Street, was almost all white; Logan Circle, altogether Black. Swann Street was a little of both.

In the 1700 block of Swann, on the south side of the street, Rupe parked the car. We headed a few houses up the block on foot, then went down a dimly lit half flight of stairs. Rupe knocked lightly on the door, then stationed himself in front of the peephole, pulling me a little closer so that whoever was inside could see me too.

The door swung open and we heard a blast of jazz from inside. The doorman, dressed in a suit with a white shirt and stickpin through his tie, gave Rupe a pat on the back. It was hard to hear anything above the sound from the jukebox. The doorman's name was Dizzy. Rupe told me later that he worked during the day as a janitor at the Supreme Court.

That was how I got introduced to Pussy Lindsay's after-hours club on Swann Street, which was said to operate with the forbearance of Deputy Police Chief Roy Blick, who was known to drop in himself now and then.

A long bar ran down the right-hand side of the room; almost all its seats were occupied by women, most of them talking with men standing behind or squeezed in next to them. Beyond the bar was another low-ceilinged room with couples sitting at tables and booths. The place reminded me of supper clubs I'd seen in 1940s movies, except there were no waiters. Almost every table had a full bottle of whiskey at its center. The crowd was probably three-quarters Black, both the men and the women.

Dizzy led us to one of the booths, and I could see, off to the side, a big buffet, which Rupert said would begin serving breakfast around five in the morning. Right now, it offered cold cuts and grits. When we'd arrived — shortly before two — there were maybe fifty or sixty people in the room and at the bar, but by two thirty people were coming through the front door in a stream. Two o'clock was the legal closing time for serving alcohol in D.C., when all the bars closed.

I didn't meet the proprietor, Pussy Lindsay, that night. Rupe told me he was probably in the gambling room, which I glimpsed at the top of the stairs. It was clear that Rupe was a favorite among the regulars at the place, some of whom — men and women — came over to our booth to say hi. I got a little embarrassed when one of the women started tousling my

325

hair, as if I were a child, though I was almost nineteen. Rupert said that maybe ten or fifteen of the women in the place were hookers, but they were almost indistinguishable, to me at least, from any of the other women there. Most were in their twenties and thirties, well-dressed. I was drawn to the aura of place: the after-hours drinking, the possibility of something dangerous; the idea of a speakeasy hidden between Dupont and Logan Circles seemed out of character for Washington, and that was part of the surprise and the charm.

I wouldn't say that I became anything like a habitué of Pussy Lindsay's, but I did stop in now and then, often with Rupe but sometimes on my own. I would get to know Pussy Lindsay well enough to have conversations with him, though I never asked him how he got his name, nor did Rupe know its origin for sure.

Riding with Rupe and Walter Gold, I'd also found out about other establishments in this part of town, which I had never known about. These were "tourist homes," which didn't do much business in tourism. They were another part of Washington's underbelly within Roy Blick's jurisdiction, which is to say that he let them operate without raiding them unless some kind of trouble developed inside. They were usually large houses on the quiet side streets between the major thoroughfares of Seventh Street and Fourteenth Street N.W.

The only thing that distinguished their exteriors from neighboring houses was a small blue or red neon sign in the front window that said TOURIST HOME. At a cost of two dollars, I was told, you could rent a room for an hour.

Our house at 6049 North Eighteenth Street in Arlington was a hub of newsroom social life, particularly in the warm months. There was a big backyard for barbecuing, with a couple of picnic tables, one for the bar and another for the food. But the real party house for the staff was in Washington, in the brick row house at 122 Duddington Place S.E., straight across the little park that separated the industrial-looking *Star* building on Virginia Avenue from the Capitol Hill neighborhood of Federal-era town houses to the north and east. The Duddington Place house was an annex of the newsroom, a five-minute walk away. The house was shared by David Breasted, whose beat was the D.C. school system; Rupe Welch; and a recently arrived rewrite man from the *Boston Globe,* Bob Leary.

At any given time, some newcomer to the paper would be in residence until permanent lodging could be found. In the winter and spring of 1963 that person was Tad Foote, who was engaged to Bosey Fulbright, the daughter of Senator J. William Fulbright from Arkansas. Foote stood out in any crowd, not least because he stood six foot six, but from the moment he came onto the dictation bank and then became a reporter on the training program, we were all convinced he was destined for big things, probably a career in politics. There was speculation — incredible as it sounded, though I was willing to entertain the notion — that he'd be president of the United States someday. (Kennedy's youth, coming after Roosevelt and Truman and Eisenhower, had people thinking in a different way about how old a president needed to be.) Even Sid Epstein seemed to feel some unease around Foote, who'd graduated from Yale in '59, then put in three years as an officer in the Marine Corps, and was torn at the moment between journalism and law school. After Foote found loftier quarters, Lance Morrow moved into Duddington Place and stayed for nearly a year.

On Saturday nights, between the first-edition deadline of the Sunday paper at seven o'clock and when the paper went to press at eleven, a stream of reporters and one or two deskmen, plus a few of the older copyboys and pretty much the whole dictation bank, would cross the little park to Duddington Place, many of them carrying bottles of booze, which they would contribute to the collection arrayed on the dining room table. Sometimes there would be bags of delicious bite-sized Little Tavern hamburgers that were sold by the dozen for a dollar. Even some of the reporters who might have had Saturday off would show up, especially the ones who were single. Some of them would already have started off the evening with dinner at Harrigan's.

The peculiar esprit of the *Star* was palpable Saturday nights at Duddington Place. Working on deadline for a newspaper could be intense, sometimes harrowing, yet here we were, friends and comrades, released from duty, the hard work done and flowing off the presses a couple of blocks away. We were relieved and ready for a drink. The rush suddenly subsided, and now it was hard not to appreciate how much fun we were having, and how hilarious were the stories we could now tell each other — inside stuff that didn't get into the paper. The joy of the work we shared, the involvement in one another's lives, even the location of the house there on Duddington Place, just on the edge of Capitol Hill — the Capitol dome was visible if you walked a few yards to the edge of the park — gave the parties a raucous glow.

The Duddington house had an air of impermanence, furnished from Goodwill Industries, with bare necessities for sleeping in the upstairs bedrooms, some Boston Red Sox pennants on the staircase wall, a big leather chair with cigarette burns on the arms, a tattered foldout couch, and a living room, dining room, and kitchen on the first floor arranged in a straight line, like a railroad car, leading to a small patio in the rear. As many as forty people would ebb and flow through this arrangement, although the seating was limited and people were mostly sitting on the floor, their backs against the wall.

Reporters and editors from the Women's Department often showed up, and most of the local staff working Saturday night — reporters, rewrite men, almost all the assistant city and state editors — were bound to drop in, along with several of the national reporters.

Phil Kelley and Tony Maggiacomo first took me to the house toward the end of my tenure as a copyboy. Ludy Werner, Myra MacPherson, Bobbie Hornig, Grace Bassett, Harriet Griffiths — almost all the women who were local reporters and editors — were certain to be there, as was Fifi Gorska, the editor of the *Star*'s new weekly *Teen Magazine*. Fifi had started at the paper as a copygirl in 1943, and as a dictationist she had taken the story reporting that the United States had dropped the atom bomb on Hiroshima. Until that day, the weapon was unknown, and unfamiliar with the term as she took dictation, Fifi typed, "President Truman today announced that the United States has dropped an Adam bomb on Japan . . ." *Adam* seemed descriptive enough, and it stayed that way in the paper through a couple editions.

The only two women on the national staff — Mary McGrory and Miriam Ottenberg

— never came to Duddington Place; though Miriam Ottenberg worked every Saturday evening, she took dinner privately with I. William Hill, the managing editor. Theirs was a relationship that the rest of us guessed at and observed with wonder. One night, upon their wobbly return to the newsroom I — and many others — saw Miss Ottenberg approach the national desk shouting and cursing about what the editors there had done to her prose. Burt Hoffman, the deputy national editor, told her that, as great a reporter as she might be, her copy needed just the kind of help he'd given it. Hearing that, Otsie (which was what we called her when she wasn't around) removed her leather belt and began lashing Hoffman about the head and shoulders until he managed to wrestle the belt from her grip.

Among those likely to show up at Duddington Place was Lucianne Von Steinberger Cummings, the PR woman whom I had first met at Harrigan's. She was good friends with a bunch of *Star* reporters and editors I was becoming closer to — ten or so colleagues in their midtwenties and early thirties, most of us single, who had flocked together, gravitating to Harrigan's after work, or sometimes (on a fancier and more expensive expedition) to Duke Zeibert's restaurant on Connecticut Avenue. We often had Sunday brunch together. Lucy Cummings had started as a copygirl at the *Washington Post* and then had worked as a press aide in Lyndon Johnson's presidential campaign in 1960, before he'd been beaten by Kennedy for the nomination and picked to be his vice president. Among Lucy's first PR accounts was the sumptuous Madison Hotel at Fifteenth and M Streets, around the corner from the *Washington Post* building. It opened to great fanfare, choreographed by Lucy and the hotel's owner, Marshal Coyne, in February 1963. Lucy had managed to get President Kennedy to cut a ceremonial ribbon to open the place. Suzy Parker, the model, sliced a cake in front of photographers to mark the occasion. We were impressed that Lucy had put the whole deal together. In the coming months she would become our ticket for a lot of nighttime socializing and champagne and caviar, all of which opened a curtain into worlds and people that were a part of Washington that, except for my grandfather's experience doing their tailoring, I knew almost nothing about.

The big local story in the first months of 1963 was the disappearance on January 20 of a schoolteacher in Laurel, Maryland. It dominated the local coverage of Washington's newspapers and television stations like few crime stories I'd seen since arriving at the *Star*. The extreme cold that winter made the search for her, over three counties, more difficult. The teacher, Allene Replane, had vanished after teaching a sewing class to an adult education group at Laurel High School, a few hundred yards from the apartment where she and her husband lived. That night he found her abandoned car nearby, headlights burning, keys in the ignition, engine turned off. There was no sign of violence.

I was working the night dictation shift about two weeks later, on February 6, when a report came across the Prince George's County squawk box that a body thought to be Mrs. Replane's had been found in nearby Howard County. Haynes Johnson, the night city editor, sent Walter Gold to Ellicott City, and by the time he'd arrived the body had been identified. It was her. On the phone to the city desk, Gold told Haynes that the cops were saying two schoolboys had found the body. A few minutes later, Gold called back with the name of one of the boys and an address.

No other city reporters were in the newsroom at that hour, and I told Haynes that I would make some phone calls. On the first try, I reached the boy's mother, who said she had seen the body herself. She was still upset and hyperventilating. I spoke to her slowly and quietly to settle her down. Finally, the story of the body's discovery emerged.

Haynes Johnson did not come naturally to being a deskman; he was doing a brief stint as night city editor, mainly to please the management. Newbold Noyes thought Haynes's excellence as a reporter might translate into being a stellar editor — which he was. But he did not like the work and was anxious to get back to reporting.

I was glad he had that temporary editing assignment. It gave me a chance to get to know him. Haynes was the single reporter at the paper I most admired and tried to learn from. (The other — also now an editor — was Ludy Werner.)

Haynes worked for both the city and national desks but was carried on Sid Epstein's payroll. The editors had dreamed up a title for him: "special assignment reporter." He had a historian's grasp and, because of that, an unusually expansive idea of what a local reporter could do. He was way more ambitious than anyone else on the staff, in my judgment. He put his raw reporting talent to work in a search for big patterns. He was thorough and never pretentious or sloppy. When he was at his best, his writing style was direct and clear and flowed as easily as a first-rate novel. No fat. Facts set forth in a vivid, purposeful manner.

In the spring of 1961, while I was still a copyboy, the Star had published his fourteen-installment series "The Negro in Washington." Haynes — a white reporter — had spent months interviewing hundreds of Black citizens about every aspect of their lives in the capital. I had never seen anything like it

334

in a newspaper. Their quotes, and his ability to convey (among other things) the deep anger and sadness at the difficulties they and their community experienced every day, were wrenching but not overwrought. His reporting was full of context; it did not pull back from complexity. There was little journalistic precedent for the ground he and the *Evening Star* were plowing in the series, in the only big American city with a Black majority. The *Star,* a newspaper without a single Black reporter, was not where most readers would have expected that series to be printed.

Much more than the *Star,* it was the *Washington Post* whose editorial policies were in line with the aspirations of the city's four hundred thousand Black citizens. Washington had long been a Jim Crow town, but it had a large and flourishing Black middle class, and a handsomely prosperous Black elite on the "Gold Coast." There were scores of Black churches across the city, which anchored a vibrant social and spiritual life, and just north of downtown stood Howard University, America's leading Black university.

The city had long been regarded by Black southerners as a great haven and destination, a place where many could get well-paying government jobs in the post office or civil service. Yet there were awful slums across large swaths of the city, especially in the alleys of Southwest and the low-rise housing projects in Northeast and Southeast, and half the capital's Black population lived in terrible poverty.

Despite the *Post*'s greater empathy in its editorial pages and the number of Blacks on the staff, the paper's reporting on the capital's Black community was (as I read it) surprisingly ordinary, with little particular depth or unusual perception. To my mind, race was the most important subject altogether for local reporting and was the constant subtext of so much that happened in our city. Yes, Washington was about politics and power, but there, too, race was a huge factor. The subject of race was largely avoided and even suppressed in public debate about the city and within its institutions, and that is why Haynes Johnson's series on Black life in Washington was so unusual.

Haynes told me that one of the reasons he had agreed to work on the desk at night was that it gave him time during the day to turn his series into a book, which would be published that spring as *Dusk at the Mountain*. Until that moment, it had not occurred to me that a local reporter could actually publish a book based on his work.

"The Negro in Washington" had run the table in the D.C. Newspaper Guild's Front Page Awards, including the grand award for public service reporting. It was a finalist for the Pulitzer Prize, and Haynes did not hide his disappointment at coming up short. His father, Malcolm Johnson, a reporter for the scrappy afternoon *New York Sun,* had won the Pulitzer Prize in 1949 for a twenty-four-part series about crime and corruption on the docks of New York City. Malcolm Johnson's series had been the basis for the 1954 movie *On the Waterfront,* starring Marlon Brando. I'd seen it three times.

The first edition of the next day's *Star* — February 7 — carried an eight-column headline: TEACHER BEATEN AND LEFT TO DIE. Late that afternoon, Coit Hendley called across the city desk to me, on the dictation bank, to take a memo from Ted Crown at police headquarters. I'd expected Crown to have picked up some information from his D.C. detective sources about the Howard County case. Instead — between chomps on his cigar and gurgling into the phone — he told me that a woman named Isabelle Crim had died and her body was unclaimed at the city morgue. Crim was the woman who for decades had sold newspapers around the corner from the old Evening Star Building at Eleventh and E Streets, and at another kiosk at Seventh and Pennsylvania Avenue. I knew her, as did everyone else, as Annie.

I typed up a quick memo based on the few particulars Crown conveyed, and Hendley told me to write an obit. She was a familiar figure to many *Star* reporters, but those colleagues I interviewed in the newsroom seemed to know almost nothing about her life except that they bought newspapers from her and that she took a motherly interest in the pigeons that flocked around her newsstand. My own memory of her was indelible from the afternoons when I'd take the Pennsylvania Avenue streetcar after Milt Grant's teenage TV dance show, but I hadn't seen her many times since President Kennedy's inauguration, when she'd complained to me about the D.C. police poisoning the birds on the avenue.

I asked Hendley if I could head over to Annie's old spot downtown. Without looking up from the copy he was reading, he told me to go ahead.

At Eleventh and E, the plywood doors of Annie's green-painted newsstand were shut, and out-of-town newspapers were bundled and stacked on the sidewalk. One of her regular customers, a clerk at a big oil company's D.C. office, showed up while I was writing in my reporter's notebook and asked what had happened.

I told him that Annie was dead. It was the middle of Washington, but it seemed like a death that had occurred in a small town. He gave me his memories of her. He talked about her shyness, but said he'd been able to get past it enough to engage in chitchat for a couple of minutes when he'd buy the paper. He said she was more drawn to children than grown-ups,

and made it her habit to give them candy —
usually in family tourist groups who'd pass by.

I walked half a block up Eleventh Street to
Draper's tobacco shop, where the manager
turned out to be a mine of information. During his decades in the store, he'd gotten to
know Annie well. He knew that she'd lived a
couple of blocks away, on Seventh Street, and
that she'd once been engaged to a man from
California who died before they could get
married. She was an orphan: born in Hagerstown, Maryland. The tobacco store manager
was adamant that I write about how smart she
was. "She was a proud and intelligent woman
with the stubbornness of a prima donna," he
said.

I was able to talk to some other customers
who added a few details to the picture before I
took a cab back to Virginia Avenue. At the office, I told Coit Hendley that I thought there
was a worthwhile tale in her death. He said to
go ahead and write the story and make it as
long as it deserved.

I turned in my copy late in the afternoon,
shortly after Haynes Johnson had arrived
for the night shift. He'd taken to calling me
Carlos of late. And I was glad he would be
the editor dealing with my copy. After he got
settled and rolled up his shirtsleeves, I could
see that he was reading it. Not long after, he
called me over to the desk.

He told me he was putting Annie's obit on

page one of the next day's paper. And he'd checked with Sid Epstein, who'd okayed that it appear under my byline. It was rare for a dictationist to get a front-page byline.

This one read: *By Carl Bernstein, Contributing Writer.* I wondered whether Coach Good would see the story.

And I called my father. He said he was proud of what I'd done, which choked me up a little, I had to admit.

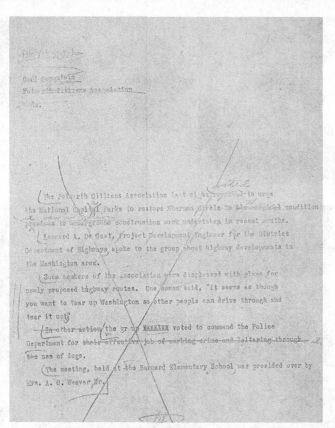

The Petworth Citizens Association last night resolved to urge the National Capital Parks to restore Sherman Circle to its original condition previous to underground construction work undertaken in recent months.

Leonard A. De Gast, Project Development Engineer for the District Department of Highways, spoke to the group about highway developments in the Washington area.

Some members of the association were displeased with plans for newly proposed highway routes. One woman said, "It seems as though you want to tear up Washington so other people can drive through and tear it up."

In other action, the group voted to commend the Police Department for their effective job of curbing crime and loitering through the use of dogs.

The meeting, held at the Barnard Elementary School, was presided over by Mrs. A. G. Weaver, Sr.

"Dry Run" story from first reporting assignment, September 18, 1960. COURTESY OF THE AUTHOR

Copyboy: photo from spring 1961. COURTESY OF THE AUTHOR

Copy desk

Haybaile

Heap

Hendley

Alexander

Werner

Porter

STATE IN

STATE OVERNIGHT

The newsroom, 1960: state, city, news, and national desks.
FROM LEFT: Mary Lou Werner, Charlie Alexander, Coit Hendley,
Belmont Faries, unknown, John Cassady, Burt Hoffman,
George Porter (ACROSS FROM WERNER), Sid Epstein, Ray Price,
Charlie Seib. In back, Earl Heap. DISTRICT OF COLUMBIA PUBLIC LIBRARY

Printers watching Red Streak sports final come off the presses. DISTRICT OF COLUMBIA PUBLIC LIBRARY

Composing room foreman Aloysius Baker. DISTRICT OF COLUMBIA PUBLIC LIBRARY

A rewrite man, at left, writes story from notes telephoned direct to the newsroom from a reporter at the scene. Other reporters dictate their stories by telephone to the dictationists at right.

COMMUNICATIONS

The newsroom communications center includes 13 Associated Press machines for city, nearby, global and financial news; one machine for weather reports and three to communicate directly with out-of-town correspondents from Gettysburg to Paris.

Rewrite man / dictation bank, at top, and wire room, at bottom. DISTRICT OF COLUMBIA PUBLIC LIBRARY

Head copyboy Phil Kelley.
DISTRICT OF COLUMBIA PUBLIC LIBRARY

A staff of seven operators runs The Star's busy telephone switchboard on the second floor. The operators handle an average of about 5,000 incoming phone calls each day.

Main switchboard. DISTRICT OF COLUMBIA PUBLIC LIBRARY

City editor Sid Epstein. PHOTO BY MARK BALDWIN

Cover of Julie London album gifted by Phil Trupp. COURTESY OF LEO MONAHAN (JULIE LONDON)

Walter Gold and Larry Krebs (in white shirts) at a crime scene. COURTESY OF LARRY GOLD

Housemates (FROM TOP LEFT): Ken Campbell, Tom Dimond, Carl Bernstein, John Fialka (*AT BOTTOM*). COURTESY OF SUZE CAMPBELL

The house at 6049 North Eighteenth Street in Arlington, 1963.

Fake obit called into the Washington Post, *September 15, 1962.*

Charles Moore, Entertainer, 84

Charles J. Moore, a Washington vaudevillian, who once received personal congratulations from President Woodrow Wilson for his ventriloquy, died yesterday following a stroke in Sarasota, Fla. He was 84.

Mr. Moore was born in Washington and attended public schools here until he was 16.

Then he collected a set of drums, a harmonica, tambourine and banjo, and set out to make a name for himself as a one-man band in the District's old burlesque circuit.

During World War I Mr. Moore offered his talents to the American Red Cross and toured Army installations here and in Europe.

A master of ventriloquy, he would dress his dummy, Van Rudy, in the garb of Kaiser Wilhelm and carry on satiric dialogues, lampooning the Kaiser.

Mr. Moore said his proudest moment came after his performance at a benefit in Washington when he met President Woodrow Wilson and received his congratulations.

After World War I, Mr. Moore gave up ventriloquy to study magic. For nearly 15 years he apprenticed under the magician, be...

INDEPENDENT TO LAST

News Public's Annie Dies

By CARL BERNSTEIN
Contributing Writer

Although they knew her only as Annie, Isabelle Crim played a daily part in the lives of hundreds of Washingtonians.

Annie, the 49-year-old vendor who operated newsstands at Seventh street and Pennsylvania avenue and Eleventh and E streets N.W., died Sunday.

And unless her body is claimed from the Morgue and she is offered burial, Annie will be cremated without religious services early next week by District medical authorities.

Most of the commuters who transferred from buses and trolleys at the busy Pennsylvania avenue corner automatically handed Annie their nickels and dimes without thinking much more about her.

Similarly, shoppers at Elev-

ANNIE

of W. Curtis Draper's tobacco shop at 503 Eleventh street, called Annie "a proud and intelligent woman with the stubbornness of a prima donna."

The stubborn streak was evident in her independence. She lived poorly in a small room at 716 Seventh street N.W., where police found her dead last Sunday.

The coroner attributed Annie's death to natural causes and neighbors said she had suffered a bad cough for the last few month. But, characterist refused to see a

The picture of Annie gave to was far from story.

She was born Md. orphaned hearted as any person could age and shut

First byline, February 9, 1963, "News Public's Annie Dies," and other stories from scrapbook. DISTRICT OF COLUMBIA PUBLIC LIBRARY (THE REST OF THE HEADLINES ARE FROM THIS SAME SOURCE)

CALLING ARLINGTON

Portable 6 on the Air; Goldwater Hams It Up

By CARL BERNSTEIN
Star Staff Writer

Having heard about Senator Goldwater's spending his time at the Republican Convention talking on the air to amateur radio operators, we decided to try it ourselves.

Does the Senator really shun the hubbub of the Cow Palace to stay in his suite at the Mark Hopkins Hotel and twiddle dials and talk with fellow "ham" operators across the country? Indeed he does.

We convinced an Arlington ham that he should put on his

Cleveland avenue, got a long-distance call 15 minutes later from a Goldwater staff member in San Francisco. "How about 2 o'clock tomorrow your time?" he asked.

"Roger. We'll by standing by at 2 EDT," Mr. Von Meister answered.

We hustled ourselves over to Mr. Von Meister's house yesterday for the big moment and found the Senator's communicant at a long desk piled high with transformers, amplifiers and what not. Then, over the loud-speaker came the

Bonn Aide Studies Nazi Files

By CARL BERNSTEIN
Star Special Writer

cessful prosecution of SS Gen. Karl Wolff was largely based on the American files. Wolff was

sentenced to 15 years at hard labor for his part in the murder of 300,000 Jews in Poland.

Calendar-Reformer Has Answer to More Holidays

By CARL BERNSTEIN
Star Special Writer

Wallace D. Barlow is a man who would like to wake up Sunday, take a three-day vacation and go back to work Mondays inter—on Monday.

And he has a way to do it, too.

The 52-year-old Navy Department engineer has proposed what he called the Barlow calendar.

If Mr. Barlow had his way, our year would have 13 months, each composed of four seven-day weeks. It has don't have a newsil handle, that means that 28 days are tell over in the 365-day year.

...

...

today. "They're just days to relax and have a little fun," their donor declares. "No clock weighing or anything. Just paradise."

Mr. Barlow's chief disagreement with the Gregorian calendar system now in use stems from holidays.

"Nothing is ever the same," he complains. "Planning is almost impossible.

"For instance, Christmas drifts from one day of the week to another each year. This coming year it will be on a Friday; in 1965 it was on a Wednesday."

"And look at Thanksgiving. It never falls on the same date, just on the last Thursday of...

fifth would be on a Friday, the 10th a Wednesday.

"This is the beauty of it all," says Mr. Barlow, a native of Blacksburg, Va. "Every month ends on a Sunday and then you get your holidays. That means that every holiday is provided by a week end. And you have more than just as many holidays as now."

The Barlow Calendar's biggest holiday comes at the end of June. "You get six days (the plus the last Saturday and Sunday of the month," he notes. "I call it June Week." As for such additional days as June 24, Mr. Barlow thinks that "people will get...

...the Yuletide celebration on December 26.

Sixth of Mr. Barlow's other holidays include Spring Day on March 26 and a two-day Music Festival at the end of October.

"There is at least one holiday at the end of every month," he says. "The reason I have amassed them are flexible and can be easily changed.

Mr. Barlow is quick to admit that his calendar "breaks completely with tradition. But, he adds, "it replaces the disorganized and chaotic pattern of errors imposed by the Gregorian calendar."

And he has an answer for arguments against his system.

Church Board Weighs Stand Critical of Md. U.

By CARL BERNSTEIN
Star Special Writer

allow the Rev. Dr. Martin Luther King to make a campus

11th Armored Comes Home to Fort Mead

By CARL BERNSTEIN
Star Staff Writer

yesterday. Luckily, more than half of the arrivals took their

than 1,100 unmarried enlisted men. They arrived at the Port

headquarters of the regiment was a crossroads of business

Win in Sweepstakes Stuns D. C. Beautician

By CARL BERNSTEIN
Star Staff Writer

General Services Administration employe for 24 years

New McLean Church Holds Fallout Shelter

By CARL BERNSTEIN
Star Special Writer

as you carry life insurance think people should be protect

D. C. Ordering Barbers Not to Refuse Negro

By CARL BERNSTEIN
Star Staff Writer

which State Department and civil rights leaders

New Welfare Store Opens

By CARL BERNSTEIN
Star Staff Writer

the cashier." The cards
specify how much food

to make it possible for peo
to pick up their food in

Super Whiz Kid, 16, Urges Navy Reforms

By CARL BERNSTEIN
Star Staff Writer

Apprentice Cooks Master the Trade

By CARL BERNSTEIN
Star Staff Writer

K2ZRK-4 at work.—Star Staff Photo.

HAM

Continued From Page A-1

operators never use last names, we were told.

The greeting seemed to break the ice and the Senator got right to the heart of the matter.

"I'm working A column 5 line with a 30 L. One," he told us.

"It's better than the rig back in

cal mobile station (the radio equipment in Senator Goldwater's airplane). All I do there is drop a 20-foot line out of the cockpit and I can call all over. I talked with Oregon when I was over Phoenix the other day."

Sees the Fog

Making sure that we were the first reporter to interview the

At the Upper End of Elkton, Maryland's Main Street,   75017₃

MINISTER MARRIAGE LICENSE

MINISTER MARRIAGE LICENSE

MINISTER MARRIAGE LICENSE

MINISTER MARRIAGE LICENSE

MINISTER MARRIAGE LICENSE

Where Thousands Have Been Joined in Matrimony

Elkton: the Maryland marriage capital

Listening to Sid Epstein, 1963: Jo Anne Mark, Carl Bernstein, Eleni Epstein.

The new Evening Star *building, 1960, 225 Virginia Avenue SE.*

Newbold Noyes Jr.

Kauffmann Is Named Star Associate Editor

Appointment of Rudolph Kauffmann II as associate editor of The Star was announced today.

Mr. Kauffmann, 49, had been production editor of the newspaper since 1957. He is secretary of the Evening Star Newspaper Co.

In his new position, he will assist the editor with the production of the editorial page and with administrative problems.

A member of one of three families which have directed The Star company since 1867, Mr. Kauffmann joined the staff of the newspaper in 1936 after his graduation from Princeton University.

He covered city planning news along with events in the Interior and Navy Departments. During World War II, he spent four and one-half years with the Navy, returning to the newspaper and in 1950 becoming assistant to the managing editor.

Among his civic posts, Mr. Kauffmann is president of Children's Hospital, first vice

RUDOLPH KAUFFMANN

president of the Hospital Council of the National Capital A and a director of Group Hostalization, Inc. He is a memb of the Gridiron Club.

He is married to the form Mary L. Wells and they h four children.

Covering civil rights (TOP TO BOTTOM): the Reverend Walter Fauntroy, Stokely Carmichael, Tony Cox, Chuck Stone (editor of the Washington Afro-American, *standing), Willie J. Hardy; pickets at the Hiser Theater, Bethesda, spring 1961; Haynes Johnson.* DISTRICT OF COLUMBIA PUBLIC LIBRARY (ALL IMAGES ON THIS PAGE)

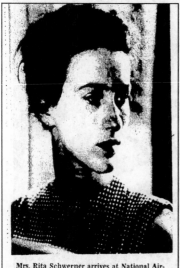

Mrs. Rita Schwerner arrives at National Airport.—Star Staff Photo.

Wife Asks All to Hunt Missing Rights Worker

By CARL BERNSTEIN
Star Staff Writer

The wife of one of three civil rights workers missing in Mississippi last night appealed to "all Americans of good conscience" to go to that State and join the search for her husband.

Mrs. Rita Schwerner, whose 24-year-old husband, Michael, has been missing for nine days, made the plea after a meeting with President Johnson which she called "very disappointing."

During her brief visit with the President, Mrs. Schwerner, 22, asked that the Federal Government send an additional 5,000 men to aid in the hunt for her husband and his two companions. She said Mr. Johnson indicated that "nowhere near that number" could be dispatched to Mississippi.

Holds Press Parley

At a press conference last night following her White House visit, Mrs. Schwerner said: "I am pleading with all Americans

replied when asked if she thinks she will see her husband alive again.

Mrs. Schwerner, who stands just five feet and weighs 95 pounds, was accompanied on her White House visit by Representative Reid, Republican of New York. Mr. Reid, Congressman from the district where Mr. Schwerner's parents live, also took her to the Justice Department for a conference with Acting Attorney General Nicholas de B. Katzenbach.

"I am afraid I found the President evasive," Mrs. Schwerner said later. "But I'm not a diplomat; I'm a woman looking for her husband."

Set Up CORE Post

Mrs. Schwerner, former junior high school teacher in Jamaica, N.Y., had worked with her husband in Meridian Miss., since January, establishing CORE's headquarters there.

Mrs. Schwerner said her

June 30, 1964, story: Rita Schwerner, wife of one of three missing civil rights workers in Mississippi, seeks help from President Johnson. DISTRICT OF COLUMBIA PUBLIC LIBRARY

The March on Washington, August 28, 1963. PUBLIC DOMAIN

At Ken and Suze Campbell's wedding, August 29, 1964, with Mary Lou Werner and her fiancé, Jim Forbes; doing the Frug with Ludy. COURTESY OF SUZE CAMPBELL

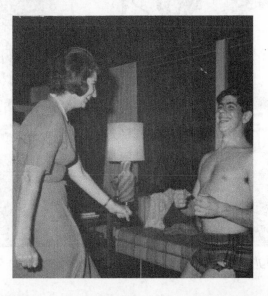

Downtown newsstand November 22, 1963. DISTRICT OF COLUMBIA PUBLIC LIBRARY

Harrigan's by night: "Waiting out the rush hour." DISTRICT OF COLUMBIA PUBLIC LIBRARY

Mary McGrory. DISTRICT OF COLUMBIA PUBLIC LIBRARY

Two Pulitzer winners: Miriam Ottenberg (LEFT) and Mary Lou Werner, 1965. DISTRICT OF COLUMBIA PUBLIC LIBRARY

Rupe Welch.
COURTESY OF JOAN EBZERY DIMOND

Mark Baldwin.
PHOTO BY HAYNES JOHNSON, COURTESY OF
MARK BALDWIN

Myra MacPherson.
PHOTO BY MARK BALDWIN

Lance Morrow.
COURTESY OF THE AUTHOR

Ted Crown and John Burch. District of Columbia Public Library

Bobbie Hornig. District of Columbia Public Library

UNIVERSITY OF MARYLAND—COLLEGE PARK, MD. 029495

Preparatory Credits From:
Montgomery Blair H.S. June,1961
Silver Spring, Maryland
Entrance Status
Regular
ISSUED TO STUDENT

Student Name: BERNSTEIN, Carl Milton
Birth Date: 2-14-44   Birth Place: Washington, D.C.
Home Address: 9340 Harvey Road, Silver Spring, Maryland
Degrees Granted:

DEPT AND COURSE NUMBER	TITLE OF COURSE	Sem. Hours Att'pd	Final Grade	Sem. Hours Earned	Qual. Pts.
By classification test, excused from Eng. 1 & 2, G&P, 1					
	COLLEGE OF ARTS & SCIENCES				
	FALL SEMESTER 1961				
S 001	BASIC AIR SCIENCE	.5	C	.5	01.0
NG 021	ADV FRESH COMP LIT	03	B	03	09.0
+P 003	PRIN OF GOV+POLITICS	03	C	03	06.0
+P 004	STATE GOV + ADMIN	03	A	03	12.0
E 001	ORIENT TO PHYS ED	01	D	01	00.0
PCH 001	PUBLIC SPEAKING	03	C	03	06.0
	SPR SEMESTER 1962				
S 002	BASIC AIR SCIENCE	02	F	00	00.0
OT 001	GENERAL BOTANY	04	F	00	00.0
NG 003	COMP + WORLD LIT	03	D	03	03.0
NG 012	INTRO CREATIV WRITNG	03	C	03	06.0
IST 054	HIST ENGL + GT BRTIN	03	IC	03	06.0
HIL 001	PHILOS FOR MOD MAN	03	C	03	06.0
E 007	RECREATIONAL SPORTS	01	C	01	00.0
	FALL SEMESTER 1962				
OT 001	GENERAL BOTANY	04	-	-	-
CON 037	FUND OF ECONOMICS	03	-	-	-
NG 004	COMP & WORLD LIT	03	-	-	-
NG 056	ENG LIT FROM 1800 TO PRESENT	03	-	-	-
I 05	HIST OF AMER CIV	03	-	-	-
S 002	BASIC AIR SCIENCE	02	-	-	-
ATH 003	FUND OF MATHEMATICS	04	-	-	-
E 001	ORIENT TO PHYS ED	01	-	-	-
REGISTRATION WITHDRAWN NOVEMBER 15, 1962					
READMITTED FEB. 1963					
	SPRING SEMESTER 63				
BOT 001	GENERAL BOTANY	04	F	00	00.0
ECON 031	PRINS OF ECONOMICS 1	03	D	03	03.0
ENG 004	COMP + WORLD LIT	03	B	03	09.0
HIST 006	HIST AMERICAN CIV	03	A	03	12.0
PE 003	DEV + COMB SPORTS	01	F	00	00.0
SPCH 022	INTRO RADIO + T V	03	D	03	03.0

DEPT AND COURSE NUMBER	TITLE OF COURSE	Sem. Hours Att'pd	Final Grade	Sem. Hours Earned
	FALL SEMESTER 63			
PE 00J	DEV + COMB SPORTS	01	F	00 00
HIST 005	HIST AMER CIVILIZATION	03	C	03 06.
ZOOL 001	GENERAL ZOOLOGY	04	F	00 00.
MUS 020	SURVEY MUSIC LIT	03	C	03 06.
FR 001	ELEMENTARY FRENCH	03	C	03 06.
ENG 150	AMERICAN LITERATURE	03	B	03 09
	SPR. SEMESTER 64			
ENG 151	AMERICAN LITERATURE	03	F	00 0
HIST 042	WESTERN CIVILIZATION	03	F	00 0
MU 131	MUS LIT SUR NON MAJ	03	F	00 0
FR 002	ELEM FRCH LECTURE	03	F	00 0
ENG 116	SHAKESPEARE	03	F	00 0
ACADEMICALLY DISMISSED 6-5-64				
Reinstated on Jr.Standing Probation Sept.1964				
	FALL SEMESTER 64			
ENG 151	AMERICAN LITERATURE	03	F	00 0
FR 002	ELEMENTARY FRENCH	03	F	00 0
ENG 055	ENG LIT BEGN TO 1800	03	F	00 0
HIST 042	WESTERN CIVILIZATION	03	F	00 0
HIST 051	THE HUMANITIES	03	F	00 0
ACADEMICALLY DISMISSED 1-27-65				

GRADING SYSTEM: A, B, C, D—Passing; F—Failure; I—Incomplete; S—Satisfactory; X—No record, off-campus course; W—Withdrew; WP—Withdrew passing; WF—Withdrew failing; WX—Withdrew during first half of semester. R—Course repeated. NR—Not required for degree. At graduate level, D is failure.

Academic record (bad), 1961–64. COURTESY OF THE AUTHOR

I. William (Bill) Hill, managing editor: "Carl, experience is no substitute for the training program." DISTRICT OF COLUMBIA PUBLIC LIBRARY

17

AMBITION

One of the first things I did after getting bounced from the university for overparking was to go to Camalier and Buckley's stationery store on Connecticut Avenue and buy myself a bunch of three-by-five index cards and alphabetical dividers, plus some fancy boxes covered in green linen to hold the whole lot. And onto these index cards I started transferring notes from my reporter's notebooks where I'd jotted ideas for stories, and the names and addresses and phone numbers of likely sources. I would number all the pages in my relevant notebooks and copy the best quotes and other essential information onto the index cards, a kind of cross-referencing system that — redundant as it might appear — kept me on track and able to locate material when I needed it.

I also bought a two-drawer metal filing cabinet for my room in Arlington and began keeping a clipping file of stories I found pertinent — from the *Star,* the *Post,* the *New York*

Times, the *Herald Tribune,* the *Afro-American, Time* magazine, the *Reporter, Harpers,* the *New Yorker,* the *New Republic,* the *Christian Science Monitor,* even the *National Enquirer* tabloid. Soon there were dozens of stories from dozens of papers and magazines in bulging manila envelopes — anything I thought would be useful to me. I studied feature stories, trying to understand better what made for good writing. That was another category in which the *Star* surpassed the *Post:* the writing. Not just Miss McGrory, or the rewrite men like O'Leary or Herndon or Herman Schaden, the Magician. There were ten or twelve other members of the staff who could compose a sentence that was as perfect as a line in a song and maintain the pitch through the whole production. Haynes Johnson would sometimes write from Olympian heights when he was covering a big breaking story, sounding a note of portent, which was much different from the way he'd written "The Negro in Washington," all clean and reportorial and dramatic in the sparseness and punch of its style. Yet both his approaches had their own elegance and brought the reader into the middle of the story.

Sid Epstein had recently made a couple of unconventional hires that were intended to raise the literary quality of local coverage. John Sherwood lived on a boat in Annapolis part of the time and trawled the Chesapeake for tales of watermen and other distinctive peoples who lived strange lives by the bay, such as the inhabitants of Tangier Island, who spoke an ancient English dialect akin to Welsh but less comprehensible. David Braaten was brought on to be something of a resident humorist, and most of the time I got the joke. Braaten could be even funnier and exceedingly companionable outside the newsroom, especially when he was with his wife, who was from Denmark, and was breathtakingly beautiful. Not long after his arrival, Braaten churned out a series of articles about his attempt to quit smoking: the surgeon general of the United States had declared cigarettes a threat to the national health and was agitating to put a deathly warning on the sides of cigarette packs. In the newsroom, Braaten was pretty much a lone horse in his quest. At any given moment someone on the staff was much more likely to be struggling to give up booze than cigarettes, usually to little effect — though the day after St. Patrick's Day 1963, Jerry O'Leary Jr. started attending meetings of Alcoholics Anonymous. In addition to his speed as a rewrite man, O'Leary was a great feature writer. Every year, he would compose an ode to the opening of oyster season on the Chesapeake, always with the same lede: "Behold, the succulent bi-valve."

John Sherwood's example spurred me to focus even more on the palette of Maryland, in particular my research into the Wesorts

343

people. My aunt Annie had explained to me that when she was a girl growing up in Charles County there were three separate school systems there: one for white children, one for Black children, and another for the Wesorts children. Every couple of weeks, I'd drive down to Indian Head or Port Tobacco and knock on the doors of people listed in the Southern Maryland phone book who were named Proctor or Swann or Johnson or one of five other surnames; there were eight core Wesorts families who had intermarried over the centuries, I'd learned early on. Often the people I sought out said they didn't want to talk to me, but there were enough who let me inside their houses for my journalistic purpose — women, usually, because the Wesorts were almost a matriarchal society. The whole community was isolated, shunned by whites and Blacks both, and had been for centuries. The Wesorts all were Catholic, Maryland having been (as Ebenezer Cooke wrote about during his laureateship) a colony founded by Roman Catholics. So I was able to trace family histories all the way back to the 1700s from baptismal and marriage records kept in the old parish churches around the county. By springtime, I'd amassed so much information about the Wesorts and filled so many notebooks that a full green box of index cards was devoted to them exclusively.

I'd dedicated another box to sources — not

344

that I had so many of them yet, but I was building up a respectable list of people, dating back to the citizens meetings I'd covered as a copyboy. Now I was getting assigned to evening meetings of local government commissions and school boards in the suburbs and some important political organizations and trade associations in the city. This whole business of courting and developing sources was almost an art form, as I saw from my study of the best *Star* reporters. It was through good sources that a reporter would happen upon first-rate stories, sometimes in a conversation about something else altogether. But just as important, a reporter's sources also possessed the kind of background knowledge and specific expertise you could depend on whenever crucial information was needed. I made it a habit to call Reverend Fauntroy, for instance, every few weeks; he seemed to know what was going on in the city's neighborhoods, from Swampoodle to Shepherd Park; he was also involved with Dr. King's civil rights work down South, and his connections with people in the District Building were formidable. I also thought he might be helpful on an idea I had for a piece for Harry Bacas's Sunday magazine.

A big part of the satisfaction of newspapering, which I would not have guessed, came from the personal relationships built up between a reporter and his sources, though

I could also see that this might be a tricky business. Some of the best sources tended to be important people, or individuals caught up in circumstances you wouldn't encounter if you didn't have a press card, and there was often a back-and-forth tug that was part of the process of trying to uncover information from them. I began to understand the value of calling up these folks from a list and checking in with them, or meeting them for lunch or a drink, not to interrogate them but just to get to know each other and perhaps to coax some useful piece of information from them in the process. For now I often decided to do it on the phone, in part because I was self-conscious about my age.

One of the most important sources I wanted to develop was Joe Rauh, the civil rights and civil liberties lawyer who had been a big player in town since the Roosevelt administration. He was on first-name terms with many of President Kennedy's closest aides in the White House. I'd met him the previous fall at a quarterly meeting of Americans for Democratic Action, the liberal advocacy outfit he ran. The meeting took place the day after JFK had finally signed a long-promised executive order outlawing racial discrimination in government-assisted housing across the country; it was being called "historic" in the headlines. Rauh literally hammered the proceedings to a close with a gavel that had been a gift from Eleanor Roosevelt. A few moments later I went up and introduced myself. I asked if he thought the president would issue another order, long rumored but never materializing, that would ban *all* housing discrimination in the District of Columbia. Rauh told me he was hearing from his friends in the White House that language was already being drafted and that Kennedy would issue it for sure in the next few months.

I asked him a lot of other questions, more to get to know him, I was thinking, and for him to perhaps remember me, than in relation to the article I would write for the next day's paper. My lede for the story — which ran above the fold on the split page — was based on the information I had gotten from Rauh and some phone calls I made as soon as I got back to the newsroom, about the likelihood of Kennedy's issuing the D.C. order.

From the time I'd arrived at the paper there was no question that civil rights was what I wanted to cover, in all its manifestations, and Joe Rauh was as well positioned as anyone in town to know what was going on at a given moment. Over the next few months I checked in with him by phone on a regular basis about the status and likely timetable of the D.C. order. Meanwhile, he offered to put me in touch with some other people involved in the civil rights movement he thought I should

347

know, including two administration officials who dealt with civil rights and desegregation: Charles Horsky, who he said Kennedy intended to name as his special assistant for all matters dealing with the District of Columbia; and Harris Wofford, who was working behind the scenes in the administration on the Route 40 desegregation problem. Rauh volunteered to put in a word for me with both of them.

Jo Anne Mark didn't know much about what I considered real newspapering, especially in a big city, even though she was almost three years older than me and had graduated from journalism school at Penn State and had studied in France in her junior year and had worked summers since high school as a reporter for the *Beaver Valley Times.* So it was natural that I tried to teach her — from the start of our spending time together — both about Washington, D.C., and what I'd learned so far about covering it.

On our first date, only a week after she arrived at the paper, she told me that ever since she was a little girl, she had always wanted to become Brenda Starr, the feisty girl reporter of the Sunday comics. And though I advised her not to say that out loud to anyone else in the newsroom, she did, quite a few times, and it wasn't long before that was what a lot of people at the *Star* were calling her. The amazing thing was that when they called her

Brenda Starr, it was said with affection and even admiration — that was how quickly she won everybody over.

I came to see why everybody fell for her. It wasn't an act, or premeditated, it was just the way she was. It helped that she was really pretty, but not the same way Brenda Starr looked in the comic strip. Which, for the first time in my life, I took to reading. Brenda Starr's hair was flaming red, but Jo Anne's was soft and blond. She also had this big throaty laugh that kind of rumbled, and her voice had almost as many octaves as an opera singer's. Tom Dimond, who was around the two of us a lot, said he had never met anybody who talked so much, and she herself liked to say she was a flibbertigibbet. Right off the bat, some people in the newsroom were saying we were like brother and sister. I would say that for the first couple of months, we carried on more like the closest of friends. Not much later she would tell me that at first, she'd actually wanted me to teach her about Washington.

The office of Charlie Seib, the assistant managing editor, was less than ten feet from the dictation bank, behind the switchboard, and from my vantage point I had a straight-on view through his door. He almost always kept it open because he'd be walking in and out to the newsroom floor to be up to the minute and preside hands-on over production of the whole newspaper through all five editions from the first-run deadline at ten o'clock until the Red Streak Final went to press in the evening. He must have legged a couple of miles a day between the Sports Department behind the hay baler and the features desk by the freeway window, plus the Women's Department across the hall, and adjacent to that, Ed Tribble's Sunday Department. He'd also pace the center aisle and veer off to talk to the reporters who were working on the day's big stories, or just to chat and keep up the morale.

Until Newby Noyes succeeded Ben McKelway as editor in chief, Charlie Seib had been the national editor; and because Bill Hill — who was close to useless, if you want to know the truth — was promoted to play at being managing editor even though he was altogether out of his league, it fell to Charlie to hold the daily news operation together.

So my first glimpse of Jo Anne Mark was through the door to Charlie Seib's office on the day he hired her, and I noted at the time that she was in that office probably longer than I'd ever seen anyone seated across from Charlie at his desk. Later that afternoon she went downstairs to see the nurse and get checked out, and took the typing test in the Personnel Department. She was a terrible typist — as I was witness to in the months we sat next to each other on the dictation bank. Downstairs, she filled out all the employment forms, and by the end of the day she was a copygirl in the Women's Department with a charter from the assistant managing editor that if all went well back there, she'd be on the training program before the end of the year.

When Jo Anne came back upstairs, Charlie Seib gave her a tour of the newsroom that, under normal circumstances, Phil Kelley or a senior copyboy would have been deputized to conduct. After Seib had rounded the perimeter with her and returned full circle to the neighborhood of his office, he brought her over to the dictation bank to explain what we did there and how essential the dictationists were to getting out an afternoon newspaper. Then he introduced me, saying he was sure I could be helpful if there was anything she needed to know about this part of the news operation, because I'd already been working in the newsroom for a few years. What registered with me was how bouncy and at ease and girlish and grown-up she seemed all at the same time, and that even though she wore glasses, she didn't look too studious. Up until then, I had been enjoying the whole show. But in my distraction I didn't catch her exact response; the heart of it was that she looked forward to asking me a lot of questions.

A few days later she came through the newsroom wearing a printer's apron on her way to the composing room to pick up page proofs,

351

and I swiveled my chair around to watch her go up the metal steps by the wire room. Later that afternoon, I went to the Women's Department to check on how she was doing — I hadn't been back there more than half a dozen times since I'd graduated from being a copyboy — and asked if she wanted to go to Harrigan's after work for a drink. She was still wearing the printer's apron and told me that Aloysius Baker himself had given it to her. I didn't burden her with a history of my dealings with him, but strangely enough, in union solidarity, he had gotten me to buy a twenty-dollar ticket to the D.C. Printers Ball of the Allied Printing Trades Council, which I had no intention of attending. At Harrigan's — where she ordered a Manhattan and I swilled beer — I asked her more questions than she did me, and I was not surprised to learn that she'd had something of a privileged upbringing. In fact, if she hadn't gotten hired by Charlie Seib, there was a job waiting for her in New York with *Mademoiselle* magazine, which somehow I connected with the fact that she had studied in both Paris and Strasbourg, which I had never heard of, in France.

Her father was the manager of a Jones & Laughlin steel plant outside Pittsburgh in Aliquippa, she told me, and he'd gotten a call just before her high school graduation from the editor of the local paper, the *Beaver Valley Times,* saying he intended to hire Jo Anne for the summer because he'd never met a girl who wanted a newspaper job so much. At Penn State, her mentor had been Gene Goodwin, the head of the Journalism Department, who had been a renowned reporter and assistant state editor at the *Star* — and greased her interview with Charlie Seib.

We were sitting on the long banquette across from the bar. Even though I had promised myself I wouldn't, I told her the story about what Al Baker had done when I touched the split page in hot type. It was past nine o'clock before I drove her to where she was staying in Georgetown. At the door I asked her if she wanted to go to the Printers Ball.

Jo Anne looked dreamy, all decked out in her fancy dress, when she answered the door of the tiny row house in Georgetown. She had to borrow the dress from her housemate Jane (her own clothes had not arrived from Pennsylvania yet). She shared the house with her Penn State sorority big sister and Jane Deegan, who was the secretary for Herblock, the great *Washington Post* political cartoonist, who also lived in Georgetown. Apparently, Jo Anne was sleeping in the kitchen.

There had to be at least five hundred people at the Printers Ball at the Shoreham Hotel — not just printers from the *Star* and the *Post* and the *Daily News,* but also from the Government Printing Office and jobbers all across town. We said hi to Al Baker, who (sad to say) greeted me as Alfalfa, and a few of the Linotype operators I knew from the composing room, but mostly Jo Anne and I kept to ourselves; she was hopeless at fast-dancing, at least the way Washington young people danced, which was okay because I was happy to dance close with her, though she was taller than me in high heels.

I also wanted to get away from the noise and talk some more with her, so we went to the Blue Room bar, and she had a Manhattan again. If we had been at Harrigan's I would have ordered a martini, but I didn't think I'd get served one in the Blue Room, because the legal age for consuming hard liquor was twenty-one; they didn't even ask Jo Anne for a driver's license. By now she was familiar with a lot of people in the newsroom, even though she'd been at the paper for just a couple weeks, and she wanted to know more about them — especially the women who were reporters on the local and national staffs. Already, she said, she wanted to get out of the Women's Department as fast as she could, though she liked a lot of the women who worked there — especially Sid Epstein's wife, Eleni, and most of the reporters. But she hated the idea of covering "society news," which was what the Women's Department specialized in. And she swore me to secrecy before confiding that almost every day, the editor of the section sent her next door to the liquor store — where most *Star* reporters cashed their biweekly paychecks — to buy a half pint of Teacher's scotch.

The only woman Jo Anne seemed to be interested in knowing more about in the department was Betty Beale, the paper's high-society reporter, whose column ran in more than one hundred newspapers across the country. I told her that, according to what I'd heard from one of the national political reporters, Betty Beale was having an affair with Adlai Stevenson, and that of all the people I'd ever had to take dictation from, she was maybe the most impatient and demanding. One time I had to stop her when she dictated — from an embassy party — that "the champagne flowed like wine." And Tom Dimond had told me that during the Korean War she had once written, "The real victims of the Korean War are the debutantes," though I couldn't find the actual story no matter how hard I looked for it in the clips.

We kept talking until the bar closed at two and never went back to the ballroom. When we got to Georgetown, at Jane Deegan's front door, I thought about how I wanted to kiss her goodnight, but not push things too much, and so I held her like when we'd been dancing and kissed her gently on the lips, and she kissed me back on both cheeks — which I guessed was something she had learned in France.

355

The next Sunday Jo Anne and I went to Dumbarton Oaks, which for somebody who had studied international economics at the Sorbonne she was not very knowledgeable about. We walked over from Jane's house. On the way, Jo Anne pointed out where Drew Pearson, the muckraking columnist, and Ted Kennedy, the president's youngest brother who now had JFK's old Senate seat, lived. Meanwhile, I explained about the Dumbarton Oaks conference, where the negotiations to establish the United Nations were held. But the real reason for us to visit there was for the flowers — Washington in springtime, I'd always thought, was about as beautiful a place as could be imagined, and nowhere was that truer than the acres of gardens and flower beds at Dumbarton Oaks.

Over the next few weeks the two of us must have done the whole outdoor tour of the great sites of the capital with me as the tour guide: the Tomb of the Unknown Soldier at Arlington Cemetery, the Lincoln Memorial, Theodore Roosevelt Island on the Potomac. We walked through Rock Creek Park and around the Ellipse and the White House. One Sunday I went with her to Mass at Trinity Church across from Georgetown University. Later, she told me her father was Catholic and her mother Presbyterian, and she was thinking

356

of leaving the Church to become an Episco-
palian. She also told me that even though she
was a virgin and intended to remain one until
she got married, she didn't like the Catholic
Church's teachings about sex.

That spring, I made a point of trying to
work as many ten-to-six shifts as possible, to
coincide with Jo Anne's hours in the Women's
Department. She became a regular part of
the lunchtime rush to Harrigan's, and usually we'd sit together. On our outings, it was
becoming clear to me how much she was
getting to appreciate the city and wanted to
know all its high and low aspects. I took her
down to police headquarters one night, and
I showed her the slums across the Anacostia,
the Cafritz estate on Foxhall Road, and all
around the Hill. With my yellow press pass, I
revealed the hidden parts of the Capitol, riding in the open subway car with the senators
and congressmen.

I could also tell by the questions Jo Anne
asked that she was going to be a first-rate
reporter — not the frilly stuff, but getting to
the heart of things, including my own history,
which she was too good at plucking out of
me in no time — the whole story, or at least
more of it than I'd ever told anyone else. She
asked me what I wanted to do as a newspaperman. I told her that, as a reporter, I wanted
to cover what was going on in civil rights. It
was the most important story in the country

and would be for a long time, I was sure. I identified with its importance for the nation. Jo Anne knew that I'd already been writing stories about the demonstrations in Maryland, and that I had gotten to know some of the students at Howard University who had gone south on the Freedom Rides.

She was envious that I'd gotten to do so many things at the *Star* already. She was penned up in the Women's Department, and they wouldn't even let her out at night to cover a citizens meeting. The biggest assignment she was looking forward to, she said, was a national day celebration at the Tunisian embassy. What she really wanted to be, she told me — and this is where Brenda Starr came in — was an investigative reporter, righting wrongs, though it wasn't clear to me how many wrongs she'd run across in the French countryside and Paris, or in the valleys of Pennsylvania.

Regarding my own ambition, I told her what I'd given a lot of thought to but had kept to myself: that if I was really successful and really lucky, someday I might become city editor of the *Star,* maybe by the time I was in my thirties. Or if that didn't work out, perhaps city editor of the *Post,* though I couldn't imagine working over there on L Street, for any number of reasons, which I would let her know later. I told her about how much I had learned watching Sid Epstein. I didn't say anything about his clothes, though that was probably part of the bargain in my vision. By now Sid Epstein had taken an interest in Jo Anne — he called her "kid" too, the only other person I'd heard him do that with. Eleni had filled him in about her being kind of an unrestrained character, certainly by the standards of the Women's Department.

I told Jo Anne that Sid Epstein had been only twenty-eight when he became city editor of the *Times-Herald,* and he was thirty-three when the *Star* put him in charge of its city coverage. I knew I didn't want to go to a paper in another city, not even the *New York Times,* though if I eventually became a national reporter for the *Times* or the *New York Herald Tribune* in Washington, it would be okay for a while; but I'd want to come back to being city editor in D.C. I was born and raised in Washington, and the way I looked at the place — as did Sid Epstein, too, I was sure — was based on my experience growing up in a city that was both a great world capital and a smallish town that was home. D.C. was unique, and I couldn't imagine there were many more cities in the world as interesting.

I also told her about a book I'd picked up from Ed Tribble's overstock a few months earlier. It wasn't too long, maybe 250 pages or so, but got at both the history and sights, plus the real life of the people of a city the way I looked

359

at Washington. After I'd read the book the first time, I went through it with a pencil and dog-eared the pages and even photocopied some of them back in the library. And I cleared out a whole file drawer in my room in Arlington for clippings and other books and pamphlets that related to an idea I was developing. The book was about Venice — a place I'd barely known existed except for some dim memory of Mr. Pioli in tenth grade rambling on about the Venetian Republic, which at the time had got me thinking about how Venetian blinds got their name and what that had to do with a great city. There was certainly nothing in the book I was reading that had anything to do with Venetian blinds.

The book was called simply *Venice* and had been written by James Morris, an Englishman who had published a previous book about the first expedition to conquer Mount Everest; he'd even gone along on the trek, up to twenty-two thousand feet. The idea taking shape in my mind was that as I worked my way up the reportorial ladder and then onto the city desk, I would also save string and write pages for a book of my own that would be a wholly different kind of volume about the capital of the United States: both a guide and a history, written for tourists and for the people who lived in the city and for anybody else who wanted to fathom the place. A lot of it would be about race. James Morris had divided his book into sections titled "The People," "The City," and "The Lagoon" — which I conjured in terms of "The Potomac." There was a ton in there about architecture and art, and a few weeks later I went with Jo Anne to the National Gallery of Art on Constitution Avenue, where she showed me some of the paintings by Venetian artists. It was a rainy day, and the marble of the National Gallery's exterior had turned a shade of pink, which was what always happened to the marble when it rained. In my book I'd write about how the Mellon Gallery turned pink in the rain, I told Jo Anne. The next day she brought me a piece of cake from the Tunisian embassy celebration.

One of the places that didn't get much attention in the usual guidebooks, and was known more to local people than to the transients of "Official Washington," was Hains Point at the tip of East Potomac Park, formed by the confluence of the Potomac and the Anacostia Rivers. I'd been going there since I was a toddler: first with my grandparents, to watch the speedboats on the Potomac, and then, after I'd gotten my English racer, I'd pedal around the park and visit the Jefferson Memorial and Tidal Basin across from the other end of the peninsula. The east bank of the park formed the Washington Channel — where Mark Baldwin had located his underwater city — and to the west, across the Potomac on the Virginia side, was National Airport. In high school, it had been an established part of the boys' curriculum at Montgomery Blair to drive to Hains Point with our dates to watch the submarine races at dusk. Very few of the girls fell for the joke.

It was a warm May evening when Jo Anne and I drove there, and I'd even told her about the joke when we parked by the willows across from the airport and watched the sun set. There was not a lot of room in my little Renault; it was smaller than the Chevy I'd had in high school. She was wearing a white blouse with a string of pearls. This time, when I turned to hold her and kissed her, there was no hesitation or kissing on the cheek. I'd say we went on holding and kissing and caressing and touching, and sometimes stopping to watch the planes land across the river while I stroked her hair, until it was almost pitch-dark outside. And I don't think we would have stopped until much later if it hadn't been for the park policeman who rapped with his flashlight on the window on my side of the car. He was very polite and said we were nice kids and there was no telling what could happen at night in the park, and we should move on. So we got ourselves together, and once he had left, we held each other again and kissed before I started the engine, and looked at each other kind of trembling. And except for the moment when Rudy Kauffmann had led me onto the newsroom floor, I had never been so sure about knowing where I wanted my life to go.

18

AMERICA

I'd never been west of West Virginia before, or south of North Carolina, or north of New York City. So in the summer of 1963, I set out to experience America in full, driving from coast to coast and then doubling back across Canada with my closest friend from Harvey Road, Stan Sitnick, in his off-white Chevrolet Corvair Coupe. Most nights, we would camp in national and state parks.

The idea had been hatched the previous winter, when it seemed fine. Now I was having second thoughts. I wasn't sure I'd like sleeping in a tent any more than I'd liked bunking in a trailer park. Besides, the trip meant two months away from the newsroom and two months away from Jo Anne.

An absurd amount of time had gone into planning our safari. We had calculated the route meticulously — mapping it out on spiral TripTik flip-cards supplied by the American Automobile Association. The expedition would cost a lot, partly because of the income

I'd be losing; the Newspaper Guild guaranteed that I got two weeks paid vacation a year, but that was it. We'd taken out the Corvair's backseat to make room for sleeping bags, camping gear, clothing, and lots of Chef Boyardee ravioli, plus my guitar. We had practiced pitching the tent in his parents' backyard.

The evening before we hit the road, President Kennedy went on television to announce — belatedly, for sure — that he would commit his presidency to passing the boldest civil rights legislation in history, putting an end to all legally sanctioned racial discrimination in America: in public accommodations, federal and state elections, public education, and employment opportunity. It had taken repeated, graphic acts of violence by state authorities and white citizens in the Deep South to get him to act. What at last moved him was a children's crusade by Black pupils in Birmingham, Alabama, and its unspeakably violent suppression. I had taken dictation from Haynes Johnson in Birmingham over the past ten days, and sometimes the screams of the little boys and girls — they were getting knocked down by the force of high-pressure water hoses — were so loud over the phone that I couldn't hear Haynes dictating, even though he was in a closed phone booth.

I was reminded of the pain of the Black children I'd held hands with at the sit-ins in downtown Washington when I was eight or nine years old. We'd spend the afternoon lunch hours sitting on swivel chairs at the counter and being refused service. Inevitably one of the Black children would have to go to the bathroom but, unlike the white children, wouldn't be allowed to use the one on the premises. Then a whole group of us would go running to the National Gallery of Art, five blocks away, but more often than not it would be too late by the time we got there, and the children would pee in their pants and cry, and sometimes their mothers and even their fathers would cry too. I'd never gotten the picture out of my head of those little children holding their legs together and the anguish in their faces.

"We are confronted primarily with a moral issue. It is as old as the scriptures and is as clear as the American Constitution," Kennedy said in his speech. Stan Sitnick and I were watching it at my parents' house in Silver Spring. The Corvair was in the driveway, awaiting our departure early the next morning.

An hour before the president spoke, two Black students were admitted to the University of Alabama under the federal protection of three thousand National Guardsmen.

At last there was a powerful ethical and historical dimension to Kennedy's words and action. His manner was somber and determined. The brevity of the thing — he spoke for barely

366

twelve minutes — added to its power. The speech felt spontaneous, not over-rehearsed. He seemed to speak from his heart and from some deep well of understanding. And despite the political risks for his 1964 reelection campaign, this was a personal assertion of principle about the country. January 1 had been the one hundredth anniversary of the Emancipation Proclamation. "This nation will not be free until all its citizens are free," he said.

A few hours after Stan and I drove off at sunrise, the news was on the radio that in Jackson, Mississippi, a civil rights leader — Medgar Evers, field secretary of the NAACP there, aged thirty-seven, a World War II veteran and graduate of a Black college who had applied for admission to the segregated University of Mississippi law school — had been shot to death in his own driveway a few hours after Kennedy's speech.

Making our way across the continent, we cooked our meals on a folding portable gas stove and read in our tent by the light of a Coleman oil lamp. We kept a diary of the trip, each of us writing alternating nights. Every morning, at the top of a page, we recorded the mileage on the Corvair's odometer.

June 18 — . . . passed through Gary, Indiana and couldn't see through the smoke from the steel mills.

Camping is fun, requires much work . . . midwestern newspapers are lousy.

Stayed in the Evanston, Illinois YMCA for $2.50, and saw an amazing number of dead fish floating in Lake Michigan.

In Chicago we stayed with friends. I went downtown and spent the day at the Old Town School of Folk Music — and bought a banjo.

In Milwaukee our log recorded sadly: "Brewery tours all closed, at Schlitz, Pabst, Blatz and all the rest. Tour book said they were open."

We crossed the Mississippi at La Crosse, Wisconsin, and the Missouri in South Dakota, where we ate buffalo burgers at the famous Wall Drugstore. In the log I noted, "All the S.D. towns are the same: one main street (usually dirt) off the main highway . . . street contains all the town's commercial facilities . . . groceries, a dumpy motel, a feed grain store, auto and farm equipment repair shop . . . and at the end of the block, railroad tracks and grain elevators . . . After supper we saw Mount Rushmore."

We climbed the Tetons in Wyoming and floated on our backs in the Great Salt Lake in Utah. In Las Vegas, the day after the Fourth of July, we stood in line for ten minutes at the Sahara Hotel and Casino to get a room "that rivals the Taj Mahal." In the room the phone rang and a sexy voice said, "Mr. Bernstein, the manager would like to buy you a drink." We had martinis. Our room cost twelve dollars a night. We dressed in our best khakis for the Folies Bergère Dinner Show at the Tropicana and I had a great run at the craps table. (My father, oddly enough, was a serious crap shooter.)

We crossed the desert to Palm Springs with a water bag on the Corvair's radiator and arrived in 115-degree heat. When we got to Los Angeles, we stayed with family friends. We took a tour of Hollywood, then rode in a double-decker bus past the homes of movie stars in Beverly Hills, and drove through Trousdale Estates, where Richard Nixon lived before he lost the governor's race to Pat Brown the year before and decamped for New York. Nixon had said he bought the house for thirty thousand dollars.

I wrote in the log: "There is not a home in that development that would go for less than $100 grand. Either Tricky Dick knew the assessor or he quoted his gardener's salary." Then we drove north to San Francisco, Portland, and Seattle, and headed to Canada.

The strangers we met in campgrounds were mostly wonderful, and often unforgettable. In Sequoia National Park, we gathered around the campfire for a guitar sing-along with, as I recorded in my log, "Bob, a 20-year-old marine who is very funny and after every girl in the park. He talks like Henry Miller writes. There's Linda, Bob's cousin, a very pretty 14-year-old who looks about 19. And Tom, a little 15-year-old who calls everyone Tarzan and really is a nice kid but also a pest. His brother is a 16-year-old punk with hair to his shoulders and a supply of liquor keeping cold in the river. All he ever says is, 'Gimme another weed, man,' And 'I'm going down to the river for awhile.' "

On the car radio, we listened — over and over — to songs from the new Bob Dylan album: "Blowin' in the Wind," "Girl from the North Country," "A Hard Rain's a-Gonna Fall," and "Don't Think Twice, It's All Right."

I was trying hard to absorb and enjoy everything. Day after day, we drove across enormous landscapes. I had never before had a sense of the breadth and ruggedness of the country, especially as we slogged on through the Dakotas and eastern Montana in the summer heat. This America was impressive and often spectacularly beautiful, but a little alien — my country, of course, but on a slightly different planet.

Being so far from Washington, I felt disconnected from what was happening in the news. While we bounced along the highways, President Kennedy traveled to Germany and raised the Cold War stakes in Berlin with his challenge to the Soviets, *Ich bin ein Berliner.* The Vietcong won a series of big battles in

South Vietnam. A new pope, Paul VI, succeeded the beloved John XXIII. Almost every day there seemed to be more violence in Alabama and Louisiana and Mississippi.

In each big city we reached, we headed to the American Express office to pick up mail and to a newsstand to buy the previous Sunday's *New York Times,* the only newspaper circulated nationally. I'd been at the *Star* for three years now, and I'd gotten used to looking out at the world from the window of a newsroom, and when I was really lucky, grabbing a notebook and going out to cover it myself.

In early August, with only two weeks left on our trip, I wrote Jo Anne a letter saying that, as excited as I was at what I was seeing and learning, I'd be glad to be back at the paper — and to see her. In Seattle, I called her from the American Express office after reading in the *Times* that Philip Graham, the publisher of the *Washington Post,* had committed suicide. Graham had been hospitalized for two months earlier in the year for a nervous breakdown, the *Times* reported. Jo Anne told me that the day after Graham's death, Jane Deegan had gotten married in a big ceremony at All Souls Unitarian Church to Bob Asher, a *Post* reporter whom I'd run across a couple of times covering fires with Walter Gold. Jo Anne said that most of the people at the wedding seemed to be in a state of shock.

371

■ ■ ■ ■

While we'd been on the road, a coalition of civil rights, religious, and union leaders had announced plans for a massive demonstration in Washington to take place on August 28: the March on Washington for Jobs and Freedom.

I slept in Silver Spring the night Stan and I got back from our trip — Friday, August 23. I'd scheduled my return to work for that Sunday, by which time we'd unloaded the camping gear and been debriefed near to exhaustion by our parents.

My whole family, including my grandmother, was gearing up for the march. I shared their excitement about a national mobilization to bring one hundred thousand citizens to Washington, whites and Blacks together, to demand equal rights and an end to the raging racial violence below the Mason-Dixon Line. Dr. Martin Luther King Jr. was going to speak. In the front line of the march would be Harry Belafonte, the leaders of every major civil rights organization, the bishops of the American Catholic Church, and the presidents of Jewish organizations, Protestant denominations, and the United Auto Workers. Tens of thousands of demonstrators were already converging on Washington by special trains and chartered buses. Bob Dylan, Marian Anderson, Joan Baez, Mahalia Jackson, and Peter, Paul and Mary were listed on the program to sing. Sally Sitnick, Stan's mother, whom I'd never considered to be remotely "political," told Stan she intended to march too, with Stan and his sister Rita.

I was relieved to get back home — to Arlington — on Saturday night. My housemates Dimond, Campbell, and Wurfel all had their assignments for covering the march. When I came into the living room with my suitcase, they were speculating about whether there would be violence. Fifteen thousand soldiers, including a thousand military policemen, were on standby in the suburbs; two thousand National Guardsmen would be riding in scout cars, manning patrol wagons, and walking beats alongside D.C. cops. If there was going to be violence, I said, it wouldn't be started by the marchers. Their leaders were all committed to nonviolence, which had given their movement its moral authority and was, in an odd way, their best protection. Any danger, I reckoned, would be from outsiders — KKK types without their robes — coming to D.C. George Lincoln Rockwell and his American Nazi Party were planning a "countermarch."

One thing was already certain. The march was going to be bigger than any previous protest or demonstration in the country's history, with at least twice as many protesters than the forty-three thousand Bonus Marchers who had come to Washington in the summer of 1932, toward the end of Herbert Hoover's administration, and camped on the Anacostia Flats. Estimates by the organizers kept growing. Nobody knew how many were coming. The Republican congressman from northern Virginia, a segregationist who sat on the House D.C. Committee and whose district included our house in Arlington, described the arriving "hordes" as an invasion — and in the interest of public safety he called for all nonessential government workers to be furloughed. For the first time since Prohibition, liquor stores in the District were ordered closed.

I was scheduled to work Sunday from noon to eight, usually the only dictation shift on Sundays. When I got to the newsroom, Jim Lee was already there, his headset draped around his neck. Half a dozen city and state-side reporters were at their desks, all of them working up stories about the march for the Monday paper. More surprising, Sid Epstein was at the desk in his little office. I had never known him to set foot in the newsroom on a Sunday.

I checked in with Jim. We were good friends, from playing music together every week or two: folk, bluegrass, and sometimes the blues, usually in trio with his wife, Carol, who could sing better than either of us. Dave Breasted and Tad Foote also played guitar, and sometimes there were five of us trying to stay in key.

Then I headed over to talk to Coit Hendley,

who was seated across from Sid Epstein's empty swivel chair on the opposite side of the city desk. Coit was the highest-ranking editor in the newsroom to be part of the regular gang who spent their lunchtimes and rush hours at Harrigan's. Over a drink, he would give me a boost and, in a confiding manner, critique something I'd written.

I wanted to spend a couple of hours catching up on the papers I'd missed, which was fine with Coit. But first he told me about his own experience as a teenager driving across the country just before the outbreak of World War II, from his home in South Carolina north to Chicago and then west on Route 66. He was twenty-one — only two years older than me — when he'd enlisted in the navy at the end of the trip.

Final editions of the *Star* from the current month were mounted full-sized atop one another and clamped together on a big chest-high table behind the hay baler. The table was slanted upward to ease turning the pages and reading on your feet. I started with that Sunday's paper and worked my way back to August 1, and then I went into the library, where monthly leather-bound volumes were kept. Kennedy and the Russians had finally reached an agreement on a limited atomic test ban treaty. The Supreme Court, in a unanimous decision, had declared that prayer in the public schools was unconstitutional — just as Madalyn Murray had demanded. In Indochina, the American-sponsored regime of Ngo Dinh Diem in South Vietnam seemed to be teetering, as tens of thousands of the country's Buddhist majority took to the streets in protest.

One story had dominated the front page for days: the birth on August 7 and death, from a respiratory weakness thirty-nine hours later, of President and Mrs. Kennedy's premature baby boy, Patrick Bouvier Kennedy.

Through the whole summer, Stan and I had heard radio reports tracking the civil rights protests in the Deep South. As we crossed the country, I'd been unaware of the intensity of the parallel struggle taking place in Maryland and Virginia, in every county adjacent to the District of Columbia. The fierce resistance to desegregation in Maryland and Virginia, from millions of citizens and even from some federal judges, was far uglier and more formidable than I'd imagined possible.

Nine years had passed since *Brown v. Board of Education*. Yet in Richmond the U.S. Court of Appeals for the Fourth Circuit had just ruled that Virginia could resume public subsidies to pupils attending private segregated schools like the whites-only "academies" of Prince Edward County that Ludy Werner had written about. Fifteen miles southeast of the U.S. Capitol, a sprawling new town in suburban Maryland had just started selling its first units; sales to Black home buyers were banned. The last dictation I'd taken before our trip was from John Barron in Cambridge, Maryland, on the Eastern Shore, reporting on the fury of racial violence there, not far from the Ocean City beaches where my Blair classmates and I had escaped (often on schooldays) as soon as the warm weather arrived. White citizens in Cambridge were using fists and clubs and baseball bats against civil rights protesters. Fifty percent of the city's population was Black, yet every aspect of life there — schools, housing, restaurants, public accommodations, the downtown department stores — was segregated. As was almost all of the Eastern Shore. While I was camping out west, the governor of Maryland had declared martial law across most of the shore counties, and National Guard troops had been dispatched to Cambridge to put down the white resistance. I'd told John Barron what Julius Hobson — who was among the organizers of the Cambridge demonstrations — had said to me when I'd first met him as a copyboy, covering the D.C. Federation of Civic Associations. We were standing with Stokely Carmichael and Walter Fauntroy, talking about the Route 40 sit-ins to integrate restaurants on the Maryland part of the highway, and about Cambridge. The power of Hobson's observation seemed to stun even Carmichael and

Fauntroy: *"Maryland is the South — not really a border state. But the Eastern Shore of Maryland is the Deep South — like Mississippi,"* he'd said.

My reading in the library was interrupted by a copyboy who told me that Sidney Epstein wanted to see me in his office. I was startled to see the city editor dressed as if he might saunter out of the building that afternoon and head straight for the track at Pimlico. I'd never seen him in the newsroom without a necktie, but this was something else again: off-white linen pants cinched with a lizard-skin belt, argyle socks descending into white leather loafers, and a paisley foulard triangle tucked at the neck into a powder-blue silk shirt with a distinct reflective sheen. So powerful was the impression that I recorded the details in a reporter's notebook the minute I got out of his office. I even drew a stick figure with each of the colorful elements labeled.

Sidney Epstein's desk and the identical one that butted against it were now overlaid with maps and papers, including a document that stretched a full five feet and looked like a rug runner made from a roll of teletype machine paper. The length of this scroll was covered with typing in two separate columns, with Sid Epstein's handwritten notes in between. His own name — *epstein,* in lower case — was typed like a reporter's "slug" at the upper left corner of the scroll. After that day, I never slugged my name at the top of a story with a capital *B*.

The rolled-out document was his battle plan for the *Star*'s reporting on the March on Washington. Reading upside down, I saw that "Assignments for March" was typed at the top. Newby Noyes had settled on Field Marshal Epstein to coordinate the paper's coverage. The city editor would command not only sixty or so reporters from the local staff, but also all of the national staff, from Garnett Horner at the White House to Bill Hines helping to write and update the lead story, and even reporters from the Sunday and Women's Departments. The left-hand column of the scroll listed almost a hundred reporters in alphabetical order with their assignments described in typed detail to the right. Handwritten at the bottom of the rug was, "Crosby Noyes, Rewrite." He'd flown in from Paris to be part of the coverage.

Sidney Epstein was explaining all this to me because the following morning, starting at six, he wanted me to sit at the city desk between him and Coit Hendley to help test the elaborate communications plan that had been laid out. Through contacts at the Chesapeake and Potomac Telephone Company, he had managed to get ten dedicated telephones installed on the Mall and the Ellipse between the Lincoln Memorial and the Capitol that *Star* reporters could use to dictate their stories. Phil Kelley's copyboys would do the test from the field, and during the actual march they would protect the phones from poachers. The *Washington Post* and the *New York Times* — morning newspapers both — didn't face the kind of logistical challenge that confronted the *Star*. Sid Epstein had also prevailed on the Park Police brass to allow seven *Star* radio cars inside the march area that, as of Tuesday, would be cordoned off to traffic. And he had convinced a deputy chief to do a reconnaissance dry run with him a couple of weeks earlier. Each car would have a driver borrowed from the Advertising Department and from one to three reporters assigned to it as a home base, so they could always be in contact with the desk. The cars would be carrying water and sandwiches — and helmets, in case of trouble.

A vexing piece of the puzzle was how to get the latest pictures from the march into each edition of the paper. Using runners on foot would be too time-consuming; they'd have to weave through the crowd and take film back to 225 Virginia Avenue, more than a mile away. The solution was a helicopter. Chic Yarbrough, the paper's aviation reporter, identified an open area between the Lincoln Memorial and the Potomac where the chopper could take off and land — and he'd fixed the arrangement with the Federal Aviation Administration. Motorcycle couriers would speed the film from designated spots just off the Mall to the makeshift helipad. The copter would fly to the *Star* building and hover over the roof, and Yarbrough would lower the cargo down by rope.

Yarbrough was a minor legend at the paper — a short, jaunty man who looked and talked like a test pilot and was ready for anything. (Like some other reporters, I discovered, he tended to take on the look of the people he covered — the way a State Department correspondent would start to dress and talk like a diplomat.) Yarbrough's most famous exploit in the sky turned into a kind of grim slapstick. Assigned the task a few years earlier of scattering the ashes of a beloved rewrite man over the Chesapeake Bay from his Piper Cub, he miscalculated a headwind, and the ashes blew back into the cockpit and covered his goggles and the plane's instruments and everything else. Yarbrough, flying blind, pushed the plane into a steep dive. It was as if the dead rewrite man wanted to take poor Chic with him. Yarbrough pulled up just in time.

Late that Sunday afternoon, after Sidney Epstein had departed for whatever occasion he had gotten himself dressed up for, I drifted to the back of the newsroom to chat with Clarence Hunter. He was the first Black reporter to be hired by the *Star,* the summer before.

Clarence had written most of the stories

about the lead-up to the march that I'd been reading back in the library, and his byline was on the page one account that Sunday. Despite his presence in the newsroom as a visible sign of progress, the *Star*'s ownership still seemed ambivalent — even schizophrenic — on the subject of race. I read an editorial from a couple weeks earlier that put the *Star* on record as opposing the March on Washington altogether. It urged its organizers to call the whole thing off and predicted that the march would lead to violence that would damage the city and the interests of its Black citizens for generations.

And yet the paper's first-rate coverage on race and civil rights — going back to Ludy Werner's work in Virginia, Haynes Johnson's "The Negro in Washington" series, the reporting from the Deep South of Paul Hope and John Barron and Cecil Holland, most of them white southerners — attested to the *Star*'s commitment to unbiased reporting. The separation of church and state — the wall between editorial columns and news coverage — was (in the view of the news staff) sacrosanct. Almost every aspect of our news coverage, we believed, was better balanced than the *Post*'s: the ideal was always to get as near to the truth as good reporting could take you, through persistence and listening and observing with an open mind, regardless of your own opinion. I was also learning about the importance of context, as opposed to stringing together mere facts. Disparate facts alone did not necessarily indicate a larger truth, Ludy Werner had lectured me. By now she had become my most assertive tutor, and there were evenings that we'd sit at Harrigan's together and talk about the meaning of reporting.

It was a complex subject, as well as part of a constant debate between reporters at the two papers. The *Post* seemed willing, especially in matters of local coverage of race, to bend the facts toward the liberal views of the paper's editorial page, and the opinions of its city editor, Ben Gilbert.

Until my family moved to Silver Spring, I spent many weekend sleepovers at the Gilbert home, because Ian Gilbert was one of my closest childhood friends. I was aware from a very young age of Ben Gilbert's exalted position in the town, not least because his car bore the desirable low D.C. license tag number 490. Also, it always amazed me when, around ten o'clock at night, a copy of the next morning's *Post* — the bulldog edition — would be dropped off on the Gilberts' front porch on Grant Road, a full eight hours before paperboys would deliver the *Post* to the doorsteps of other city residents. Ben and Maureen Gilbert had been close friends of my parents, too. I hadn't realized until I went to work at the *Star* and read through the files on Ben Gilbert that he'd become city editor of the *Post* at age twenty-seven. Most of the men in the *Post* newsroom had gone off to war, including the city editor, and Gilbert — who had a medical deferment — was put in the job. But the admirable fact remained that Ben Gilbert and the *Washington Post* had hired the paper's first Black reporter in 1952; and by the time of the March on Washington, the *Post* had five Black reporters.

I didn't know how or exactly when the *Star* finally decided to bring a Black reporter onto the staff — or even, in precise terms, why. The Washington Redskins were the last professional football franchise to integrate, and it was only under pressure from the Kennedy administration that it happened, just the year before. Washington's baseball team, the Senators, were also among the last to add a Black player to their roster — fully seven years after Jackie Robinson broke the color barrier. Even now, in 1963, the capital of the United States was still, in many respects, a segregated southern town.

About a year before Clarence Hunter came to the paper, we were joined on the dictation bank by a young man Sid Epstein had hired upon graduation from Columbia J-school. He'd gone to Howard University as an undergraduate and went on the training program that summer. He was going to be the *Star*'s first Black reporter. Then suddenly he was gone, before he'd had a byline in the paper

— though it was obvious to all of us that he had the talent to be a fine reporter. Coit Hendley later explained that our new colleague had been picked up on a morals charge by one of Roy Blick's undercover agents in a men's room downtown. Charlie Seib, the assistant managing editor, then began a search for a Black reporter whose experience was already established at a major paper. Clarence Hunter was thirty-six when he came to the *Star,* after extensive work as an associate editor at *Ebony* and *Jet* magazines and then as a reporter for the *Post-Tribune* in Gary, Indiana, where he'd been the first Black person on that paper's staff.

His front-page story that Sunday was focused on how many people would be participating in the march — a hundred thousand or more, its organizers predicted. City officials called that estimate "rather high."

Driving into the city at dawn on the day of the March, I took the Fourteenth Street Bridge from Arlington. A General Services Administration cop, when I showed him my *Star* ID, let me park inside the Department of Agriculture compound at Independence Avenue. From there it was a five-minute walk to the Washington Monument grounds, where two thousand or so people had already gathered as the sun rose over the Capitol. Thousands more were making their way along Constitution Avenue and the Mall. I tried to estimate the ratio of Blacks to whites — probably five to one, I scribbled in my notebook. I spoke to two white teenagers who had hitchhiked from New York and arrived at three in the morning. Most of the crowd here — and, almost everywhere, as I could see later on television — were well dressed. Many families came with small children, some in strollers. Often, the Black women looked as if they were dressed for church, in hats and fine dresses, and most of the men wore suit jackets and ties. By Washington standards, it was going to be a very pleasant summer day, with temperatures from the midsixties in the morning to the mideighties later in the afternoon. Many men wore straw hats, either wide-brimmed or porkpie.

What struck me most was the quiet determination of the people, their words and attitudes — expectant and fervent, but also at ease and even gentle. They projected an enormous moral dignity, as if everyone understood this to be the culmination of a drama that had been building for a long time. Many carried signs.

WE MARCH FOR INTEGRATED SCHOOLS

FREEDOM NOW

UAW SAYS JOBS AND FREEDOM FOR EVERY AMERICAN

BAPTIST MINISTERS CONFERENCE OF
WASHINGTON, D.C.

FREEDOM '63

WE DEMAND EQUAL RIGHTS NOW. WE
DEMAND DECENT HOUSING NOW.

JIM CROW MUST GO

WE SHALL OVERCOME

TRUTH SHALL SET US FREE

The elaborate planning for the March had been accomplished in only eight or nine weeks, though the root cause was centuries in the making. The primary organizers — Bayard Rustin, a champion of the civil rights movement since the 1930s, and A. Philip Randolph, president of the Brotherhood of Sleeping Car Porters union — had for decades envisioned a massive march on the capital for equal rights and economic opportunity for Black Americans. In the late 1940s, my father, as a leader of the government workers union, had been involved in discussions with Randolph for such an event. Propelled finally by the demonstrations and violence in the Deep South — and the one hundredth anniversary of the Emancipation Proclamation and President Kennedy's introduction of a sweeping civil rights bill — the organizers began contacting religious and labor leaders, celebrities from film and TV and music, and all the leadership of the civil rights movement, to make the march a reality.

At the cusp of rush hour, Independence Avenue was almost empty. Government workers weren't coming to work. When I arrived at the *Star*'s newsroom for my seven-thirty a.m. shift, three portable TV sets had been set up on the state, city, and national desks, with a fourth in Sidney Epstein's office. An expanded complement of six or seven rewrite men (and Harriet Griffiths) had been mustered, and additional deskmen pulled in to edit copy.

Charles Puffenbarger, the assistant city editor who I'd become closest to, gave me my assignment: Beginning around nine o'clock, Bill Hines would be stationed inside the Lincoln Memorial near the front steps that led to the Reflecting Pool. He would locate the *Star* phone installed inside the memorial and dictate copy or give notes as the crowds arrived and the focus of the march moved to the memorial. Because I was accustomed to taking dictation from Hines on Martha Angle's days off — and could manage his rapid-fire delivery from Cape Canaveral or Houston — I, along with Martha, would be handling him from the memorial all day, and also picking up anyone else dictating from the phone inside Lincoln's temple. Clarence Hunter and David Broder were assigned to stay with the march leaders through the day and might also be calling from the red phone across from Abraham Lincoln's feet.

Meanwhile, I wrote a memo with details from my visit to the Washington Monument grounds and handed it to Herman Schaden, who was putting together a sidebar that would get bigger through the day, of scenes from the crowds.

When I wasn't taking dictation, I watched the live television coverage. The network cameras at the West Front of the Capitol sighted down the Mall all the way to the Lincoln Memorial. The crowd had swelled exponentially in the couple of hours since I'd left the monument grounds. I now saw an ocean of people, moving like a wave down Constitution Avenue. They had begun marching on their own, ahead of schedule, while their leaders were inside the Capitol talking to members of Congress. For long moments on television, there was no commentary, only the music from the front of the line of march — "Down By the Riverside," "This Land Is Your Land," "Blowin' in the Wind," and "We Shall Overcome."

The next few hectic hours in the newsroom became intense, even bizarre. Chic Yarbrough's helicopter came and went, maybe fifty feet above us; the noise and wind of its blades rattled the windows. Jerry O'Leary, on rewrite, watched the TV screen and asked people around him to quiet down so he could type notes from what Walter Cronkite was saying. Blanche at her switchboard presided over a tangle of wires, connecting reporters to rewrite men. Myra MacPherson was on the line reporting about Charlton Heston and Bob Dylan and Joan Baez and Sammy Davis Jr. and the other celebrities Sidney Epstein had assigned her to keep track of. As the leaders of the march reached the Lincoln Memorial, David Broder kicked Bill Hines off the red phone with me just as Hines had been describing how women were sitting by the reflecting pool with their bare feet in the water while Mahalia Jackson led a choir of thousands singing "We Shall Not Be Moved." Ted Crown checked in from police headquarters to report that apprehension about violence was, thus far, misplaced. Earl Voss, who ordinarily covered the State Department, and John Barron were reporting on the American Nazis' "counterdemonstration," which the cops had kept marooned on the opposite side of the Lincoln Memorial. By three o'clock, Miriam Ottenberg at the Justice Department got word that Bobby Kennedy and the White House were gratified at how the day was progressing — that the multitudes of demonstrators, overwhelmingly Black, marching peacefully hand in hand with tens of thousands of white citizens, were making their cause felt. The symbol of the march, worn on the lapels and shirt pockets and dresses of tens of thousands

390

of the marchers, was a pin depicting a black hand and a white hand clasped together.

Dick Fryklund at the Pentagon command center reported that the troops on standby had nothing to do by the time Martin Luther King began speaking. Haynes Johnson, who was writing the main story with Crosby Noyes, stood in tears at the national desk as King spoke in his rolling, preacher's cadences. The cameras panned over the thousands upon thousands of rapt listeners.

The police now estimated the crowd at more than 175,000. At the close of the march, its leaders went to the White House to meet with President Kennedy. Their remarks, too, were covered live on television. A. Philip Randolph declared the march "a great American experience."

Sidney Epstein's coverage plan had gone like clockwork, and by the time the Red Streak Final edition came off the presses around five in the afternoon, its front page had chronicled the day in every column under a huge headline announcing 175,000 MARCH PEACEFULLY FOR RIGHTS. Looking around the newsroom, watching and listening as the event had developed on the TV screen, I thought it would be hard for almost any reporter not to be moved. Especially as the largest crowd ever assembled in one place in American history began singing "We Shall Overcome" in unison at the conclusion of the march.

Yet by the time I read through the Red Streak Final, it was clear to me that our entire front page communicated comparatively little of what had really happened. King's speech, replayed over and over on the newscasts, was not mentioned in the lead story, nor in Mary McGrory's accompanying column. He'd spoken too close to deadline, perhaps. And yet, astonishingly, King's speech was not mentioned in David Broder's front-page lead story for the next day's paper either. I remembered once reading that Lincoln's address at Gettysburg had been more or less ignored at the time.

There was something monumental about the power of television news, I was coming to realize. There were things that TV could do, the combined impact of pictures and sound, that newspapers couldn't. But there were also things that television could never do that newspapers could, given the time and editing and power and craft of the written word. But on this day it was television that had delivered.

Later that evening, I went to the back of the newsroom, where Haynes had returned to his own desk, after writing all day by the rim of the news desk. By then, the Park Police estimated the crowd at 250,000 people. The march, he said, was transformative. But he had not used that word in his copy. This day *might* change the course of American history, he said. His emphasis was on the conditional, but he was by nature, he said, an optimist about the country.

For me, listening to Dr. King's speech, with its emotive power, and witnessing the sheer numbers of Black and white people marching together, I was certain I had experienced the most powerful moment of my lifetime — the "someday" from "We Shall Overcome" was drawing nearer.

19

MONUMENTAL

The first week of September, Sid Epstein summoned me to his little matchbox office and told me he was making me city desk clerk, which was a very big deal. The next week I began — on academic probation — yet another semester at the University of Maryland, and promptly fell asleep in my first French class.

There was too much going on. I was working five eight-hour shifts a week on the dictation bank, days and evenings, plus going to class three days a week. Most nights Jo Anne and I saw each other, and often we had lunch together at Harrigan's and spent our days off together. Being a son of the labor movement, or so I imagined, I got myself bamboozled into serving on the Newspaper Guild negotiating committee, which was having unpleasant discussions with the *Star* management over a new contract for newsroom employees. The Noyeses and Kauffmanns seemed adamant that their newspaper would not be the first in America to pay journeyman reporters ten thousand dollars a year. The possibility of a strike around Christmastime looked more than plausible.

The position of city desk clerk carried considerable responsibility (and for someone nineteen years old an unusual measure of power) because the primary element of the job was to schedule, in extensive consultation with Sidney Epstein, all the city reporters' work shifts and vacation days for the upcoming week, and the same for the dictationists. Tom Dimond had been city desk clerk for more than two years when he was still going to school. But after he'd become a reporter nobody else had been able to do the job to Sid Epstein's satisfaction. Or so Sid Epstein said to me, and he was going goddamned crazy from it, which were his exact words; he expected me to straighten things out. He said Puffenbarger had thought I'd be right for the job — though Puff had never mentioned it to me.

Whoever was city desk clerk was also granted the title of chief dictationist, although I never quite understood what that meant, and neither did Tom Dimond — except that with the title came a fifteen-dollar raise and the prerogative of telling Blanche you were too busy to take dictation from Betty Beale or an obit from the stringer in Purcellville. There were stretches of several hours when I'd be sitting at the second desk in Sid Epstein's office trying to manufacture a coherent workweek for a staff of fifty reporters and more than a dozen dictationists, most of whom did not want to work nights or Sundays. And some of them needed Tuesdays off because it was their regular day for going to the beauty parlor. I spent more time at that big desk than Coit Hendley did. Each Thursday, after the final-edition deadline, I'd meet with Sid Epstein, and he'd go over the whole thing with me, which took an hour at least.

One bonus was that I got to make up Jo Anne's schedule. She had gone onto the dictation bank at the end of summer; I made sure that we had the same two days off every week. When she finally went on the training program that winter, I scheduled her for a couple of shifts working night police when Walter Gold was off. She said she wanted to get the whole experience of what went on in the city after dark. Sid Epstein got red in the face and told me that Jo Anne Mark might think she was Brenda Starr, but there was no way the city editor of the *Evening Star* could send a woman — much less a twenty-two-year-old woman — out at night chasing the cops around on a double homicide in the dicier parts of town.

People on the staff appealed to me for favors. I was amazed at how many of them had regular appointments with their dentists and doctors on Mondays or Fridays. Not to mention the unusual number of funerals they attended.

After a few afternoons sitting across from Sid Epstein in his office, it became apparent to me that I was now talking with him on a different level, though he still called me "kid." Sometimes he'd share his judgments about people on his staff. For instance, he'd say that X or Y ought to work a later shift because they were better and faster than Z during the afternoon deadline crunch; or, in the winter, that Z couldn't write a weather story worth a damn, which required a lot of prose in a hurry when a big snowstorm hit; or that because so-and-so often came back loaded from dinner at Harrigan's or Julie Hall's Seafood Restaurant at Buzzard's Point, we couldn't schedule that reporter from four to midnight.

He'd also give me glimpses of his journalistic and social accomplishments, at least the parts he liked to talk or even boast about, which was how he came to tell me about hiring Jackie Kennedy to be an inquiring photographer at the old *Times-Herald*.

Some friend of the publisher had arranged a job interview for her. She was twenty-two years old. He told me she'd wanted to be a reporter, but when he pointed out to her that she didn't have any experience, she said, "I'm also a photographer and used a Leica at the Sorbonne."

"I said, 'Kid, we don't have anything that

fancy. You'll use a Speed Graphic here'" is how he told the story to me. In fact, he needed a new inquiring photographer. "If you can learn how to use the Speed Graphic by tomorrow, I'll hire you." She did, and he hired her at twenty-five dollars a week. He also told me that when she asked to go on an extended summer vacation, he said no, but then she explained she'd been invited to the coronation of Queen Elizabeth, so he said okay — if she'd send him copies of her letters to her family and a pencil sketch back by airmail. And she did. By then he'd given her a daily column called "Inquiring Camera Girl by Jacqueline Bouvier." Back home, she became good at tracking down people of interest in the city, well-connected ones usually, and getting them to talk with unusual candor. "She had a knack," he said. "A real knack for getting to people, and then getting them to unburden themselves. She understood how to be a very good listener."

I wasn't quite sure what he expected me to learn from all this, since I most definitely wasn't heading for the Sorbonne, but I could see he was trying to convey something important that he thought I'd do well to understand about reporting. It was hardly what I'd had in mind when I asked him about Jackie Kennedy.

I was also a college student — again. And it was no surprise that the single course that held my interest was English Literature, because we were reading Charles Dickens. At the close of the last class before Thanksgiving vacation, I headed out the door pleased at the prospect of a week and a half off campus altogether.

And then I noticed a commotion in the hallway. Thirty or forty people were clustered around a portable radio. When I got closer, I heard Walter Cronkite's voice saying "There's been confusion but no panic," and something about the scene outside a hospital. My first thought was maybe there had been a terrible explosion at a hospital somewhere. Then Walter Cronkite said the president had been shot in the head during his motorcade in Dallas.

I started running to my car, which was more than a quarter mile away, at Student Parking Lot B. Still, I made it to the *Star* building in less than twenty minutes, speeding down the BW Parkway, past the National Arboretum on Kenilworth Avenue and through a couple of red lights just east of Capitol Hill. On the car radio, Cronkite was saying that the president's wounds appeared very serious, and that Governor John Connally of Texas, who was riding in the front seat of the presidential limousine, had also been severely wounded. I parked in the loading zone in front of the liquor store next to the *Star* building. Bobbie Hornig came running out the door with her reporter's notebook in her hand. "He's dead," she said. Her voice sounded hollow. "Jerry O'Leary got word from the CIA. He's dead."

It had not occurred to me that President Kennedy might actually die from whatever his wounds were, so impossible did that seem.

Upstairs, everybody in the newsroom seemed to be in motion, either typing or shouting or on the phone or taking notes by hand around a TV set that had been rolled out between the city and national desks. A dozen people were crowded into the wire room reading over one another's shoulders, teletype bells were going off, and all the dictationists were on their headsets. The newsroom was operating on the certainty that Kennedy was dead — O'Leary was on the phone and typing notes that Burt Hoffman, the deputy national editor, snatched out of his typewriter every couple sentences. Walter Cronkite was saying on the television that there was no definitive word yet on the president's condition. In the middle of this, Newby Noyes was conferring with Sid Epstein, John Cassady, Bill Hill, and Phil Price, the news editor. From my seat on the dictation bank, I was near enough to gather that a decision had been made to publish an "Extra": the next edition would not be the regular Night Final, but would announce in oversized type on the masthead — twice — "Extra." Burt Hoffman, who had returned to his seat on the rim side of the national desk and was on the telephone, hollered suddenly in my direction, *"Bernstein, take Broder from Dallas!"* I put on my headset as Blanche put the call through.

I was used to taking dictation from David Broder, and he was always pretty much unflappable, and polite and precise in his words. As he was now, though he said to me, "Ready?" And, as if he were taking a deep breath, then started dictating without a pause.

"Two priests announced outside Dallas Parkland Memorial Hospital at 1:32 p.m. today Central Standard Time, comma, quote, The president is dead. Period. End quote. Paragraph."

My hands were shaking, and I mistyped *Hospitol* without having time to correct it. Broder told me to get that graf to the desk right away, and then he picked up with the next. Even before I could holler *"Copy!"* I saw Phil Kelley himself crouched next to me, and I ripped the page from my typewriter and handed it to him.

After a few more sentences, Broder got off the phone in midparagraph and, from what I could infer, rushed back to the hospital entrance, where the White House deputy press secretary announced officially that the president had died at one o'clock Central time; Kennedy had been given the last rites by one of the priests. A few seconds later, the wire room bells went haywire with the report — a FLASH — that the president really was dead. Around the TV set on the city desk, there

401

was a sudden hush. I think it was then that Walter Cronkite said, "From Dallas, Texas, the Flash . . . President Kennedy died at 1 pm Central Standard, 2 o'clock Eastern Standard Time, some thirty-eight minutes ago." And, though I didn't see it, Jo Anne told me later he had taken off his glasses twice and put them back on again and struggled for a moment to keep his composure.

Right after I put down my headset from taking Broder's dictation, Puffenbarger called me over to the desk and told me to get to the Capitol as fast as I could. My mission was to find John McCormack, the Speaker of the House. It was unclear where Vice President Johnson, who had been in the presidential motorcade and was unhurt, was at this moment. But Johnson was now the president of the United States, and the Speaker was next in the line of succession to become president if anything happened to Johnson. No one knew if what had occurred in Dallas might be part of some kind of larger conspiracy, perhaps still ongoing, Puff said. That was one of the things Jerry O'Leary was working on.

I'd intended to drive my Renault to the Capitol's East Front parking area. Instead, I spotted someone getting out of a cab as I went running out of the *Star* building — and I jumped inside. Straightaway, I realized I had no idea where on the Hill the Speaker might be. In the Speaker's Rooms in the Capitol, just off the House floor? In his congressional office in one of the two House Office Buildings? (I didn't know which.) Perhaps he'd been escorted to some secure hiding place? I entered the House side of the Capitol Building and showed my *Star* ID to a couple of Capitol policemen inside the revolving door. They examined it closely this time. The first thing I noticed was the silence. Usually crowds of tourists and legislative assistants and members of Congress would be hurrying through the hallways in a clamor. The corridors were almost empty now, and the few people I saw talked in whispers, if it all. I headed for the press elevator and went up to the press gallery. Somebody there, I guessed, would know where the Speaker might be. The House page operating the elevator told me he'd heard that when the shooting of the president was first reported, the chief of the Capitol Police had ordered Speaker McCormack to crawl underneath his desk and take cover. But one of the aides in the gallery upstairs said this was an unfounded rumor that had raced around the Capitol in the first moments of shock. The Speaker had, in fact, been at lunch with two assistants in the members' dining room when two reporters informed him of the shooting. He had then taken his reserved elevator to approximately where I was standing in the press gallery to read the news bulletins on the tickers. When he read that last rites had been

403

given to the president, McCormack left immediately for his office in the Speaker's Rooms downstairs. The press aide didn't want to say anything else about how the Speaker had looked or reacted.

McCormack was old. Both JFK and McCormack were Boston Irish, but McCormack was about the same age as JFK's father. The previous November, the Speaker's nephew Eddie McCormack had run for JFK's old Senate seat against the president's youngest brother, Ted, and lost. Less than two hours had passed since I'd arrived in the newsroom from school: Jeremiah O'Leary Sr. was dictating from the other side of the Capitol that Ted Kennedy had been presiding over the Senate when a press liaison officer walked up to the dais and told him that his brother had been shot.

Now I went down a flight of stairs to the House floor level and got about as far as the Speaker's Lobby, where a formation of Secret Servicemen had been posted, blocking any access to the Speaker's Rooms. I took the elevator back upstairs and phoned the city desk. Puffenbarger told me to dictate my notes as fast as I could about everything I'd learned; there might still be time to make the Extra. Sam Eastman, whose regular beat was the District Building, was on his way to the Hill and would be writing a long piece about the Speaker and his subsequent movements for the next day's paper. As soon as I finished dictating, Puff said, I should head to the Pennsylvania Avenue side of the White House. Large crowds were gathering there and across the street in Lafayette Square. Myra MacPherson was already there.

I had to walk down Capitol Hill toward Pennsylvania Avenue to hail a cab. Policemen were now stationed around the Capitol parking areas and were letting very few cars in. I told the hack to drop me off at Treasury — on the Fifteenth Street side, so I could find a place on G Street or New York Avenue to buy a transistor radio. Just before I'd left the Capitol I'd crossed from the print-press section of the gallery to look at television for a few minutes, in the smaller area where the TV reporters had their desks. Air Force One had just left Love Field in Dallas with JFK's body and his widow aboard, bound for Andrews Air Force Base outside Washington. Before takeoff, Lyndon Johnson had been sworn in as president — on the plane, the reports said. There weren't many more details. Puff had told me that O'Leary was hearing there might have been an arrest in Dallas connected to the president's murder.

With my transistor radio playing in my pocket — I'd bought it in a souvenir shop for fifteen dollars — I made my way to the East Executive Avenue gate of the White House.

In the setting sun, the flag flying over the mansion was at half-staff; lights were on in the East Room. A crowd filled most of the sidewalk along Pennsylvania Avenue from the North Lawn fence to the curb. It was rush hour and traffic continued to stream by, though tens of thousands of people had already left their offices downtown and exited federal government buildings soon after the president's death had been announced. On the opposite side of Pennsylvania Avenue, in Lafayette Square, a hushed crowd was also gathering. I guessed there were about two thousand people on both sides of the avenue. They were of all ages and races. I felt awkward about interviewing them. The quiet — broken only by the sound of some portable radios — was conspicuous. At the White House fence, a few people took pictures. I again remembered my mother telling me that when FDR had died, she had brought me — a one-year-old — to this place as his body was carried on a caisson in a military procession from Union Station. On the radio, the network reporters were saying that Air Force One would arrive at Andrews about six o'clock. Already senior members of President Kennedy's staff and cabinet, and the congressional leadership — including Speaker McCormack — were waiting there.

I'd seen a circle of people gathered around a small portable TV near Andrew Jackson's statue in the center of the park, and as six o'clock approached I crossed the avenue to join them. Transfixed, I watched the black-and-white images of President Kennedy's casket being lowered from the hold of the plane by his closest comrades and colleagues. And then, behind the casket, the president's widow and brother, the attorney general, came into focus, holding one another's hands. Bobby Kennedy had boarded Air Force One as soon as it landed, unseen by the press.

Around me in the square, from the light of the portable TV, I could see that tears were streaming down the faces of many of those watching. Some sobbed.

As inconspicuously as I could, I started writing in my notebook. My *Star* ID dangled from the chain around my neck.

Then President Johnson addressed the nation, briefly and with grace. But the attention of those around me was on President Kennedy's widow, not the new president. This was real tragedy — sudden, irrevocable, and continuing in real time.

On the TV, the casket was placed in a gray navy ambulance-hearse, to be taken for an autopsy at Bethesda Naval Hospital; Jacqueline Kennedy and Robert F. Kennedy got into the hearse just afterward. People in the crowd were obviously planning to stay where they were, in front of the White House and in the square opposite, until Mrs. Kennedy and the casket arrived. I set out to find Myra MacPherson. She was talking to people in the crowd by the Northwest Gate, and to the White House policemen just inside. It had not occurred to me that Lyndon Johnson, the new president, would be coming by helicopter straight from Andrews to the White House; but Myra, who had a White House press pass and was keeping in touch with the desk from the *Star*'s cubicle in the pressroom, said she was heading for the South Lawn, where the presidential helicopter should be arriving in a few minutes.

As its lights came into view over the Ellipse and the roar of its rotors broke the silence, hundreds of people started running to get a view of its landing — and it was only then, listening to some in the crowd, that I understood that many of them thought Mrs. Kennedy might also be aboard and returning to the White House now. I was so far back behind the pack that it was impossible for me to see the new president, or anyone else, get out of the helicopter.

In the lull that followed I decided to phone the desk, and I headed across the park for the comfort of one of the Hay-Adams Hotel's old wooden telephone booths and its cushioned seat. Blanche put me through to Puffenbarger. He said to stay outside the White House through the night — that it was likely that President Kennedy's body, and presumably Jackie Kennedy as well, would be returning at some time in the morning. A television had been set up in the Hay-Adams lobby. Every chair and sofa was occupied, and some people were reading the Extra editions that both the *Star* and the *Post* had put on the streets. I managed to get a copy of the *Star*'s when someone finished reading it and could tell it was, in fact, a second replate Extra. A portrait of Kennedy, with the dates of his life below, was on the front page, framed by thick black rules; I saw there were a couple of paragraphs based on my notes about Speaker McCormack. Before heading back to Pennsylvania Avenue I went into the bar and ordered a bourbon on the rocks — something I wouldn't have done at any other time except at Harrigan's or Julie Hall's. But no one behind the bar wanted to check the age on my draft card on this night.

At about four thirty in the morning the gray ambulance-hearse, followed by several black limousines, arrived outside the Northwest Gate of the White House. By then rows of policemen were keeping the crowd from getting too close to the driveway. Pennsylvania Avenue had finally been closed to traffic altogether. Floodlights illuminated almost all of the North Lawn and the surrounding grounds. The North Portico doors of the Mansion were draped in black crepe. The procession seemed to part the crowd. All was silent. The side windows of the hearse were curtained, but through the back window I could see the flag covering the casket. At the portico the procession came to a halt and a battery of marines moved to the front. An honor guard lifted the casket and carried it inside. Behind it, the president's widow and his brother, who had been in the hearse, followed.

I got back to the newsroom about an hour later, drained. Phil Robbins, one of the assistant city editors, told me that Myra was writing from the White House pressroom and that I should do a long memo on what the scene had been like for additional details that would be folded into her story.

She wrote a great, moving piece for the Saturday paper. Later I heard that Sid Epstein was frustrated that Mary McGrory's story, about the arrival at Andrews, had run on page one, stripped across the bottom, and that Myra's was inside the A section. He was right: Myra's was better. But for the rest of the weekend, no print reporter came close to matching McGrory's perfect grasp of the story.

I went home to Arlington for a few hours' sleep and a change of clothes. When I returned to the newsroom at one o'clock in the afternoon, more people were there than I'd ever seen on a Saturday. In fact, more than I'd seen on any day. Usually, the Saturday paper was a thin, single-edition prelude to the fat Sunday edition, with a few pages of local, national, and foreign news, a couple of sports pages, and a two-page church section. On this day, there were more than fifteen pages of type and photographs conveying an extraordinary account — journalistic, historic, nearly novelistic in its wrenching details — of this shared national experience that had begun less than twenty-four hours earlier. Overnight, advertisers had converted their ad copy into black-bordered memorials to the president. Even the abbreviated sports section was almost all about the athleticism of JFK and the Kennedy clan. A revised Sunday edition — with the latest shattering news and pictures and outlines of preparations for the president's funeral — was taking shape upstairs in the composing room. Beneath its front-page headline (PRESIDENT JOHNSON TAKES OVER / KENNEDY LIES IN WHITE HOUSE) was a *Star* photographer's picture of the flag-draped coffin in the East Room. At the bottom of the page was an AP wirephoto of the new president taking the oath of office aboard Air Force One, the murdered president's widow at his side.

Late Saturday morning the First Lady and her children had attended a private Mass in the East Room. I took dictation throughout the day and into the evening, mostly from Jack Horner at the White House and Jerry

411

O'Leary, who had flown to Dallas by chartered plane Friday night and — through his closeness to the top of the FBI chain of command, I was sure — was learning a lot about Kennedy's suspected assassin, Lee Harvey Oswald. Though David Broder was already in Dallas and was a great political reporter, Sid Epstein had argued to Newby Noyes that the *Star* needed a reporter there who knew his way around cops and murders. Overnight, O'Leary had managed to spend some time with the Dallas police chief, who had shown him a snapshot of Oswald holding up copies of the Communist Party newspaper the *Daily Worker* and a Trotskyist paper. Oswald's fingerprints were on the suspected murder weapon, a rifle that had been traced to his purchase through a mail-order gun dealer.

From the White House, Horner dictated a series of inserts, his tone tremulous and his cadence more halting than I was accustomed to hearing as he tried to describe the transition of power and the new president's meetings with the cabinet and foreign leaders arriving in Washington. Ike and Truman had arrived to confer with Johnson and to pay their respects to Mrs. Kennedy. So many heads of state were coming that Earl Voss, the paper's senior diplomatic reporter, and Daisy Cleland from the Women's Department were both trying to keep track — in part through the State Department Office of Protocol — of the list of arrivals of dignitaries and were writing inserts and sidebars about the most prominent.

Jo Anne was working on this project with Daisy. I was able to get back there only a couple of times during the afternoon and late in the evening to spend a few minutes with her and catch up. When Walter Cronkite had announced to the nation that the president was dead, Jo Anne had asked for a moment of silence in the Women's Department and led her colleagues in reciting the Lord's Prayer. She'd been queasy — morbidly so for a couple hours after the shooting, she said — but now was okay and "cried out," as she put it. She was hoping the women's editor would assign her to the funeral procession or a spot outside at St. Matthew's Cathedral on Monday. It was evident that the funeral of President Kennedy would be attended by the most remarkable congregation of world leaders ever gathered together in one place.

Puff told me to come in Sunday morning around eleven o'clock. That way I'd be in the newsroom when the procession behind the president's casket departed the White House for the Capitol just after midday. Reading the lead story in the paper that morning, I knew something of what to expect. A flag-draped caisson, drawn by pairs of gray horses and followed by a riderless one, would carry the president's body from the White House to the Capitol, where he would lie in state until his funeral on Monday. Like the setting of the bier itself in the East Room and the black crepe draped over the North Portico, the procession and arrangements to lie in state in the great Rotunda of the Capitol were almost identical to what had taken place when Abraham Lincoln had been assassinated a century before. And the catafalque in the Rotunda was the one that had been used for Lincoln's casket. By the time I arrived at the *Star,* more than a quarter million people were lined up on Pennsylvania Avenue, according to the D.C. police chief, and tens of thousands more were converging on the Capitol from other avenues.

The newsroom was eerily empty. Because it was Sunday and the next deadline wouldn't hit until six the following morning — for a huge special Monday edition with several replates planned around the president's funeral and then his burial at Arlington Cemetery — there was no need for extra complements of dictationists and rewrite men until late afternoon. Plenty of time would be available for the reporters covering the procession and the ceremonies in the Rotunda to get back to the newsroom and write their stories and file their memos. Or, late in the day and into the morning, to dictate from the White House and the press galleries on the Hill or from police headquarters.

I settled in at the desk, near where Ludy

Werner would usually be sitting, to watch the preparations for the procession on television along with several deskmen and reporters who had rolled up chairs. Only NBC had been doing nonstop coverage since the shooting in Dallas, and the network was going back and forth between the White House and its anchors and other correspondents. There was some on-air discussion about the three speeches to be delivered in the Rotunda — by Senate Majority Leader Mike Mansfield, Chief Justice Warren, and Speaker McCormack. I wasn't paying much attention. Like much of the country, I was anticipating seeing live pictures of Mrs. Kennedy and the children. So when the image on the screen went from an anchorman to a correspondent in Dallas who was narrating the imminent transfer of Lee Harvey Oswald from one jail to another, I looked up and didn't quite understand what was happening in the pandemonium, even after the *pop-pop* of gunshots, until someone — Tom Petit of NBC, standing near Jerry O'Leary, as it turned out — hollered, "Oswald has been shot!"

The next few hours might as well have been broadcast from a distant planet, so strange was the juxtaposition of events. The TV coverage cut from Dallas to the North Portico with the widowed First Lady standing next to Caroline and John Jr. as the casket was carried in front of them, and then the muffled drumbeats as the procession began its journey past a quarter of a million mourners in a dismal rain falling over Washington. Then back to Dallas, where Oswald had been taken to the same emergency room at Parkland Hospital as the fatally wounded president two days before. And this, interspersed with information about the assassin of the assassin (as someone put it), a Dallas strip club owner named Jack Ruby. Then back to the Rotunda, where Senator Mansfield gave the most poetic of the day's eulogies. He described the man, his wife, their children, the nation, the moment of death, and how the First Lady had placed her wedding band in her husband's coffin. And after Mansfield had spoken, Jacqueline and Caroline Kennedy knelt by the casket and kissed it.

And then to the official announcement of Oswald's death in Dallas, ten feet from the hospital room in which Kennedy had died.

By nightfall, the line to view the president's body in the Rotunda was more than two miles long, despite the official schedule that called for the Rotunda to be closed at nine. The newsroom, so silent only hours before, was in a state of exhaustion and a kind of disciplined chaos, trying to deal with the murder of the president, and the murder of his murderer on the eve of his funeral, and the meaning of all that was happening.

The national desk got word that the Rotunda would remain open all night to accommodate the people waiting in line. There were some two hundred thousand of them. Puffenbarger told me to go to the end and talk to those who were still arriving in the cold and rain. The line now reached the D.C. Armory at the end of East Capitol Street and doubled back along Pennsylvania Avenue to Seventh Street. I joined it two blocks from where I'd watched the presidential limousine pass in the inaugural parade — with the new president and First Lady waving on their way to the White House.

At about nine o'clock, with lights flashing and motorcycles at the front, a limousine carrying Mrs. Kennedy and Robert F. Kennedy passed us at the end of the line on their way to visit the Rotunda again. An hour later, the president's mother went by in another limousine. By now, those in the line were ten abreast — talking quietly, listening to radios. Some were in wheelchairs, some dressed as if heading to church, others in overalls and soiled work clothes, many in military uniform, small children on the shoulders of their parents, teenagers in groups without their parents. A large number were Black. Soon after midnight — by which time we had moved only three blocks — I called the desk from a phone booth, and Phil Robbins told me to come back to the newsroom and

417

file a memo. It took me about an hour to write it.

Jo Anne had been moving between the Women's Department, writing inserts, and the newsroom, taking dictation. She and I went back to her house and — slumped together on the couch in the living room — talked about Kennedy. I hadn't realized until then how much I'd been consumed by the turbulence of covering the story; yet in other moments, I absorbed it with a kind of sadness I'd never experienced. The feeling wasn't grief, exactly, but a heartache beyond anything I'd known in my nineteen years, certainly since Buddy Holly's plane had gone down not five years before. But this was different — monumental. What was similar, however, was knowing that something that was part of the shared experience of Americans was gone and not coming back. I'd come to feel connected with the president and with what I saw as the goodness of his struggle. He was a much bigger part of my life than I'd thought. The loss now seemed deeply personal, even familial.

The last time I had seen President Kennedy in person had been in September, at his first press conference after the March on Washington. In the initial questions, a couple of reporters had tried to pin him down on Vietnam and what the mission of the sixteen thousand American troops he'd sent there really was. My seat was way at the rear of the auditorium, so I could see only the backs of the heads of the reporters during the exchange. I was surprised that senior members of the Washington press corps would be so aggressive toward a president. He'd pushed back, saying the United States wanted the war to be won against the Communists.

Then the subject switched to civil rights, and he seemed more thoughtful — as if after the march ("a great historical event," he declared it) he and much of the country had crossed over into new territory. He delivered something of a history lesson, going back to Lincoln, then citing Theodore Roosevelt, who (he said) had recognized the need for an America that was racially and socially and ethnically mixed. Kennedy's lesson was informed by historical nuance in a way that his perspective on Vietnam was not, I thought. I'd never considered him an idealist. But he left no doubt he thought it essential to lead the country through what he now called a "grueling" moral test on race. He expressed faith that southerners would respect the law during that test, though he said he recognized that most were opposed to integration.

Three days later, on the Sunday after the president's press conference, a bomb exploded at the Sixteenth Street Baptist Church in Birmingham, killing four little girls. Kennedy's professed faith — and Dr. King's dream — had seemed an awfully big stretch to me after that, and the country appeared heading into darkness. And now the president himself had been assassinated and lay in state at the other end of the Mall from Lincoln's temple.

I slept on the couch. We returned to the office before eight Monday morning. The cortege from the Capitol to the White House was to begin around ten thirty, followed by the procession to the funeral service at St. Matthew's. We each took dictation through the day, focused more (we noted later) on the television than on the typewriter keys and pages of copy. Jo Anne was in the Women's Department; I was in the newsroom. The images were indelible, both the pictures on the TV which all of America was watching and those formed by the *Star*'s reporters through our headsets. As the funeral procession reached Arlington Cemetery, almost all work in the newsroom ceased, and reporters from the Women's Department and Sports Department and Sunday Department gravitated to the newsroom, quiet as I'd never seen it. We all gathered around the TV sets. Cardinal Cushing prayed, in Latin and then in English, for the soul of "John Fitzgerald Kennedy, the thirty-fifth president of the United States." The reporters and dictationists and others who were still at their desks now stood, and the newsroom fell silent as Mrs. Kennedy was

420

presented with the flag that had covered his casket. The only sound I could hear was the playing of *Taps* and the din of the teletype machines in the wire room.

20

GROWING UP

Except for seeing Senator Lyndon Johnson inside Wagshal's fancy delicatessen when I was little, and riding my bike past his house in Spring Valley (where he slept the first night of his presidency), plus listening to No-Label Louie brag about him as a customer every time I tried on a suit jacket, my knowledge of the new president of the United States was limited.

Most of it came from reading the newspapers and listening to reporters talk about him — always in larger-than-life terms and often in clichés about him being the greatest majority leader and arm twister in the history of the United States Senate. Plus tales suggesting he could be uncouth, in various personal ways. But I'd never gone back to the library to read up on him in the clips, or asked serious questions of the people who'd covered him — until the assassination. And I'd done it then in large measure because of the Bobby Baker case.

Bobby Baker had been Johnson's "young

protégé," as he was referred to by the press, when LBJ was majority leader. After his mentor was elected vice president, Baker continued to wield outsized influence from his position as secretary of the Senate. He'd been forced to resign in August because of "alleged financial improprieties" and unwholesome conduct in the company of call girls and United States senators. *Life* magazine had done a solid series of exposés suggesting that Baker knew dark secrets about Lyndon Johnson's financial dealings (and other matters). A hush-hush investigative team at the *Star* — John Barron, Paul Hope, Cecil Holland, and occasionally Miriam Ottenberg at Bobby Kennedy's Justice Department — had been digging into the Baker-Johnson relationship for months. I'd tried to get Sid Epstein to tell me during one of our Thursday scheduling meetings whether the *Star* was about to break a big story about Baker and Johnson. "We'll see" was all he would say, but the way he tilted his head back and looked up at the ceiling was a pretty easy read. I'd also overheard Miss Ottenberg and the national editor discuss hints she was getting from Bobby Kennedy that the president might drop LBJ as his running mate in the 1964 election because of the Baker troubles.

On the first full day of Lyndon Johnson's presidency, Cecil Holland wrote an eight-column takeout about the life of the new president and the struggles he'd overcome as a young man and, later, as a seasoned politician. I knew Cecil more from the telephone than in person. Usually he was either in the Senate or on the road covering political campaigns. I liked taking his dictation. He was a fine storyteller with a low-country southern accent and a silky, conjuring voice that turned his dictation into real entertainment.

During a moment of relative quiet on November 23, after Cecil had finished writing his LBJ piece, I drifted to the back of the newsroom with a hopeful notion of finding out what he thought about Lyndon Johnson and what lay ahead for the country. This was another thing about being a dictationist: you could form relationships with the reporters you admired just from being on the phone, and then when you would see each other, there was enough of a bond that you could ask them pretty much anything you wanted to know or understand better. Cecil was high up on my list in that regard.

Cecil said that for most of Lyndon Johnson's political life, he had wanted to become president — and he'd come close, in 1960, when he'd lost the nomination to Kennedy. LBJ had the skill and the kind of determination and instincts about what was good for the country that should serve him and the nation well in this terrible moment — which was the way Cecil talked even when he wasn't dictating. Then I asked him where he thought the *Star*'s

Bobby Baker investigation would go now that Johnson was president. He didn't seem surprised that I knew about it. The Baker case was "the other side" of Lyndon Johnson, he said. There was a lot of disturbing information that had been developed by the *Star*'s investigative team over the past three or four months — really serious stuff — and he hoped it would see the light of day. But he wasn't at all sure that it would.

I never typed so much as I did in the next month. There was no letup. And a lot of overtime. It didn't matter that it was Thanksgiving — or how sad the country was in observing it. And then we were into Christmas season, which in ordinary times was slow and leisurely in the newsroom, but not this year.

Five or six intertwined story lines dominated the news day after day, on almost every page in the A section, and all through the local pages, even the women's section. I wrote a page one story about a group of nuns who sprinkled too much holy water on President Kennedy's grave and extinguished the Eternal Flame.

Probably twenty-five reporters were assigned to weightier stories, many about Jackie Kennedy and her children moving out of the White House and going to Georgetown; and the complicated, emotional transition from JFK's presidency to Lyndon Johnson's; plus who was staying and who was going, and whether Johnson would be faithful to Kennedy's civil rights priorities, and whether he would continue to expand the U.S. military role in Vietnam.

Jerry O'Leary was still in Dallas, and most days I took dictation from him, whether it was related to Oswald's years living in the Soviet Union or about bystanders in Dealey Plaza who claimed they heard too many shots fired from too many directions to have come from one gunman holed up in the Texas School Book Depository building. O'Leary had managed to find Oswald's widow and interview her. Within a week, the FBI had concluded that Oswald was the lone shooter.

To ensure confidence in the official investigation, President Johnson appointed Chief Justice Warren chairman of a commission to investigate every aspect of the assassination, including the possibility of foreign involvement in a plot to kill Kennedy. Dana Bullen, our Supreme Court reporter, told me that the chief justice had resisted taking the assignment, but Lyndon Johnson had twisted his arm, talking about the national interest. David Broder, meanwhile, had gone almost straight from Dallas back to covering the campaign for the Republican presidential nomination — which meant I took heaps of *his* dictation from the road as he jumped from Barry Goldwater's campaign to Nelson Rockefeller's and off to Maine, where Senator Margaret Chase Smith planned to announce her candidacy. She was a hero there — but not beloved by her own party in Washington because she had been the first Republican senator to condemn Senator Joseph McCarthy in public a decade earlier.

Aside from all that typing, I had to juggle the schedules of almost the whole local staff because of the special assignments Sid Epstein and Coit Hendley were inventing in the assassination's aftermath. Orr Kelly, who had been a six a.m. rewrite man, now had a full-time beat covering the political and aesthetic debate about a national cultural and performance center to be built on the Potomac riverbank at Watergate. It was going to be named after President Kennedy. I tried to promote my roommate Ken Campbell from covering police headquarters to the rewrite bank, but Sid Epstein said that somebody more experienced would have to fill Kelly's spot.

The tone of much of the coverage — nationwide and at the *Star* — was set almost in stone in the first week of December when Theodore H. White wrote an "Epilogue for Kennedy" in *Life* magazine. It also ran verbatim on the *Star*'s front page under the headline "For One Brief Shining Moment There Was Camelot." The piece was based on an interview Jackie Kennedy had granted seven days after Dallas.

427

In fact, her wedding ring hadn't been buried with the president in Arlington, she told White. In the emergency room in Dallas, she had taken the ring off and put it on her husband's finger. "Do you think it was right? Now I have nothing left," she'd asked Kenny O'Donnell, one of JFK's closest aides. Then at one o'clock the next morning at Bethesda Naval Hospital in Maryland, O'Donnell went back to the room where Kennedy's body lay, removed the ring, and returned it to Mrs. Kennedy.

Theodore White's piece wasn't long, maybe five hundred words or so, brief enough to run on the front page without a jump. Jacqueline Kennedy told him how at night, before she and the president went to sleep, he would play records on a phonograph in their bedroom. And the song he liked the most, from the Broadway musical about King Arthur and his knights, ended, "Don't let it be forgot, that once there was a spot, for one brief shining moment that was known as Camelot."

She (and White) wanted to make sure the point wasn't lost: there would be great presidents again, and the Johnsons had been wonderful to her, he quoted her as saying. "But there will never be another Camelot again."

I read and reread that piece. I was amazed that White could achieve such a powerful effect in so few words. The country had been overwhelmed by images of Jackie Kennedy's grief and bearing during the assassination weekend and through the procession and funeral and burial of the president at Arlington. But here, in type and not on television, was the magic of the written word. I especially admired this touch: that she kept twisting her wedding band as she talked to White.

Although I disliked the place, I had to admit that the University of Maryland was a good beat for a reporter. What I despised was not the university per se, but being a student. The university was a fine place in terms of its colonial architecture, the Dairy Bar, and a chance to sing "Maryland, My Maryland." And there were some great professors, if what you were interested in was great professors. In my whole time at the university I had gone to only one football game, and that was because I wanted to sit with Rita Sitnick, who'd said I could tag along with her and her friend Jane Magidson.

My freshman year, measured by academic credits, was stretching into three years, which is to say I was still a freshman at the time of President Kennedy's assassination, though I was on track to end the semester with the best grades I'd gotten yet.

I should admit here that the only reasons I stayed enrolled — or tried to, even in fits, what with my suspensions and reinstatements and academic probations and periodic dismissals and appeals of dismissals — were:

(1) To maintain my 2-S draft status with General Hershey's Selective Service people in order to avoid being conscripted into the U.S. Army.

(2) The memory of how emotional my father had become when he described how he'd scrimped and saved to put himself through Columbia University and then Columbia Law School by working on a loading dock across from Penn Station in New York. So it was obvious that my graduating from college was a big deal for him and my mother.

(3) Though Sid Epstein had never said it to me directly, I was developing the impression that I might never get to be a reporter at the Star unless I had a diploma. When I looked around the newsroom, there wasn't a single reporter who'd been hired after, say, the late 1950s who didn't have a college degree. Even in the Sports Department. And most of the young reporters going on the training program now had been recruited from Ivy League schools. Or, like Jo Anne with her junior year in France, they had some kind of academic asterisk in their

430

personnel file that Bill Hill, the managing editor, and maybe Charlie Seib too, believed made you a better prospect by having stewed in academe till you came out knowing about things that, to my mind, would be of no use whatsoever in a whole career in the newspaper business.

But a big generational change was occurring in the journalism trade. Editors wanted college graduates now. My view was that you might be better prepared by graduating from horticultural school than from Yale or Princeton. At least that way you could write the gardening column. So I figured it would not be wise to raise the subject with Sid Epstein, or even Puff or Coit or Mr. Porter, all of whom had a say in evaluating the work of the dictationists and deciding who went on the training program. Or fell off it, because some of the flashiest recruits had flunked out of the dictation bank after graduating cum laude somewhere in the Ivy League.

The idea percolating in my mind — though I never talked about it with anybody, not even Jo Anne — was to achieve a variation of what Tom Dimond himself had accomplished: get promoted to reporter while still going to school, say by the time I was twenty-one. Because at the rate I was going, I wouldn't graduate until 1970 or so.

Meantime, I exploited the university in my own way. By the time of the assassination, there were twenty or so good stories in my scrapbook about things happening at the school, including a recent split page feature, above the fold, about student cave explorers who went spelunking — which I had not enjoyed reporting because the cave into which I had crawled was damp, dark, claustrophobic, and populated by bats. I'd also gotten my second page one byline, on a piece about a retired government engineer inventing a new calendar to replace the faulty and inconsistent Gregorian mess that had been in use in America since the eighteenth century. His big idea was to make each month twenty-eight days long, with holidays distributed at the end of each month.

In January and February 1964, I produced a series of what might be regarded as investigative pieces. The stories were, in part, about the Christian chaplains of the university concluding that the on-campus fraternity system was promoting decidedly unchristian conduct.

The origins of my reporting on the chaplains went back a year, when I had done a feature for the Saturday church page about religious life not taking a backseat to football games and textbooks at Maryland. The evidence for this improbable idea was a survey claiming that one out of every three students who lived on campus attended Christian services each week, most of them at the University Chapel. It was the only story that I had ever done in which I was skeptical of the premise I advanced. But knowing that I might get a byline on the piece, I did nothing to urge the church page editor, Caspar Nannes, to kill the story or tell him I thought more reporting might be called for. The premise of the piece was preposterous: a big state university where students were as interested in religious practice as in football and grades.

A year later — in January 1964 — I got a call in the newsroom from the preacher I'd quoted at length in the piece, the Reverend Jesse Meyers, the Presbyterian chaplain, asking if I would meet with him in secret somewhere off the main campus. He said he had a very big story that reflected on the conduct of the president of the university, Dr. Wilson Elkins. I suggested the Dairy Bar. This would be the first of half a dozen "clandestine" meetings in the next month (he wore a jacket zipped above his religious collar) — all at the same location. On this occasion, Reverend Meyers told me that President Elkins was determined to undermine the traditional independence of the school's chaplains, who reported to their denominational leaders and not to the state university system. He said that a series of "authoritarian" actions by Elkins over the past year — some of which Meyers was reluctant to reveal, but promised he might later — were an affront to religious and academic freedom.

Elkins was intent on muzzling the chaplains because of a letter Meyers had written to the parents of incoming Presbyterian students warning about a fraternity-circulated "Code of a Frat Rat" that celebrated sexual promiscuity, heavy drinking, vulgarity, and bad study habits. The code's distribution, said Meyers, demonstrated the university's lax supervision of the fraternity system.

Elkins had responded that the chaplain's letter was irresponsible and conveyed a distorted picture of fraternity life at College Park. (However, I could tell you from my high school classmates who lived in the Tau Epsilon Phi house that Rev. Meyers had understated the reality.) Elkins announced he was recommending to the university Board of Regents that chaplains, like deans and professors, should be considered part of the administrative apparatus of the university, reporting ultimately to the Office of the President.

Within twenty-four hours of my first story on this dustup, the Catholic archbishop of Baltimore expressed his displeasure with Elkins's assertion of authority over priestly matters. Then the *Catholic Review* of Washington and Baltimore weighed in and went after Elkins for flouting the separation of church and state. This was followed by the American Civil

Liberties Union, which said that Elkins was guilty as well of violating the Constitution's guarantee of freedom of speech. The *Star* editorial page, too, took offense, observing that the fraternity system was not above reproach and expressing astonishment that Elkins and the university administration would go to such lengths to protect what Gould Lincoln or someone back there referred to as "a social anachronism."

I tried to keep a straight face through some of the thunderous denunciation, including proclamations by the Student Senate condemning Elkins for his "authoritarian" actions. Meyers's co-chaplains, meanwhile, told me that Elkins had tried to get the whole lot of them replaced by their respective synods and presbyteries and bishops with more malleable clergymen.

The controversy went on for a full two months, until Rev. Meyers resigned, but not before he and his brethren told me (and I reported) what Elkins most feared becoming known: that he had ordered the chaplains to withdraw an invitation to Martin Luther King Jr. to speak on campus and had told them they could not participate in the March on Washington.

I wondered if Elkins or someone on his staff had bothered to put two and two together about the reporter of these stories — my byline was on half a dozen of them, all on

435

page one or the split page — being a miscreant freshman who had previously been suspended at the university for excessive parking violations.

The Baltimore *Sun* had by now assigned a reporter to come down to College Park, and my stories — with my byline — were running on the state AP wire. Ludy Werner, in a memo to Sid Epstein and Bill Hill, suggested I might have the makings of an investigative reporter someday. Bill Hill agreed — once I'd finished school, he said.

Through all this, I'd been studying how Paul Hope, John Barron, and the rest were reporting on the Bobby Baker case. Their stories were running under six- and eight-column headlines on page one, to the fury of President Johnson, his press secretary, and his most senior White House staff. Hearings on Baker's financial machinations were scheduled on Capitol Hill, initiated by gleeful Republicans. On a congressional salary of $22,500 he had managed to amass a fortune in the millions, including ownership of the Carousel Hotel in Ocean City, Maryland, where those call girls and members of Congress were said to have partied.

When Hope and Barron won the Washington Newspaper Guild's Front Page Award for their stories, Sid Epstein sent me to cover the luncheon at the National Press Club at which they were honored. It gave me an excuse to ask them a lot more questions about investigative reporting.

I had my doubts about the notion that investigative reporters were different from other good reporters, except that some of them (though not Hope and Barron) acted at times as though they were looking to put notches on their belts. Miriam Ottenberg was accused of it, but — hard-boiled as she was — I thought she was more complicated than that. David Broder and Haynes Johnson, who were not regarded as "investigative reporters," seemed to me exemplary models of how to do the work.

I'd gotten it in my head that all good reporting was pretty much the same thing: the best version of the truth you could come up with. It wasn't just stringing together disparate facts, an approach that could actually undermine the truth (witness my story on religion versus football at the University of Maryland), but it was also about finding a way to put context into a story.

There was another thing I'd noticed about the best reporters at the *Star:* they didn't get fooled by conventional wisdom. I knew enough from talking to them — and from my own limited experience — that they were constantly surprised by where the facts took them. After doing the reporting, rarely did a story fit with their first assumptions of where it would lead.

Jo Anne was fascinated — more than I was, for sure — by this business of investigative reporting. It was part of her identification with Brenda Starr. She got the idea of going undercover as a teenage resident at D.C. Junior Village, a notorious city-run compound for orphaned, abandoned, neglected, and abused children sent there by the courts and the District of Columbia Welfare Department.

It wasn't that she would be undercover as far as the staff of Junior Village was concerned — the Welfare Department had consented to the arrangement — but to the children she'd be living with, disguised as a seventeen-year-old. I drove her there with her bags in the early morning on Lincoln's birthday. She wasn't wearing makeup and her hair was in pigtails. The previous night, we'd been up late because we'd gone to watch the Beatles arrive at the British embassy after their show at Uline arena — their first concert appearance in the United States. A crowd of hundreds of screaming teenagers was kept behind barricades by police on the other side of Massachusetts Avenue. Our press credentials got us just inside the embassy gates with a scrum of photographers. John, Paul, George, and Ringo were in a playful mood as the windows in the back of the Rolls-Royce limousine were lowered and we got a glimpse of them waving to

438

the crowd. I was surprised at myself. Fandom went against what I regarded as my detached reportorial nature. But Jo Anne's enthusiasm was contagious, and I was relieved on this occasion not to take myself so seriously.

The next night, at the end of her first shift at Junior Village, she called me at the house in Arlington. Everything she'd heard and read about Junior Village understated how awful the conditions truly were: nine hundred needy children jammed together in a space intended for three hundred, many of them with obvious mental and physical disabilities, and woefully few counselors struggling to maintain a semblance of order.

A few nights later she called and told me she was scared. Some of the children kept scissors under their pillows; bloody fights broke out daily. Troublemakers were sent to the infirmary and came back heavily sedated. Her "cottage" — one of a dozen, organized by age, from six months to eighteen years — was adjacent to a fetid dump and a sewage treatment plant. Many of the children had been ripped from living at home with their mothers because of what was known as the "man-in-the-house" rule: it had been promulgated by Senator Robert Byrd of West Virginia, who was chairman of the subcommittee that presided over the city's budget and the Welfare Department. Under the rule, investigators were sent to welfare recipients' homes, often at night; if a man was found to be living or visiting there, aid to dependent children was almost immediately revoked and, under court order, the children were sent to Junior Village or foster care. By coincidence, I had covered a hearing in which a D.C. Superior Court judge had ordered the Welfare Department not to cut off aid to a family with nine children because the father of several came to visit them regularly in their apartment. Contradicting other court decisions, he called the Byrd rule "inhumane."

Jo Anne intended to spend two weeks at Junior Village. On the eleventh or twelfth day she phoned and said, "I don't want to be here anymore. Come get me." She'd seen more than enough to write the story. Above all else, the suffering of the children was unbearable. And she said that for the first time she was having doubts about wanting to be Brenda Starr.

Jo Anne and I were in a celebratory mood that Saturday night, February 29, not least because the first part of her Junior Village series had run on the first Metro page that day, and the experience was at last behind her. As usual, a post-deadline party had been put together — at Puff's house that week — attended by most of the local staff and others meandering in after their shifts ended for the Sunday paper's first-edition deadline. We were also celebrating, belatedly, my twentieth birthday, which had occurred on Valentine's Day, when she was at Junior Village.

By now, Jo Anne and I had become something like inseparable, though there had been a period in the summer, while I was on my cross-country trip, when her old boyfriend from Penn State had gone to work at WMAL as a radio producer and had seen her a bit. This had unnerved me, and I was happy when I learned that he'd gotten another radio job out west and was gone.

As usual, there was a lot of drinking — including, on this occasion, some birthday toasts. Because Jo Anne and I hadn't seen each other much for a couple of weeks, we spent a lot of time pressed in a corner by ourselves, talking. Somebody near us — I don't know who — mentioned that it was Sadie Hawkins Day, February 29, a reference that passed by me altogether. I had never heard of Sadie Hawkins Day. I had been a regular reader of comic books since I'd gone to sleepaway summer camp for two weeks at age nine — *Superman, Archie, Betty and Veronica, Batman and Robin* — and continued to read a good number of comic strips in the *Post* and the *Star* — *Dick Tracy, Popeye, Dennis the Menace,* and, for the past year without missing a day, *Brenda Starr.* But I had never taken to *Li'l Abner.* Dogpatch had no appeal to me. I didn't quite get the joke, the sensibility of the whole enterprise.

Jo Anne explained to me that Sadie Hawkins Day was ordinarily in mid-November; on that day, all the single women in Dogpatch proposed marriage to the men. When she was at Penn State there were annual Sadie Hawkins Day dances, huge affairs where the women asked the men to dance. But the really special Sadie Hawkins Day was in a leap year, when it was observed on February 29.

I said that that was interesting.

"Well, what do you think — will you marry me?" Jo Anne said, and she said it with an Ozark twang meant to be from Dogpatch, which made it sound like, *"Wail, wutteryew think — Wull you murry me?"*

Which I considered for a moment and said, "Sure." I told her, dead serious, that nothing would make me happier than us being married and that I hoped she felt the same. She said she did. And maybe we had another drink in there somewhere while this was going on.

Then I told Jo Anne that we could probably get married by midnight if we got in my car and drove straight to Elkton, Maryland, which was less than two hours away. Elkton was famous for its wedding chapels, with no waiting period needed to get a marriage license, and round-the-clock weddings. She had never heard of the place; I'd known about it for years. A lot of movie stars and big entertainers had gotten married there; it was sort of an East Coast Las Vegas in that regard, where couples up and down the Eastern Seaboard went to get married in a hurry without any frills. When I mentioned that Rock Hudson and Doris Day had gone off to Elkton to get married in a movie called *Lover Come Back,* it rang a bell.

Elkton was a tiny town on the Elk River that flowed into the Chesapeake a couple of miles downstream, with a population of less than two thousand. In the first half of the twentieth century, weddings there had become the basis of a thriving local economy. You paid your money for the license, a justice of the peace or a minister married you with a witness, there was another charge for the ceremony, and — from start to finish maybe forty-five minutes after arriving in town — you were man and wife. There were horse-drawn buggies to rent for the newlyweds to celebrate. Billie Holiday and Willie Mays and Martha Raye and Debbie Reynolds were among those who'd gotten married there, I'd read. In "Marry-land — the Free State."

"Okay, let's go," Jo Anne said.

I said, "I'll get our coats — I'm really serious about doing this, are you?" — and reminded her, "You're the one who asked."

She looked straight at me and nodded her head and said yes. I kissed her and said let's go.

It was cold outside, even for February, and the heater in the Renault took even longer than usual to warm up the car. I held her hand on the gearshift as we headed on the Beltway for the Baltimore-Washington Parkway. It was about ninety miles to Elkton — maybe an hour and a quarter ride if we made good time.

As we passed College Park, I slowed down and said, "If you have any doubts, let's turn around now. Because I'm really sure — are you?"

She said yes. We had also brought some whiskey in a cup to keep warm.

By the time we reached Baltimore, we were speculating about what Puffenbarger would say the next day when we got back and told him we were married. We didn't discuss the question of where we might live. A honeymoon was out of the question, since we both had to be back at work on Monday.

I was absolutely calm and steady — and at the same time, maybe more excited than I could ever remember being — and just hoping with all my might that we would go through with this and not change our minds at the last minute. I knew there was no chance I would change mine.

We checked to see how much money we had between us — maybe seventy-five dollars; I was relieved — because I had no idea how much the marriage license would cost, or the fee for the justice of the peace. We would also need to stay somewhere on our wedding night. I wasn't about to raise the question again about going through with this. Instead I said how happy I was that she had known all about Sadie Hawkins and *Li'l Abner* and how lucky we were to be on our way to Dogpatch. She agreed, as we drove through the night, and I accelerated to get us there faster.

I had never actually been to Elkton — the town itself was a mile or two off Route 40, which we were barreling down, the storied cross-country highway that began in California and ended in Atlantic City and connected with the New Jersey Turnpike to New York.

We talked about what a weird state Maryland was. Slot machines, quickie weddings, Wesorts, Vincent Godfrey Burns — the poet laureate of anticommunist pentameter of my childhood. I told her all about Ebenezer Cooke, the virgin poet laureate of Maryland and his other profession as a tobacco "factor" for Lord Baltimore himself. When we passed a sign that said ENTERING CECIL COUNTY, of which Elkton was the county seat, I explained that people hereabouts pronounced it *Sissal,* as had the seventeenth-century English colonists who first settled the Delaware-Maryland-Virginia peninsula between the great bays — the Chesapeake and the Delaware. And that my history class that semester convened in Taliaferro Hall, named after an old Maryland family dispersed over the centuries through the bay counties — and still pronounced *Toliver.* I wondered — aloud

— whether the justice of the peace would pronounce us man and wife in the "Del-Mar-Va" accent that prevailed in these parts.

We crossed over the Elk River and headed to Main Street, passing a couple of "wedding chapels" with signs saying MINISTER, MARRIAGE LICENSE, but they looked dark at this hour. In fact, except for three or four motels with neon signs, and an almost empty diner, the whole town looked shut down. There were two or three more wedding chapels — one of them a big stone house with Gothic windows and a sign — dark — that said CHAPEL. Maybe we had to wait till morning to get married, Jo Anne said. Perhaps they were finished for the night, for some reason.

After one more drive around some backstreets, I stopped the car at a motel that called itself a motor court and Jo Anne waited in the car. I went inside and asked the desk clerk where we could go to get married. He explained, matter-of-factly, that the marriage law had been changed by the state legislature in Annapolis and that a forty-eight-hour waiting period was now required. We could still get our license in the morning and be married by Tuesday. He said this happened all the time — people from up and down the Eastern Seaboard still showed up to get married on the spot and had to kill time in town for two days or come back after forty-eight hours for the ceremony.

This was not the news I'd hoped to hear — it felt crushing, in fact — and I asked him for a room for the night. I had never before stayed in a roadside motel, nor had Jo Anne, but the place was cozy and had knotty pine walls and calico pillows. It was the first time we had slept together in the same bed, after discussing our options.

We were also out of liquor. And, in the morning — hungover, she more than me, it appeared, because she was not usually a big drinker — we considered our situation in a different light. I was — more than Jo Anne perhaps, I wasn't sure — sad beyond depth. As if some momentous life-changing opportunity had passed. She was sad too, she said. But it was her opinion that we needed to do a lot more thinking before we made any decisions about being married. And we had to be back at work the next morning.

The drive back was through rain and fog, and we, tender and awkward, though we laughed some about the experience, debated whether to tell Puffenbarger. No one else, that was for sure.

Before taking Jo Anne back to her place in Georgetown, we stopped at Hofberg's delicatessen on the D.C.–Silver Spring line and ate bagels and lox and cream cheese. I went across the street to Mousie's newsstand — where Ben Stein and I, in our early teens, had bought copies of the Sunday *New York Times* to stuff in the Hofberg's bags and deliver with our neighbors' smoked fish. I was now altogether finished being a teenager — by two weeks. On this day, I bought the *Star,* the *Times,* and the *Post* and brought them back to our table.

I presented Jo Anne the *Star* and pulled out the comics section from the *Post.* I went straight to *Li'l Abner* to see what had happened in Dogpatch the day after Sadie Hawkins Day.

She passed me back the *Star* split page. Above the fold was a story about Leap Year's Day and women asking men to marry them, with the headline IT'S ALL OVER, GIRLS; LEAP DAY IS GONE BUT TRADITIONAL ARGUMENTS REMAIN.

21

CIVIL RIGHTS

The day after Jo Anne and I got back from
Elkton, Coit Hendley hollered to me to pick
up a call from the deputy superintendent of
Walter Reed Army Hospital with information
about General Douglas MacArthur being
rushed to the hospital and admitted there.
Hendley told me to stay with the story. A week
or so later, the deputy superintendent told me
that the general's condition was weakening
and should be considered "serious." His liver
was failing. The *Star*'s medical writer was enlisted for additional details. Try as I might, I
couldn't restrain myself from including refer-
ences to MacArthur's famous words — "old
soldiers never die, they just fade away" — in
my updates. The general was "fading into
a coma," I reported near the end of March;
family members were at his bedside. And,
in the final hours, "The life of Gen. Douglas MacArthur is slowly but steadily fading
away."

There was more dictation than all of us

could handle during March and April, owing to the political calendar, and because of developments in Vietnam. Secretary McNamara had gone to Saigon and said the United States would never leave until there was victory over the Communists. At the very same time, the president had launched his war on poverty in America. To accommodate this news crunch, the dictation bank needed to be expanded by at least three or four new people, who came on board that spring. Which freed me up when anti-civil-rights demonstrations in Maryland turned violent after the governor signed the first law south of the Mason-Dixon Line guaranteeing Black citizens the same access as whites to all public accommodations, including restaurants, hotels, public bathrooms, and the waiting rooms of bus and train stations.

Mr. Porter told me to commandeer one of the *Star* radio cars and drive to Cambridge on the Eastern Shore.

My instructions were to hook up with Jim Rowland, the Maryland statehouse reporter, and help him with whatever he needed. The National Guard was firing tear gas when I got to Cambridge after dark, and it took me two hours to find Rowland. By then I had a notebook full of repellent details about the scene behind the white demonstrators' side of the line — which I had been unable to cross because of the troops. One reason the whites had attacked Black protesters marching through downtown Cambridge was that they'd been incited by Governor George Wallace of Alabama, who was running for president of the United States and had decided the way to show serious appeal to voters outside the Deep South was to enter the Democratic presidential primary in Maryland. He had announced he would come to Cambridge, whose Black citizens had led much of the Maryland civil rights movement and the fight for equality in public accommodations. Now they were back in the streets to demand that Wallace stay out of Cambridge.

Over the next couple of weeks, Mr. Porter sent me to several Wallace rallies — usually to help Rowland, but sometimes on my own if it was a smaller event. Wallace was careful to avoid outright hateful speech about Black people. He talked instead about "outside agitators" and "pointy-headed college professors," but such phrases were enough to set off bursts of racist epithets from the audience.

Wallace's crowds became huge, and the polls showed him gaining strength in the primary. He was out to prove there was an ingrained aversion to racial integration among northerners as well as southerners. It was the first time I'd seen a demagogue inflame the emotions of American citizens who I'd thought were familiar to me.

On May 12, Jo Anne and I went to the

University of Maryland to watch Wallace deliver his last big speech before the primary. She said she wanted to see for herself what I'd described. I got press credentials from the Wallace campaign for both of us — though I wasn't working that night. The night before, Wallace had shown up at a rally in Cambridge. Hundreds of National Guardsmen, with fixed bayonets and firing tear gas canisters, had stopped Black demonstrators marching to disrupt his appearance.

Jo Anne and I arrived on campus in the late afternoon to hear Senator Daniel Brewster of Maryland speak first, from the steps of the university library to a crowd of several thousand students. Brewster was President Johnson's stand-in on the state primary ballot. The event was sponsored by the campus chaplains — who had managed to elude the governance of the university administration after the stories I had written for the *Star*. As the crowd sang "We Shall Overcome," several hundred students led by a flag bearer waving the Confederate battle flag emerged over a hill from the south, shouting *"We want Wallace!"* and screaming denunciations of Senator Brewster. A solid line of state troopers separated them from the upcoming main event while Brewster urged that Governor Wallace be accorded a courteous welcome. I was dumbstruck by the senator's refusal to answer Wallace with any fire of his own.

Instead, he seemed content to attack Wallace merely for "misrepresenting" the contents of the landmark civil rights bill — initiated by President Kennedy and embraced and expanded by President Johnson — that, all year, had divided the Congress and the country.

Our press credentials allowed us to enter Cole Field House through the locker room door used by the Terps basketball team. Governor Wallace, guarded by dozens of state troopers, was forced to delay his speech for about ten minutes after he arrived because of the volume and persistence of an unrestrained crowd of more than ten thousand, which seemed divided almost evenly between supporters and detractors. Hoots, whistles, and rebel yells bounced from the rafters. Jo Anne was unnerved by the ferocity. I'd seen Wallace enough times by now to recognize his pugilistic stance at the podium. He'd been an amateur boxer. The disdain of his detractors added drama to his performances. If the crowd would "just shut up and listen," he hollered back at them, maybe they'd be converted. "Go to the back of the bus," thousands in the field house were chanting. "Don't have a heart attack over there," he shouted back.

When the bedlam subsided, he repeated his boilerplate speech about federal encroachments on states' rights and his opposition to the civil rights bill, saying it would mean death to labor unions and private property.

He promised that Maryland would deliver him a much more convincing moral victory than the 33 percent of the Indiana vote he'd won. In Wisconsin, the first state in which he'd competed, he said, he'd shaken the eye teeth of the liberals by getting almost a third of the vote — but in Maryland those eye teeth were going to fall out.

Jo Anne was amazed at how polished and respectable his message was on the surface, even while his followers responded to the emotions boiling beneath it. There was not a hostile word per se against Black people or his famous mantra, "Segregation today, segregation tomorrow, segregation forever." He made it sound as if all this was a lofty discussion of constitutional principle.

On primary election night a week later, I worked in the newsroom. Mr. Porter had assigned me to stay on an open telephone line with the Associated Press headquarters in Baltimore. As precinct-by-precinct returns reached the AP from around the state, they were dictated to me and I passed them on to Paul Hope, who was already writing B-copy for the main story in the next day's paper. By eleven o'clock it was evident that Wallace would make a mighty showing. He was on his way to capturing at least 40 percent of the vote, including a clear majority of the white vote in the state. Most of the white neighborhoods of Baltimore were supporting Wallace.

I'd also been helping Hope with some inserts about Maryland history. Though it fought with the Union, Maryland remained a slaveholding state until almost the end of the Civil War. In the library I had found an old article from the Baltimore *Sun:* on the day of the emancipation of Maryland's slaves in 1864, almost exactly one hundred years before, the Baltimore City Council had ordered a celebration with bells ringing, flags displayed through the city, and the firing of five hundred guns to observe the "deliverance" of its Black people.

Around one in the morning, John Barron phoned the desk from Wallace headquarters in Baltimore County. He had spent almost the whole evening by the candidate's side, somehow gaining Wallace's confidence. Apparently, Barron was the only reporter to have heard virtually everything Wallace said while the votes were coming in. Final tallies showed Wallace winning 43 percent of the statewide vote. Mr. Porter told me to take Barron's dictation. It was an astonishing story, in which Barron himself figured as "a reporter who had been present" and had listened keenly as Wallace analyzed incoming returns.

If it hadn't been for "the nigger vote," said Wallace, he would have won the primary outright. And, even more spectacular, he would have carried a majority of voters in the whole state had this been a general election in which

Republican votes were added to his total. He slammed the "incompetent press" that had failed to recognize his appeal, and all the institutions and prominent individuals who had written him off — the Church, the unions, Ted Kennedy, and every other Democratic senator from the North.

I hadn't seen a classroom for three months. I'd stopped going to school altogether back in February and March — after Elkton and the chaplains' stories. I would get my grades for the semester — all F's, for sure — and a formal notice of academic dismissal from the university in a few weeks, I knew. I was already calculating how long it would be before General Hershey's people got notified and changed my 2-S college deferment status to 1-A: eligible to be drafted at any time for two years' active duty in the U.S. Army. I did not tell Jo Anne any of this — in fact, we hardly ever talked about my being a student, even when she was on campus with me for the Wallace event.

That spring, she'd met my parents — and my grandparents and my great-aunt Rose and great-uncle Itzel, plus my sisters, Mary and Laura, and family friends. I'd brought Jo Anne to Harvey Road for the family Passover Seder, an observance that celebrated the ancient liberation of the Jews from slavery in Egypt, and, for my family, the prospect that soon, in our time, the descendants of American slaves from Africa would likewise be truly free. At some point during the reading of the Haggadah, my grandmother noticed a ring Jo Anne was wearing on her left hand, and after dessert took her aside to ask if it was an engagement ring from me. I was grateful for the uncharacteristic discretion shown by my grandmother in at least stepping away from the table. Jo Anne told me later there had also been a pretty funny conversation driven by my grandmother's skills as an interrogator. This was another thing about Jo Anne: I had never known a girl so unintimidated by any kind of situation, no matter how difficult or awkward by other people's measure. She could also charm her way through any thicket, often clearing obstacles with her booming laugh. I could see how taken by her my grandmother was — a woman capable of finding fault in almost anyone. And Jo Anne and my mother seemed as comfortable as if they'd known each other for years. As we left my parents' house that day, I was astonished to find that my mother had given Jo Anne her copy of Simone de Beauvoir's *The Second Sex.* The hilarious but indecipherable implications of the gift set off another booming laugh from Jo Anne.

A few days after the Maryland primary, Jo Anne, Charlie Puffenbarger, and I were at

Harrigan's sharing a pitcher of beer in the outdoor "garden," the fenced-in courtyard where Phil Trupp still sat in with his old band some nights. Puff told me to bring my scrapbook in to the office the next day. Every so often, he would review the dictationists' work. He said to include everything to date.

Looking at the scrapbook that night in Arlington, I saw that since Easter I'd written or legged a lot more page one and split page stories than I'd thought. Probably three-quarters of them were about race and civil rights. In April, I'd reported on the refusal by the Episcopal bishop of Washington to allow the burial of a Black parishioner in Oak Hill Cemetery on the edge of Georgetown — until public pressure changed the bishop's mind. Then Ludy Werner dispatched me to ceremonies observing the one hundredth anniversary of the Battle of Spotsylvania County Courthouse, near Fredericksburg, where Grant and Lee's forces — 150,000 soldiers in all — had fought the third-bloodiest battle of the Civil War, with more than 30,000 casualties on both sides. Lee's second-in-command at Fredericksburg was General A. P. Hill, the ancestor of my childhood friend Powell Hill. I'd seen old daguerreotypes and documents handed down in the family about the battle. And a few days after I'd been in Spotsylvania County, I'd revisited my (and Powell's) elementary school to do a story on the tenth anniversary of *Brown v. Board of Education* and *Bolling v. Sharpe.*

Several recent clips were about the D.C. Democratic primary campaign: come November, the citizens of Washington were going to vote for president for the first time in American history. I'd gotten some good information from a new source: the daughter of F. Scott Fitzgerald, Scottie Lanahan. She was the co-chair of the city's Democratic Committee.

I was more interested in doing a story about Scottie and her family than about the Democratic primary. Her father and her mother — the flamboyant Zelda Fitzgerald — were buried in a cemetery not far from the Montgomery County courthouse in Rockville. The convolutions of how they came to rest there were considerable. Scott Fitzgerald's full name was Francis Scott Key Fitzgerald, after his ancestor who had written "The Star-Spangled Banner." And the novelist's father was born and buried in Rockville. The Fitzgerald family cemetery plot was in the old St. Mary's Catholic cemetery there. But because F. Scott Fitzgerald was a notorious drunk and hadn't received the sacraments in decades before his death, he was denied a place in that consecrated ground. Instead, he (and, later, Zelda) ended up a mile down the road in the Anglican cemetery, which agreed to take them in.

Scottie told me the story of how she'd come down from Vassar College for her father's burial.

When I met with Sid Epstein to do the scheduling for the last week of May, my scrapbook was on his desk. Janet Kolton, the paper's chief obituary reporter, who was responsible for preparing long obits on prominent figures whose demise appeared imminent, was pregnant and would be taking the summer and part of the fall off. I asked who we should schedule to take her place.

"You," said Sid Epstein.

He'd gone through my clips, he said, and they were good. It was Puff's idea. I would be taking Janet Kolton's place as a full-fledged reporter on the city staff, until she came back and I returned to school in the fall. I'd be making eighty-eight dollars a week — Guild scale for a first-year reporter, a thirty-dollar raise from my salary as chief dictationist and city desk clerk. Assuming I did all right, I'd keep the increased salary when I went back on the dictation bank. And during the summer, I'd still do all the city reporters' scheduling with Sid Epstein.

He handed me back my scrapbook. I was dumbfounded. I was now an actual reporter for the *Evening Star.*

I went back to my desk and phoned my mother with the news, and told her to tell my father as soon as he got home from work.

460

■ ■ ■ ■

As the historic civil rights bill headed toward a final vote in the first days of summer, the headlines in the *Star* and newspapers across the country were about the disappearance in Mississippi of three civil rights workers: James Chaney, Michael Schwerner, and Andrew Goodman. Coit Hendley dispatched me to National Airport, where Schwerner's wife was arriving from New York. She'd gotten an appointment with President Johnson — to pressure him to order more federal assistance in the search for her husband and his companions. Coit instructed me to stick with her all day. He handed me a schedule from the office of her congressman, who was coordinating the arrangements for her visit.

The first thing I noted at the airport was how tiny she was, and how young — not much older than me, I guessed. I was the only reporter there, but the congressman said she would not say anything to the press until after her meeting with the president later in the day.

In the congressman's reception room, I asked one of his legislative assistants if he could get me a full biography of Mrs. Schwerner — and that I'd be very appreciative if he could find out her height and weight.

After almost an hour or so, the door to the congressman's private office opened and he

461

and another assistant walked Mrs. Schwerner out. They were now heading to the Justice Department to meet with Deputy Attorney General Nicholas Katzenbach. The congressman instructed one of his secretaries to call over to Justice to clear me for admission as well. On the way out I was handed a typewritten biography of her — with a handwritten note at the top. She was five feet tall and weighed ninety-five pounds, it said. I was curious how they'd gotten the information. As we walked down the long hallway, she looked purposeful and sad-eyed, but not unsteady or dazed. She was twenty-two years old.

Before hailing a cab to the Justice Department, I found a telephone booth at the House Office Building entrance and called Coit. At the airport I'd been with Tom Hoy, a *Star* photographer whose twin brother, Frank, was a photographer at the *Post*. A couple of times, on police stories, I'd been on the scene when both were covering the same event. They were called the Hoy Boys. I told Coit he should send a photographer to the Justice Department — and that somebody should try to find out if Bobby Kennedy had engineered the visit with Katzenbach, his deputy. It made sense that Kennedy was putting pressure on the president to meet with Mrs. Schwerner and force more action to find her husband and his two colleagues. She had worked in Mississippi too, that spring, registering Black

462

citizens to vote. On the day the three had disappeared, Andrew Goodman had written a note to his parents about how friendly the residents of Meridian, Mississippi, were. The three had last been seen alive in Meridian. Michael Schwerner had called the other two that week to come to Mississippi to help investigate the burning of a Black church in a neighboring town. There had been a multitude of church burnings in the Deep South that spring.

John Barron was in Meridian, writing the lead story about their disappearance and the search there. Three hundred college students, most of them white and from the North, had arrived to live in the homes of Black Mississippians, helping them register to vote and joining their protests against the state's Jim Crow laws.

I told Coit Hendley that depending what time the meeting at the Justice Department concluded, I would try to dictate for the final edition. Around three, Mrs. Schwerner's meeting with Katzenbach ended, and she stood next to him in an anteroom to answer questions from the press. He towered above her as Tom Hoy snapped pictures. There were a dozen or so reporters present now, most of whose beat was the Justice Department. A year before, Katzenbach, accompanied by federal marshals and the Alabama National Guard, had pushed past Governor George

463

Wallace "standing in the school house door" to accompany two Black students to register for classes and desegregate the University of Alabama. Now Katzenbach said Mrs. Schwerner would take a few questions before she left for the White House and, after that, a formal press conference at SNCC — the Student Nonviolent Coordinating Committee — headquarters near Howard University. She had one message: the government wasn't doing enough to search for the three missing civil rights workers. Their burned-out car had been found on Tuesday, June 23, six days earlier. Only a couple hundred military personnel from a nearby naval base were searching the swampy, wooded backcountry. She had been there Friday and was dismayed at the response, she said.

A reporter from one of the wire services asked her if she thought the men were dead. I was incredulous. Would I have asked that question? I didn't think so. "I'd rather not say," she answered.

There was a pressroom on another floor and I called the city desk. I read the quotes back to Coit Hendley. I had only a few minutes to dictate, I said, before Mrs. Schwerner and the congressman headed to the White House. I was hoping Hendley would tell me to go there. Instead, he said I should hold off on a story for the final and come back to the office after her press conference at SNCC to write an overnight that would cover everything.

He also said that I should go straight to SNCC headquarters rather than the White House. Jack Horner could file a memo about whatever took place there, and I would use it in my story. I was disappointed. I didn't know what I expected to see at the White House — maybe the president, though that seemed unlikely. Since my copyboy days, I'd been there a dozen times running some errand or other. I'd never gotten much closer to the Oval Office than the pressroom — or the South Lawn once, to see JFK arrive by helicopter. But just walking on the grounds or entering the pressroom, and sometimes being allowed to wander a few feet into the West Wing, where the president's top aides worked, was a powerful experience. There was never a time on those visits that I didn't feel amazement, or awe, or something like that, looking at the pictures on the walls, and knowing the history made in the house, and that the Oval Office was only a few yards away.

I knew SNCC's headquarters from when I'd first met Stokely Carmichael in 1961. At the time, he'd been organizing the Route 40 Freedom Ride protests in Maryland. I'd last seen him in Cambridge — he was one of the principal leaders of the demonstrations there — and he was now in Mississippi, organizing.

Coit Hendley had finished for the day when

465

I called from a phone booth near the SNCC office. Emerson Beauchamp, the night city editor, filled me in on what had happened at the White House: Mrs. Schwerner had met for five minutes with the president; George Reedy, the presidential press secretary, then told reporters that Johnson had also conferred with J. Edgar Hoover and that the search perimeter in Mississippi would be expanded. Reedy said nothing about increased government manpower.

Hoover was no friend of the civil rights movement. I knew enough about his mindset of late — in part from Sid Epstein and Jerry O'Leary, who was in frequent contact with Deke DeLoach — that at almost every turn until recently Hoover had resisted getting the FBI involved in meaningful investigation of attacks on civil rights workers. In fact, Miriam Ottenberg and O'Leary had said Hoover's priority for years was to investigate supposed Communist influence in the civil rights movement, not to assist it in any way.

TV cameras and batteries of microphones were set up in the SNCC office when Mrs. Schwerner arrived in the sweltering Washington summer heat. Twenty-five or thirty reporters crowded into a small room with folding chairs. She sat behind a small table, looking exhausted and forlorn. I made a note that she folded her hands for a moment, and touched her wedding ring.

466

She spoke softly, almost inaudibly. I was seated in the front row and could hear her and see her clearly. From the first question, she was unequivocal about the inadequacy of President Johnson's response and that of the whole federal government. She was un-intimidated by the president of the United States. "Very disappointing," she said of the five minutes they spent together. She had found President Johnson "evasive." Two hundred military people on the ground in Mississippi were not nearly enough. She was unfamiliar with the protocols of Washington, she said. Rather, she described herself as a woman looking for her husband. She told the president that five thousand more searchers — federal marshals, FBI agents, soldiers — were needed. But without expla-nation, he'd said nowhere near that number could be sent.

I looked around the room and could see that some of the reporters were having trouble with their emotions. It was hard to take notes without tears.

She was pleading — and she used that word — for all Americans of good conscience to come to Mississippi and organize search par-ties to do the job the government couldn't or wasn't willing to do.

I thought about how young she was — and that she was heroic.

There was no way to look at Rita Schwerner,

and weigh the facts on the ground in Washington and Mississippi, and not feel a personal identification with her and the rightness of what was being fought for at this moment in history. It leaped out at you and transcended the particulars of the scribblings in your notebook. It was tangible. And that was being reflected in the stories filed from the South by the *Star*'s reporters and in other newspapers. The old fifty-fifty, down-the-middle, half-on-one-side-half-on-the-other approach was giving way to real reporting that was closer to the truth. Because, for all the right reasons, the truth was not neutral.

The desk had given me only sixteen column inches to work with. It took me about three hours of struggling to write my story. I didn't want a single false note in there.

In the last two grafs of the story, Rita Schwerner had expressed an awful truth.

Mrs. Schwerner said her experience "has left me wondering just how long it will take" before violence ceases to be part of the struggle for Negro rights.

"I thought when those little girls were killed in Birmingham that that would be the end," she said. "And I thought that Medgar Evers would be the end and I thought and I thought and I thought. But now I think that when people in this country decide they want it to be the end it will be the end."

■■■■

Three days after I'd covered Rita Schwerner's visit to Washington, the momentous Civil Rights Act of 1964 — the most consequential such legislation since Reconstruction — at last passed both houses of Congress. In Mississippi, more Black churches were being burned. The disappearance of Chaney, Schwerner, and Goodman — and the gathering concern and outrage in response — had been the final impetus for the bill's passage. Live television from the East Room of the White House that evening carried President Johnson's signing of the legislation. He used seventy-five pens, handing the first one to Martin Luther King Jr. and the rest to other civil rights leaders and to congressional leaders of both parties who had shepherded its difficult passage.

That afternoon I wrote a bylined story for the front page of the next day's paper reporting that the District of Columbia commissioners would issue orders within two weeks banning racial discrimination in Washington barbershops, many of which continued to refuse to cut Black people's hair. The commissioners had delayed acting until there was a national civil rights act to back them up. Now, in law at least, Black citizens could no longer be denied access or service in any public accommodations in the United States

— restaurants, hotels, theaters, buses, parks, sports arenas, swimming pools, and all federally funded programs. Likewise, discrimination by race, religion, sex, or national origin in hiring and promotion was outlawed.

I'd phoned the D.C. head of the Master Barbers and Beauticians of America union for a comment. White barbers, he said, weren't qualified to cut a Black person's hair. He said that the commissioners would now be held responsible for the quality of "Negro haircuts" once the regulations were adopted. I'd also called the Reverend Walter Fauntroy. In the three years since I'd met him with Julius Hobson and Stokely Carmichael, Fauntroy had become an invaluable source. As Dr. King's deputy and the Washington director of the Southern Christian Leadership Conference, he was in the East Room that evening. He told me that the success or failure of the Civil Rights Act would depend in large measure on the rigor with which the Justice Department and the president immediately enforced its provisions. This was not the first time Black Americans had won such rights, he noted.

During Reconstruction, a civil rights law passed by Congress in 1875 had similarly guaranteed Blacks equal access to public facilities, including hotels, theaters, transportation, and eating places. That law had also made it a crime for anyone to facilitate the denial of accommodations or services on the basis of "colour [or] race." Then, eight years later, the Supreme Court declared the act unconstitutional.

Within days of passage of the new rights law, Fauntroy's admonition looked prescient. I wrote another front-page story at the end of the week, ordered up on deadline by Ludy Werner, about four white men arrested in rural Clarke County, Virginia, after they fired shots at a bus carrying Black parishioners back to Washington from a prayer meeting in the county. It took me a couple of hours working the phones with state and town police around Berryville to get the details. Berryville was the home of Senator Harry Flood Byrd, the architect of massive resistance to desegregation in Virginia.

The bus had stalled on Route 50. The four white men drove up and asked two of the Black men walking down the road seeking help whether they were Freedom Riders. The white men then drove away and returned with shotguns and fired at the wheels of the bus while terrified passengers threw themselves down on the floor inside.

In Cambridge, on the Eastern Shore of Maryland, most white-owned cafés for the first time served Blacks — but the sodas and milkshakes they'd ordered arrived in paper cups, not glasses. A few days later, Cambridge voters elected a new mayor who had brought Governor Wallace to speak there, and had led successful opposition to a local public accommodations law. In Mississippi, the governor warned of "real trouble ahead" and said that hotel and restaurant owners should not comply with the Civil Rights Act until it was tested in the courts.

Then in Georgia, before dawn that Saturday, Lemuel Penn, an assistant superintendent of the D.C. school system, was killed by a shotgun blast fired from a passing car as he drove from his summer Army Reserve training at Fort Benning.

By the time Charlie Puffenbarger told me to try to reach members of Penn's family and any co-workers and fellow reservists I could get hold of, Clarence Hunter was on the way to Penn's house on Upshur Street; Jerry O'Leary was on the phone with the FBI; Gerry Herndon had reached someone at the Georgia Bureau of Investigation; the national desk had sent a second reporter to the White House; and Miriam Ottenberg was summoned from home to go to the Justice Department. Dick Fryklund, on his day off, was dispatched to the Pentagon. Because Penn had been murdered traveling from his Army Reserve training at Fort Benning, it had been Secretary of Defense McNamara who notified the president in the early morning of the shooting. Sid Epstein sent Charlie Pierce, whose beat was the District Building, to Athens, Georgia, by chartered airplane.

I got through to Penn's house the first time

I dialed. The man who answered said he was a close friend of the family and told me that Lemuel Penn's wife had learned of her husband's death around nine thirty that morning, in a telephone call from one of two fellow Black reservists, both D.C. schoolteachers, who had been riding in the car with her husband, a lieutenant colonel. Mrs. Penn had to tell their three young children that their father was dead. She presumed that the death of her husband was somehow "related to civil rights." To be safe, Col. Penn had even timed the group's departure and route from Fort Benning to avoid possible trouble.

I was able to put together the beginnings of a full biography from what the friend told me. The details of Lemuel Penn's life, in some regards, were as telling about my native city as the remarkable man himself. After graduating from Armstrong High, the combined vocational and academic high school in the old "Negro Division" of the D.C. school system, Penn had earned his bachelor's and master's degrees at Howard University. He was about to receive his PhD from New York University in public education and was on track to become the third-highest-ranking official in the D.C. system, in charge of vocational education.

He was forty-eight years old, a second-generation native of Washington, the son of a laborer at the Interior Department and a homemaker. He began his career as a teacher of science and math in the city's Black schools before World War II. During the war, he served in New Guinea and the Philippines campaign with the rank of captain and was awarded a Bronze Star for bravery. Returning home, he became principal of Phelps Vocational High School in 1954. He was a Boy Scout leader, a member of the Black Masonic lodge, a trustee of one of the city's biggest Methodist churches, and an officer of his neighborhood civic association, and he had been instrumental in organizing a Black Boy Scout camp on the Chesapeake. There had been a white Boy Scout camp since the 1920s, but none for Black children. His wife, also from Washington, was a home economics teacher at a junior high school in the District. All these details were prominent in the column-and-a-half obituary I wrote that afternoon for the Sunday paper, adjacent to the jump of the page one stories about the killing of Lemuel Penn.

In the main story for the Sunday edition, Mrs. Penn was quoted at length by Clarence Hunter. She said she had talked to her husband by phone Thursday night, and he told her that he had stayed on post throughout his tour of duty at Fort Benning to avoid encountering any racial problems in the neighboring Georgia towns. She told Clarence that she and her husband were "just quietly involved" in civil rights through their jobs and civic activities. "I just guess it's the ignorant people of the South. They think they are doing right. . . . I have been thinking that maybe this [her husband's death] will go down in history, though it's a great loss. . . . Our loss. It might be a real gain for the Negro," she said, because of increased awareness of violence against Black Americans. "I think it's going to be a long, long time before the violence ends. People need a lot of education."

Her husband, she said, "was about the most perfect person you could meet. . . . It was such a pity. You know, he lived through engagement after engagement, fighting in the South Pacific during the war. And then he couldn't even come home safely to his own country."

22

SUMMER

Barry Goldwater was heading toward the Republican nomination for president. I didn't have much doubt that he would be a danger to the country if he was elected. I talked to David Broder who thought Goldwater had no chance of reaching the White House.

I was fascinated by Goldwater. In junior high school I'd been a photography nut, and one of the magazines I read, along with catalogs for the cameras and darkroom equipment that left me broke (though my poker losses also helped), was an understated journal of mostly black-and-white photos called *Arizona Highways*. Many were taken by Senator Barry Goldwater. I thought he was a great photographer. He also was half Jewish, which made his candidacy even more exotic in my mind. He drove a Corvette. And he was a ham radio operator — I knew this from talking about him and his quirkier aspects with Broder and some of the other reporters.

Then I read that Goldwater planned to

take his ham radio equipment with him to the Republican National Convention in San Francisco.

I decided that it would make an interesting story if, from Washington, I could somehow hook up with the senator and have a chat with him via ham radio.

I looked up the name of a ham radio association in Arlington, got hold of its president, and told him my idea: Would he send a message by ham radio to some co-hobbyist in San Francisco, to deliver to the senator at the Mark Hopkins Hotel there? Since the message was in a foreign tongue, I drafted it with the help of the Arlington ham operator: "Sir. Understand you are now Portable Six. Would like to arrange schedule for one of these mornings on 14.340 megacycles. K2ZRK-4."

Fifteen minutes later we got a long-distance phone call from a member of Goldwater's staff in San Francisco who seemed intrigued by the idea of an interview via ham radio with the Washington *Evening Star*. "How about two o'clock tomorrow?" he said. To which my ham radio expert — we were in his basement, filled with dozens of pieces of heavy radio equipment — responded, "Roger."

The next day I told Sid Epstein that I was going to interview the Republican candidate for president of the United States over ham radio — twenty-four hours before he was to be officially nominated.

Sid Epstein's face turned red. "You're not making this up, are you, kid?" he said. I thought he might be remembering the fake obituary we'd foisted on the *Washington Post*.

I explained the whole deal and, shaking his head, Sid Epstein went over to the national editor and told him what I had in mind.

At two that afternoon, my co-communicator in Virginia was ready to go, seated at a long desk piled high with amplifiers and transformers and speakers and stuff. I sat down next to him, and he fired up the rig.

Then, over one of the loudspeakers, came the unmistakable voice of President Lyndon Johnson's opponent: "This is Kilowatt Seven Uncle George Able Portable Six from the Mark Hopkins Hotel in San Francisco."

The senator, the Arlington ham, and I proceeded in a similar vein for the next half hour or so.

"Where are you calling from?" Goldwater asked. We told him that we were in Arlington and that he was coming in loud and clear.

"That's good. Which Arlington?" the senator wanted to know. "Arlington what? What state? King Seven Under Georgia Alaska Portable Six standing by."

I told him we were in Arlington, Virginia, across the river from where he lived, and asked him how the ham rig in his Corvette was working. He gave me an answer that included a lot of information about ignition shielding. He said he also had a rig in his campaign plane and that on his way to the convention he'd dropped a twenty-foot line out of the cockpit and talked with someone in Oregon when he was over Phoenix. He was co-piloting the plane at the time.

The conversation went on from there, and came down to earth when I asked him how solid his nomination looked. There were around eight hundred votes that looked "pretty hitched," he said. "I lost one from Georgia today, but it looks good."

I got back to the office and gave Sid Epstein an exhaustive account of what the senator had said, and his face got red again. "How are you going to write this?" he asked.

I'd been giving it some thought. It was unusual for a news story to be written in the first person in any newspaper. At my typewriter, I tried it out, but the result was too jarring and too much about me, to my ear.

I tried a straight-news version in the third-person about the ham operator in Arlington sitting next to "a reporter" while the two of them conducted an interview over ham radio with the prospective nominee for president. It was okay, but then I thought I'd try something else, hardly original. I'd write it in the first person plural, like the *New Yorker* magazine's "Talk of the Town" pieces. Sometimes John McKelway and George Kennedy, who alternated writing the *Star*'s local "Rambler" column on the split page, would use the first person plural. So I thought I could get away with it. And it seemed to work.

Having heard about Senator Goldwater's spending his time at the Republican Convention talking on the air to amateur radio operators, we decided to try it ourselves.

Does the Senator really shun the hubbub of the Cow Palace to stay in his suite at the Mark Hopkins Hotel and twiddle dials and talk with fellow "ham" operators across the country?

Indeed he does.

The story ran at the bottom of page one on the afternoon Goldwater became his party's nominee for president of the United States, as noted in the eight-column headline across the top of the page.

"Okay, kid," was all Sid Epstein said to me when the first edition of the paper came off the press. And he grinned and shook his head.

Though I now had a charge account at Saltz Brothers and had built up a considerable wardrobe from its wood-paneled premises, I continued to visit No-Label Louie's on a regular basis. And I made it my business to introduce Sid Epstein's hires for the dictation bank or training program to its bargain racks. So at twenty-five or thirty dollars a crack, most of us owned shiny tuxes or white dinner jackets, put into service during that spring and summer for the four hundredth anniversary of Shakespeare's birth, with cocktails and dinner at the Folger Shakespeare Library; for the arrival of "Whistler's Mother" at the National Gallery; for a dinner-dance at the U.S. Open golf championship at Congressional Country Club; and for the state visit of the shah of Iran, which set off a round of partying at a dozen embassies and dizzying displays of Persian culture, cuisine, and dancing at the Corcoran and Mellon galleries. Barely a week went by without high-toned freeloading at embassy soirees, symphony concerts, art openings, theater, and cabaret.

Warren Hoge arrived at the *Star* that spring out of Yale and two years in the army, full of Whiffenpoof charm and commanding an exceptional baritone singing voice. Hoge was good-looking and jive-talking on a level above the scruff of any of us, so when he'd enter a ballroom or shake hands with the embassy protocol officer (with the rest of us lined up behind him) there were never any questions about what this bunch was doing there. He pulled it off even with the beyond-obviously frayed shirt collars that, for reasons of complicated upper-class chic, I guessed, he wore with Louie's finest productions. Of all the new dictationists and reporters, I became closest to Hoge and Lance Morrow. You could not find two more opposite characters except in the Ivy League credentials they shared (Lance went to Harvard), their readiness for slick mischief, and their talent for getting away with it.

Jo Anne, after graduating from the training program, had been shuffled back to the Women's Department, where her assignments were not the stuff of Brenda Starr's dreams. Instead, her editors sent her on an outing to a French Country Fair fundraiser for the Maret School and to Patti Page's show at the Shoreham Hotel (after Jo Anne had interviewed the singer about being on the road with a baby). She also got assigned to a new *Star* venture, the *Weekender Magazine,* another implausible attempt by the managing editor, Bill Hill, to stanch the hemorrhage of ads and paid circulation benefiting the *Post.* So through May and June, the two of us did a lot of walking on the C&O Canal towpath, revisiting the gardens at Dumbarton Oaks (where we had gone on our first date), and hitting a couple of furniture fairs and fashion trade shows, all subjects of what-to-do-this-weekend features by Jo Anne.

The fact that we hadn't gotten married did not seem to cloud our situation. In and out of the office, we were in each other's regular company until one or two in the morning, when I would drop her off at the Georgetown house and head back woozy to Arlington. In early May, there had been a five-day printers' strike at the paper in which members of the Newspaper Guild — virtually all of us who worked in the news departments — refused to cross their picket line. While management-level editors and production executives put together a single-section paste-up version of the *Star* that looked more like a high school newspaper than a Washington daily, Jo Anne and I drove in the Renault to Virginia Beach and stayed by the ocean in a house owned by a family friend of hers.

In the months since our trip to Elkton, we'd talked about the experience a few times, with some seriousness, sometimes laughing about it, and both of us concluding that had we been sober and had the chapel been open for business, we'd have gone through with it. But there was also a view setting in — that she expressed better than I did — that we were pretty young, not to mention that I was still in school (sort of). By now she was twenty-three and I was twenty.

There was another thing she'd said, back when I was scheduling her work shifts on the training program, and I hadn't heard it again until the beginning of summer. As fond and admiring as she was of the women in the newsroom, she didn't want to live the life she perceived they had chosen: focused almost altogether on their careers like Miriam Ottenberg or Mary McGrory, or having affairs with some of the men on the staff (whether married or not), as she thought a couple of the others were doing. She also told me that a senior editor of the *Star* had given her a ride home after work one night and tried to make a move on her, and she had been really saddened — and repelled — by the experience.

In June, her housemate in Georgetown, Posey Bresnehan, got a new assignment abroad from the CIA, and over a weekend we loaded up all of Jo Anne's stuff and moved her into the apartment of Polly Dranov, a reporter for UPI she'd known for years.

I hadn't thought anything was amiss until a couple weeks later, when Jo Anne seemed uncharacteristically moody and once got visibly furious at her boss, who was too drunk to edit her story, which for sure wasn't the first time. And there were a couple of occasions, after we'd arranged to meet up at Harrigan's after work, when she said she wasn't feeling well and was going home to Polly's.

Then, after we'd been walking on the towpath for her story for the *Weekender,* she told me she'd made a decision to leave the paper and go back to Pennsylvania. She didn't see any future in covering furniture fairs, she said, and maybe she'd blown her big chance because the Junior Village story didn't turn out to be the powerful series she'd envisioned. She'd called Gene Goodwin at Penn State and explained to him that as much as she'd loved her time at the *Star,* it wasn't working out as she hoped, and could she come back to graduate school. He'd made all the arrangements and offered her a job as a teaching assistant in the Journalism Department. She was leaving in a week. Charlie Seib had tried to persuade her to stay, and she'd said no. And she hadn't wanted to tell me until now because she knew I might be able to get her to stay. But her mind was made up.

I will not say how I felt when she told me, but it was a lot worse than when the desk clerk in Elkton said we couldn't get married until Tuesday.

I took her to Union Station on a Saturday for the train to Harrisburg. We'd packed up her things at Polly's, and a moving company was going to pick them up. In the Renault, I felt like I couldn't breathe, but we both tried to be light about it all, and she said that she'd call as soon as she was settled. And explain more to me. Inside the station, when we hugged each other good-bye, I could see she was starting to cry, and I gave her a kiss, and she waved back to me before she got on the train.

Nobody in the newsroom — or maybe even in Washington journalism — could compete with Mary McGrory's ability to cast a spell with words. She had a way of being both deadly and genteel in her writing, suggesting that the reader shared her own higher standard of intelligence and discernment. Yet she was too smart to sound stuffy or superior when she did this. She was one of those writers who set up a little conspiracy between themselves and the reader.

Both the *Washington Post* and the *New York Times* had tried to woo her away. But she had a better understanding of the *Star* probably than any of us, an idea of the place as a big extended family, and sometimes a dysfunctional one at that: with a messy living room — the newsroom — in which any kind of family squabble or backbiting was liable to end with siblings and cousins laughing and rolling their eyes. And all of us agreeing that we lived in the best house in the neighborhood, even if it was kind of ramshackle and the foundation was getting creaky.

Miss McGrory also cast a spell over the men in the newsroom, including the ones who counted the most. Not just the best reporters on the staff like Haynes Johnson and Bill Hines and David Broder, or the most refined souls like Ed Tribble, or the editors she admired like Newby Noyes (maybe more than he deserved, in the view of some colleagues) and old Ben McKelway and even the tyrannical Earl Heap on the copy desk. But also Phil Kelley, the head copyboy, whom she appreciated and depended on almost as if he were the head of the household staff.

How she cast her spell was a bit mysterious.

She knew her worth. She used the authority of her talent. It's true, she acted a little too preoccupied and needy in the fetch department, which seemed excusable because everyone was aware she operated on a higher plane and was too nice and sometimes too genuinely abstracted to be a real prima donna. Once, in my first year at the paper, she hollered *"Copy!"* on deadline, and I raced to her desk; she said she couldn't write the rest of her story because she couldn't find her glasses, and I located them on the string that hung around her neck.

She was Boston Irish, but one of the things I liked best about her was her appreciation of the city of Washington and its history, in ways that were matched by few other reporters, even on the local staff, except maybe Lance Morrow and Tom Dimond. On the few occasions when she and I would find ourselves alone together — if I was helping her get to the airport in a cab, for instance, and then waiting to assist her at the gate to board — she would ask me about myself, with genuine interest, it seemed to me. After she learned I was a native of the city, and my mother too, we established an easy manner of conversation and would talk about aspects of the town, usually things she had discovered in her reporting. At times she'd be writing about a matter of grave national importance, and her story would pause to mention Washington's springtime flowers and gardens or, say, the grandeur of a particular room in the Capitol, implying that the senators convening there were unworthy of their surroundings.

And though I didn't qualify as the most *anything* in the newsroom, she'd put her spell on me, too. Somehow — because of scores of errands and getting-her-cabs and carrying-her-bags, plus being the dictation-ist she asked for when she was on the road — I'd gotten myself included in the circle of people who were invited to her house parties on St. Patrick's Day, and who on Christmas delivered presents along with "Mary Gloria" (from Mary McGrory, a name the kids had trouble pronouncing) at the St. Ann's Infant and Maternity Home. On Wednesdays in the hot months, we'd take a bus full of the children to go swimming and picnic at Hickory Hill, the home of Robert and Ethel Kennedy in McLean, Virginia. The first time I'd gone was toward the end of summer in 1962; Bobby Kennedy had been there, acting as sort of a ringmaster around the pool, toss-ing some of the children into the water and, at a long picnic table, slicing pieces of cake and handing them out. I was fascinated by a beige telephone on a stand a few feet from the edge of the pool. It had a row of buttons, one of which was labeled WHITE HOUSE. With some frequency, the attorney general would step aside from his ringmaster role and sit in a chair next to the telephone with his feet on the stand and talk on that phone.

Now, in the first summer after the assassination of his brother, and in the midst of murderous events in the Deep South, Attorney General Robert F. Kennedy was getting ready to announce his candidacy for senator from the state of New York. But he responded like all the rest of us to the spell of Miss McGrory and showed up for her and the children.

I watched him closely that Wednesday afternoon. He looked hollowed out, pushing himself to be the ringmaster, as he moved between the picnic table and the phone next to the pool.

After four years at the paper, I understood the lengths to which a *Star* reporter, especially a good one, was expected to go to get the story, short of breaking the law or misrepresenting himself as another person on the phone or in someone's office, which I knew happened sometimes in journalism but would not be tolerated in our newsroom. (Still, it seemed okay to me in a pinch to read a piece of paper upside down on someone's desk if you were sitting across from him.)

In my earliest months as a copyboy, Phil Kelley had sent me out frequently to get a photograph of the deceased in difficult or sensitive situations, for instance immediately after a murder or a car crash, or for an obituary of someone who had otherwise died tragically. I was a freckled teenager with a flattop haircut and, when I wished, an earnest and sympathetic manner. I became adept at talking myself into the homes of bereaved spouses or siblings or parents. Usually when I arrived on their doorstep, they'd had only a few hours in which to absorb the awful news that the police or the emergency room had delivered to them.

The task was to borrow a photograph of the deceased, with a promise to return it. Families were usually remarkably cooperative, and giving a photograph to the newspaper seemed often to help them in some way. Sometimes I would record the mournful reactions of the immediate survivors in my notebook. All this I assigned to the category of "human interest." By the time I had moved on to the dictation bank, Sid Epstein was aware of my talent for such unpleasant chores. I knew how to talk with genuine sincerity about my deep sadness at a family's loss before making off with a framed eight-by-ten photo.

After I was on the premises and the bereaved had agreed to bring out a picture, it was easy to start asking questions about the deceased or the circumstances of his or her demise. I learned that grieving people often want to talk at such moments. And it was in these encounters that I recognized that a reporter could usually find out much more by being a good and sympathetic listener than by aggressively interrogating or interrupting or pushing a person in one direction or another. Spontaneous information was often more reliable and nuanced than what you might get by tightly focused interrogation.

On a Saturday afternoon that August, word reached the state desk from a stringer in Charles Town, West Virginia, that two teenage boys from D.C. had drowned in the Shenandoah River, after one had tried to save the other in thirty-foot-deep water.

Sid Epstein dispatched me to their homes to get a picture of each from their families. Even more than usual, it was an assignment I dreaded.When I was in eleventh grade, I'd had a good friend, Ralph Penn, who had drowned in the James River near Williamsburg. I'd often thought about him since, imagining the horror of how he died and the devastation to his family.

I took a car from the *Star*'s fleet of blue Ford Falcons and drove to MacArthur Boulevard, where the family of one of the boys, Dennis Donovan, lived in a small frame house near the Dalecarlia Reservoir. I knocked on the open screen door, and a man of perhaps thirty answered. I explained that I was from the *Evening Star* and, as much as I didn't want to burden the family, the newspaper was hoping to obtain a picture of his brother.

He said his parents didn't wish to be

disturbed, but he would get the photo for me. He came back a moment later with a picture of a youngish man who was obviously older than the teenager who had died that morning in the Shenandoah River. I said he must have misunderstood, I'd come to get a picture of his brother, and he looked at me confused — though he was no more confused than I at that moment. I repeated I was there for a picture of his brother Dennis — and I thought he was going to faint. He asked me what was I saying, why did I want a picture of his brother Dennis, it was his brother Marty whose picture I wanted and which he had brought me.

Now it began to dawn on me what was happening, and I did not know what to do next. But I certainly couldn't leave without explaining in full why I was there. I also kicked myself for not adding everything up and doing my homework before I had left the newsroom. And this was a rare moment when I felt real anger at the ugly aspects of the profession I had chosen and the cavalier way it exploited other people's pain and hurt.

"Oh my God, no, no, God," he cried, trying to absorb the truth: he had lost two brothers in the space of two weeks. His older brother was a cop, Martin Donovan, who had been shot to death chasing a robbery suspect near Thomas Circle; the story had been on the front page. I had read every detail about the shooting of his brother. Now his younger brother had drowned.

"I have to tell my parents," he said. "How do I tell them?" He asked me if Dennis really was dead — was I sure? He explained that Dennis and a group of friends had gone to Charles Town for a weekend of swimming and fishing at a youth club there. And then he asked me how he had died. There was nothing I could do but tell him. His brother had drowned trying to save a friend who couldn't handle the current because he was swimming with an injured arm. I told him there was no need for him to get me another picture — the right one, as it were. I must have blocked the next few minutes out of my mind because I remember little else except driving back to the office in a daze.

I told Sid Epstein what had happened and said that I wanted to think twice about going on any more picture-grabbing expeditions. In fact, I resolved to myself that I would hold to a higher standard: that in such obvious conflict between the humane and the journalistic, I would make the more thoughtful choice. But I relented after a while, and I continued to look on such incidents as part of the job.

And I had brought back the right picture from MacArthur Boulevard.

Sid Epstein decided that the split page was too dull and contrived — a mix of predictable crime, bureaucratic bumbling, and over-wrought stories about thunderstorms, brightened only by an occasional gem from his best writers: John Sherwood, unanchored on his sloop on the Chesapeake; Herman Schaden, whose prose was still most deeply inspired by the creatures at the National Zoo (sometimes with me tagging along); and Gerry Herndon, when he could free himself up from early-morning rewrite. And a few others.

Sid Epstein's new idea was to run an eight-column feature story above the fold every day. This was a major break for me. Especially because of summer vacations, there weren't seven reliable feature writers to carry the weight each week. So between mid-July and mid-August I did five such stories. The first was about apprentice chefs learning their trade, with photos of them in their big toques taken by the Star's only woman photographer, Rosemary. That was her whole professional name and byline: Photo by Rosemary.

My next piece was about U.S. Air Force "weekend warrior" reservists flying from Maryland to Germany and back — it was fun to report because, a few hours prior to their takeoff from Andrews Air Force Base, I'd squeezed myself into and out of the cockpit of an F-18 fighter jet before twenty of them roared down the runway and broke the sound barrier overhead.

For another feature — about a Maryland

State Penitentiary rehabilitation program for felons — I went to art and English classes behind bars in Baltimore. And there was a profile of a single residential block and its inhabitants, in a Northwest D.C. neighborhood called Trinidad. The story compared Wallach Place to a checkerboard, with one row of houses occupied by middle-class Black professionals, and across the street transients sitting on the steps of dilapidated quarters sipping from half pints of whiskey. After this, I got the idea of making a specialty of writing profiles about different neighborhoods and streets around the city. I was especially interested in Anacostia, in Southeast D.C., on the bluffs high above the river, where Frederick Douglass had lived in a big frame house and where St. Elizabeths Hospital dominated the landscape. I remembered my night there with Walter Gold back in my early copyboy days. Given the number of stories I imagined resided at St. Elizabeths, I was incredulous that no one on the city staff had claimed the hospital as part of their beat.

Among the eight thousand patients at the hospital was Dallas O. Williams, known to every D.C. homicide detective (and newspaper headline writer) as the Badman of Swampoodle. I'd wanted to write about both Swampoodle — the impoverished neighborhood just east of Union Station — and its most famous resident for months. The Badman

495

had killed at least two people, maimed many more, and was arrested more than a hundred times and convicted in fifty-nine cases. He told the judge that he had committed his violent crimes because visions came to him in his sleep. The U.S. Court of Appeals had cited cases like his as a model in its decision that criminals judged insane at the time of their crimes should be found not guilty by reason of insanity. But lawyers for the Badman were able to win his release from St. Elizabeths on numerous occasions, when psychiatrists there found him sane after spending some time at the hospital. Then, repeating the cycle, he would go on another violent rampage through the city and get arrested again.

Also, as part of my apprenticeship, I filled in occasionally for rewrite men on vacation, a job I assigned to myself as clerk in charge of scheduling the staff. Sid Epstein raised no objection. I learned how to write front-page weather stories about an approaching storm or its aftermath: the trick was to make the weather dramatic, full of vivid effects — clouds like gunpowder, that kind of thing. I was assigned to a coroner's jury inquest: convened to determine whether the cause of death of a D.C. policeman was murder or accident. In Chevy Chase, on what had once been a driving range where I'd shagged golf balls for a nickel apiece near Chesapeake Street, I covered the opening of Saks Fifth

Avenue, the first "plush" (a word I misused in the lede) out-of-town department store to locate in a capital city long regarded as a fashion backwater. And, with firsthand information I'd gotten from Reverend Fauntroy, Julius Hobson, and Harris Wofford, I wrote a story for the national desk about the Mississippi Freedom Democratic Party fighting to be seated at the Democratic National Convention, in place of the segregationist regular state party delegation. It ran the same week that the bodies of Michael Schwerner, James Chaney, and Andrew Goodman were found. An informant had disclosed to the FBI that the bodies had been buried, facedown and side by side, deep under a levee in Neshoba County, Mississippi.

23

FORT HOLABIRD

It did not take General Hershey's people long to learn that I'd been bounced from the University of Maryland. In August, I was notified by certified mail that my draft status had been changed from 2-S to 1-A, meaning that I was now eligible to be drafted for two years of active military duty, plus four years in the reserves.

This notice arrived on almost the same day that the U.S. Navy destroyer *Maddox* was attacked in the Gulf of Tonkin in the South China Sea off the coast of North Vietnam. By now there were more than twenty thousand American servicemen in South Vietnam, and President Johnson, Secretary of State Rusk, and Secretary of Defense McNamara were making clear that many more thousands were about to follow. I did not want to be one of them, a guilt-inducing position that was nonetheless consistent with my belief that Vietnam was not worth America fighting for.

After Johnson ordered a series of retaliatory

bombings of North Vietnam, the Congress passed the Gulf of Tonkin Resolution, giving the president broad war powers to meet any attacks on American forces. Dick Fryklund reported from the Pentagon that this was a blank check to initiate further escalation and commitment of U.S. ground troops and support from air and sea.

The certified letter from the Silver Spring Selective Service Board directed that I report again in mid-August to its headquarters at Blair House. From there, I would be taken by bus to the Military Entrance Processing Station at Fort Holabird in Baltimore for a physical examination and a battery of psychological tests that would determine whether I was fit for military service.

Bad as the news was, it wasn't quite as awful as it sounded. Even if I passed the physical — which I was gearing up to fail, for legitimate reasons, I believed — my draft lottery number was high enough to stave off being called to active duty for another few months. And in that interim, I figured I could find a reserve unit to take me in — which would mean I'd do six months' active service in the army and another five and a half years of weekend reserve duty, plus two weeks of summer training every year.

On the appointed day, with about twenty other young men from Silver Spring, I boarded a yellow school bus. We were informed that

until we returned that night from being processed, we were under the command of the
United States Selective Service System, and
that we'd best pay attention. This greeting
was delivered by a civilian martinet not tall
enough, I reckoned, to be eligible to serve in
the military himself.

Fort Holabird came into view an hour
later, at the end of the Baltimore-Washington
Parkway and off an exit ramp leading to the
Dundalk Marine Terminal, a landfill island
with dozens of barracks-like buildings made
from plasterboard, and even more dozens of
yellow school buses disgorging young men of
approximately the same age from throughout
the state.

All of us were herded into adjacent lines of
about fifty individuals, then each line snaked
into one of the plasterboard buildings. A row
of a couple dozen oscillating fans from one
end of place to the other generated more noise
than cooling against the 90-plus-degree heat.
Behind the fans were long tables pushed together end to end, like in a school cafeteria,
with at least fifty clerks thumbing through
stacks of paperwork and calling out names in
no particular order.

The business end of this operation was
behind these clerks: a curtained medical
theater as wide as a football field was long,
with white-clad doctors — maybe sixty of
them — standing next to examination tables

and medieval-looking instruments hanging from coatracks. I was told to strip down to my underpants, put my sweat-soaked clothes on the rack, walk in front of the examination table, and bend over with my hands on my knees. *This won't hurt,* I was assured, and the elastic waistband of my shorts was pulled down. The same doctor, in the space of less than a minute and a half, examined my eyes, took my pulse, told me to take a series of deep breaths, ran a stethoscope over my chest and back, took a blood sample, and pronounced me in good shape. Then he thumbed through my paperwork, which included a note from my physician about the migraine headaches I'd begun suffering around age eighteen, and asked me if there was any reason I thought I couldn't fight in the army.

I told him, truthfully, that the headaches would usually come in the afternoon or night, sometimes once a week, sometimes two or three, almost out of the blue, and that I'd have to lie down in the dark until the pain went away, at times for almost two hours, and that there was also nausea that came with them, and dancing spots of light when I closed my eyes. He asked if I ever threw up, and I said no, which probably was the wrong answer. The only thing I didn't tell him was that often I'd get the headaches after I'd been drinking. Which meant that sometimes, after lunch at

Harrigan's and a couple martinis, I'd have to go up to the fifth-floor cafeteria and lie down on the slinky blue sofa that curved around the employees' lounge. Most days, from about twelve thirty to one, the sofa was occupied by Sid Epstein, who was dutiful about taking a midday nap and almost never went out for lunch.

The Selective Service doctor asked me a few more questions, including whether I thought I could crawl on the ground like a reptile in the middle of a headache attack, about which I had some doubt.

In another building, which smelled like the boys' gym at Montgomery Blair on account of everybody sweating through their clothes, they gave us IQ and psychological tests. *Was there anyone in my family I liked to scream at?* Uncle Sam wanted to know.

A number of guys put their heads down on their test papers as if the pages were pillows, and some of them were snoring. When the forty-five minutes were up, a few civilian monitors went down the rows to wake or shake these guys, and they got to their feet, unsteady.

On the bus ride back, the little man in charge said he was pleased that none of us from Silver Spring had nodded out. He explained that it was common, especially for bad kids from Baltimore, to get high on heroin before they boarded the bus to Holabird, knowing that if the drugs showed up in their bloodwork, they'd never be accepted into the army.

Meanwhile, I had passed my physical with flying colors.

The Arlington house was breaking up. Ken Campbell had gotten engaged, and Tom Dimond had won a scholarship, paid by the *Star,* to grad school at the University of Wisconsin to study political journalism the coming fall. We put word out that at the end of August there would be a farewell party and tribute to the house and its history with the *Star.*

We'd thrown a couple dozen big parties and barbecues there during the two and a half years since I'd moved in, almost all in the summer months. Unlike the house on Duddington Place, where Lance Morrow and Bob Leary and Rupe Welch lived, ours had a big backyard. And on a Saturday night it was only fifteen or twenty minutes by car from the *Star* building: across Memorial Bridge to the GW Parkway and then straight up Spout Run.

The thought of leaving the house was wrenching — something like graduating from college, I imagined, and for the others a different kind of milestone altogether. We had paid a hundred and forty dollars a month total rent — twenty-eight bucks apiece. Then there were the women who had been de facto members of the household. Tom Dimond was going out with Ginny Koerber, a former dictationist who'd graduated from the training program the previous summer and was now a general assignment reporter on the city staff. Norma Eneim and John Fialka had dated for a year; she worked in the Sunday Department and was the sister of Jerry O'Leary Jr.'s wife, Maria. The sisters were stunningly beautiful. Norma helped out part time at Maria's Mexican craft shop in Alexandria, which accounted for whatever decorative aesthetic had evolved in our house. Suze Thurston was a twenty-year-old sophomore at Connecticut College for Women when she started commuting from New London to stay with Ken in the upstairs front bedroom for long weekends and the summer months. We were all the luckier for it. She was a great cook, knew how to shop for fresh seafood, and invariably planned our meals for the weekend upon her arrival. And she lent much-needed ebullience to our overly self-serious focus on our careers and endless discussion of the burdens of the nation. Another regular presence was our neighbor Jean Sonen, a maternal figure who often cooked and shared dinner with us while we took turns helping her teenage daughter with her homework. We relied on Jean for peacekeeping duty when other neighbors complained about noise and the cars blocking their driveways on summer Saturday nights.

I'd just started seeing Judy Scribner, who

was willowy and blond (she stood just over six feet) and who'd worked in the Women's Department with Jo Anne before moving to the dictation bank. She was twenty-three, adventurous, hilarious, and inclined toward the intellectual. (She insisted I read *The Lord of the Rings,* which I never managed to finish.) Judy had grown up in Western Maryland and was the sister of Norman Scribner, the assistant director and organist of the National Cathedral Choir, where she too sang; I'd go with her on occasion to listen to the choir rehearse. Our friendship was sealed when, at her request, I agreed to schedule her for the eleven-to-seven dictation shift because she was chronically late for work in the morning.

Close to a hundred people showed up for the farewell party: almost the whole local reporting staff and the deskmen and their wives (but not Sid Epstein, of course), plus Ludy Werner and her boyfriend (but not Mr. and Mrs. Porter), and pretty much everybody from the Sunday Department and younger members of the Women's Department staff.

The party was not entirely a success. It went on too long. The wife of one of the assistant city editors left the premises with a dictationist, and in the morning, when I got up for work, just after sunrise, there were still a few people stumbling around the lawn or passed out on Adirondack chairs.

I'd scheduled myself to work the seven o'clock Sunday morning shift — something I had to do on a semi-regular basis because I was the juniormost reporter on the staff. So when I got up, a little wobbly and parched, I grabbed a nearly full pitcher of ice water from the refrigerator and drank it straight down without bothering to get a glass. It didn't register on me until I was almost finished that I was consuming the better part of a quart of Tom Dimond's martinis left over from the night before.

I arrived at the *Star* in time to start making the morning police checks. But I began to fall asleep in midconversation with the Prince George's County fire dispatcher. When the assistant city editor that day, John Koepeck, arrived, I confessed I wasn't feeling well and told him about drinking the pitcher of martinis. He gently suggested that I go upstairs to the employees' lounge to lie down. I also felt a migraine headache coming on. By the time I woke up, it was midafternoon and almost the end of my shift. Koepeck was understanding and said he'd finished the police and fire checks himself.

John Fialka and I found new places to live in houses three doors apart near Dupont Circle, in the 1600 block of Nineteenth Street — about four blocks from where my mother was born, and just down the hill in Adams

Morgan from the little apartment where I'd lived with her and my grandparents until I was two years old and my father came back from the South Pacific after the war.

As much as I'd loved living in the Arlington house, I was happy to get out of the suburbs once and for all. My interest in Arlington County, Virginia, was minimal, except on those occasions when Ludy sent me on a really good assignment, or on an evening after work when I'd go up to the great lawn of Robert E. Lee's mansion on the Arlington Heights and sit and watch the sunset cast its glow on the city below and its monuments.

I'd been surprised — a couple of weeks before the farewell party — when a letter arrived from the Office of the Dean of the Faculty of Arts and Sciences inviting me to seek readmission on academic probation to the University of Maryland for the fall semester. The catch was that by the end of the following semester, I would need to achieve junior standing or be expelled for good. It was impossible to imagine how I'd ever get that many credits. (The amount of studying would have been near-fatal or require that I retire from the newspaper business.) But I was happy to accept the dean's invitation, knowing that readmission would buy me a draft deferment for another five or six months. I calculated that once I finally and irrevocably got expelled from the university, I'd have had ample time to find a reserve unit to take me in. So I drove out to College Park, reenrolled, chose half a dozen academic subjects I had no intention of studying, and stopped the Selective Service clock.

24

GENERAL ASSIGNMENT

There had been no letup in the *Star*'s Bobby Baker coverage through the spring and summer. Cecil Holland told me that, so far as he knew, there hadn't been any heavy-handed moves or intimidation from the White House to stop it. A torrent of damning stories by John Barron forced the Democrats on Capitol Hill to give in to the Republicans who were demanding hearings to investigate Baker's financial dealings — and the sexual favors of young women that he'd supposedly promised to politicians and politically connected businessmen.

I took note of how Barron, through the close reportorial relationship he'd established with the Republican vice chairman of the Senate Rules Committee, John J. Williams of Delaware, had helped bring about the thing the White House feared the most: a congressional investigation.

But in the first half of October, pressure to kill a different kind of story by Barron seemed, for a moment, to be succeeding. It was about the arrest of Lyndon Johnson's closest White House aide, Walter Jenkins, on charges of engaging in an "indecent" act in the men's room of the downtown YMCA, two blocks from the White House.

Roy Blick, the commandant of the Morals Division, and his sleazy deputy Louis Fochett were behind the arrest by detectives from the Prostitution and Perversion Squad. Every aspect of the story was disturbing, including the timing of Jenkins's arrest a few weeks before the presidential election. I knew from Rupe Welch, who was (again) determined to get the story out, that it had originated with sources in the Goldwater campaign who had been fed information by Lieutenant Fochett. Rupe, in a state of agitation, told me the whole backstory at Harrigan's one night.

No one among the president's innermost circle — not even Bobby Baker — was closer to Johnson than Walter Jenkins. For twenty-five years, since Lyndon Johnson had been a young congressman, Jenkins had been his confidant and most trusted and skilled aide. Few major players in the town were as universally admired. He was not only beloved by the Johnson family and colleagues on Capitol Hill but also celebrated for his honesty and decency by the reporters who had covered LBJ for decades. He was a devout Roman Catholic and the father of six children.

Plainclothesmen, working under Blick and Fochett's command, arrested Jenkins and another man on October 7 in the YMCA restroom on disorderly conduct charges for "making indecent gestures," according to the police paperwork that Fochett passed on to his Republican contacts. A week later, at four in the morning, Rupe Welch was awakened at the house on Duddington Place by a phone call from Sid Epstein. He told Rupe to get dressed in a hurry and head straight to police headquarters, where Ted Crown was working on a story John Barron was writing about the arrest of Lyndon Johnson's chief aide. Sid Epstein was already in the office trying to engineer the story into the paper. He directed Rupe to get a firsthand look at the arrest record and confirmation of whatever additional details Crown was hearing from his police sources.

At headquarters, Crown told Rupe where to locate the arrest book of Roy Blick's Prostitution and Perversion Squad. And in the process, to be sure to keep himself invisible to Al Lewis and Johnny Burch, in case the *Post* and the *Daily News* were also on the trail.

In the anteroom outside Blick's office, a deputy led Rupe to the book — and its arrest entry, under the name "John W. Jenkins: occupation, clerk," with no indication that he was a White House official.

Rupe asked the deputy for Lieutenant

511

Fochett's home address, in the far Virginia suburbs, and headed out there. No one was home. A neighbor told Rupe that half an hour earlier, Fochett and his family had packed up their car for what looked like a vacation. Rupe surmised that the deputy had tipped off Fochett that a *Star* reporter was on the way.

Rupe found a phone booth and called Sid Epstein. "Fochett is gone," he reported. By then it was after nine in the morning. Sid Epstein said, "We're going to kill the story." He explained that Abe Fortas and Clark Clifford — LBJ's personal lawyer and his unofficial White House counsel, both esteemed Washington hands — had persuaded someone near the top of the *Star*'s chain of command not to run the story of Jenkins's arrest. Fortas and Clifford were now on their way to the *Daily News* and the *Post*.

After that, Rupe told me, he took action to make sure that the story wouldn't stay buried; he was furious. At lunchtime, at the National Press Club bar, he ran into a UPI reporter with whom he'd attended Georgetown University. The UPI man told him the wire service had gotten a strange tip they were running down — about the arrest of a White House aide on a morals charge. Rupe, furious that the White House was trying to suppress the story, swore the UPI man to secrecy, pulled out his notebook, and provided all the details.

By early afternoon, both UPI and NBC

512

News had broken the story — which, as Rupe had intended, freed the *Star* to run John Barron's full, detailed account in the final edition.

By seven o'clock, Jenkins had resigned as the president's assistant and entered George Washington University Hospital, suffering from fatigue, according to the White House press secretary. Meanwhile, Lyndon Johnson had been informed that afternoon — as Jerry O'Leary Jr. had learned from Deke DeLoach at the FBI — that Jenkins had been arrested in 1959 at the same YMCA on a similar morals charge. At that time, he had been charged with "disorderly conduct (pervert)," paid a twenty-five-dollar fine, and was sent home.

By the end of the evening, Barry Goldwater charged that the White House was "dark with scandal" and mashed up the Jenkins story with the Bobby Baker mess. The Republican national chairman insisted that the FBI investigate whether Jenkins might have been compromised in some kind of blackmail operation, and the president announced later that night that he'd asked J. Edgar Hoover to conduct a full FBI investigation.

Goldwater said he would not make any comments about Jenkins specifically or his arrest. The reason was revealed in the *Star*'s first edition the next morning: Walter Jenkins was a colonel in the Air Force Reserve squadron founded on Capitol Hill in 1961 and commanded by Major General Barry Goldwater. (Goldwater liked to head out to Andrews on weekends and fly F-18s.)

What struck me in the *Star*'s exhaustive coverage that day — three stories on page one — was at once the determination to report all the discomfiting circumstances of how Jenkins had been arrested and for what, and at the same time quoting the president, members of Congress, and White House colleagues about the human tragedy that had befallen Walter Jenkins and his family.

But part of me wondered if there wasn't another story that really deserved to be in the paper: the role of Roy Blick and his Prostitution and Perversion Squad in the life of the nation and its capital city.

About a dozen of us were just ordering lunch at Harrigan's when the saloon's owner, Morris Engel, hollered that Coit Hendley was calling for whoever could get to the phone quickest. Bill Basham, a former marine who stood over six foot three, bounded from the banquette, cradled the receiver to his ear, and ran his eyes down the table. There had been a shooting on the C&O Canal towpath near Georgetown, probably fatal. Hendley was dispatching Basham immediately to the scene and wanted Charlie Puffenbarger, me, and a couple of others to get back to the newsroom right away.

There, Hendley reported the scant details: a well-dressed white woman had been shot and a Black man apprehended soaking wet near the Potomac riverbank. From police headquarters, Lance Morrow had gotten to the scene faster than the homicide detectives. He'd seen the woman's body close up, standing right over her for ten or twelve minutes, in fact, before the cops arrived and shooed him away. The woman looked to be in her late thirties or early forties, and there was a bullet hole in her head and another in her back, the cops were saying. Hendley told me to get down to headquarters right away and fill in for Morrow.

A desk sergeant and a lieutenant were in the homicide squad room when I arrived, and all they knew was that the victim didn't appear to have any identification on her. K-9 units, Park Police, and some of the top brass from the department were at the scene.

And Lance Morrow, I told them.

A few minutes later an inspector whom I'd met on the street a couple of times walked into the squad room. He told me that a woman's glove was found near the body. And that a white jacket, possibly worn by the killer, was found on the bank of the canal farther downstream. The inspector took a phone call in his inner office, walked back out, and told the three of us that there was a tag sewn into the glove with the name Meyer.

I phoned the information to Gerry Herndon on rewrite. A replate of the final edition included those details in a front-page story with an oversized headline. Meanwhile, Hendley told me to come back to the office and work the phones into the night.

Seven or eight reporters and editors were on aspects of the story when I got there, and Sid Epstein was in his chair, his sleeves perfectly rolled. The victim had been identified: Mary Pinchot Meyer of Georgetown, a highly regarded artist and socialite from a famous family. Her father, Amos Pinchot, had been a founder of the Progressive Party in Theodore Roosevelt's time, and her uncle was Gifford Pinchot, one of America's most renowned conservationists and a former governor of Pennsylvania. Lance Morrow was explaining this genealogy to Sid Epstein.

Perhaps of greater significance at the moment, Mary Meyer was the sister of Toni Pinchot Bradlee, the wife of Ben Bradlee, the Washington bureau chief of *Newsweek* magazine. Bradlee, a close friend of the late President Kennedy, had identified the body of his sister-in-law.

I called the homicide inspector. He said that detectives, working with their only identifying clue — the tag in the glove — had sought out all the Meyers in Georgetown and Upper Northwest, leading to her address. Neighbors had said that she was divorced, that she

516

lived alone, and that her sister was married to Bradlee.

I made calls through the night to Mary Meyer's friends and neighbors, among them Scottie Fitzgerald Lanahan, who had been her classmate at Vassar College. She said that Mary had often walked that stretch of the towpath with her friend and former neighbor Jacqueline Kennedy during the White House years. And that she was a talented painter. She and her ex-husband, Cord Meyer Jr., a World War II hero who had since served in and out of government, were upper-crust fixtures of the Georgetown and official Washington social circuit.

The vivid portrait Scottie Lanahan painted — reduced to a small box I wrote for the jump page — emphasized Mary Meyer's physical beauty, her sense of daring (she had worked on the night copy desk of the New York *Daily Mirror* just out of college and rode the subway to and from the job), and her intellect.

My role in the story was, in fact, minor. What made the *Star*'s coverage extraordinary was Lance Morrow.

By that summer, and with Tom Dimond's departure for the University of Wisconsin, Lance had become my closest friend at the paper. He had grown up in D.C., too, in more rarefied circumstances, in a big shingled house in Cleveland Park. Hugh Morrow, his father, was an ex-newspaperman and

517

Washington editor of the *Saturday Evening Post* who now was New York governor Nelson Rockefeller's principal aide-de-camp and press spokesman. At age thirteen, Lance had been a Senate page assigned to Bobby Baker's staff. He'd graduated from Gonzaga High downtown — the first-rate parochial academy run by the Jesuits — and from Harvard, magna cum laude, in the spring of '63. When he was seventeen and eighteen he'd worked at the *Star,* in the old building on Pennsylvania Avenue, as a copyboy and dictationist. Sid Epstein had hired him to come back that fall as a dictationist, with a promise of going on the training program in the spring of '64.

It was apparent from his first stories in the paper that Lance possessed a kind of native writing talent that, had he chosen, could have been expended as easily on great fiction as journalism. So much so that Ted Crown, John Burch, and Al Lewis had taken to calling him Hemingway, which they did not necessarily intend as a compliment. Partly it was because he showed up at the police headquarters pressroom wearing a tweed jacket and carrying copies of *Encounter* and *Commentary* magazines and also because Hemingway was a novelist known to them. They saw that he had a superior reporter's eye, discernment, and instincts. Plus he had a capacity for fun and playful misconduct that — as became evident during the months we spent together

518

on the dictation bank — was a good fit (or so others noted) with my less restrained and refined manner.

At police headquarters that Monday, Lance had heard the radio dispatcher direct cruisers 25 and 26 to the C&O Canal. He recognized them as homicide squad cars and right away called the city desk. Then he drove fast to Georgetown, parked on Canal Road just west of the bridge, and found two men who had been fixing a car and had seen the shooting from a distance. Standing by the wall overlooking the canal, Lance could see a body curled up in a ball on the towpath. There were no cops by the body. They were far in the distance, forming a dragnet to look for the killer.

From playing in the area as a boy, he remembered a tunnel that went under the canal and exited on the towpath not far from where the body lay.

Lance ran through the tunnel and found himself standing alone over the body. The woman was lying on her side, and he knew she was dead, but the bullet holes were turned away from him, and he could not see any blood. So he waited until cops finally approached and held up his reporter's notebook to identify himself — although some of the cops already knew him from the homicide squad.

A few days later, I pasted the Scottie

Lanahan sidebar, and the page one story to which I'd contributed, into my scrapbook. And I also slipped a loose copy of Lance's first-person story inside, as a reminder to keep studying — about the possibilities of breaking journalistic convention. He'd written that, a dozen years earlier, he and his brother had chased butterflies on that stretch of the towpath — recalling the fishermen with their live bait and tackle on the banks of the canal, and the red admiral butterfly his brother had caught and asphyxiated in his little lepidopterist's killing jar.

For the next few days, half a dozen reporters — Lance and me included — continued adding details to the Walter Jenkins story and the Mary Pinchot Meyer saga. Then, in the course of a single week, the Russians launched a spacecraft with three cosmonauts aboard (it was the first time more than one person had been sent into space); Nikita Khrushchev was deposed as the leader of the Soviet Union; China became a nuclear power with the explosion of its first atomic bomb; Martin Luther King Jr. won the Nobel Peace Prize as churches continued to be bombed in the South; and Lemuel Penn's accused killers — three members of the Ku Klux Klan — were acquitted of murder by a Georgia jury. At week's end, former president Herbert Hoover died, and his casket lay in state in the

Capitol rotunda. Again, I stood outside with my notebook.

By now I was a bona fide general assignment reporter, or at least Sid Epstein and his deputy city editors seemed to regard me as such. I had never much liked doing old-fashioned man-on-the-street interviews, but Sid Epstein, pushing the principle of *all news is local,* had the idea that Khrushchev's fall deserved such a downtown send-off. He sent me to G Street outside Woodward & Lothrop to record the reactions of random Washingtonians. I thought it was the stupidest assignment I'd been handed since I was a copyboy, and after half an hour of filling my notebook with the requisite quotes, I marched down the street to find Eddie Bernstein on his skateboard. I took more notes on what he had to say than on the remarks of the full-bodied people on the street.

It didn't take a Hebrew school graduate (which I wasn't) to figure that the circumcision of Michael MacPherson Siegel was on the fringes of traditional Judaic territory. Before that October, I had never been to a bris except my own, which was attended (I was told years later) by my mother, my grandparents, and my great-aunt Rose and great-uncle Itzel. My father, because he was off at war in the South Pacific, missed the event. Michael Siegel's circumcision, on the other hand, was like a state occasion — one that might have been organized by Damon Runyon. It drew a crowd of close to a hundred. The guest list included the likes of Goldie Ahern, the boxing promoter and ex–bantamweight fighter whose name had once been Isidore Goldstein. Duke Zeibert, the restaurateur who patterned himself and his establishment after Toots Shor in New York, was there; Father Hartke had been assigned a vague ecclesiastical purpose in the ceremony; Sid Epstein, his eyes averted squeamishly, helped pin the wailing baby down; Bobbie Hornig performed the same task with more competence; Judges Tom Scalley and John Sirica, both known for the lengthy jail sentences they liked to impose, stood by in witness to the scene; a pair of photographers from the *Evening Star* Picture Department were on hand to record the event; and old buddies of the baby's parents hung in the background like photogenic props, among them Shirley Povich, the *Washington Post* sportswriter, and the great Gil Hodges, beloved in Brooklyn but now suffering as the manager of the hopeless Washington Senators.

Nine months before the bris, Myra MacPherson — the gorgeous and hilarious (and at times hilariously profane) feature writer — married Morrie Siegel, whose byline had migrated to the *Star* after his years across town as the premier sports columnist at the *Daily News*. Their wedding had been planned for early December, but the assassination and its aftermath had caused a postponement. My own fantasies about Myra MacPherson had gotten me no farther than a great friendship, but not for lack of trying and seeing a lot of movies together and hanging out at Harrigan's late into the night. Now and then she found it necessary to remind me that I was either nine or ten years younger than she was, depending on the month of the year we were in.

The *mohel* running the MacPherson-Siegel bris was Rabbi Chaim Williamowski, a character well known around town quite apart from his precision with a knife. He was the Jewish chaplain at St. Elizabeths, rabbi to the Police and Fire Departments (with a combined congregation tiny by comparison to those assembled for Michael Siegel's bris), and consultant to a couple of ceremonial winemakers and matzo bakers. His son Ben, a dentist, lived down the street from my parents on Harvey Road, and his grandson — my friend Sammy — was a couple of years behind me at Blair.

After the ceremony, as everyone sipped champagne and nibbled on Duke Zeibert's pastrami and chopped liver hors d'oeuvres in the dining room, I approached Rabbi Williamowski and told him that I was myself a graduate of his practice, class of 1944. He looked at me and said (for the four thousandth time, I guessed), "I never remember a face." After which I informed him of my Harvey Road connection with his mishpachah and asked if I could come visit him at his St. Elizabeths office.

Over the next weeks, the rabbi took me to the Anacostia police precinct for a personal introduction to its commanding officer; got the St. Elizabeths brass to allow me a meeting in a rubber-walled room with the Badman of Swampoodle, Dallas O. Williams; and greased visits with the general and admiral in charge of Bolling Air Force Base and the adjacent Naval Air Station, which occupied the length of the Anacostia flats by the river. I was determined to be the *Star*'s unofficial chronicler of Anacostia affairs, fertile journalistic territory long ignored.

Around that time, the city desk was handing me assignments focused on urban planning and renewal. The sleepy southern town of my childhood was undergoing transformative changes. Even some World War II "tempos" on the Mall were being torn down. The final section of the Beltway had just been completed — with a ribbon-cutting ceremony I was sent to. I covered endless National Capital Park and Planning Commission meetings at which plans for a futuristic subway system were taking shape. I rewrote — with flourishes drawing on my experience as a child of the disappearing city — handouts from the Pennsylvania Avenue planning authority about the gigantic new FBI building designed, in part, to level all the peep show emporiums and tattoo parlors on Ninth Street. In grade school our fourth-grade class had taken the tour of the FBI's headquarters at the Justice Department. The highlight was the shooting range in the basement, where G-men fired hundreds of rounds from tommy guns at bull's-eyed paper targets of the bureau's Ten Most Wanted. J. Edgar Hoover had prevailed on Lyndon Johnson to break federal budget guidelines for construction of a new headquarters and promised that the next FBI firing range would be an even flashier display for America's children.

Much of Southwest Washington, where my grandparents and other immigrant "greenhorns" had first settled, was being razed. Harrigan's was now a lone lighthouse on a ghostly cleared concrete peninsula. Permits and contracts were being authorized for the construction of redbrick public housing developments for tens of thousands of the city's poor in the back portion of the peninsula. Glass-fronted luxury apartments with views of the Anacostia and Potomac Rivers were given enthusiastic approval by the city authorities, and a gigantic departmental complex on the scale of the Federal Triangle built fifty years earlier was planned along Independence Avenue.

When I wasn't writing about Anacostia or being sent to planning meetings, I was working — often at home, or out doing interviews on my own time — on the long-term projects I was nurturing. Among them were the life and times of Eddie Bernstein; the tribulations of the Wesorts; the political ambitions of the Big Train, Walter Johnson; the burial of Scott and Zelda Fitzgerald in their Rockville graves.

And there was one story that filled an entire drawer of my metal filing cabinet: the Giles-Johnson rape case in Maryland. I knew a lot more about the case than what was in the newspapers because the lawyer for the accused rapists — two young Black men sentenced to death for raping a white woman in rural northern Montgomery County — was Joe Forer. I'd known Joe for as long as I could remember. He was my parents' friend. When I was little and went with my mother and father to the downtown lunch counter "sit-downs," he had been the attorney who won the court case that had finally desegregated Washington's restaurants. He'd given me reams of documents and transcripts from depositions about the Giles-Johnson matter. He compared the case to *To Kill a Mockingbird,* the novel that had won the Pulitzer Prize and been made into a movie starring Gregory

526

Peck. Joe Forer did not look like Gregory Peck, and he smoked big cigars and lisped a little. But I knew how good a lawyer he was, and thought if anybody could save the lives of the accused he could.

25

THE WHEEL

Charlie Puffenbarger, who knew my academic situation inside out, and a lot of other things about me — especially because he and I would go together to Harrigan's after work now that Jo Anne had left — advised me not to say anything about flunking out of school. Not even to Sid Epstein, or to any of the other editors. Puff was a slim, somehow sinuous and insinuating man with an air of crafty amusement about him. He looked as if he were brimming with secrets, possibly salacious and maybe hilarious. He was a great pal to the younger members of the staff, and especially to me.

Once, a few days just after the end of the semester, Mr. Porter asked me how it was going at school; I just said okay and that I was waiting on my grades, which technically was true, though I knew they were going to be all F's. Puff figured, and I hoped he was right, that by the time my academic status became known, I'd have a pretty good argument for remaining a reporter on the staff — a scrap-book full of stories, plus the confidence of pretty much every editor in the newsroom that I could handle almost any assignment thrown at me. I'd even become good at dictating stories myself.

On the third Thursday of September, after Sid Epstein and I had finished the newsroom schedule for the following week, he told me — and I couldn't imagine him saying anything more devastating — that I'd have to go back to the dictation bank. He said he had met with Bill Hill about new staff hires, including the next round of recruits for the training program. Sid had proposed to Hill that since I was already on the staff and thriving at it, they could just eliminate one of the hires and everything would even up. But Hill had said no: I couldn't be a reporter until I graduated from college, even though he knew full well I'd been a reporter with stories plastered all over page one and the split page since June.

Sid scrunched up his face and the corner of his mouth when he told me this, a really skeptical look, shaking his head as if to say he didn't understand it either. "Hill doesn't want anyone new on the staff without a college degree," he said.

I may have raised my voice. I was already on the staff and I wasn't new, I said, and Sid Epstein didn't answer but rolled his eyes, which I had always thought was pretty funny when I'd seen him do it, up until this moment. What I really thought — and it made me sad and hurt — was that Sid Epstein hadn't fought hard enough for me.

I asked him if he'd pointed out to Hill that the *Star*'s city editor — Sidney Epstein — and deputy state editor, Mary Lou Werner, who'd won a Pulitzer Prize, were both college dropouts. But I could see that Sid didn't want to go into more detail. I told him I wanted to talk to Hill myself, which he said was fine.

As far as I knew, Bill Hill had never done anything that made the *Star* a better paper, certainly not in the four years I'd been there, though he had been the co-editor of a book called *Mirror of War: The* Washington Star *Reports the Civil War*. It was a very good book, in an oversized format, with more than three hundred pages of the *Star*'s original coverage from a century before, battle after battle, campaign after campaign, in pictures and stories, with the old headlines reproduced above all the articles. I had used it to prepare when I was sent to the battle reenactments. I was sure the book was so good because John Stepp, a first-rate feature writer and its co-editor, had written commentary for each chapter.

Hill was on the newsroom floor, talking to John Cassady, the national editor. I parked myself about two feet behind him, so if he turned around he'd run straight into me. I figured I had nothing to lose at this point.

And when he did turn, I asked if I could talk to him for a minute in his office. To which he seemed to agree, reluctantly.

Bill Hill, who stood two or three inches over six feet, had a loping but slightly menacing way of moving around the newsroom, as if he were off to correct some grievous wrong or chastise someone. His body tended to list to one side or the other, and he seemed to be pushing through a crowd even though none was there. His face was either blank or angry; I'd never seen him laugh, except in a horsey kind of way. Nor could I ever figure out why he had a responsible position at the paper, but then I thought the same about two or three other senior people, who gave you the feeling that they'd been promoted for some long-forgotten nineteenth-century reason that had ceased to make any sense in the twentieth.

It occurred to me once we got inside his office that I had never set foot in it. If Rudy Kauffmann's office was a shrine to geology, Bill Hill's was a museum of Bill Hill glad-handing. He'd been on the board of the American Association of Managing Editors and several similar outfits, and his surroundings suggested a keener interest in their doings than running a newsroom. There were framed photos tacked up on the walls of him presiding with a gavel over the managing editors, and others with his cronies at this convention or that.

I looked around for a second, thinking that there might be a picture of him and Miriam Ottenberg together. There wasn't, though there was a photo of her and Ludy Werner at some event for the Pulitzers. The romantic pairing of Bill Hill and Ottsie (assuming our speculation was accurate) was hilarious, first of all because he was tall and rangy and sort of goofy and she was short, compact, bustling — like a tightly packed sausage. Both of them usually appeared to be irritated at something, and of course they seemed to like to fight when they had a drink or two. Charles Dickens would have had a lot of fun with them.

Now he leaned back in his slatted wooden chair — sort of like Johnny Burch's at police headquarters, except that Bill Hill's was of polished mahogany — and asked me what was on my mind. I thought it was actually possible that he hadn't guessed why I might be in his office for the first time in the four years I'd been at the paper.

I told him why right off the bat: that Sid Epstein had just told me I couldn't stay on the staff — despite the fact that my scrapbook was full of clippings that might hold their own against those of a fair number of cityside reporters. And that I was pretty sure that Coit Hendley and Charlie Puffenbarger and Harry Bacas — and Sid, too — would agree. I was surprised at my own boldness.

Hill gave me an unconvincing smile of what

he meant to be sympathy or understanding or something in that neighborhood, I suppose, and uttered a line that I knew I would never forget.

"Carl," he said, "you've really put your shoulder to the wheel, and your work has been great. But experience is no substitute for the training program."

He told me that once I graduated from college and got my diploma, I could go straight on the training program the very next day.

I would like to tell you that I got angry on the spot, but the anger would come a little later. I was feeling pretty bad about the whole thing, a little stunned and confused (which wasn't like me), and I pondered again if Sid Epstein could have kept this from happening. I knew I was never going to graduate from college. And now, for the first time since Rudy Kauffmann had marched me down the aisle that, at this moment, I was looking at to keep my eyes from looking at Bill Hill, it occurred to me that I might not be making my newspaper career at the *Evening Star*.

Hill got up from his desk, letting me know that was all there was to it. I don't remember what I said on the way out. Puff was still marking up overnight copy on the city desk, and I told him what had happened. When he heard the part about "experience is no substitute for the training program," Puff asked, "Hill really said that?" He went over to Ludy

Werner and told her what had happened, and the two of them thought it would be a good idea to take me to Harrigan's to commiserate and discuss the matter.

We went in Ludy's car, and by the time we got there I was finally really mad, and though usually in the evenings I would only drink beer, we all ordered martinis.

What added to my fury was that I knew that Hill himself had, a couple of days earlier, been singing my praises about a story I'd written, one that he took credit for. Here's what happened. He had just initiated another harebrained idea to invigorate the split page — prevailing on Sid Epstein to run a new series above the fold for a couple of weeks, about people who had unusual government jobs.

Sid Epstein had thrown up his hands when he told me about it, during one of our meetings to do the schedule. He said Hill's real reason for wanting the series was to show off the capabilities of the *Star*'s new color presses, which had been installed at a cost of hundreds of thousands of dollars. So Hill had found somebody in the civil service who'd come up with a list of government jobs that had exotic picture possibilities. Sid offered me a crack at the story initiating the series: about a woman taxidermist — the only taxidermist on the federal payroll, the idea being to also emphasize that this wasn't the usual women's work, plus having a splashy picture (as Sid put it) of this dame with a stuffed cheetah.

Actually it was a leopard.

The leopard appeared on page one, not the split page, because the new color presses could (for now) print color only for the front page, not inside the paper. A banner headline ran across all eight columns, above the *Star* masthead — STARTING TODAY: A SERIES ON UNUSUAL GOVERNMENT JOBS, PAGE B-1.

Beneath the masthead, in glorious color, were the leopard and the taxidermist — Sybil Greenwell, she in orange blouse and blue smock, applying extra spots to the beast with a paintbrush. Below the photo ran this copy:

Unusual Occupation

In all the vast hierarchy of the federal government, Sybil Greenwell may have one of the most unusual jobs. She is a taxidermist and considers touching up a leopard as part of the day's work. (Story and other pictures on page B-1.)

Above the fold on the split page, under my byline and the headline GIRL LOVES HER JOB IN EERIE JUNGLE SETTING were black-and-white photos of Miss Greenwell dusting off a whooping crane and painting the feathers of a stuffed parrot. My lede said,

535

If the average government girl were to open the office supply closet some morning and find several dozen dead rats, lizards, skunks, toads and snakes, she might reasonably be expected to react drastically. Scream. Faint. Jump out the window. Take the pledge.

During part of my interview with her, and more for the benefit of the photographer than for me, Miss Greenwell showed us how she installed a glass eye on the leopard, which involved screwing it into the leopard's stuffed eye socket almost like a lightbulb. As she did it, I thought about my childhood friend Ian Gilbert's glass eye, and about his father, Ben Gilbert, Sid Epstein's competing city editor, across town at the *Post*. Ian would always be taking his eye out and then putting it back in.

By now I knew a few reporters from the *Washington Post* who drank with Rupe Welch when I'd tag along, among them Harry Gabbett, the famous (for his droll wit) rewrite man, and Phil Casey, who could hold his own with any feature writer in the city. They'd meet up with Rupe either at Harrigan's or more often downtown not far from the *Post* at the Golden Parrot, which was owned by Goldie Ahern, the fight promoter. They were old-timers, and probably had fifteen years each on Rupe, but together the group was a hoot, even though Gabbett and Casey would complain endlessly about what a dull place the *Post* was, and how almost none of the reporters went out drinking together, and they hoped we appreciated how good we had it at the *Star*.

Which of course was true: we did have it good. Really good. But the part of the equation that they hadn't considered was Bill Hill, who as far as I was concerned was as big a reason as any that the *Post* was pulling farther and farther ahead of the *Star* on too many fronts.

That night after I got back home, I went straight to my room and pulled out my scrapbook. I wanted to see if I was right about the work I'd done in my months on staff.

The headlines of my stories were the stuff of any solid cityside general assignment reporter.

OFFICER SHOOTS MAN WITH GUN

WIN IN SWEEPSTAKES STUNS
D.C. BEAUTICIAN

STUDENTS URGE 'FREE LITHUANIA'

PORTABLE 6 ON THE BEAM
(GOLDWATER HAMS IT UP)

COLD CAPSULES SEIZED BY FDA

INTRUDERS TIE 2, ROB HOME
IN SPRING VALLEY

NOTRE DAME HEAD HITS
COLLEGES ON COLD WAR

DR. T.H. CARROLL DIES:
PRESIDENT OF G.W.U.

11TH ARMORED COMES HOME TO FORT
MEADE AND A HOUSING SHORTAGE

APPRENTICE COOKS
MASTER THE TRADE

MISSISSIPPI NEGROES PUSH
CONVENTION BID

WEEK-END D.C. WARRIORS
FLY ATLANTIC

HELICOPTER BUSINESS CAN'T GET
ALOFT [LEAD ON BUSINESS PAGE]

THE ROUTE TO OUTDOOR FUN
[SPECIAL BELTWAY SECTION]

52 STRANDED BY STEWARDESS
STRIKE REACH D.C.

FOUR CHILDREN DIE AS FIRE
ENGULFS HOME IN N.E.

MARYLAND PRISON SCHOOL
REHABILITATES FELONS

DISTRICT'S FINAL VOTER DRIVE
TOPS THE 218,000 MARK

TWO YOUTHS SHOT TO DEATH
IN WOODED AREA

FAMILY OF PILOT SLAIN IN VIETNAM
IS LIVING IN BETHESDA

PRESIDENT HONORS 121 PUPILS

CLERGYMEN FIGHTING FOR CIVIL
RIGHTS BILL GIVE THANKS

COOL HOLIDAY FORECAST
FOR EVENTS HERE

And so forth.

For four months my byline had read:

By Carl Bernstein
Star Staff Writer

In the coming weeks and months, I continued to be assigned to just as many stories as
before, and I was treated by my editors as if
my shoulder was still on the wheel. But my
byline reverted to

By Carl Bernstein
Star Special Writer

My pay remained the same reporter's salary, and I was still the city desk clerk, but I
did have to take dictation again, though not
nearly as much as before.

At times, it was still fun to be there. There
were intense friendships among us — the work
and our professional lives were all mixed up
with our personal lives; we shared the stories,
the labor, the gossip and politics. Working for
the *Star* was a little like being part of a troupe
of actors in a repertory company, all of us

absorbed in the same project, all wrapped up in the stories, the work, and the editors, the cast of characters. We were smart, we never had enough money, and we often had too much to drink. There were hangovers, and dreary times at police headquarters, and sometimes the early men on the city desk would call at seven in the morning to tell you that you had overslept and had been due in the newsroom at six thirty.

My first "Star Special Writer" byline after walking out of Bill Hill's office was on Election Day, on a story about the snafus caused by the huge turnout of D.C. citizens casting ballots for president for the first time. I'd taken cabs to half a dozen voting places, and the situation was the same at each precinct: for hours that Tuesday morning, the crush of people overwhelmed the poll workers. At one elementary school, twenty-five hundred voters were already waiting in lines that snaked around the block and beyond when the polls opened at seven.

The situation was inflamed by Republican poll watchers. My story noted,

The local GOP placed three "poll watchers" at each precinct as part of a national Republican "Operation Eagle Eye" program to challenge votes thought to be cast irregularly.

I'd known and covered the D.C. Republican chairman, Carl Shipley, since I was a copyboy attending citizens meetings. Now he told me — disingenuously, I believed — that election officials were prejudiced against his poll workers. He claimed "the election board people were overly anticipating Republican goon squads." Yet his earlier threat of Republican poll watchers initiating wholesale challenges alleging voter fraud never materialized; only twenty-three hundred of almost two hundred thousand ballots cast were challenged by the time the polls closed.

Some election board officials and poll workers told me the voting process was hampered by intimidation from Republican "Eagle Eye" functionaries demanding that they be allowed to make challenges before individual voters cast their ballots.

The election results — in the District, as in the whole country — were of historic proportions: LBJ took 61 percent of the nationwide popular vote, the largest margin since the almost uncontested presidential election of 1820; Barry Goldwater won only four states, giving Johnson an Electoral College victory of 486 to 52. "Extremism in the defense of liberty is no vice" — the mantra of Goldwater's campaign — had made it easier for Johnson and the Democrats to paint the Arizona senator as a nuclear-trigger-happy warmonger; and they turned his other campaign slogan, "In Your Heart You Know He's Right," into another boomerang: "In Your Guts You Know He's Nuts."

541

That night, I worked at the *Washington Post,* which is to say that its newsroom on L Street was the local election night pool headquarters for the *Star,* the *Post,* the *Daily News,* and the Associated Press. Results from every county and municipality in Maryland, Virginia, and West Virginia poured into the newsroom over the wires and on phone lines from court-houses across the states. Every two years on election night, the pool headquarters rotated.

My job was to relay the Maryland results through the night back to the *Star* newsroom by phone, and I'd been given a seat on the *Post* state desk from which to work.

The *Post*'s newsroom was packed beyond capacity because along with the twenty-five or thirty people working in the pool, the whole *Post* reportorial staff was covering — on deadline — the presidential election, the U.S. House and Senate elections, and the state and local elections, including D.C.'s first vote for president. Yet the place seemed strangely quiet compared to what the *Star* newsroom was like on deadline even on a non–Election Day. No one yelled *"Copy!"* Reporters walked their own stories up to the desk. And people talked in almost hushed tones, as if the place were a public library and not a great daily newspaper.

The newsroom was smaller than the *Star*'s grand open space. The *Post* had been putting out a newspaper from this newsroom since

1951. Instead of a hay baler to carry copy to the composing room, there were pneumatic tubes at the news and copy desks that made a whooshing sound each time a piece of copy went on its way. The *whoosh* punctuated the weird quiet of the place, and you heard the faintest clicking of the teletype machines coming from a separate enclosed room just off the newsroom floor.

LBJ's victory was so overwhelming that the *Post* was able to close its first edition by ten o'clock, declaring the president's massive reelection victory. During the lull after that deadline I heard someone call "Carl!" and looked up to see Ben Gilbert standing beside me. I hadn't seen him since I was ten years old, and I'd forgotten, from seeing him come home from work on Friday nights when I would spend the weekend in the Gilbert house, that he wore bow ties. The round tortoiseshell eyeglasses were also the same. Instinctively I said, "Hi, Ben," and got up to shake hands. It was a confusing moment for me.

The Gilberts had been the one family in our D.C. neighborhood with whom my parents felt a particular kinship, a sense of shared values. At the Gilberts' dinner table, as at ours, adult talk was likely to be about the issues of the day — discussed in terms understandable to children. The larger concerns of the Gilberts seemed not unlike those of the Bernsteins.

Aside from our house, theirs was the only one in the neighborhood in which I had ever seen Black friends.

Then, in 1954, my mother was called to testify before the House Committee on Un-American Activities, which was investigating purported Communist Party associations in the District of Columbia. After her testimony, the lead story on page one of the next day's *Washington Post* carried a six-column head-line (RED PARTY 'HARD CORE' IN CAPITAL, VELDE SAYS) set off by six one-column headshots. Harold Velde, a Republican congressman from Illinois, was chairman of the HCUA. My mother was in column 4: ". . . invoke Fifth Amendment to duck questions put by House Un-American Activities Group," said the caption.

The next day, at the Giant food store, my mother was picking out a head of lettuce, and right next to her, also picking out a head of lettuce, was Maureen Gilbert, Ben's wife and my mother's close friend. Maureen Gilbert walked away without a word, and thereafter the Gilbert family's contact with the Bernstein family ended. (It was indicative of the time that on that same day, my younger sister was thrown out of her nursery school.)

My parents attributed the end of our relationship with the Gilbert family to the fact that Ben Gilbert had had a left-wing background while a student at City College of New York, and so perhaps he feared that his job might be in jeopardy if he associated with friends who had invoked the Fifth Amendment before the Un-American Activities Committee.

Now, ten years later, Ben Gilbert obviously appreciated that I'd put my shoulder to the wheel at the *Star,* because after we shook hands he told me how terrific my stories were and how pleased he was that I seemed to have chosen the newspaper game as my profession.

He asked after my parents, and I told him they were fine. There wasn't time, happily, for any more small talk, because the next batch of election returns was pouring in, and Gilbert had his own staff's work to edit.

26

FLACK

I'd come to know the Reverend Walter Fauntroy quite well since our introduction at that civic association meeting in 1961. He was a small, fiery man, pastor of the New Bethel Baptist Church in Northwest D.C., in the Shaw neighborhood where he grew up. I went to Sunday services there a few times, at his invitation. He would sometimes sing "You'll Never Walk Alone" in a dramatic near-falsetto voice with such enthusiasm that even his own congregants laughed good-naturedly and studied the stained-glass windows.

He was well regarded in the civil rights movement, especially because of his closeness to Dr. Martin Luther King Jr. and his role as Washington director of King's Southern Christian Leadership Conference. Physically and emotionally, Fauntroy struck me as the opposite of his mentor. In contrast to King's rolling, biblical oratory, Fauntroy's voice was high-pitched; he was a small man, wiry, and had none of King's commanding presence

546

and self-assurance. Fauntroy tended to push his way to the front, not subtly, but he had a keen intelligence and the ability to size up people and situations in a hurry.

Though I was eleven years younger, we'd established an easy relationship that went beyond simple give-and-take/question-and-answer journalism. We always spoke on a first-name basis. Every month or two we would have a long conversation about what was happening in the city and the country, though sometimes he wandered into theological territory that was beyond me.

He'd helped coordinate the March on Washington and was in constant touch with all the major civil rights leaders and organizations. Fauntroy was one of half a dozen clergymen, union representatives, and civic leaders who had formed an organization called the Coalition of Conscience that, for the past five years, had been at the forefront of every civil rights battle in the city. As SCLC's man in Washington, he was deeply involved in the voting rights campaign that Dr. King and hundreds of young people were currently waging in Alabama, keeping up the moral and media pressure on Congress and the president to get a voting rights bill signed into law.

Bad things were happening very fast in Alabama. On February 26, a civil rights worker named Jimmie Lee Jackson was killed by police in the city of Marion. On March 5,

Dr. King met with President Johnson at the White House and told him of the march he was planning from Selma to the state capitol in Montgomery to protest the killing. Dr. King confided to Fauntroy privately that he was worried the march would end in violence, using much stronger terms than the ones quoted in an AP story that the *Star* ran about the meeting with the president. Fauntroy had told me about this conversation and I'd shared the information with John Cassady, the national editor.

Two days later, about six hundred marchers led by Hosea Williams and John Lewis — the young activist who was the chairman of the Student Nonviolent Coordinating Committee — started marching out of Selma to cross the Alabama River on the Edmund Pettus Bridge. At the far end of the bridge, state and county police, reinforced by a horse-mounted posse of local white men, beat and gassed the marchers and scattered them. John Lewis got a fractured skull. Dozens of other marchers went to the hospital. That was Bloody Sunday.

Haynes Johnson flew to Alabama on Monday to cover the story, and I took his dictation on deadline from Selma and Montgomery all that week. Most days, I'd check in with Fauntroy to help fill in details that would supplement what Haynes was seeing and learning down there. Haynes was amazed at the arrival of hundreds and hundreds of ordinary

Americans, Black and white, who'd witnessed the violence on TV and decided to give their support and show up in Alabama. On Tuesday night he had coffee after dinner with a white clergyman we both knew from Washington, James Reeb. A few hours afterward, Reeb was savagely beaten by Klansmen in Selma. He died two days later.

In response, and in consultation with Dr. King in Selma, Fauntroy and other leaders of the Coalition of Conscience met with President Johnson in the White House to discuss what was to be done in the crisis — especially how to get federal protection for the demonstrators in Selma. The meeting was tense. Johnson said at one point that he did not "want to be blackjacked" into action. Fauntroy gave me a briefing on all of it. I told Cassady, the national editor, that Fauntroy's information was far more detailed than the AP account that had run on page one of the first edition. He had me do a lengthy memo, which the national desk rewrote and combined with the AP's information and became the guts of the lead story, under an eight-column banner headline, in the Red Streak Final that evening.

Fauntroy also told me that a private plane was flying down to Montgomery with people from the Coalition. He said there was a seat available and he'd hold it for me.

I told Cassady. But he said if there really

was only a single seat remaining, he'd need to give it to Mary McGrory. And he did. She flew down on the plane to join Haynes Johnson in covering the story.

I was angry. I had vacation time accumulated, and I immediately claimed it. In the heat of the moment, I arranged with Fauntroy to become a sort of public relations man for the Coalition of Conscience for the duration of the crisis.

Which is how I wound up in the midst of the big demonstration in Lafayette Square across from the White House on a sunny March 15, hours before Lyndon Johnson went before a joint session of Congress and urged passage of the Voting Rights Act, declaring (in his emphatic Texas accent), *"And we shall overcome!"*

Fifteen thousand people were packed into Lafayette Square to demand federal intervention in George Wallace's Alabama. I was not a reporter now, but a flack — though for a cause in which I believed with fervor — handing out mimeographed press releases and briefing reporters. Walter Reuther of the United Auto Workers spoke. He and the others wore black armbands to mourn the death of James Reeb. Stokely Carmichael objected that the armbands were for a white man and not for the Black man, Jimmie Lee Jackson, who had also died.

I stood in the crowd next to the statue of Andrew Jackson mounted on a rearing horse and waving his hat. I talked to Paul Moore, the Episcopal bishop of Washington and co-chairman with Fauntroy of the Coalition of Conscience, and to Fannie Lou Hamer of the Mississippi Freedom Democratic Party. Clarence Hunter, still the *Star*'s lone Black reporter, came up to us and I drew him aside and gave him a rundown — all the information I had about King and Fauntroy's discussions with the White House, the Coalition's role, and what was likely to come next.

In the four and a half years since I'd been at the *Star,* I had never felt so uncomfortable. Almost out of my own skin. I'd covered the Coalition of Conscience since it was founded — initially to fight Senator Byrd's man-in-the-house rule, after a welfare recipient was evicted from her home under its provisions and froze to death her first night on the street. Paul Moore by then was also a good source.

I wanted to be a reporter covering the Selma story, with a notebook and a typewriter. Not someone handing out mimeographed press releases and whispering in journalists' ears.

Two weeks after Bloody Sunday, in a triumphant march led by Martin Luther King Jr. and protected by federal marshals, twenty-five thousand people — including hundreds of celebrities and reporters and escorted by the Alabama State Police — set off from Selma, crossed the Edmund Pettus Bridge, and headed east toward Montgomery, fifty miles away. They made it five days later.

I slunk back to the dictation bank, wondering if I was going to get a lecture from Sid Epstein — or even fired by Bill Hill — for crossing the reportorial line. I heard not a word.

In the midst of the battles in Alabama, Miriam Ottenberg had written a massive front-page special report about right-wing violence in America perpetrated by the Klan, the Minute Men, and other vigilante groups. The headline was THE HATERS: THEIR CALL TO ARMS CAUSES NEW CONCERN IN WASHINGTON.

As if to confirm what Miriam Ottenberg had written, on the day the march reached Montgomery, three Alabama Klansmen in a car caught up with a white housewife from Detroit, Viola Liuzzo, as she drove on the road between Selma and Montgomery. She had come to Alabama to join the march. They gunned her down from the passing lane.

27

LEAVINGS

Sometime that spring — perhaps during the season's first hot spell — Bill Hill determined that a way to slow the *Star*'s eclipse by the *Post* would be to provide readers with two full newspaper pages of weather and astronomical information every day, including elaborate maps and charts and diagrams of the moon rising and the sun going down and tide tables and related matters of meteorology and maritime phenomena. That would mean that, on a given day, an unusual amount of the paper's available news hole would be given over to weather.

The managing editor and I had not exchanged a word since he'd told me I could never be a staff reporter without a college degree. Then, one afternoon in early May, he planted himself in the doorway of his office — directly across from the dictation bank — called my name, and beckoned me to join him. I sat and, without further prelude, he announced that I was just the man he was looking for — to research, design, and produce a set of mock-ups for the greatest weather pages in any daily newspaper in America, or probably the world.

He brought forth a loose-leaf binder with the *Star*'s logo on the cover, slid it across his desk to me, and said the contents — a dozen or so pages separated by dime-store dividers with plastic tabs — would give me some idea of the subject areas and types of illustrations and tables and written matter he had in mind.

"Carl, everybody is interested in the weather."

I gathered from his tone and enthusiasm that he thought I'd welcome this special assignment, and possibly that he figured it would salve my disappointment at being demoted back to the dictation bank. He'd told Sid Epstein that I'd have all the resources — Art Department people, photographers, unlimited funds for research — and two months to work on the project.

Then he dismissed me without asking if I had any questions.

I went into Sid Epstein's empty office to study the contents of the binder. There were pages of dense technical prose and graphs from the Naval Observatory's library, from NASA, from the *Bulletin of the American Meteorological Society,* from the National Weather Service. Most of it was unintelligible to me. My experience in the science of weather was limited to dialing the forecast each morning, or now and then glancing at the daily forecast on the *Star*'s weather "ear" — the little summary in the upper right-hand corner of page one.

At first, my approach to the project was scattershot. I went to National Airport's control tower to study the forecasts the air traffic controllers received on teletype machines to warn them of impending snow or crosswinds or whatever. (Hill wanted to know if it was feasible to update our pages in each edition of the paper.) Then I camped at the Library of Congress to study books on basic meteorology. I tried to learn about isobars. I studied marine forecasts and pored over maps from the Coast and Geodetic Survey. This was worse than going to college. I toted stacks of professional journals and illustrated textbooks back to the *Star* for use by the Art Department.

Finally, I hit on how to better comprehend my subject: I bought a copy of *The Golden Book of Weather,* for children.

In the end, I presented Bill Hill with the goddamnedest weather proposal any newspaper had ever seen, I'm pretty sure. And he loved it.

Soon he had dummy pages pasted all over his office walls. He called long conferences with the other editors to pick their brains for ideas on how weather stories — actual tales of snow and ice and rain and fog — from all over the United States, from everywhere in the world, might enliven the new pages he was contemplating. The editors came out of his office scratching their heads and exchanging glances.

Pretty soon people were joking about it at Harrigan's — and commiserating with me (and asking me for the forecast).

Almost as abruptly as Bill Hill had dreamed up this idea, he began to let go of it — I gathered because Newbold Noyes and some wiser heads had doubts about sacrificing precious newspaper real estate to in-depth coverage of the changing tides and hidden phases of the lunar cycle.

The longer I had been city desk clerk, the more I'd looked forward to my Thursday meetings with Sid Epstein. Our sessions started at four in the afternoon, after the final-edition deadline, except when big news was breaking late and we had to move it to the next day. A big part of my newsroom education had taken place in those meetings. I asked questions, and Sid, as easy and informal as he ever was, would take the time to discuss how I'd covered this event or that, sometimes without my raising the matter first. Or he'd tell a story about covering local gangsters when he was at the *Times-Herald*. Still, there was always a reserve about Sid Epstein. He didn't want you to get too close. He was wary, self-contained. Coit

Hendley once told me at Harrigan's that even though he'd been Sid Epstein's deputy for five years, he didn't feel he really knew the man. He wasn't sure anybody really did, including Eleni, though the two of them seemed to have a wonderful life together.

Not long after Easter, Sid and I were talking about some wrinkle in the next week's schedule when the phone on his desk rang. He picked it up and listened for a second and then, with unusual abruptness, told me we'd have to finish the schedule the following day. He almost pushed me out of the office.

I went back to my desk at the end of the dictation bank. I watched Jerry O'Leary go into Sid's office, which was surprising, because — unless there was a late-breaking story — O'Leary would be out of the building by two thirty or three at the end of his shift. A few minutes later I saw Deke DeLoach, the deputy director of the FBI, come into the newsroom from the hallway. He walked straight into Sid Epstein's office and closed the door behind him. It was not unusual for DeLoach to be in the newsroom — I'd seen him there probably ten or fifteen times. Usually he'd sit down next to O'Leary on the rewrite bank, or occasionally they'd go into Sid's office, and Coit Hendley would join them. Almost always, if Miriam Ottenberg was at her desk, he'd stroll back there and pull up a chair.

DeLoach — his real first name was Cartha,

though I never heard anybody call him that — was a big, sleepy-eyed man from Claxton, Georgia. He was the number three man at the FBI, and it was said around FBI headquarters that DeLoach, born in 1920, was like the son that J. Edgar Hoover never had. There was never a doubt that when he was doing FBI business, even with Jerry O'Leary, what he said came from Hoover; he was known for giving speeches now and then to right-wing audiences.

DeLoach had helped lead the FBI's investigation of the killings of Chaney, Goodman, and Schwerner, and of Viola Liuzzo. He'd become the bureau's point person in civil rights matters. So I figured perhaps he'd come to the *Star* to talk about Selma or one of the investigations into the continued violence down South.

It was more than an hour later that the door to Sid Epstein's office opened and DeLoach, dressed like every other G-man in a dark suit and white shirt, exited. He was carrying a briefcase. O'Leary and Sid remained in the office. A few minutes later Newby Noyes joined them, and the door closed again. It was another hour before the three of them finally emerged.

The next day Sid was in his office, on and off, for several hours — with the door closed, which was something I'd seldom seen. Again, Newby came and went a couple of times. So did Clarence Hunter. All very mysterious.

A few weeks later, at Harrigan's after dinner, Coit Hendley and I sat together on the patio. Coit sipped a martini, not his first. I was drinking beer. Since I'd gone on the dictation bank, I'd always been drawn to Coit, probably because of his easy generosity. "Let me show you something," he'd say. And he'd correct a piece of copy I'd written. Or on a paper napkin at Harrigan's, using the Parker 51 fountain pen that he kept in his jacket pocket, he'd illustrate a story he was telling, often about something that happened in World War II, when he'd been a navy lieutenant driving a landing barge at Normandy on D-Day at the age of twenty-three, and half the men he'd brought ashore were gunned down as they hit the beach.

I'm not sure why I asked him what I did on this evening, probably because I suspected he would know the answer. I asked what was so secret and important about that business in Sid's office, with O'Leary and Deke DeLoach and Newby and Clarence Hunter.

Coit said he wasn't supposed to talk about it — no one was. He said DeLoach claimed to have transcripts from secret tape recordings of Martin Luther King Jr. in hotel rooms having sex with various women.

DeLoach had held out the possibility that, if backup tape recordings were necessary to confirm what was in the transcripts, he might be able to provide a sampling. Coit said it was obvious that DeLoach had come to the *Star* with the intention of getting the paper to investigate what might be on the tapes while at the same time keeping their connection to the FBI a secret — and then publishing a sensational report about King's infidelities, as if on the *Star*'s own authority.

After the discussions that afternoon and the following day, Newby Noyes decided — apparently with the concurrence of everybody else involved — that the *Star* would have nothing to do with the story.

In mid-April, the draft board sent me a certified letter to let me know that I had lost my student deferment. I was reclassified 1-A.

The bad news arrived at a hectic time. That same week, I covered the so-called March on Washington to End the War in Vietnam and the observance downtown of the hundredth anniversary of Abraham Lincoln's death.

The march was sponsored by Students for a Democratic Society, which our page one story described as "a self-proclaimed left-wing radical but non-communist organization." Twenty thousand demonstrators, mostly students, had come to Washington from all over the country. I was posted at Fifteenth Street and Pennsylvania Avenue, a block from the White House. The marchers streamed by waving signs, shaking fists, shouting slogans, and then moved on to the

Washington Monument, where Joan Baez gave a concert.

I certainly identified with their cause. A few days later, General Hershey's Selective Service let me know that my draft lottery number would be called within days. And that not long after that, I would be inducted into the United States Army for two years of active duty. The only way out would be to find a reserve or National Guard unit in which to enlist. In that case, I'd only have to do the requisite six months' active duty and attend weekend meetings for six years, plus a month each summer at an army base on active reserve duty.

I sought out friends in the newsroom who were in reserve units: O'Leary, McAleer, Tom Dimond, a few others. Precious days passed. They all came back with word that their units were full, no vacancies. Tens of thousands of men my age were trying to do the same thing: find a unit in which to shelter from the war. I was frantic, and that drew the attention of a new dictationist whose husband — a *Washington Post* reporter I'd met a couple of times covering police headquarters — was in an Army Reserve unit that drilled at Andrews Air Force Base. I phoned him immediately and, as it happened, he was scheduled to drill over the coming weekend. He promised to check with his commanding officer on the off chance there might be room in his unit.

There was — and so the following Monday I drove out to Andrews to meet with Colonel Bo Thwat, the commanding officer of the unit. From the name, I'd expected Colonel Thwat to be Southeast Asian, but instead he turned out to be a tall, muscular Swede — maybe six foot two or three — who stood ramrod-straight and let me know he ran a tight outfit that demanded discipline and physical effort, but if I could take it, there was a place for me. I filled out the paperwork on the spot. Colonel Thwat told me to raise my right hand, and I became a member of the U.S. Armed Forces.

A few days later, Lance Morrow told me he was leaving the *Star* to be a writer for *Time* magazine at its headquarters in New York. He'd seemed in some faraway place for a couple of weeks. There was no one I was closer to at the paper, and for a year and a half there probably hadn't been a stretch of three or four days when we hadn't spent hours talking or drinking together or conjuring some kind of adventure, whether intellectual or helping each other on assignment or simply going out to look for trouble. Between the two of us — Washington natives with our distinctly different upbringings and shared experience as copyboys and dictationists and ambitious reporters at the *Star* — there wasn't much territory in the city we weren't familiar with, or too many categories of people we didn't know or want to get to know. We took advantage of all that and our (usually) good luck.

Lance was the smartest person I thought I'd ever met, which from my perspective had almost nothing to do with his academic credentials, though his were notable and he was unquestionably the best-read person I knew as well. He'd seemed to have had every kind of experience, enhanced by the ability to be assertive and extroverted at one moment, and then — almost in the same setting or among the same people — he could strike you as almost shy five minutes later. People gravitated to him for the range of his thought and conversation, and for his immense curiosity and genuine interest in whomever he was encountering, and I'd say they were also drawn by his sweetness and caring, which was given with no fanfare.

I could not have been more stunned or felt more shaken by Lance's news, though I'd had the sense for a while that the *Star* might not always be the place for him to build on his talents, nor was there any sign that Newby Noyes had experienced the same extraordinary flash of recognition about Lance Morrow as he'd had about Mary McGrory.

We had a big, long, boozy party for Lance on Saturday night at the house on Duddington Place where he had been living with Rupe Welch and Bob Leary. It spilled out onto the patio and lasted until three in the morning, when the neighbors informed us — politely enough, under the circumstances — that if we didn't break it up they would call the cops.

Lance slept for a few hours and then packed his car — a ramshackle little Mercedes sedan that he'd bought from Gerry Herndon for $500 — and headed for New York.

I began seriously reconsidering my own situation. Jo Anne was gone. Lance had left. Bill Hill was determined to block my way at the *Star* until I had a college degree — and that was not going to happen. I loved the *Star,* but it did not quite love me back. I woke up those days feeling a heavy sadness.

In June, for two weeks, I became the church editor of the *Evening Star.* Going back to when I was a copyboy, I had written stories for the Saturday church page. And as a dictationist, when the *Star*'s policy became more generous about giving bylines, I discovered that the church page was a good place to practice writing feature stories — and to get my name in the paper. There'd been a profile I wrote of a "night-club pianist" (actually he played at a strip club) who taught music in the nursery school at St. Agnes Episcopal; a story about ballet for seniors at the Asbury Methodist Home; and a piece about a fallout shelter built beneath a McLean Baptist church not long after the Cuban missile crisis.

My editor on those stories had been Caspar Nannes, who ran the *Star*'s religion pages. He was a remarkable character. For years he had simultaneously edited the church page and been the tennis editor of the sports section — while also serving as vice president of the Middle Atlantic Lawn Tennis Association. He had a PhD in English literature, and his first name seemed too good to be true. He was a wisp of a man, about the same age as Mr. Porter, and appeared almost ghostly in his manner. He rarely spoke, but rather seemed to hum a little, in an abstract, half-conscious way, and he wore a vague smile that was indicative of his kindness. He recognized how restless and bored I was becoming, after my return to the dictation bank. His invitation to edit the church page during his two-week vacation was a relief. With help from his regular deputy, I learned how to design every element of a newspaper page. I wrote the headlines, chose pictures with the Photo Department, assigned stories, and edited almost every bit of copy those two weeks.

Coit Hendley was also restless, and perhaps weary of working in Sid Epstein's shadow. That June, after twenty-five years at the *Star,* he accepted an offer to become editor of the *Elizabeth Daily Journal,* in Elizabeth, New Jersey, a newspaper with a circulation of about fifty thousand. Whatever the *Star*'s difficulties, it still sold four times as many copies as the paper in Elizabeth, a grim town wedged between Newark and the largest oil refinery on the East Coast. But Coit would be his own boss, and that appealed to him.

Shortly after Coit accepted the job, he asked me if I'd come to work with him in Elizabeth. I could do anything I wanted, he said — cover whatever I wished, write a column, be an editor. My pay would be equal to that of a journeyman reporter with eight years' experience. I discussed his proposal with no one, not even Puff or Ludy. I did not want to be dissuaded, or to remain at the *Star* much longer. Sid Epstein had tried once more to persuade Bill Hill to keep me on the staff as a reporter. It was no use. Hill was adamant. I accepted Coit's offer to go to Elizabeth, sight unseen.

Sid Epstein was not there when I left. He had gone on his summer vacation. On my last day at the paper, I wrote him a note to say I was leaving, and to thank him for all he'd done for me. I said I would miss him.

I packed some clothes and bought a footlocker into which I loaded two bulging *Star* scrapbooks, my notebooks, and my files about the Wesorts, Scott and Zelda Fitzgerald, Walter Johnson, and Eddie Bernstein, among others. By then, I'd learned that Eddie was actually close to a millionaire, from his earnings on the street and investments he'd made in Florida, where he'd spent his winters for

566

years. He told me most of the story after I got a tip from a rival street vendor downtown who was suspicious about a lot of things about Eddie.

I wasn't sure where I would eventually write all these stories — or whether any of them might fit into the realm of Jersey journalism — but I thought there was gold in their telling and that I would find a way to get them into print one way or another.

Coit had offered to drive me to Elizabeth. The last thing I did before we left was take the red Renault to the dealership, which offered me three hundred dollars for it. I took a few things from the glove box, checked to see that there was nothing wedged in the driver's seat or underneath, and did the same around the front passenger seat. I felt something with my hand beneath the seat, bent down to try to see, and managed to pull it out.

It was a broken string of pearls. Jo Anne's pearls.

EPILOGUE

On the third Saturday of July, Coit Hendley and I drove up to Elizabeth in his new Chrysler LeBaron, a symbol of his improved status (and paycheck) as editor in chief.

As we approached Exit 13 — marked ELIZABETH — on the New Jersey Turnpike, the giant Bayway Standard Oil refinery loomed ahead, belching flames and clouds of smoke from a hellish tangle of storage tanks and pipes and gas flares. The air became so noxious that we hurried to close the car's windows.

The Exit 13 off-ramp led to a potholed avenue that wound its way through a neighborhood of dilapidated frame houses.

A few minutes later, I checked into the Winfield Scott Hotel, the second-tallest building in downtown Elizabeth. Coit and I walked across the street to the *Elizabeth Daily Journal*'s squat brick headquarters, and up a single flight of stairs to a door with a glass panel marked newsroom. I saw through the glass that the entire newsroom was smaller than the Sports Department of the *Star,* with old wooden desks for the paper's thirty reporters and editors.

The *Elizabeth Daily Journal* — an afternoon paper — published two editions six days a week. Because there was no Sunday paper, the newsroom on this Saturday evening was unoccupied except for a copyboy tending the wire machines. Coit unlocked the door to his office at the far end of the newsroom, grabbed some work papers, and suggested we go back to the hotel for a drink.

He'd been there for only two weeks as editor. "It's not the *Star,* that's for sure," he said. "But we" — and now he looked at me and pointed — "can make this a scrappy little newspaper." He said there were half a dozen good reporters on the staff. "And a couple of editors who really understand the town."

The next day — Sunday — I walked around the three-block commercial core of "downtown Elizabeth." There were two department stores, a luncheonette-tobacconist called the Pipe Shop, a lace-making business, a shoemaker, and several hardware stores. The tallest building in town was the Union County Courthouse, an early-twentieth-century tower seventeen stories high that loomed over the surrounding landscape. On the city's edges lay Port Elizabeth–Port Newark, the busiest container port in the world; the pleasant Weequahic neighborhood of Newark's southernmost tip; and, like an escape valve, the Goethals Bridge connecting Elizabeth to the borough of Staten Island, New York City. Beneath the northern span of the bridge was the Singer Sewing Machine factory, which employed several thousand people.

That Thursday, after I'd settled into the newsroom and met my new colleagues, Coit arranged for me to attend a big lunch convened weekly in the back room of Christine Lee's Chinese restaurant by the town's mayor, Tom Dunne. I was seated between the mayor — a jovial but intense Irish pol who previously had founded the Electrical Workers Union at the big Western Electric plant in nearby Kearny — and Tony Provenzano, the head of the Teamsters Union that ran the docks in Elizabeth and elsewhere in North Jersey. Others at the table were Elizabeth's chief of police; the owner of the local bowling alley; the chief judge of the municipal court; the floor manager of the Singer plant; the proprietor of the town's Chevrolet dealership; and the monsignor from St. Anthony of Padua Catholic Church, the city's biggest. Elizabeth — I was told that day — had the highest proportion of Catholic citizens of any city in America — maybe 90 percent — half of them of Polish descent and the rest of Irish, German, Italian, or Spanish ancestry.

Those first days, I scoured Elizabeth's residential neighborhoods looking for a place to live. What I encountered was a series of dank, musty apartments carved out of the parlor floor of small houses, with heavy furniture that must have been handed down for generations.

On Saturday I took the train to Manhattan. It was the first time I had been to New York as an adult. I was transfixed. From Times Square I took the subway to Greenwich Village. I went into the White Horse Tavern and had a beer. A picture of Dylan Thomas hung above his regular booth.

Later in the afternoon, walking on Sixth Avenue with my nose buried in the "For Rent" columns of the *Village Voice,* I stopped at an Italian restaurant called La Groceria to eat at a sidewalk table. I thought I heard someone call my name. I was startled: sitting a few tables away was Lucianne Von Steinberger Cummings. I'd last seen her in Washington at one of her PR soirees.

When I told her I had gone to work with Coit Hendley in Elizabeth, New Jersey, and was looking for a place to live in the Village, she suggested that I stay temporarily at the apartment a block away that she was sharing with a girlfriend who worked for TWA, and two Pan Am stewardesses. There was a spare bedroom.

The apartment was above Emilio's restaurant, and reeked from the smell of chicken cacciatore seeping up through the floorboards.

The two stewardesses flew the Toledo Turn-around, and each night came home with their flight bags stuffed full with whiskey minia-tures from the plane. I stayed there for three months.

Coit kept his word: I wrote a weekly column — patterned after the *Star*'s "Rambler" col-umn about local life, and called it "Of This and That." I learned a lot — about Elizabeth's neighborhoods and characters and especially its history. I covered the docks, the Teamsters, Tony Pro, the mob, and a colorful cast of poli-ticians. My best sources — the ones who put me on to my best stories and columns, often without realizing they were doing so — were the men and women I lunched with every week at the mayor's table at Christine Lee's. I ate there several times a week. She and the regular customers at what became her famous restaurant were likewise invaluable sources and subjects. Some days I would head over to the Singer plant and watch the sewing ma-chines come off the assembly line. The final piece to be assembled would be the iron foot treadle with the iconic Singer stamp: the same as the treadle my grandmother rocked back and forth in the shop in Adams Morgan.

The Singer factory and its workers were always good for a column. Elizabeth, it turned out, was a reporter's dream waiting to be discovered, at least for this reporter whose previous experience had been in the comparatively genteel precincts of Washington, D.C. Gentility was not what Elizabeth, New Jersey, was about. It was gritty, working class, with a stew of rich ethnic cultures, and — to my mind — it felt a lot more exemplary of America than did the nation's capital city.

Each day after work, at about four o'clock, Coit and I would go next door to the Winfield Scott Hotel bar and drink till about seven. Both of us had switched from martinis to bourbon on the rocks. Then he'd go back to his house in suburban Plainfield and I'd take the train back to Manhattan.

Still, Elizabeth was difficult for both of us. Despite all of Coit's efforts, the paper — compared to what we were both used to — was bush league, subject to a whiff of ingrained local corruption and mired in the muck of provincial Jersey journalism. (Rightly or not, I became convinced the proprietor of the bowling alley had found a way to pay off someone at the paper for the unusual amount of coverage his lanes received.)

At times I was disdainful of the paper, and colleagues noticed. I became known to some of them as "the rotten kid"; the term was coined by my favorite reporter there, Joan Haggerty, whose desk was next to mine. I understood how they felt. I was only twenty-one, an outsider who had come on board as the friend and protégé and drinking buddy of the new boss. I chose to live in Manhattan, not Elizabeth. I often worked a four-day week and seemed to make my own rules.

But I delivered. Mondays, I'd arrive at the office and hand in my copy — written at home over my three-day weekends. Almost invariably, it ended up on the front page. I did a series about teenagers from Elizabeth crossing the Goethals Bridge at night by car and on foot to drink in bars on Staten Island. The legal age to drink beer and wine in New York was eighteen, compared to twenty-one in Jersey. And these kids were getting hammered, not sipping delicately. Some died in car wrecks, and there were bar fights every weekend, knifings, occasional shootings, and a lot of throwing up. Closing time for bars in New York City was four o'clock, and hundreds of teenagers were still there at that hour, many of them passed out. After the series ran, the New York City Police Department put together a special unit to try to impose order on the situation.

The highlight of my time in Elizabeth was covering the Great New York Blackout of November 9, 1965. When the lights went out I was uptown, in the twenty-sixth-floor apartment of my old next-door neighbor Ben Stein, who was attending Columbia Law School.

Hitchhiking, walking, hitting the candlelit bars, covering the surprising celebratory aspects (and some real hardships) of a giant swath of the darkened city from 140th Street to the Battery, I kept at it until four thirty in the morning. Then I took a bus from the Port Authority to the bright lights of New Jersey and Elizabeth, where I wrote a first-person account that filled the whole front page — eight full columns — of the newspaper. How I managed to write five thousand words by the ten o'clock deadline I could not imagine afterward.

The following May, the State Newspaper Association (it did not occur to me that such an organization would have any reason to exist before I came to New Jersey) awarded its annual reporting prizes. I won first prize in three categories: investigative reporting (for the Staten Island series), news on deadline (for the blackout), and feature writing.

I'd been in Elizabeth for less than a year, but I was already looking for a way back to the major leagues. The State Newspaper Association prizes, I thought, might be my ticket.

I applied for reporting jobs at the *New York Herald Tribune* and was turned down (I already knew the *New York Times* would never hire me without a college degree); the *San Francisco Chronicle* (turned down); the *Washington Daily News,* which immediately offered me a job; and the *Washington Post.*

Ben Gilbert had become the *Post*'s metropolitan editor. In July I got a phone call from the city editor who'd succeeded him — Steve Isaacs — asking me to come down for an interview. I studied up on Isaacs. He had gone to Harvard and played halfback on the varsity football team.

In the *Post*'s rinky-dink old building, I found his office next to the wire room. The previous year, Katharine Graham had recruited Ben Bradlee to be the *Post*'s managing editor. He was one of the reasons I wanted to work there. Bradlee was hiring great writers for the national staff and letting his subeditors — like Steve Isaacs — run with their imagination and create their own staff. And it was clear that Bradlee would soon take command of the paper altogether as executive editor.

Isaacs told me he'd read my clips from Elizabeth and the *Star*. He'd liked my point of view as a native of the capital — it came through in my *Star* stories, he said.

I told him I thought my best credential to work at the *Washington Post* was not having finished college. That during those years from age sixteen to twenty-one, I had gotten the best education a reporter could get, from the greatest teachers — across town at the *Star*.

He hired me on the spot, based in part on a letter of recommendation from Charlie Puffenbarger, who had left the *Star* to become a professor of journalism at the University of Illinois. He read it to me.

Puff said that the *Star* had made a major mistake letting me go. Isaacs said he'd greatly admired the *Star*'s local coverage when he took over from Gilbert, and had the highest regard for Sid Epstein.

Six weeks later, in September 1966, I went to work at the *Washington Post*.

As for the *Star,* its fate was probably sealed as early as March 1954, when the *Washington Post* acquired its morning rival the *Washington Times-Herald,* along with many of that paper's readers, popular comic strips, and advertisers. It did not occur to the *Star*'s owners to bid on the *Times-Herald* themselves. They assumed that their own preeminence was unassailable.

For some years after that, the *Star* remained arguably the nation's best afternoon paper, with a superb staff (Mary McGrory, Haynes Johnson, David Broder, Bill Hines, and all the others). But beginning in the mid-1960s, an ominous symptom appeared. Some talented younger people in choice positions were leaving the staff. Another factor: the *Star* remained an afternoon paper — at a time when the city's suburbs were rapidly expanding into the Maryland and Virginia countryside, where timely afternoon newspaper distribution was more difficult (delivery trucks got tied up in rush hour traffic) and where commuters, after the long drive home, were now apt to turn on the television evening news instead of opening a newspaper.

Meanwhile, the *Washington Post* under Ben Bradlee and Katharine Graham was becoming a great — and exciting — newspaper, with only the *New York Times* in serious competition as the best in America.

At the *Star,* there followed a long, gradual decline, not so much in the paper's editorial quality, which remained often remarkable and enjoyed a lovely Indian summer, but more fundamentally in its financial position. In 1974, the owning families (the Noyeses and the Kauffmanns) — a numerous bunch who had long been accustomed to their dividends and at one time had been part of the *Star*'s obsolescent charm — sold their interests in the paper to Joe Allbritton, a multimillionaire from Texas.

Four years later, after misadventures and misunderstandings (and plundering), Allbritton sold the *Star* to TIME Inc. for twenty million dollars. That didn't work either. In its arrogance, TIME Inc. thought that because its flagship magazine was stronger than Mrs. Graham's *Newsweek,* it could also beat her newspaper. TIME Inc. lost eighty-five million dollars on the paper over the next three and a half years and at last abandoned the project.

On August 7, 1981, the *Star* ceased publication. The *Washington Post* purchased the *Star*'s land and buildings and printing presses.

My young friends followed their own remarkable paths.

Jo Anne Mark, after leaving the *Star,* had a long career in journalism, including an investigative series in 1974 for the *Philadelphia Inquirer* about teenage cults, which later was the basis of a book she wrote on the subject. She became the editor of a suburban Pittsburgh weekly, a reporter for the *St. Petersburg Times,* and the publisher of a group of twenty trade magazines. For many years she owned an investment firm in Chestertown Maryland, thirty miles down the road from Elkton, which she drove past regularly.

In the spring of 1966, a year after I'd left the *Star,* I went to visit Jo Anne in State College, Pennsylvania. By then she was married to her old boyfriend, had a baby (the first of two children), and was working in the Journalism Department at Penn State. In the half century since, we've stayed in touch. She was divorced in 1985, is now married to her second husband of many years, and lives in Florida.

Lance Morrow occupies a unique place in the journalism of our time. In the early 1970s, *Time*'s managing editor Henry Grunwald created that magazine's essay page for the purpose of showcasing his writing talent and his shimmering intelligence. Lance wrote hundreds of pieces at *Time* over a span of forty years and later began contributing periodic essays to the opinion pages of the *Wall Street Journal*. His commentaries adapt the ways of the classical essay to the work of journalism. "He created the form, and he's still the best," Jim Lehrer of the *PBS News Hour* said. Weighing the ethical and moral dimensions of war and peace and race and presidential politics and the ways of American society, his essays have made their way into the culture. Lance is the author of nine books, including a couple of memoirs and two collections of his essays.

Tom Dimond stayed at the *Star* through its final edition. He'd been the paper's education reporter, assistant city editor, business editor, and, from 1978 to 1981, assistant managing editor. He then went to the *Washington Post* as assistant business editor and supervised the paper's Pulitzer Prize–winning investigation of the Securities and Exchange Commission in 1989, retiring as deputy business editor in 2002. We remained friends over the years. In 2013, I spent two wonderful days at his house in Chevy Chase, Maryland, talking nonstop about the *Star*. It was the last time I saw him. He died on July 31, 2020.

Not surprisingly, **Mark Baldwin** made unorthodox choices that served him well. Despite being awarded the *Star* college fellowship, he dropped out and quit the paper.

He became managing editor of *Washingtonian* magazine, then gave up journalism to take (amazing) photographs, manufacture wooden bathtubs, and build houses in Maine and sail. He also designed and manufactured a successful "honey log" — a chunk of spruce cunningly seeded with pockets of honey. Placed in the cage of a bear in a zoo, the log would occupy the beast for hours in creative foraging and stop him from pacing back and forth and driving himself crazy. The honey pockets could be refilled as needed. In 1984 Mark started the Borealis Press — a specialty greeting card manufacturer that has built a huge following.

John Fialka finished his law studies at Georgetown University, became a reporter for the *Star,* and then went on to a spectacular twenty-five-year career at the *Wall Street Journal.* He was the paper's lead reporter in the first Gulf War, worked in its London bureau, and became a specialist, based in Washington, covering energy, the environment, and politics and money. Since retiring from the *Journal,* he has been editor of *ClimateWire,* an Internet newsletter about global warming.

Ken Campbell's last day at the *Star* was the week before his wedding to Suze in 1964. He then became a correspondent for UPI in London and, next, an investigative reporter for the *Boston Globe,* where he also wrote a column and covered the statehouse for five years. Later he was the public information officer for the Massachusetts Transit Authority. He and Suze live in New Hampshire.

Warren Hoge left the *Star* in 1966 to become the *New York Post*'s Washington correspondent. Ten years later, he joined the *New York Times,* where he built a career as foreign correspondent, London bureau chief, and finally the paper's foreign editor. We've remained close friends and occasionally sing 1950s doo-wop songs together.

Phil Trupp, characteristically, became something of an adventurer. He wrote and edited a dozen books, from spy thrillers to studies of undersea life. He became the jazz critic for the *Washington Times* and led searches for sunken treasure. I'd forgotten the name of the subject of our fake obit and couldn't trace it in the *Post* archives, so I called Trupp one day to ask if he might remember the details. Amazingly enough, he had kept a copy of the obit — a trophy of his youth.

Tony Maggiacomo died in 1974 at the age of thirty-seven, of an aneurysm. He'd left the *Star* before I did, to become an English teacher at a prep school in Connecticut. Later he taught at the University of Rhode Island. In 2020, when I spoke with members of his family, I learned that he'd been a four-letter athlete — including playing football at Brown — and that he had graduated from the Columbia School of Journalism.

After the *Star* folded, **Rupe Welch** was hired as a rewrite man at the *Washington Times* (owned by Rev. Sun Myung Moon's Unification Church) by its new managing editor, Coit Hendley. He then (successively) became assistant metro editor, assistant national editor, and spent two years on the *Times'* investigative team looking at corrupt contract practices in the administration of D.C. mayor Marion Barry. He left the *Times* — because of his distaste for its right-wing politics showing up in news columns — and joined Thomson Newspapers as editor of its *Traffic World* publication. Thereafter, he edited several trade magazines until his retirement in 2001.

Ben Forgey became a distinguished critic of art and architecture, first at the *Star* (he stayed until the paper's end) and then at the *Post,* where he specialized in architecture and urban development.

Tad Foote became a leading educator, first as dean of the law school at Washington University in St. Louis, and then, after 1981, as president of the University of Miami, which he took over as a mediocre "suntan university" and led to academic, financial, and athletic preeminence. He died in 2016 at age seventy-eight.

Walter Gold continued playing the night for the *Star* until the paper went out of business, then did the same for the *Washington Times* and WTOP television for a few more years. He showed up at fire and crime scenes for decades as a member of the Bethesda–Chevy Chase Rescue Squad. He became a public information officer for the D.C. Police Department and helped create the D.C. Fire and EMS Museum. In 1991 Walter began dating Bobbie Parzow, my Blair classmate and dancing partner on *The Milt Grant Show,* where we actually had won a major teenage dance contest. They married in 2007. Walter died at age eighty-four in October 2020, with Bobbie at his side.

Ben Stein went to work in the White House as a speech writer and lawyer for President Richard Nixon seven years after I'd seen him on the night of the Great New York Blackout. His father, **Herb Stein**, served as chairman of Nixon's Council of Economic Advisors. Despite our fundamental political differences, Ben and I have managed to remain friends and see each other almost every year. After Watergate, there was much speculation that Ben had been "Deep Throat," which he rightly denied but (not so rightly) claimed was a fictional character Bob Woodward and I invented. Ben's career as an actor (including as the economics teacher in *Ferris Bueller's Day Off*), TV game show host, right-wing political commentator, polemicist, and writer is well known.

My own path at the *Evening Star* intersected with a few "historical footnotes," as I think of them — people who came to figure in consequential or curious events of our time.

More than a decade after her murder in 1964, it came to light that **Mary Pinchot Meyer** had had a secret love affair with John F. Kennedy through much of his presidency. Over the decades that followed, conspiracy theories proliferated, including one in which someone from the CIA committed the murder in order to keep Meyer quiet about something to do with JFK's assassination. The young Black man arrested at the scene of her murder, Ray Crump Jr., was acquitted the following summer for lack of evidence. Lance Morrow, who was there on the towpath of the C&O Canal when an eyewitness identified Crump and followed his trial closely, remained convinced that Crump was the murderer.

Lucianne Von Steinberger Cummings married Sid Goldberg, the executive editor of the North American Newspaper Alliance, in 1966, the year I left Elizabeth, New Jersey, to work at the *Washington Post*.

Among the stories Bob Woodward and I missed in our coverage of Watergate was Lucianne's role as a spy for the Nixon reelection campaign in 1972. With the code name Chapman's Friend, she was embedded in the campaign of Nixon's opponent Senator George McGovern. Using her "cover" as a supposed columnist and would-be campaign book writer, she traveled on the McGovern press plane and phoned in hundreds of gossipy reports to Nixon's old-time political dirty tricks specialist Murray Chotiner. Many of her reports were read with gleeful enthusiasm by Nixon and his chief of staff, H. R. Haldeman. Lucianne's role as a spy was revealed not by Woodward and me, but in the *Star* in August 1973, in a story written by Bob Walters, the husband of my former colleague on the dictation bank Martha Angle.

In the 1980s, Lucianne opened a literary agency in Manhattan that specialized in "right-wing, tell-all attack books," in the words of the *New York Times*. In 1987 she was the ghostwriter of a romance novel called *Washington Wives* by Maureen Dean, the wife of John Dean, whose Watergate testimony played a crucial role in Richard Nixon's downfall.

In 1997 Lucianne advised Linda Tripp to secretly record Monica Lewinsky, who had told Tripp about her sexual relationship with Bill Clinton. Tripp had come to Lucianne with the idea of selling a book about the White House intern and the president. The rest — as the cliché has it — is history.

Milton Pitts, the barber who tended both Walter Gold's and my flattop haircuts when we were teenagers, went on to become Richard Nixon's White House barber in 1970. By then, he operated the Pitts Hairstylist shop in the tony Sheraton Carlton Hotel, where his regular customers included Senator George McGovern and my father. Several hours before announcing his resignation, President Nixon summoned Mr. Pitts for a last haircut. He'd be resigning that day, Nixon told him, settling into the barber's chair. "Well, we've made some mistakes and we've done a lot of things right, too, and I'd like to thank you for your good service over the years." The emotional scene, based on my interview with Mr. Pitts, is recorded in *The Final Days*. He continued to cut my father's hair until the Sheraton shop closed shortly before Mr. Pitts's death at age eighty-two in 1994.

My story about the **Wesorts** community of Southern Maryland, based on interviews I did at the *Star* as well as the *Post*, ran on page D-1 of the *Post* on November 29, 1970.

In his later years, **Walter Fauntroy's** story became sad and somewhat bizarre.

He'd been one of Martin Luther King Jr.'s principal aides, a recognizable and effective figure in the civil rights movement of the 1960s. As the *Post*'s District Building (city hall) reporter, I covered Walter when he was vice chairman of the City Council in 1968–69, a position appointed by the president. In 1970 he became the first elected delegate to the House of Representatives. After he was defeated in his campaign for D.C. mayor in 1990, he formed a lobbying and consulting firm that represented, among other clients, Nelson Mandela's African National Congress.

But in 1995, he pleaded guilty to falsely claiming he had made a twenty-four-thousand-dollar donation to a Washington church. In 2012, he wrote a bad check for fifty-five thousand dollars to help pay for Barack Obama's second inauguration festivities. A judge issued a bench warrant for his arrest and Fauntroy fled the country, abandoning his wife of many years, Dorothy, who, in her eighties, was left burdened with debt and eventually forced into bankruptcy. For four years, Fauntroy hid out in the Persian Gulf states, sometimes sending strange and, some said, delusional emails. In 2016, he returned to the United States and lives with his family.

Eddie Bernstein died in Pensacola in 1979, leaving an estate worth $691,676 (about $2.5 million in today's dollars), according to records of the D.C. Superior Court, including $364,000 in a Merrill Lynch bond account.

I last saw him in 1971. He told me he was spending much less time in D.C. His life in Florida was the antithesis of his panhandling existence in Washington. In Pensacola he wore prosthetic legs, drove a Cadillac, and owned three bars, including the Red Garter, a gay bar with "the South's finest in the art of female impersonation."

In the winter months, when he went to

Pensacola, Eddie arranged for his monkey, Gypsy, to be cared for at the National Zoo. He was an Orthodox Jew, and when Gypsy died, he wouldn't allow her to be cremated, but instead had her buried at Aspin Hill Memorial Park, a pet cemetery in Silver Spring. It turned out that Gypsy had been given to Eddie by Evelyn Walsh McLean, the mining heiress whose alcoholic husband had once owned the *Washington Post* and who had bought her the famous Hope Diamond. She'd met Eddie in the 1940s when she was shopping downtown and encountered him begging on his skateboard.

For twenty years, Eddie had deposited up to a hundred dollars a day when he was in D.C. at the McLachlen National Bank downtown. He was seventy-nine years old when he died.

About the extraordinary reporters and editors who became this kid's teachers and mentors and, really, extended family:

Coit Hendley left the *Elizabeth Daily Journal* to become editor of the *Camden Courier Post* and then was executive editor of the *Passaic Herald-News*. In 1982 he was hired as the first managing editor of the *Washington Times* and was its associate editor when he died in 1985 at age sixty-four. In 2019, his son Peter published an archive of his papers describing what it was like when Lt. (jg) Coit Hendley commanded LCI-85 (landing craft infantry) as

590

it plowed ashore under heavy fire on Omaha Beach on D-Day, June 6, 1944.

Charles Puffenbarger left the *Star* in 1965 to teach journalism at the University of Illinois. He returned to Washington as a deskman at the *Post* in 1969 and our close friendship resumed. Until his retirement in 1985 he remained at the *Post* as an editor in the business section, but his real vocation was mentoring young journalists. Until his death in 1997 at age seventy, he was an adjunct professor of journalism at George Washington University.

Mary McGrory won the Pulitzer Prize in 1975 for her Watergate commentary. She remained at the *Star* through its final edition. The following day, she went to work at the *Washington Post*. The last of her eight thousand columns was published in 2003, the year before her death at age eighty-five. At her funeral service at the Blessed Sacrament Catholic Church, her colleagues from the *Star* and the *Post* were asked to sit on their respective sides of the aisle. I was not sure which side to choose. Finally, I sat with Bob Woodward on the *Post* side. Mary had never felt altogether comfortable at the *Post,* grateful as she was, in particular, for Katharine Graham's friendship and the platform that the *Post* gave her. But her heart always remained with the *Star.*

Miriam Ottenberg's most remarkable piece of work was perhaps *The Pursuit of*

Hope, her book published in 1978 about her twenty-year battle with multiple sclerosis. The disease had forced her to retire from the *Star* three years earlier. It described her attitude — and those of dozens of others she interviewed — about living life to the fullest possible despite the crippling effects the disease. Two years after its publication, she was diagnosed with cancer and began planning a similar book about people responding with hope and the fullness of activity, but she died in 1982, at age sixty-eight. Miriam once described her role as a journalist this way: "A reporter should expose the bad and campaign for the good. That's the way I was brought up."

Mary Lou Werner shared the byline in the *Star*'s final-edition story about the paper's history and its death. By that time, she had left the state desk and become an editorial writer. In 1984, she joined the *Washington Times* as the chief of its commentary pages. We always stayed in close touch until her death in 2009 at age eighty-three.

Myra MacPherson left the *Star* in 1968, when she was hired by Ben Bradlee to be a feature writer in the *Post*'s new style section, and retired in 1991. Her half dozen books include a masterful biography of the radical journalist I. F. Stone (the basis of a film), an account of Vietnam veterans' struggles with post-traumatic stress disorder, and a study of the marriages of major U.S. politicians. Our close friendship is in its seventh decade.

Ted Crown, after forty-six years as a reporter for the *Star*, retired at age sixty-five in 1973. Even while covering police, he'd been town treasurer of Seat Pleasant, Maryland, and he continued his local civic work after retirement. He died in 1987. A street in Seat Pleasant was named in his honor, and his family endowed the J. Theodore Crown Sr. Scholarship to support students at the University of Maryland College of Journalism.

David Broder was hired by Ben Bradlee in 1967 as the *Washington Post*'s chief political reporter. In 1963, I had taken David's dictation from Dallas. Nine years later, several days after the Watergate break-in and the Nixon campaign's denial that it had anything to do with it, David came to me with the name of an official of the Republican National Committee and suggested that I contact him. I called the man, who knew a lot about the inner workings of the White House and the Nixon reelection campaign. I asked if he believed the denials. As described in the early pages of *All the President's Men*, "The man laughed. 'Bob Dole and I were talking on the day of the arrests and agreed it must have been one of these twenty-five-cent generals hanging around the committee or the White House who was responsible. Chotiner or Colson. Those were the names thrown out'."

This early, insider's hunch was of crucial importance to Bob Woodward and me at a moment when conventional wisdom held that the Nixon apparat had nothing to do with the break-in. As it turned out, Charles W. Colson was the Nixon deputy who had hired the chief Watergate burglar, E. Howard Hunt, to work for the White House. Dave Broder's tip was invaluable. He remained at the *Post* for the next thirty-seven years, and we remained friends until his death in 2011.

Jerry O'Leary Jr. (Jeremiah Aloysius Patrick O'Leary Jr.) was the *Star*'s chief White House correspondent when the paper folded — forty-four years after he'd gone to work there as an eighteen-year-old copyboy earning ten dollars a week. Within days of the *Star*'s demise, he began an unhappy eight-month stint in the Reagan administration as a special assistant to the president's national security adviser — unhappy because he was asked to lie to the press on a critical occasion and he quit. He then joined the *Washington Times* as its White House correspondent, working under its associate editor Coit Hendley. In 1989 he began writing a column for the *Times,* "O'Leary's Washington," as well as pieces for the paper's commentary pages, which were edited by Ludy Werner. When he died in 1993, he had been a sober member of Alcoholics Anonymous for thirty years — and was responsible for bringing numerous

594

colleagues at the *Star* and other news organizations into AA's fold.

Ben Gilbert edited *Ten Blocks from the White House,* a definitive book by the local staff of the *Post* about the riots in Washington that followed the assassination of Martin Luther King Jr. in 1968. (I wrote a chapter about white-owned liquor stores.) Eased out of the paper's management by Ben Bradlee in 1970, he became the head of Washington's municipal planning agency, then moved to Tacoma, Washington, where he was chairman of the city's Landmarks Preservation Commission. His legacy at the *Post* was in his pioneering initiative to hire African American reporters.

Haynes Johnson won the Pulitzer Prize in 1966 for his stories from Selma, Alabama. Three years later, Ben Bradlee lured him to the *Post*. There we resumed our dialogue — a delight to me — about newspapering, about America, about writing and reporting. He still called me Carlos. His reporting — and position — at the *Post* was unique: looking at the "big picture" of America, traveling across the country and finding out what was on people's minds, especially in election years. His books and series for the *Post* were often written with his old *Star* colleague David Broder. He retired from the *Post* in 1994 and took up the Knight Chair in Journalism at the University of Maryland. He died at age eighty-one in 2013. Haynes and his father, Malcolm

Johnson, were the first father and son to have both been awarded Pulitzers.

Sid Epstein became managing editor of the *Star* and then its executive editor and associate publisher in its final stages. Every few years, he and I would get together and catch up. He knew that — from that summer of 1960 when I went to work at the *Star* — he had been my role model, my idea of what a newspaperman should be. One night in 1997, he invited me over to his house — it had been his parents' house, the house he grew up in on Woodley Road; Eleni had died in 1991. And we spent an evening talking about the *Star* of the 1960s. Out of the blue, he jabbed a finger at me and said, "Kid, I want you to speak at my funeral." He wasn't maudlin about it, just affectionate. He died five years later, in 2002, and was buried at Arlington with a twenty-one-gun salute.

In my eulogy, I said, "In my life, I've been blessed by great editors. It's important today to remember what Sid's work was about: putting out five editions a day of a great newspaper, whose reporters, most of them under his command, routinely beat the hell out of the *Post* in that day and age — and did it with standards and style and honesty, and a kind of esprit and joy that I have never seen since in journalism. The heart of that esprit was Sid — our commander in a pink shirt. I loved him, and I owe him — big-time."

ACKNOWLEDGMENTS

Chasing History is, on the simplest level, the tale of my apprenticeship in the newspaper trade from ages sixteen to twenty-one, between the years 1960 and 1965. Its narrative defines a momentous epoch in American life and culture, as I witnessed and experienced it in those days in the capital of the United States, which happened to be my native city.

Virtually everything of import that occurred afterward in my life as a reporter and as a man — whatever I was able to accomplish, or failed at, or struggled with — had its nascent formation in those years. A remarkable measure of the same can be said of the nation as we know it today.

My understanding of journalism, and basic view of the world I've covered and written about and my relation to it, crystallized in five incomparable years at a uniquely great American newspaper. It was a time of amazing change and historic events in the city of my birth and in the nation, and I was lucky enough to share that experience with a group of extraordinary people, all older than I, who became my teachers and closest friends and lovers and, really, my family. They were, and remain indelibly in my memory and heart, a colorful, wonderful, happy (generally) lot: the "heroes" of this book, and of my formative years.

Working on this memoir, I was lucky enough to revisit at length or have a series of extended phone conversations with more than thirty people I worked closely with at the *Star*. My debt to them is twofold: for their lasting influence on my life and for reliving those days with me a half century later.

Three friends need special mention: Lance Morrow, Jo Anne (Mark) Gerhardt, and Tom Dimond.

Over almost sixty years, my friendship with Lance has been an incomparable joy of my life. When I first thought of writing about my years at the *Star,* I took the idea to Lance. He has since been present at every stage of the book's development. His wisdom, remarkable memory for detail, and wonderful sensibility are essential to the story I have told here.

When it came time to begin writing, Jo Anne and I spent many hours recalling our time together at the *Star*. I could never have pieced together the events — personal and professional — I describe between March 1963 and July 1964 without our conversations. Perhaps more than any other person, she was able to help me understand who I was at the height of my time at the *Star*.

Tom Dimond's perspective, memory, friendship, and his unique experience at the *Star* had huge influence on my perceptions of the paper, its characters, and the time we lived together in the Arlington house, which was a sort of rollicking journalistic commune. My special thanks, also, to Tom's wife, Joan Ebzery Dimond.

My recorded interviews with Haynes Johnson, Roberta Hornig (Bobbie), Myra MacPherson, Rupe Welch, and Ben Forgey fill a bookshelf's width of binders. My gratitude to them over half a century is beyond expression.

Two of my other housemates, John Fialka and Ken Campbell — and Ken's wife, Suze — provided a loving and curated record of life at 1609 North Adams. The Campbells' photos are an integral part of the record.

Mark Baldwin and Phil Trupp were great colleagues and friends who played an outsized role in my *Star* education. Their recollections and impressions of that time and place have enhanced this record and my own memories. Mark, too, contributed to the photographic archive.

These colleagues from the dictation bank also spent many hours with me reconstructing the milieu and tales of our experience together: Warren Hoge, Martha Angle and Bob Walters, John Stacks, Judy Scribner, Clare Crawford, Richard Slusser, and my great friend Ron Oberman, who bridged my experience from junior high school through Montgomery Blair and the *Evening Star*.

Others who provided memories and perspective: Regina Ottenberg Levin, Arnold Taylor, Martha Grigg, Ann Wood, Walter Pincus, Bruce Kinsey, Boris Weintraub, David Breasted, Tad Foote, Walter Gold, Larry Gold, Bobbie Parzow Gold, Maria O'Leary, Timothy O'Leary, Elizabeth Eastman, Brooke Bacas Waldron, Kathy Crown, Lisa Gorska Kowalski, Mary Herndon Junda, Christian Kauffmann, Mike Mosettig, and Robert G. Kaiser.

I owe special thanks to Jerry Ceppos, Sid Epstein's nephew and former dean of the journalism department of Louisiana State University.

Barbara Cochran, my friend of more than fifty years and the *Star*'s last managing editor, shared her invaluable knowledge of the paper and its history.

Evelyn Duffy was there with advice and the keenest eye when it was most needed. As was Suzy Hansen. Thanks also to Evelyn's colleague Ben Gambuzza. And to Darien Brahms for her research work.

I am the beneficiary of the constant generosity of Faye Haskins, former director of the Washingtoniana Collection of the D.C. Public Library. Faye is also the author of an authoritative history of the *Evening Star*.

Thanks, also, to Mark Greek, the Archival Collections coordinator of the D.C. Public Library, who has come through with answers to my questions at every juncture and hour.

In addition to her research work, Anna Fitzgerald has been the perfect tech adviser and multitasker.

Edith Barreto's kindness and generous spirit have brightened our household and office for fifteen years.

Lucy Horowitz started working with me on this project when she was sixteen. Now twenty-one, she was exactly the right person to call on again during the final part of this process. She is wise beyond her years, steadying in the storm and bringing ebullience into the room with her. Thanks, too, to Glenn Horowitz and Tracey Jackson.

Special thanks to Ambrose Powell Hill III and Johnny Gianaris, who shared their recollection of our growing up together in Tenleytown.

From Harvey Road and Silver Spring, a tight group of us have remained the closest of friends and hardly a year has passed without our seeing each other: Allan Akman (who worked at the *Star* after high school as a tour guide) and Janet Akman, Jerry and Susan Akman, Stan and Peggy Sitnick, Phil and

Beverly Sklover, Ed Goldman, and Frank and Irene Schubert.

Also from Silver Spring and friends since high school: Gerry Rebach, Roberta Greenblatt Krasner (who also helped with old photos), Annie Groer (who became a reporter at the *Star*), Gloria Kozak, and Sheila Katz Linken.

Nancy (Immler) Luscombe has occupied a special place in my heart for sixty-five years, since seventh grade — a unique and enduring bond, with a lifetime's wonderful twists and turns.

Cydney Cort has the eye and ear of a great editor. And she is a friend like no other. Her mind and presence enrich my life.

Peter Osnos, my old *Washington Post* colleague and founder of Public Affairs Press, was the first person in publishing with whom I discussed my idea for this book. His enthusiasm convinced me to go forward.

Steve Rubin, former publisher of Henry Holt, has been the essential advocate of this project. Not for the first time, he understood a book I proposed from its inception and shepherded it through its critical phases. Every author should be so lucky.

Three editors at Holt — John Sterling, Paul Golob, and Sarah Crichton — have helped me at every step, and I'm enormously grateful.

Also at Holt, I've had a great team shepherding the book to publication: Amy

Einhorn, publisher; Natalia Ruiz, editorial assistant and my savvy navigator there; Chris O'Connell, production editor; Meryl Sussmann Levavi, designer; Bonnie Thompson and Emily DeHuff, copy editors; Lisa Kleinholz, indexer; and Patricia Eisemann, director of publicity.

This is my second book on which Elizabeth Shreve has provided generous counsel on matters of publicity.

Special thanks to my friend of almost five decades the great graphic designer Walter Bernard, who stepped in on a moment's notice to create the cover of this book.

And to Joan Didion, Amanda Urban and Ken Auletta, Mary Karr, Richard Cohen, Jon Segal, Sally Quinn, Judith Thurman, Allison and Leonard Stern, and Eve Ensler (V).

Bob Woodward and I are in our fiftieth year of almost constant dialogue and unique friendship; thanks, too, to Elsa Walsh.

This is the second book on which Kristina Goetz, a great reporter and editor, has worked with me from beginning to end. Her insight and skill and calm are essential to my work.

For a decade, Amanda McCollam has been my assistant, friend, counselor, and right hand. She is also a superb reader and editor. This project could never have been undertaken without Amanda's patience and dedication — like so much I do.

■■■■

My cousin Sonia Stirman Herson — who remembers my great-great-grandmother — has been a wonderful guide and touchstone through all these years.

Love and thanks — for a lifetime — to my sisters, Mary Bernstein and Laura Bernstein Ikonen. And my gratitude to my brother-in-law Stanley Ikonen.

There is no prouder father than I: Jacob and Max Bernstein are, hands down, as good as a dad gets in this life. Period. And I'm also blessed by my daughter-in-law Rachel Rohac Bernstein and my wonderful stepson, Marc Kuehbeck.

For almost twenty years Christine Kuehbeck, my wife, has been my rock. She brings to our lives her wisdom, immeasurable kindness, practicality, sense of adventure, and boundless curiosity. She was the first person to read this memoir — with deep insight and two decades' worth of gentle understanding. My love and appreciation cannot be overstated.

INDEX

ABC News, 186, 225
Accokeek, Maryland, 154, 204
Adams family, 22
Adelman, Mr., 195–97, 217, 244–46
African National Congress, 589
Afro-American, 342
Agriculture Department, 163, 385
Ahern, Goldie, 522, 536
Aid to Families with Dependent Children, 440
air raid shelters, 289–90
Alabama, 546–52
Alabama National Guard, 463
Alabama State Police, 551
Alaska, 178
Alcoholics Anonymous, 343, 594
Alexandria, Virginia, 99
Alexandria Gazette, 119
Allbritton, Joe, 579
All the President's Men (Woodward and Bernstein), 593
American Automobile Association, 364

American Catholic Church, 372
American Civil Liberties Union, 434–35
American League, 69
American Nazi Party, 211, 373, 390
Americans for Democratic Action, 346
Anacostia, 148, 367, 524–26
Anacostia Naval Air Station, 524
Anderson, Marian, 184, 372
Andrews Air Force Base, 285, 321, 405, 410,
    494, 561–62
Angle, Martha, 253, 388, 587
Angleton, James Jesus, 587
Annapolis Capital Gazette, 61
Annie's newsstand 16–17, 180, 338–39
anti-civil-rights protests, 449–51
Aquasco Speedway, 201
Arizona Highways, 476
Arlington Cemetery, 477–78, 482
Arlington house, 273–75, 315–16, 327, 373,
    503–6
Armstrong High School, 473
Army-McCarthy hearings, 35, 66
Asbury Methodist Home, 564
Asher, Bob, 371
Associated Press (AP), 38, 58, 69, 411, 436,
    454, 542, 548–49
Association of the Oldest Inhabitants of the
    District of Columbia, 167, 195

Bacas, Harry, 234, 247, 249, 253, 257, 298,
    322–23, 345, 532
Baez, Joan, 372, 390, 561

Baker, Aloysius E., 31, 158–62, 164–66,
    220–22, 352–53
Baker, Bobby, 422–25, 436, 509–11, 513
Baldwin, Mark, 70, 87, 223–24, 228–30,
    257, 279, 361, 581
Baltimore, 76, 163, 455
Baltimore City Council, 455
Baltimore News-American, 61
Baltimore *Sun,* 61, 436, 455
Barnard Elementary School, 89
Barron, John, 377–78, 382, 390, 436, 455,
    463, 509–13
Barry, Marion, 584
Barth, John, 241
Basham, Bill, 514
Bassett, Grace, 220, 330
Bay of Pigs invasion, 232–39, 285, 291
Beale, Betty, 355, 395
Beatles, 483
Beauchamp, Emerson, 79, 93–95, 141–43,
    147, 167, 216, 322, 466
Beauvoir, Simone de, 457
Beaver Valley Times, 348, 352
Belafonte, Harry, 372
Belgian Congo, 39–41, 69
Berlin crisis, 250, 259–61, 269, 286–87, 321
Berlin Wall, 259
Berman, Peter, 198, 205, 219
Bernstein, Alfred (father), 80, 174
    barber and, 469–70
    Carl's career and 19–20, 96, 340, 460
    college and, 19, 430

Bernstein, Alfred (*continued*)
  Cuban missile crisis and, 291, 296
  sit-ins and, 12–13, 526
  elections of 1948 and, 189
  Gilberts and, 383–84, 536
  Jo Anne Mark and, 456–57
  jobs of, 11–12, 19–20, 52, 291
  March on Washington and, 373, 387
  World War II and, 521
Bernstein, Charlie (uncle), 156
Bernstein, Eddie (pencil vendor), 12–14, 18,
    44, 85, 195, 521, 526, 566–67, 589–90
Bernstein, Laura (sister), 102, 291, 456, 544
Bernstein, Leonard (composer), 188
Bernstein, Leo (real estate owner), 37
Bernstein, Mary (sister), 102, 291, 456
Bernstein, Sylvia Walker (mother), 62, 80,
    120, 174
  Carl's career and, 86–87, 96, 460
  Central High and, 37
  Cuban missile crisis and, 291, 296
  D.C. sit-ins and, 526
  death of FDR and, 406
  Gilberts and, 383–84, 536
  HCUA and, 544
  Jo Anne Mark and, 456–57
  March on Washington and, 373
  presidential elections and, 218
  Women Strike for Peace and, 259
Berry, Chuck, 203
Bethel Tourist Home, 125
Bethesda, 210–11

Bethesda–Chevy Chase High School, 144
Bethesda–Chevy Chase Rescue Squad, 141,
      585
Bethesda Naval Hospital, 407, 428
Bible, Alan, 11, 67, 103, 190, 219–20, 304–5
Bible, Billy, 11, 67
Bible, Loucile, 67, 219
Bible, Paul, 11, 67
Birmingham, Alabama, 365, 419–20, 469
Black churches, 336, 463, 469, 520
Black Masonic lodges, 474
Blacks. See also civil rights movement;
      desegregation
   Anderson concert and, 184
   cab companies and, 231
   Civil Rights Act and, 470–75
   D.C. and, 12, 90–91, 190–91, 210, 262,
      334–37, 469–70
   family friendships with, 544
   fight vs. segregation, 181
   Giles-Johnson rape case and, 526
   JFK and, 231, 417
   Lafayette Square police brawl and,
      132–33
   March on Washington and, 385–93
   Maryland and, 209–13
   Montgomery Blair and, 198–200
   murder of Chaney, Schwerner, and
      Goodman and, 461–68
   as reporters at Star and Post, 215–16, 231,
      381–85
   school integration and, 89, 106–8, 299

Blacks (*continued*)
  Swann street jazz club and, 324–25
  voting rights and, 548
  Wallace and, 450–53
Blair, Montgomery, 276
Blair, Preston, 276
Blair family, 199
Blair Mansion, 275
Blanche (switchboard operator), 231, 253,
    271, 390, 395, 401, 408
Blick, Roy Early, 124, 129–34, 195, 214,
    324–26, 385, 510–11, 514
Bloody Sunday, 548–51
Bogley, Ron, 119
Bolling Air Force Base, 148, 524
Bolling v. Sharpe, 38, 89, 191, 299, 459
Bonus Marchers, 373–75
Borealis Press, 582
Boston Globe, 61, 327, 582
Boy Scouts, 179–82, 474
Braaten, David, 343
Bradlee, Ben, 516, 577–80, 592, 594–95
Bradlee, Toni Pinchot, 516
Brando, Marlon, 337
Breasted, David, 327, 374
Bresnehan, Posey, 484
Brewster, Daniel, 452
Brightwood Civic Association, 219
Broder, David, 73, 208, 254, 284–85, 388–
    93, 401–2, 412, 426, 437, 476, 486,
    578, 593–94
Brotherhood of Sleeping Car Porters, 387

Brown, James, 202
Brown, Pat, 369
Brown, Tom, 322
Brown v. Board of Education, 38, 89, 98, 191, 299, 376, 459
Bullen, Dana, 312–15, 426
Bulletin of the American Meteorological Society, 554
Burch, Johnny, 126–33, 511, 518
Burning Tree Country Club, 62
Burns, Vincent Godfrey, 241–45, 445
Byrd, Charlie, 77, 204
Byrd, Elbert, Jr., 269, 273
Byrd, Harry Flood, 36, 98, 471
Byrd, Robert, 439, 551

C&O Canal towpath, 193, 514–20, 586
Cambridge, Maryland, protests, 376–78, 452, 465, 471
Camden Courier Post, 590
Camelot (musical), 174
Camp Airy, 243
Campbell, Jo Anne, 203
Campbell, Ken, 318, 373, 427, 503, 582–83
Camp David, 243
Capital Beltway, 200–5, 240
Capitol Cab Company, 231
Capitol Police, 142, 403
Cardozo High School (*formerly* Central High), 38
Carmichael, Stokely, 215–16, 377, 465, 550
Casey, Phil, 536

Cassady, John, 207, 222, 400, 530,
    548–50
Castro, Fidel, 46, 69, 208, 218, 227–28, 238,
    291
Casualty Hospital, 45
Catholic Church, 117, 344, 356–57
Catholic Review, 434
Catholic Standard, 298
Catholic University, 263
Census, 244
Central High School (*later* Cardozo), 37, 81,
    104
Central Intelligence Agency (CIA), 68, 232–
    34, 238, 285, 317, 400, 586
Chaney, James, 461–68
Chapman's Friend, 586
Charles County, Maryland, 65, 154–55, 242,
    344
Chesapeake and Potomac Telephone
    Company, 379
Chesapeake Bay, 242, 381
Chevy Chase Saks Fifth Avenue, 496
Chicago Tribune, 61
Chile, 197
China, 113, 229
  atomic bomb and, 520
Chotiner, Murray, 587, 593
Christian Brothers, 299
Christian Science Monitor, 342
church-state separation, 313, 434
City College of New York, 544
civil defense, 286

612

Civil Rights Act (1964), 453, 461–62, 469–71

civil rights movement, 13, 69, 117, 191, 210, 216, 344, 346–48, 357–58, 366, 349–63, 419–20, 426, 451, 461–68, 546–49. *See also* desegregation; *and specific events and individuals*

Civil War, 36, 120, 455, 458
  centennial of, 196–97

Clark, James, 308

Clark, Mrs. James, 308

Clarke, Edwin W., 252

Clarke County, Virginia, shootings in, 471–72

Cleland, Daisy, 412

Clifford, Clark, 512

ClimateWire, 582

Cline, Patsy, 202

Clinton, Bill, 587

Coalition of Conscience, 547–51

Coast and Geodetic Survey, 555

Cohen, Richie, 201

Cohen, Ronnie, 201

Cold War, 258–61

Colson, Charles W., 594

Columbia University, 430
  Journalism School, 258, 318, 348, 583
  Law School, 430, 575

Communists, 20, 52, 114, 191, 229, 238, 450, 466, 544

Confederacy, 120

Congressional Directory, 31

Congressional Quarterly, 254

Congressional Record, 64, 164
Connally, John, 399
Constitution Hall, 184
Coolidge High School, 108
Corn, Herb, 222
Country Gentlemen, 203
County Juvenile Court (Rockville), 205
Coyne, Marshal, 332
Crawford, Annie, 256
Crawford, Clare, 258
Crim, Isabelle "Annie," 337
Cronkite, Walter, 390, 399–402, 413
Crown, J. Theodore "Ted," 124–39, 143–45,
    154, 214, 337, 390, 511, 518, 593
Crump, Ray, Jr., 586
Cuba, 41, 69, 82
  Bay of Pigs and 227–38, 285–86, 291
  missile crisis and, 284–97
Cuban exiles, 232–34
Cummings, Lucianne Von Steinberger (*later*
    Goldberg), 263, 331–32, 572, 586–87
Cushing, Cardinal, 420

Daily Worker, 412
Dallas Parkland Memorial Hospital, 401, 416
Dallas Police, 412
Dartmouth College, 258
Daugherty, Jane, 13 1 228
Daughters of the American Revolution, 184
Davis, Sammy, Jr., 390
Day, Doris, 443
Dean, Jimmy, 202

Dean, John, 587
Dean, Maureen, 587
Death and Life of Great American Cities, The (Jacobs), 156 271
Deegan, Jane, 204–5, 214 371, 353
DeGast, Leonard A., 50 93
de Gaulle, Charles, 125, 135 218, 237
DeLoach, Cartha "Deke," 50, 295–96, 466, 513, 557–60
Democratic National Convention
  of 1960, 73
  of 1964, 497
Democratic Party, 66, 509
Democratic primaries of 1964, 450–56
Depression, 7 19
desegregation, 36, 38, 97–99, 181, 192, 210–11, 220, 269–70, 348, 357–58, 365, 376–78, 419–20, 450, 464, 471–72. *See also* civil rights movement; *and specific locations*
Diamond Cab Association, 231
Dickens, Charles, 113, 399, 532
Diem, Ngo Dinh, 376
Dillard, Don, , 108, 202–4, 220
Dimond, Tom, 247, 249, 258–59, 269, 273, 286, 318–21, 349, 355, 373, 395, 431, 503, 517, 561, 581
Dirksen, Everett McKinley, 64–67
District of Columbia
  Black population in, 335–37
  childhood in 10–13, 192–94
  congressional representation and, 190

District of Columbia (*continued*)
    desegregation fight in, 12, 181, 210, 335,
        365, 526–27
    home rule and, 219–20, 304
    newspaper strike of 1958, 161
    police (*see also* Metropolitan Police
        Department) 92, 124–28, 142, 145,
        524, 583
    printing industry in, 161–62
    public housing and, 262, 525
    riots of 1968 and, 595
    sacking of 1814 and, 88
    school system, 473–475
    segregation and, 12, 38, 49, 86–92, 150–
        51, 191, 210, 346–47, 384
    streetcars and, 91, 167
    transients vs. permanent people, 49
    urban renewal and, 262, 524
    voting in presidential elections and, 189–
        90, 218–19, 457–59, 541
D.C. Board of Commissioners, 304
D.C. City Council, 588
D.C. Commissioner, 469–70
D.C. Democratic Committee, 459
D.C. Engineer Commissioner, 252
D.C. Fire and EMS Museum, 585
D.C. Fire Department, 523
D.C. General Hospital, 275
D.C. Highway Department, 91, 93, 176
D.C. Junior Village, 438–41, 484
D.C. Newspaper Guild Front Page Awards,
    336

D.C. Printers Ball, 352–53
D.C. Recreation Board, 74
D.C. Stadium
  Opening Day and, 322
  Thanksgiving Day Riot, 298–306, 310
D.C. Superior Court, 440, 589
D.C. Transit Company, 91
D.C. Welfare Department, 438–40
"District Line, The" (Gold), 144
Dole, Bob, 593
Donovan, Dennis, 491–92
Donovan, Marty, 491–92
Douglas, William O., 192, 312
Douglass, Frederick, 495
draft, 430–31, 456, 498–503, 560–61
Dranov, Polly, 484
Draper's tobacco shop, 339
Duddington Place house, 327–31, 511, 563
Dumbarton Oaks, 356, 482
DuMont network, 12
Dunne, Tom, 571
Dupont Circle apartment, 506
Dusk at the Mountain (Johnson), 336
Dylan, Bob, 370, 372, 390

Eastern High School Ramblers, D.C.
    stadium riot and, 299–306
Eastern Market, 104
Eastland, James, 52, 79–80
Eastman, Sam, 286, 404
East Potomac Park, 361
Eastwood, Laura "Aunt Laura," 256–57

Ebony, 385
Edelman, Dickie, 197
Edmund Pettus Bridge, 548, 551
Eichmann, Adolf, trial of, 208
Eisenhower, Dwight, 40, 62–63, 113, 115–
        16, 117, 149, 227, 252–53, 328
    Bay of Pigs and, 235, 285
    Cuba and, 208
    JFK assassination and, 411–412
    JFK inauguration and, 177–78, 187
    Khrushchev visit and, 68
    second inauguration and, 174
Eisenhower, Mamie, 187
Eleanor Roosevelt Institute for Cancer
        Research, 291
elections
    of 1948, 189
    of 1956, 108, 122
    of 1960, 18, 40–41, 68–69, 73, 106–21
    of 1962, 284
    of 1964, 367, 423, 426, 452–55, 510–12,
        540–43
    of 1972, 586–87
Electoral College, 541
Electrical Workers Union, 571
Elizabeth Daily Journal, 565–75, 590–91
Elizabeth II, queen of England, 398
Elkins, Wilson, 433–36
Elkton, Maryland, attempt to marry Jo Anne
        Mark in, 441–49, 483
Ella, Hurricane, 285

Ellicott City, passenger plane crash near,
       306–10
Ellington, Duke, 202
Eliot, T. S., 113
Emancipation Proclamation, 367, 387
Eneim, Norma, 504
Engel, Morris, 264, 514
Engle, Clair, 112
"Epilogue for Kennedy" (White), 427
Epstein, Abe, 80–81
Epstein, Eleni Sakes, 76–77, 194, 207, 354,
       359, 557, 596
Epstein, Ida, 80–81
Epstein, Sidney, 94, 296, 322, 505, 565–66,
       578
    Al Baker's fight with, on touching type,
       164–71, 220–22
    Bay of Pigs and, 234
    Black dictationist and, 384–85
    Bobby Baker scandal and, 423
    civil rights and, 466
    college degree and, 430–31, 529–30
    Crown and, 127, 131–32, 134
    Cuban missile crisis and, 285, 289
    D.C. association meetings and, 88
    D.C. home rule and, 220
    D.C. stadium riot and, 303–7
    dictation bank and, 247, 249
    Ellicott City plane crash and, 306–10
    eulogy for, 596
    fake obit for Post and, 282, 478

Epstein, Sidney (*continued*)
  FBI's King sex tapes and, 557–60
  Foote and, 327–28
  Goldwater ham radio interview and,
      477–80
  Hope and Barron Front Page Award and,
      436–37
  Jackie Kennedy hired by, 398
  Jenkins arrest and, 511–12
  JFK assassination and, 402, 409–11, 427
  JFK inaugural and, 171, 175, 182, 186,
      190, 194
  Jo Anne Mark and, 359
  Lafayette Square police brawl and, 137
  last note to, on leaving *Star,* 566–67
  later career of, 596
  life of, beyond office, 207–8
  local coverage and, 342–43
  March on Washington and, 374, 378–80,
      387–91
  Mary Meyer murder and, 516–17
  Morrow and, 517–18
  naps and, 502
  obits writing and, 255–56, 339–40
  pencil editing by, 82
  photos of deceased and, 490, 493
  promoted to city desk clerk by, 394–98,
      557
  promoted to reporter by, 460, 521
  promotion to reporter revoked by, for lack
      of degree, 528–33, 551
  reporter training program and, 233

as role model and mentor, 43–47, 50, 71,
  73–78, 80–84, 109, 158, 206, 359–59
Siegel bris and, 523
split page and, 493–94
thumbsuckers and, 207
unusual occupations stories and, 534–35
weather project and, 554–55
Woodley Park home of, 315
Esquire, 74
Evangelical Protestants, 117
Evers, Medgar, 367, 468
Executive Protection Service, 142

Faries, Belmont, 51, 56, 69
Fauntroy, Dorothy, 589
Fauntroy, Walter, 215–16, 345, 377, 471,
  496–97, 546–52, 589
Federal Aviation Administration, 380
Federal Aviation Police, 142
Federal Bureau of Investigation (FBI), 18,
  50, 169
  civil rights and, 465–66, 472, 496–97, 558
  Ellicott crash and, 308–10
  Jenkins arrest and, 513
  JFK assassination and, 412
  King sex tapes and, 556–60
  McCarran Act and, 293–97
  new building for, 525
  Oswald and, 426
Federation of Citizens Associations, 91, 93
Federation of Civic Associations, 91, 213–16,
  377

Fialka, John, 318, 504, 506, 582
Final Days, The (Bernstein), 588
FIRE, 140
Fitzgerald, F. Scott, 459, 526–27, 566
Fitzgerald, Zelda 459, 526–27, 566
Fochett, Louis, 135–37, 214, 510–12
Folger Shakespeare Library, 481
Foote, Tad, 327–29, 374, 584
Ford's Theatre, 11
Forer, Joe, 526
Forgey, Ben, 258, 584
Fortas, Abe, 512
Fort Benning, 472–73, 474
Fort Holabird, 498–503
Fort Meade, 258
Fort Stevens, 88
Frankfurter, Felix, 312
Freed, Alan, 110, 203
Freedmen's Hospital, 45
Freedom Riders, 358, 471
Fryklund, Dick, 260, 284–85, 289, 298, 391,
    472, 499
Fulbright, Bosey, 327
Fulbright, J. William, 327

Gabbett, Harry, 536
Gagarin, Yuri, 221, 223, 227, 231–32
Gallaudet College, 162
Garfinckel's department store, 11
Garroway, Dave, 221
Gary, Indiana, *Post-Tribune,* 385
Gay, Connie B., 202

Gayety Burlesque Theater, 243
General Services Administration, 385–86
Georgetown University Law School, 318
George Washington High School
    (Alexandria), 54 99
George Washington University, 81, 257, 591
  Hospital, 513
Georgia Avenue streetcar line, 91
Georgia Bureau of Investigation, 472
Gianaris, Johnny, 58, 77, 103
Gianaris, Pete, 103
Gifford's Ice Cream Parlor sit-ins, 212–13
Gilbert, Ben, 66–67, 383, 536, 544–45, 595
Gilbert, Ian, 383, 536
Gilbert, Maureen, 383, 544
Giles-Johnson rape case, 526
Gimble, Gil, 250
Glen Echo Amusement Park, 144
  desegregation of, 211
Gold, Bill, 143–44
Gold, Walter, 133, 140–55, 169, 183, 301,
    326–27, 333, 495, 584–85
Goldberg, Lucianne. *See* Cummings,
    Lucianne Von Steinberger
Goldberg, Sid, 586
Golden Book of Weather, The, 322 555
Golden Parrot, 536
Goldstein, Louie ("No-Label Louie's"), 14–
    16, 422, 480–81
Goldwater, Barry, 426, 510–14, 541
  ham radio interview of, 476–77
Gonzaga High School, 518

Good, Joe, 196–200, 239, 244–46
Goodman, Andrew, 461–68, 497, 558
Goodwin, Gene, 353, 484
Gorska, Fifi, 330
Government Printing Office, 163, 353
Graham, Katharine, 577–80, 591
Graham, Phil, 320, 371
Grant, Cary, 298
Grant, Milt, 116, 204, 338
Grant, Ulysses S., 18
Grant, Ulysses S., III, 195–96, 227, 458
Greek Americans, 76–78
Green Bay Packers, 322
Greenwell, Sybil, 535–536
Gregorian calendar, 432
Griffith, Clark, 102
Griffiths, Harriet, 330, 388
Griffith Stadium, 69, 193
Grunwald, Henry, 580
Guantánamo, 82–84
Guarino, Phil, 219
Guback, Steve, 305
Gulf of Tonkin Resolution (1964), 498–99
Gulf War, first, 582
Gusti's restaurant, 77

Haggerty, Joan, 574
Hains Point, 361–62
Haldeman, H. R., 587
Haley, Bill, 203
Hall, Julie, Seafood Restaurant, 397, 409
Hamer, Fannie Lou, 551

Harpers, 342

Harrigan's saloon, 261–65, 273–74, 278,
   293, 317–18, 331, 352, 357, 375, 394,
   397, 409, 457–58, 484, 501–2, 510,
   514, 522–25, 528, 536, 559

Hartke, Father, 263–64, 522

Harvard Crimson, 258

Harvard University, 258, 482, 518, 577

Hay-Adams Hotel, 408

Heap, Earl, 55–57, 100, 221–23, 250, 255

Hecht Company department store, 200

Hemingway, Ernest, 151, 155, 518

Hendley, Coit, 78, 168, 220, 283, 322, 337–
   40, 374–75, 379, 385, 396, 427, 431,
   449, 461–466, 514–16, 532, 556–60
   Elizabeth Daily Journal and, 565–74
   Washington Times and, 584, 590–91, 594

Hendley, Peter, 590

Herb H. (dictationist) 278

Herblock, 353

Herndon, Gerry, 137–38, 164, 298–99, 303,
   342, 472, 494, 516, 564

Hershey, Lewis B., 276, 316, 430, 456, 498, 561

Heston, Charlton, 390

Hickenlooper, Bourke B., 254

Hickory Hill picnics, 488

Hill, Ambrose Powell, 226–27, 458

Hill, I. William "Bill", 331, 350, 400, 430–
   31, 436, 528–40, 552, 553–56, 564–65

Hill, Powell, 226–27, 458

Hines, Bill, 71, 222, 253, 379, 388, 390, 486,
   578

Hiroshima, 330
Hiser, John Henry, 213
Hiser Theater protests, 211–13, 216
His Girl Friday (movie), 298
Hobson, Julius, 215–16, 377, 470, 497
Hodges, Gil, 522
Hofberg's delicatessen, 103, 122, 447
Hoffman, Burt, 331, 400
Hoge, Warren, 481, 583
Holiday, Billie, 443
Holland, Cecil, 230, 382, 423, 509
Holly, Buddy, 203, 418
Holtzoff, Alexander, 252
homosexuals, arrests of, 130–31, 215
Hoover, Herbert, 373, 520
Hoover, J. Edgar, 18, 38, 50, 76–78, 558
   Blick's sex offenders files and, 131, 138
   civil rights and, 466–67
   FBI headquarters and, 525
   Jenkins arrest and, 513
   McCarran Act and, 292–97
Hope, Paul, 105–7, 114–23, 382, 423, 436,
      454
Hope Diamond, 590
Horner, Garnett D. "Jack," 72, 224–28,
      252–53, 289, 379, 411–12, 465
Hornig, Roberta "Bobbie," 330, 399, 522
Horsky, Charles, 348
Hot Shoppes, 88–89, 108, 212
Howard Theater, 202
Howard University, 45, 211, 215, 335, 358,
      384, 464

Howdy Doody Show (TV show), 210
Hoy, Frank, 462
Hoy, Tom, 462–63
Hudson, Rock, 443
Humphrey, Hubert, 293
Hunt, E. Howard, 594
Hunter, Clarence, 381–82, 384–85, 388,
    472, 474, 551

Immler, Nancy, 199
Indiana primaries of 1964, 454
Indian Springs Country Club, 113
Indochina, 113, 218, 376
"Inquiring Camera Girl by Jacqueline
    Bouvier" (column), 398
International News Service (INS), 38, 69
International Typographical Union, 161, 170
Iran, shah of, 481
Isaacs, Steve, 577–78
Italian Americans, 76–77

Jackson, Andrew, 550
Jackson, Jimmie Lee, 547, 550
Jackson, Mahalia, 372, 390
Jackson, Mississippi, 367
Jackson, Sonny, 199, 212
Jacobs, Jane, 271
Janney Elementary School, 38, 101, 192,
    226, 289, 313
Japan, 21
Jefferson Memorial, 361
Jenkins, Walter, 510–14

Jet, 385
Jews, 149, 372
Jim Crow, 463. *See also* desegregation;
    segregation
Jim Myers Silver Spring Recreation Center
    (pool hall), 60
Johnson, Colonel, 196, 244, 276
Johnson, Haynes, 296, 333–34, 437, 486,
    578
    civil rights reporting and, 211, 334–35,
        365, 382, 391–93, 548–49
    later career of, 595–96
    mentoring by, 339
    Replane murder and, 332–33
    writing style of, 333, 342
Johnson, Lady Bird, 192
Johnson, Lyndon B., 192–93
    Baker and, 422–25, 509–10, 512
    civil rights and, 192–93, 452, 461, 466–74,
        548–49
    Cummings and, 331–32
    early presidency of, 422–27
    elections of 1960 and, 332, 424
    elections of 1964 and, 453, 541–45
    FBI headquarters and, 525
    Graham and, 320
    Jenkins and 509–14
    JFK assassination and 402–8, 411–12
    JFK inauguration and, 191–92
    as Senate majority leader 15, 423–24
    Vietnam War and, 498–99
    Warren commission and, 415

Johnson, Malcolm, 337, 596–97
Johnson, Walter "the Big Train", 104–5,
    526, 566
John XXIII, Pope, 371
Jones & Laughlin plant, 352
Joseph P. Kennedy, Jr., USS (destroyer), 285
Justice Department, 423, 462–63, 471–72,
    525

Katzenbach, Nicholas, 462–64
Kauffmann, Jack, 278
Kauffmann, Rudolph, Sr., 104
Kauffmann, Rudolph Max, II "Rudy," 20–
    27, 203, 282, 321, 362–63, 531–32
Kauffmann, Sam, 278
Kauffmann family, 22, 49, 195–96, 394,
    579
Keegan, Paul, 203
Kefauver, Estes, 111–12
Kefauver Committee, 36
Kelley, Phil, 257, 330, 351, 380
    cab companies and 231
    JFK assassination and, 401
    McGrory and, 486
    mentoring by, 30–45, 48, 55–56, 62–64,
        67–68, 70, 75, 78–79, 97, 159–62, 195–
        96, 221, 223–24, 228, 234, 247–48,
        489
Kelly, Orr, 427
Kennedy, Caroline, 415
Kennedy, Ethel, 106, 189, 488
Kennedy, George, 479

Kennedy, Jacqueline, 133, 187
　　death of son Patrick and, 376
　　as inquiring photographer, 398
　　inauguration and, 186–88
　　JFK assassination and, 407–12, 415–16,
　　　　420, 425–29
　　Mary Meyer and, 516
　　sister Lee and, 237
　　trip to France and, 218
　　White interview of, 428–29
Kennedy, John F., 274–77, 328, 516
　　affair with Mary Meyer and, 585–86
　　assassination of, 398–421, 425–29, 586
　　Bay of Pigs and, 227–39
　　Broder on, 208–9
　　Camelot and, 427–28
　　Castro and, 208
　　charm and glamor of, , 230, 320
　　civil rights and, 191, 365–67, 387–88, 452
　　Communism and, 229–30
　　Cuban missile crisis and, 284–87, 291–97
　　D.C. home rule and, 219
　　Eleanor Roosevelt and, 184
　　elections of 1960 and, 18, 40–41, 68–69,
　　　　73
　　elections of 1962 and, 284
　　funeral of, 413–16, 419–20, 425
　　Horner on, 252–53
　　inauguration of, 171–94, 200, 338
　　Madison Hotel and, 332
　　March on Washington and, 386–87, 390,
　　　　419

McCarran Act and, 295–97
Montgomery Blair rally and, 105–23, 186
Post and, 320
racial discrimination order and, 346–47
Rauh and, 346–47
southerners and, 191
Soviet manned space flight and, 223–31
Soviet nuclear tests and, 259–60, 375
televised press conferences and, 225–26,
    238–240
trip to Berlin and, 370–71
trip to France and, 218
Vietnam and, 238, 275
Washington sports teams and, 322, 384
Kennedy, John F., Jr., 187, 415
Kennedy, Joseph P., 190–92
Kennedy, Joseph P., Jr., 285
Kennedy, Patrick Bouvier, 376
Kennedy, Robert F., 423
  civil rights and, 391, 462
  Hickory Hill picnics and, 488–89
  JFK assassination and, 407–9, 417
  JFK inauguration and, 189
  Senate race and, 488–89
Kennedy, Rose, 456
Kennedy, Ted, 356, 404, 456
Kennedy Center, 427–28
Key, Francis Scott, 459
Khrushchev, Nikita, 218
  Cuban missile crisis and, 291, 297
  deposed, 520–21
  fall of Stalin and, 260

Khrushchev, Nikita (*continued*)
  space race and, 223, 227
  spelling name of, 249–52
  visits U.S., 68, 72
Killebrew, Harmon, 69
King, Martin Luther, Jr., 345, 419–20, 435,
    470, 546, 547
  assassination of, 595
  Civil Rights Act and, 469
  Fauntroy and, 588
  FBI sex tapes of, 560
  March on Washington and, 372, 391–92,
    435
  Nobel Peace Prize and, 520
  Selma-Montgomery March and, 548–52
Klutz, Jerry, 20
Koepeck, John, 506
Koerber, Ginny, 503
Koltun, Janet, 290, 460
Kondracke, Mort, 258
Kookogey, Gover M., 195–96
Kopeck, John, 147, 151
Korean War, 260, 295, 321, 355
Krebs, Larry, 145–47, 153
Ku Klux Klan, 373, 520–21, 550–52

Lady Chatterley's Lover (Lawrence), 135
Lafayette Square
  beautification of, 133
  JFK assassination and, 404–5
  JFK inauguration and, 177
  police brawl at, 132–37, 214–16

Selma protests and, 549–52
Lanahan, Scottie Fitzgerald, 459–60, 517–20
Laos, 218, 229
Laurel High School, 332–34
Lawrence, D. H., 135
Leary, Bob, 327, 503, 563
LeDroit Park, 146
LeDroit Park Civic Association, 96–97
Lee, Blair, III, 111–16
Lee, Carol, 374
Lee, Christine, Chinese Restaurant, 571–72
Lee, Gypsy Rose, 174
Lee, Jim, 263, 269, 278–79, 283, 374–75
Lee, Robert E., 458
  Arlington mansion of, 120, 507
Lehrer, Jim, 581
Lewinsky, Monica, 587
Lewis, Al, 126–32, 511, 518
Lewis, Gladys, 129
Lewis, Jerry Lee, 110, 203
Lewis, John, 548
Lewis, Robert J., 270–71
Lewis & Thos. Saltz, 74, 297
Library of Congress, 555
Life, 423, 427
Li'l Abner comic strip, 441, 445
Lincoln, Abraham 320, 419
  assassination of, 11, 21, 414, 560
  Gettysburg address and, 392
  inauguration of, 18
  JFK and, 117–18
  Old Soldier's Home and, 10, 88

Lincoln, Gould, 24, 29, 231, 435
Lincoln Memorial, 120, 389
  Anderson concert at, 184
Lindbergh, Charles, 21
Lindsay, Pussy, 324–25
Linotype machines, 158–60, 159, 221, 354
Lippmann, Walter, 234–35
Liuzzo, Viola, 552, 558
London, Julie, 278
Lord of the Rings, The (Tolkien), 505
Lover Come Back (movie), 443
Lyman, Frankie, 203

MacArthur, Douglas, 21, 449
MacPherson, Myra, 330, 390, 405, 408, 410,
    522–23, 592–93
Maddox, USS (destroyer), 498
Mademoiselle, 352
Mafia, 36, 77, 294
Maggiacomo, Tony, 48–55, 66–67, 70, 74–
    75, 99, 206–7, 224, 257, 330, 583–84
Magidson, Jane, 429
Maine Avenue Waterfront, 262
Malachi, Detective Sergeant, 152–53
Mandela, Nelson, 589
Mansfield, Mike, 415
March on Washington for Jobs and Freedom
    (1963), 372, 379, 385–93, 418, 435, 547
March on Washington to End the War in
    Vietnam (1965), 560–61
Marciano, Rocky, 174
Maret School, 482

Marine, Larry, 205
Mark, Jo Anne, 371, 431, 505
 dating and, 348–63, 394
 JFK assassination and, 400–1, 414, 418–19
 Junior Village and, 438–40
 later career of, 580
 leaves for grad school, 485–86, 564, 567
 meets family, 473–75
 near marriage to, 440–48, 482–83
 night police shift and, 396
 personality and charm of, 456–57
 Wallace rally and, 450–55
 Women's Department and, 482–83
Maryland, 101, 358
 county boards, 270
 desegregation and, 209–10, 269–70, 358,
  376–77, 451
 elections of 1964 and, 541
 history of slavery and, 455
 JFK campaign of 1960 and, 105
 land use policy and, 270
 poet laureate of, 241
 slot machines and, 242
 Sot-Weed Factor and, 242
 Wallace campaign and, 451–56
Maryland and Virginia Milk Producers
  Association, 99
Maryland Court of Appeals, 311
Maryland National Capital Park and
  Planning Commission, 205, 270
Maryland state legislature, 269
Maryland State Penitentiary, 494–95

Massachusetts Transit Authority, 583
Master Barbers and Beauticians of America,
    470
Mays, Willie, 443
McAleer, Charles, 259, 561
McBride's, S. N., job at, 9, 14–15, 86, 103,
    162, 198
McCarran Internal Security Act (190),
    292–97
McCarthy, Joe, 11, 35, 66, 184, 293, 296, 427
McCormack, Eddie, 404
McCormack, John, 402–6, 409, 415
McGovern, George, 586
McGrory, Mary, 35–36, 251, 296, 330–31,
    392, 483, 550, 563, 578
  JFK and, 188, 208–9, 410
  later career of, 591
  spell cast by, 486–87
  writing style of, 342, 486–87
McKelway, Ben, 234, 304, 319, 350, 486
McKelway, John, 479
McLachlen National Bank, 590
McLean, Evelyn Walsh, 590
McLean Baptist Church, 564
McMillan, John, 220
McNamara, Robert, 449, 472, 498
Meet the Press (TV show), 116
Meridian, Mississippi, 463
Metropolitan Police Department (MPD),
    133, 142, 166
  D.C. stadium riot and, 301–5
  homicide detectives and, 515–20

March on Washington and, 391

Nichols Avenue shooting and, 151–54

Metropolitan Police Department,
  Prostitution and Perversion Squad

Jenkins arrest and, 509–14

Lafayette Square police brawl and, 130–39,
  215

Metropolitan Washington Park and Planning
  Commission, 251

Meyer, Cord, Jr., 517

Meyer, Eugene, 319

Meyer, Mary Pinchot, 514–21, 586

Meyers, Jesse, 433

Middle Atlantic Lawn Tennis Association,
  565

Milt Grant Show, The, 12, 16, 204, 585

Milton, John, 37

Minute Men, 552

Mirror of War (Hill and Stepp), 530

Mississippi, murder of civil rights workers in,
  461–68, 496

Mississippi Freedom Democratic Party, 497,
  551

Montgomery Blair Blazers, 115, 199–200, 321

Montgomery Blair High School, 118–19,
  144, 176, 195, 212, 313, 321, 362

  drag racing and, 200–5, 239–41

  JFK rally at, 106–23

  senior year at, 85–89, 99–101, 195–200,
    217–18, 234, 242–46

  typing classes at, 29

  slot machine gambling and, 242–43

Montgomery County, 65, 102, 526
  school prayer and, 313–14
Montgomery County Board of Education,
  102
Montgomery County Council, 104
Montgomery County Democratic Party, 111
Montgomery County Juvenile Court, 19
Montgomery County Police, 118, 213
Montgomery Hills Junior High School, 101
Moon, Sun Myung, 584
Moore, Paul, 551
Mormons, 184
Morris, James, 360
Morrow, Hugh, 517
Morrow, Lance, 328, 481–82, 487, 503,
  515–21, 562–64, 580–81, 586
Moser, Jim, 46
Mousie's newsstand, 103, 122, 447
Mr. Smith Goes to Washington (movie), 177
Murray, Madalyn, 311–14, 376
Mussolini, Benito, 155

Nannes, Caspar, 433, 565
National Aeronautics and Space
  Administration (NASA), 222, 554
National Airport, 307, 555
National Association for the Advancement of
  Colored People (NAACP), 367
National Capital Park and Planning
  Commission, 524
National Capital Parks, 93
National Cathedral choir, 505

National Enquirer, 342
National Gallery of Art, 361, 366, 481
National Guard, 200, 366, 377, 450–51
National Institute of Dry Cleaning, 66
National Press Building, 263
National Press Club, 436, 512
national security, 238–39
National Security Council, 286
National Transportation Safety Board,
    309–10
National Weather Service, 554
National Zoo, 126, 494, 590
National Zoo Police, 142
Naval Observatory, 554
NBC News, 237, 415, 512–113
"Negro in Washington, The" (Johnson), 211,
    334–36, 342, 382
New Arena Stage Theater, 264
New Bethel Baptist Church, 215, 546
Newcomb, Colonel, 269
New England Restaurant, 262
New Republic, 342
Newspaper Guild, 43, 365, 394
  strikes and, 161, 483
Newsweek, 516, 579, 584
New York
  move to, 572–73
  Great Blackout of 1965, 585
New York City Police Department, 575
New York *Daily Mirror,* 517
New York *Daily News,* 49, 60
New Yorker, 342, 479

New York Herald Tribune, 60, 342, 359, 579

New York Journal American, 61

New York Post, 61, 583

New York Sun, 337

New York Times, 60, 180, 254, 260, 342, 359, 371, 380, 486, 576, 579, 584, 587

  lox-and-bagel, Sunday *Times* delivery service and, 103

New York University, 473

Nichols Avenue shooting, 151–52

Nixon, Pat, 192

Nixon, Richard M., 236

  California gubernatorial race and, 284, 369

  elections of 1960 and, 18, 40–41, 68, 73, 109, 113–16

  Watergate and, 587, 592–93

North American Newspaper Alliance, 39, 586

Noyes, Crosby S., 54, 261, 240, 379, 391

Noyes, Newbold, Jr. "Newby," 35, 55, 58, 222, 240, 304, 319, 350, 379, 400, 412, 486, 556–60, 563

Noyes family, 22, 49, 168, 196, 394, 579

nuclear weapons, 259, 286, 330, 520

Oak Hill Cemetery, Black refused burial in, 458

Obama, Barack, 589

Oberman, Ron, 62, 65, 198, 201–5, 219, 272, 301

Occidental Restaurant, 16–17

Ocean City, 242, 377
O'Donnell, Kenny, 428
Office of Price Administration, 80
"Of This and That" (Bernstein), 573
Ohlheiser, Pete, 197
Old Post Office Tower, 16, 208
Old Soldier's Home, 10, 88
O'Leary, Jeremiah Aloysius, Jr. "Jerry," 46,
        50, 259, 285, 293–97, 303, 309, 389,
        466, 472, 504, 513, 561
    JFK assassination and, 381–85, 406–7,
        411–12, 415, 426
    King tapes and, 556–58
    later career of, 594–95
    writing style of, 342
O'Leary, Jeremiah Aloysius, Sr., 50, 63, 67,
        294, 404
O'Leary, Maria, 504
"O'Leary's Washington" (column), 594
On the Waterfront (movie), 337
Organization of American States (OAS),
        289
Oswald, Lee Harvey, 412, 414–16, 426
Ottenberg, Miriam, 36–38, 50, 294, 330–31,
        390, 423, 437, 466, 472, 483, 532, 552,
        557, 591–92
Ottenberg, Regina, 28, 36–39
Ottenberg rye bread, 36, 122
Our Gang (movie series), 165–66

Page, Patti, 482
Papas, Sophocles, 204

Paradise Lost (Milton), 28, 239
Parker, Suzy, 332
Parkside Elementary School, 102, 119, 241
Parzow, Bobbie, 585
Passaic Herald-News, 590
Paul VI, Pope, 371
Pay, Detective Sergeant, 119, 205, 212
PBS News Hour, 581
Pearson, Drew, 356
Peck, Gregory, 527
Peeler, Bill, 304
Penn, Lemuel, 472–75, 520–21
Penn, Mrs. Lemuel, 472–75
Penn, Ralph, 591
Penn State Journalism School, 348, 353, 442, 484, 580
Pentagon, 259, 260, 284–85, 289, 391, 472, 499
Pepper, Chili, 243
Peter, Paul and Mary, 372
Petit, Tom, 415
Petworth Citizens Association, 88–95
Phelps Vocational High School, 474
Philadelphia Inquirer, 60–61, 580
Phil's Tavern, 62, 219
Pinchot, Amos, 516
Pinchot, Gifford, 516
Pioli, Mr., 360
Pitts, Milton, 144, 587–88
Plato, 274
polio, 226

Port Elizabeth–Port Newark, 576
Porter, George, 73, 174, 276, 306, 311–12, 322, 431, 451, 455, 505, 528, 565
  Bethesda protests and, 209–13
  mentoring by, 97–106, 245–46, 254
  JFK rally and, 112–13
Porter, Mrs., 103–4, 209
Pound, Ezra, 151, 155
Povich, Shirley, 522
Powers, Francis Gary, 41, 72
President's Commission on Pennsylvania Avenue, 133
Price, Phil, 400
Prince George's County, 125, 153, 201–2, 242, 333, 506
Prince George's County Greenbelt Preservation Board, 270
Princeton University, 431
Proctor, Jimmy, 119, 240
Proctor brothers drag racing, 200–1, 240
Proctors-Swanns feuds, 153–57, 344
Progressive Party, 189, 516
Protestants, 372
Provenzano, Tony, 571
public accommodations, desegregation of, 376–77, 450, 470–72
Puerto Rican nationalists, 189
Puerto Rico, 285
Puffenbarger, Charlie, 290, 302–3, 310, 322, 388, 395, 402–8, 413, 417, 431, 440, 444, 447, 457–60, 472, 514, 528, 532, 577, 591

Pulitzer Prize, 526, 532
  Dimond and, 581
  Haynes Johnson and, 337, 595–96
  Malcolm Johnson and, 337, 596
  McGrory and, 591
  Ottenberg and, 36
  Werner and, 36, 42, 97, 530
Pursuit of Hope, The (Ottenberg), 591–92
Pustilnik, Bobby, 270

Radziwill, Lee, 237
Randolph, A. Philip, 387, 391
Rauh, Joe, 346–47
Rayburn, Sam, 191
Raye, Martha, 443
Reagan, Ronald, 594
Rebach, Gerry, 319
Reconstruction, 469–70
Red Garter bar (Pensacola), 589
Reeb, James, 549, 550
Reedy, George, 466
Reeves Bakery, 14, 85
Replane, Allene, 332–33
Reporter, 342
Republican National Committee, 219, 593
Republican National Convention of 1964,
    477
Republican Party, 190
  Baker and, 436, 509
  civil rights and, 191
  elections of 1960 and, 115–16
  elections of 1964, 427, 476, 540

644

HCUA and, 544
Jenkins arrest and, 510–11
Reuther, Walter, 550–51
Reynolds, Debbie, 443
Richmond, desegregation and, 376
Richmond News-Leader, 61
Richmond Times-Dispatch, 61
right-wing violence, 552
Robbins, Phil, 410, 417
Robertson, Sherry, 102–3
Robinson, Jackie, 284
Rock Creek Park, 75
Rockefeller, Nelson, 426, 518
Rockville, Maryland, Fitzgerald grave in,
    260, 526–27
Rockwell, George Lincoln, 211, 373
Roosevelt, Alice, 190
Roosevelt, Eleanor, 184, 190, 347
Roosevelt, Franklin D., 62, 113, 149, 226,
    328, 346
Roosevelt, Theodore "Teddy," 190, 419,
    516
Roosevelt High School, 89
Rosemary (photographer), 494
Rosson, John, 209
Route 40 protests 210, 215, 348, 377, 445,
    465
Route 50 shootings, 471–72
Route 301, 242, 274
Rowland, Jim, 450
Rubin, Buddy, 198, 219, 301
Ruby, Jack, 416

Rusk, Dean, 232, 498
Rustin, Bayard, 387

Sadie Hawkins Day, 441–42, 448
Salinger, Pierre, 111–12, 230, 284–85
Salk polio vaccine, 226
Salvation Army drum player, 256
San Francisco Chronicle, 576
Saturday Evening Post, 518
save-the-streetcar movement, 91
Scalley, Tom, 522
Schaden, Herman, 125, 164, 342, 389, 494
  JFK inauguration and, 171–74, 179–94
Schmick, Paul, 62–63, 300–1, 305
school desegregation, 36, 38, 98–99, 376
school prayer, 312–15, 375
Schwerner, Michael, 461–68, 296–97, 558
Schwerner, Rita, 462–68
Scribner, Judy, 504
Scribner, Norman, 505
Scripps-Howard company, 126
Scull, Betsy, 111
Scull, David, 111
Scull, Elizabeth Lee, 111
Second Sex, The (de Beauvoir), 457
Secret Service, 62, 105, 224, 404
Securities and Exchange Commission,
    581
Seeger, Pete, 184
Segovia, 204
segregation. *See also* civil rights movement;
    desegregation; *and specific locations*

646

D.C. and, 191, 210
    Maryland ends, 451
Seib, Charlie, 349–53, 385, 431, 485
Selective Service, 276, 430, 499–503, 560
Selma–Montgomery march, 548–52, 595
Sequoia National Park, 369
Shamrock Irish Bar, 202
Shaw, Daryl W., 108, 119–23, 246
Shaw neighborhood, 546
Shenandoah River drownings, 491
Shepherd Park neighborhood, 345
Sheraton Carlton Hotel, 587
Sherman Circle, 92–93
Sherwood, John, 342–43, 494
Shipley, Carl, 540
Sholl, Evan, 13
Sholl's Cafeteria, 13, 180–81
Shor, Toots, 522
Siegel, Michael McPherson, 522–23
Siegel, Morrie, 522
Silver Spring, Maryland, 10–11, 65, 77, 89
    Blair Blazers parade, 198–200
    drag racing and, 200–5, 240–41
    move to, 102
    streetcars and, 91
Silver Spring Selective Service Board,
        499–500
Sinatra, Frank, 173
Singer Sewing machine, 571–74
Sirica, John, 522
Sitnick, Rita, 272, 373, 429
Sitnick, Sally, 373

Sitnick, Stan, 364–72, 376
Sixteenth Street Baptist Church bombing
    (Birmingham), 419–20, 469
Sklover, Phil, 243, 301
slavery, 117–18, 125, 455
Sligo Creek Park, 102
Slye, Mrs., 313
Smathers, George, 191
Smith, Howard K., 186
Smith, Margaret Chase, 427
Smithsonian Institution, 12
Social Register, 31
Social Security, 117
Sonen, Jean, 504
Sot-Weed Factor, The (Barth), 240–45, 273
Sousa, John Philip, 183
Southeast Freeway, 277
Southern Christian Leadership Conference,
    470, 546
Southern Democrats, 190–92, 303–4
Southern Manifesto, 220
South Vietnam, 371, 376
Southwest Freeway, 262
Soviet Union (USSR)
  Bay of Pigs and, 232, 237
  Berlin and, 250, 259
  Cuban missile crisis and, 287–90, 297
  Eisenhower and, 40, 69
  JFK and, 108, 229
  Khrushchev deposed in, 520
  nuclear tests, 258–59, 375
  Oswald and, 426

space race and, 68–72, 78, 217, 220–29, 520

space program, 73, 222

Spanish-American War, 197

Sparkman, John, 176, 191

Spillane, Mickey, 277

Sporting Bulletin, 104

Spotsylvania County Courthouse, Battle of, 458

Sputnik, 72, 217

St. Agnes Episcopal Church, 564–65

Stalin, Joseph, 260

Stanford University, 318

St. Ann's Infant and Maternity Home, 35, 488

State Department
  Blick on homosexuals at, 130
  Cold War and, 258–59, 260
  Cuban missile crisis and, 290
  JFK press conference at, 224–25, 230, 235
  Office of Protocol, 412

State Newspaper Association prizes, 576

St. Bernadette's Academy, 258

St. Columba's Episcopal Church, 313

Stein, Ben, 102–3, 111, 447, 575, 585

Stein, Gertrude, 277

Stein, Herb, 102, 585

Stein, Rachel, 102

Steinbeck, John, 106 188

St. Elizabeths Hospital (*formerly* Government Hospital for the Insane), 148–51, 155, 495–96, 523

Stepp, John, 530
Sterman, Dave (great-uncle), 149
Sterman, Lena (great-grandmother), 11–13, 149
Stevenson, Adlai, 108, 121–22, 184, 232, 355
Stewart, Jimmy, 177
St. John's College High School, 204
    Cadets D.C. stadium riot and, 299–307
St. Mary's Catholic Cemetery (Rockville), 459
St. Mary's County, Maryland, 242
St. Matthew's Cathedral, 413, 420
St. Michael's, 244
Stone, I. F., 592
St. Patrick's Church, 263
St. Petersburg Times, 580
Student Nonviolent Coordinating Committee (SNCC), 464–67, 548
Students for a Democratic Society (SDS), 560
Supreme Court, 38, 89, 191, 299, 324, 471
    school prayer and, 311–15, 376
Sura, Tante Haya (great-aunt), 275
Swampoodle, 96–97, 345, 495–96
Swann-Proctor feuds, 153–57, 345
Swann Street jazz club, 324–25
swimming pool electrocution story, 72
Symington, Stuart, 65, 73

Taishoff, Itzel (great-uncle), 88, 456, 521
Taishoff, Rose (great-aunt), 88, 456, 521
Takoma Park, Maryland, 199

650

Tangier Island, 343
Tau Epsilon Phi fraternity, 434
Taylor, Arnold, 306
Teamsters Union, 571, 573
television news, 392, 405–9, 420
Ten Blocks from the White House (Gilbert),
      595
Tenley, Bootsie, 197
Tenleytown neighborhood, 101–3, 120
Texas School Book Depository, 426
Thomas, James E., 138, 214
Thomson Newspapers, 584
Thurston, Suze, 504, 582–83
Thwat, Bo, 562
Tibet, 113
Tidal Basin, 361
Time, 342, 562, 580
TIME Inc., *Star* sold to, 579
Tobriner, Walter, 303–4
Today (TV show), 221
To Kill a Mockingbird (movie), 526
Toscanini, Arturo, 173
"tourist homes," 326
Traffic World, 584
Treasury Department, 11, 182, 189
Trenton Terrace union picnics, 149
Tribble, Ed, 294, 321, 350, 359, 486
    Capitol Beltway and, 239–41
    salon of, 208–9, 225–26, 239–41, 251–52,
      261, 320
    Sunday Department and, 206–8, 239
Trinidad neighborhood, 495

Trinity Church, 356
Tripp, Linda, 587
Troup, Bobby, 277
Truman, Harry S., 73, 149, 181, 328
   civil rights and, 191
   JFK assassination and, 411
   JFK inaugural parade and, 189
   McCarran Act and, 292–94
Truman, Margaret, 189
Trupp, Phil, 262–63, 279–83, 458, 583
Twenty-Third Amendment, 218

U-2 spy plane, 41, 72
Uline Arena prizefights, 103
Unification Church, 584
Union County Courthouse (Elizabeth, New
      Jersey), 570
United Airlines plane crash, 308–9
United Auto Workers, 372
United Federal Workers/United Public Workers
      of America, 19–20, 21, 43–44, 52
United Nations, 21, 229, 232, 289
United Press International (UPI), 38, 58,
      484, 512, 582
U.S. Air Force Reserve, 513
U.S. Army, 148
U.S. Army Intelligence Corps, 258
U.S. Army Reserves, 472, 561
United States Civil War Centennial
      Commission, 196
U.S. Congress, 68, 92, 105, 178, 192, 293,
      389, 402–3, 499, 513–14

civil rights and, 192, 453, 470
D.C. rule and, 131, 219–20
Gallaudet and, 162
Voting Rights Act and, 550
U.S. Constitution, 218, 366, 435
U.S. Court of Appeals, 496
Fourth Circuit, 376
U.S. District Court, 252
U.S. House of Representatives
Committee on Un-American Activities
(HCUA), 544
District Committee, 220, 374
Fauntroy as first elected D.C. delegate to,
588–89
government printing office and, 163
JFK assassination and, 404–5
U.S. Marine Band, 182
U.S. Marine Corps, 81, 328
U.S. Navy, 148
U.S. Navy-Marine military exercises,
284–85
U.S. Park Police, 142, 515
Lafayette Square brawl and, 131–35, 136–
37, 212–14
March on Washington and, 380
U.S. Senate, 50, 64–67, 163, 252, 404
Committee on the District of Columbia, 11
LBJ and, 422–23
Rules Committee, 509
University of Alabama, desegregation of,
366, 464
University of California, Berkeley, 258

University of Illinois, 578
University of Maryland, 99, 144, 258, 263
  Christian chaplains and, 432–35
  studies at, 246, 266–74, 315–17, 394, 398–
    99, 429–33, 456, 498, 507, 528, 595
  Wallace speech at, 451–52
University of Miami, 584
University of Mississippi Law School,
    desegregation of, 367
University of Rhode Island, 583
University of Texas Longhorns' marching
    band, 173, 193
Upper Marlboro, Maryland, 153, 242

Vallens, Ritchie, 203
Vanocur, Sandy, 237
Velde, Harold, 544
Venice (Morris), 360
Vietnam War, 238, 370–71, 418, 426, 449–
    50, 498–500, 592–93
Village Voice, 572
Virginia
  desegregation and, 36, 97–98, 211, 376–77,
    470–71
  elections of 1964 and, 542
Voss, Earl, 390, 412–13
Voting Rights Act (1965), 551–52

Wagshal's, 192, 422
Waldorf, Maryland, 156, 242
Walker, Annie (great-aunt), 65, 156, 204,
    242, 344

Walker, Mary "Ooma" (grandmother), 16, 80, 149, 175, 178–79, 372, 457
Walker, Stanley (cousin), 149, 155–56
Walker, Thomas "Popsy" (grandfather), 11, 16, 80, 149, 175, 178–79, 193, 457
Wallace, George, 451–456, 463–64, 471, 550
Wallace, Henry, 189
Wall Drugstore, 368
Wall Street Journal, 60, 581–82
Walter Reed Army Hospital, 449
Walters, Bob, 587
Wardman Park Hotel, 314–15
Warren, Earl, 191, 314, 415
Warren Commission, 425–28
Washington, Dinah, 202
Washington, George, 119
Washington Afro-American, 61
Washington Channel, 361
Washington Daily News, 49, 61, 126, 353, 511–12, 523, 542, 576
Washington *Evening Star. See also specific events and individuals*
  Advertising Department, 380
  Art Department, 554
  Black reporters and, 216, 231, 335, 381–84
  books and carbon copies, 53
  buildings, 17–18, 22, 180, 261–62
  BULLETIN, FLASH and URGENT bells, 39–40, 69
  business desk, 163
  cab companies used by, 230
  carbon paper hazing at, 52–59, 66

Washington *Evening Star (continued)*

ceases publication, 579, 592–96
church editor, 564–65
church-state separation at, 382
city desk, 33, 42, 44–5, 48, 80, 143, 164, 460
city desk clerk, 394–98, 556
college Ivy League hires by, 258, 430
color presses at, 534
composing room, 31, 56–59, 158–66, 221
copyboy job, 18, 20–47, 53–63, 67–68, 78–80, 85–87, 380
copy desk, 32–36, 55–56
copy editors, 55–56
critics, 209
D.C. upper crust and, 49
decision to leave, 564–67
decline of, 145, 319–20, 482, 536–37, 553, 578–79
dictation bank, 29, 40, 209, 228–29, 236–37, 247–65, 270–79, 297, 322–23, 349–51, 401, 424, 505
dictation bank chief, 396
editions and deadlines, 40, 45, 58, 224–30, 261
employee ID card, 62
Epstein moves to, 80–81, 359
Extra edition, on JFK assassination, 400, 405, 409
fashion editor, 76
father's preference for, 19–20
FBI offers King sex tapes to, 556–60

features and, 49, 349–50
first attempt as reporter at, 89–95
first glimpse of newsroom at, 25, 30–34
first published story in, 96–98
foreign desk, 39–40, 48, 259–61
galley proofs and, 41–42, 58
geography of newsroom at, 33–34
government publications and, 163
hay baler at, 57–58
historical footnotes to, 585–90
history of, 20–21, 101
Hoover at FBI and, 50
later careers of colleagues at, 580–85,
    590–96
linotype operators at, 56
local coverage, 49–50, 260–61
loss of streetcars and, 91
Maggiacomo as unofficial historian of,
    48–50
morgue, 31
national desk, 34, 164
news desk, 34, 51, 76
news editor, 34, 42
night city editor, 79, 143
obituaries, 255, 337–38, 395
obituaries, fake, 70, 279
owners of, 20–21, 382
paper route and, 10
paste pots and, 41
pay at, 161, 297, 395
permanent vs. transient D.C. and, 49
Personnel Department, 350

Washington *Evening Star (continued)*

Photo Department, 231

Picture Department, 522

police and fire reporting, 42, 79, 124–25, 143–44

presses, 33, 42–43

printers, 160–66, 353, 482–83

race coverage by, 381–84

"rambler" column, 479–80

Red Streak Final, 45, 350, 391–92, 549

religion pages, 565

reporter, promoted to, 460

reporters, 33, 161, 259–61, 270–71, 384

reporters' degree requirements, 257, 430, 528–40, 551

reporters' scholarships, 257, 504

reporters' training program, 233, 235, 247, 327, 351, 384, 504, 518, 529, 533

restaurant critic, 209

rewrite bank, 34, 41, 45–46

scrapbook and clippings from, 96–99, 323, 341, 432, 458–59, 520, 529, 532, 537–38, 566

sold to Allbritton, then TIME, 579

split page, 165, 170, 347

Sports Department, 34, 298–306, 350

squawk box, 78–79

Star Magazine, 323

state desks, 48, 72, 97–98, 104, 183

strikes and, 161, 395, 482–83

stringers, 254

style book, 253–54

Sunday Department, 51, 206–9, 350, 379, 504, 506

Teen Magazine, 330

telegraph desk, 48

type setting, 34–35

weather stories, 496, 553, 555–56

Weekender Magazine, 482, 484

"Week in Perspective," 207

wire room and, 39–40, 58–59, 67–73, 76

WMAL and, 145

women reporters, 330, 354, 503–4

Women's Department, 34, 49, 258, 330, 350–51, 354–59, 379, 412, 418–20, 482, 505

writing quality at, 342–43

Washington *Globe,* 276

Washington Herald, 81

Washingtonian magazine, 582

Washington Monument, 12, 148, 385, 388–89

Washington Newspaper Guild Front Page Award, 436

Washington Post, 10, 20, 50, 60–61, 122–23, 126, 143–44, 181, 251, 260, 318, 331, 353, 380, 383, 409, 486, 511, 512, 537, 543

Blacks and, 216, 335–37, 384, 595

Bradlee as managing editor, 577

buys *Star* buildings, 580

buys *Times-Herald,* 50–51, 81, 319, 578

elections of 1964 pool and, 542–43

fake obit in, 279–82, 478, 583

Washington Post (*continued*)
  former *Star* staff at, 581, 584–85, 590–96
  move to, from *Elizabeth Daily Journal,* 575–78, 589
  rivalry vs. *Star,* 49–51, 537, 553
  suicide of Phil Graham and, 371
  Victory Baby and, 80
Washington Post and Times-Herald, 51, 319
Washington Redskins, 298, 384
Washington Senators, 21, 69, 102–6, 322, 384, 522
Washington Times, 584, 590–95
Washington Times-Herald, 49, 81, 319, 359, 556
Washington University, 584
Washington Wives (Dean), 587
Watergate affair, 586–87, 590–95
WDON, 108, 202
Weaver, Annabelle Gustavson, 90–94
Welch, Rupe, 232–36, 323–27, 503, 510–13, 536, 563, 584
welfare, 437
Werner, Mary Lou "Ludy," 50, 254, 296, 322, 330, 376, 382, 414–15, 458, 471, 505, 507, 533–34
  lack of college degree, 530
  later career and, 592
  mentoring by, 254–55, 334, 436
  personality of, 99
  Pulitzer prize and, 36, 42, 73, 98–99, 530
Wesorts people, 156–57, 243–44, 445, 526, 566, 588

Western Electric, 571
Westmoreland County, Maryland, 242
WGAY, 202
Whatever Julie Wants, Julie Gets (album), 278
Wheaton High football team, 115
White, Theodore H., 427–28
whites
    children and school desegregation and, 99
    Wallace campaign of 1964 and, 454, 455
White House
    Cold War and, 259, 260–61
    JFK assassination and, 405–9
    visits for *Star* and, 464
White House News Photographers
        Association, 230
White House press corps, 224–26
Willard Hotel, 16–17, 179
Willenson, Kim, 318
Williamowski, Ben, 523
Williamowski, Rabbi Chaim, 523–24
Williamowski, Sammy, 523
Williams, Dallas O. (Badman of
        Swampoodle), 163, 171, 495–96, 524
Williams, Hosea, 548
Williams, John J., 509
Wilson, Dagmar, 259
Wilson, Edith, 190
Wilson, Woodrow, 64, 189–90, 280–81
Windsor, Bob, 199
Winfield Scott Hotel (Elizabeth, New
        Jersey), 569, 574
Wisconsin primaries of 1964, 454

WMAL, 145, 202, 441
Wofford, Harris, 348, 497
Women Strike for Peace, 259
Woodward, Bob, 586, 591, 594
Woodward & Lothrop "Woodies," 9–14
World War II, 21, 79–82, 155, 197, 259, 285,
    474, 475, 559, 590–91
WTOP, 584
WTTG, 12
Wubnig, Sylvia, 244–45, 246
Wurfel, Walter, 318–19, 373
WWVA Radio Jamboree, 202

Yale University, 258, 318, 328, 431, 481
Yarbrough, Chic, 380–81, 389
YMCA, Jenkins arrest in, 510–11
Young, Joseph, 20

Zehring, Robin, 217
Zeibert's, Duke, restaurant, 331, 522–24

ABOUT THE AUTHOR

Carl Bernstein is the author or coauthor of five bestselling books, including *All the President's Men* and *The Final Days,* both written with Bob Woodward. He, Woodward, and the *Washington Post* were awarded the Pulitzer Prize for Public Service for their coverage of the Watergate story, which led to the resignation of President Richard Nixon and set the standard for modern investigative reporting. He is also the author of biographies of Pope John Paul II and Hillary Clinton and of a memoir about his family's experience during the McCarthy era. For a decade he has been an on-air political analyst for CNN, and he is a longtime contributing editor at *Vanity Fair.* He lives in New York.